O9-CFU-210
3 8077 1002 0437 3

Environmental Tobacco Smoke

Environmental Tobacco Smoke

Proceedings of the International Symposium at McGill University 1989

Donald J. Ecobichon
McGill University

Joseph M. Wu
New York Medical College

Editors and Organizers of the Symposium

Lexington Books
D.C. Heath and Company/Lexington, Massachusetts/Toronto

Library of Congress Cataloging-in-Publication Data

Environmental tobacco smoke : proceedings of the international symposium at McGill University / Donald J. Ecobichon, Joseph M. Wu, editors.
p. cm.
ISBN 0-669-24365-5 (alk. paper)
1. Passive smoking—Health aspects—Congresses. 2. Tobacco smoke pollution—Health aspects—Congresses. 3. Tobacco smoke—Congresses. I. Ecobichon, Donald J. II. Wu, Joseph M. III. International Symposium on Environmental Tobacco Smoke (1989 : McGill University)
RA1242.T6E58 1990
616.86′5′071—dc20 89-49011
CIP

Published simultaneously in Canada
Printed in the United States of America
International Standard Book Number: 0-669-24365-5
Library of Congress Catalog Card Number:

The paper used in this publication meets the minimum requirements of American National Standard for Information Sciences—Permanence of Paper for Printed Library Materials, ANSI Z39.48-1984.

89 90 91 92 8 7 6 5 4 3 2 1

The International Symposium on Environmental Tobacco Smoke, held on November 3 and 4, 1989, at McGill University, Montreal, Canada, was made possible by a tobacco industry grant and by grants and other support from the following co-sponsors:

Department of Pharmacology and Therapeutics, McGill University, Montreal, Canada

Healthy Buildings International, Fairfax, Virginia, U.S.A.

Institut Fresenius, Neuhof, Federal Republic of Germany

Institut Universitaire de Technologie de Dijon, University of Burgogne, Dijon, France

Institute of Environmental and Industrial Medicine, Hanyang University, Seoul, Korea

Institute for International Health and Development, Geneva, Switzerland

National Energy Management Institute, Alexandria, Virginia, U.S.A.

The National Federation of Independent Business, Washington, D.C., U.S.A.

The National Federation of Independent Business Foundation, Washington, D.C., U.S.A.

RCC Research and Consulting Company AG, Itingen, Switzerland

School of Pharmacology, Sunderland Polytechnic, Sunderland, Tyne and Wear, U.K.

Contents

Participants

Dr. Pamela Allen
RCC Research and Consulting Company AG
Basel, Switzerland

Dr. Peter Atteslander
Professor, University of Augsburg
West Germany

Dr. Alan Armitage
Toxicologist
Yorkshire, England

Dr. John Bacon-Shone
Professor of Statistics
University of Hong Kong

Dr. G. R. Betton
Professor, Department of Pathology
Royal Veterinary College
University of London

Dr. Robert Brown
MRC Toxicology Unit
Surrey, England

Dr. William J. Butler
Failure Analysis Associates
Palo Alto, California

Dr. Guy Crepat
Professor of Biological Science, IUT—University of Burgogne
Dijon, France

Dr. Hector Croxatto
Chilean Academy of Sciences
Pontifica Universidad Catolica de Chile
Santiago, Chile

Dr. John Dilley
Occupational Physician
Chilvester Hill House
Wiltshire, England

Dr. Alan K. Done
Pediatrics and Clinical Toxicology
Salt Lake City, Utah

Dr. Delbert Eatough
Professor, Department of Chemistry
Brigham Young University
Provo, Utah

Dr. Donald J. Ecobichon
Professor, Department of Pharmacology and Therapeutics
McGill University
Montreal, Quebec

Dr. Lorenzo Figallo Espinal
Professor of Medicine
Central University of Venezuela
Caracas, Venezuela

Susan Eyre, M.Sc
Goodfellow Consultants, Inc.
Mississauga, Ontario

Dr. Andre Fave
Dr Veterinaire
Paris, France

Dr. George Feuer
Professor, Department of Clinical Biochemistry
University of Toronto
Toronto, Ontario

Dr. Edward Field
Toxicologist
Surrey, England

Dr. W. Gary Flamm
Science Regulatory Services International
Washington, D.C.

Dr. Joseph L. Fleiss
Professor and Chairman, Division of Biostatistics
Columbia University, School of Public Health
New York, New York

Dr. Roland Fritsch
Lecturer in English and Communications
IUT—University of Burgogne
Dijon, France

Dr. Austin J. S. Gardiner
Monklands District General Hospital
Airdrie, England

Dr. Howard D. Goodfellow
Goodfellow Consultants, Inc.
Adjunct Associate Professor, Engineering, Applied Chemistry, Occupational Health and Industrial Hygiene
University of Toronto

Dr. Gio Gori
The Health Policy Center
Bethesda, Maryland

Dr. John Gorrod
Professor, Department of Pharmacy
King's College (KQC)
London

Dr. Stanley M. Greenfield
Systems Applications, Inc.
San Rafael, California

Dr. Alan J. Gross
Professor, Department of Biometry
Medical University of South Carolina
Charleston, South Carolina

Dr. Lawrence Holcomb
Environmental Toxicologist
Olivet, Michigan

Dr. Ronald D. Hood
Professor, Biology Department and Adjunct Professor of Environmental Toxicology
The University of Alabama
Tuscaloosa, Alabama

Dr. Edward Lee Husting
Occupational and Environmental Epidemiologist
St. Petersburg, Florida

Jolanda Janczewski, MPH
President, Consolidated Safety Services, Inc.
Oakton, Virginia

Roger Jenkins
Oak Ridge National Laboratories
Oak Ridge, Tennessee

Dr. Irving I. Kessler
Professor, Department of Epidemiology and Preventive Medicine
University of Maryland School of Medicine
Baltimore, Maryland

Dr. James Kilpatrick
Professor of Biostatistics
Medical College of Virginia
Richmond, Virginia

Dr. Yoon Shin Kim
Associate Professor, Environmental Sciences
College of Medicine
Hanyang University
Seoul, Korea

Dr. Flemming Kissmeyer-Neilsen
Professor of Clinical Immunology
University of Arhus
Arhus, Denmark

Dr. Maxwell W. Layard
Layard Associates
Mountain View, California

Peter Lee, M.A.
Biostatistician
Surrey, England

George B. Leslie, FRC Path.
Pathologist
Bedsfordshire, England

Dr. Maurice Le Vois
Risk Assessment and Epidemiology
San Francisco, California

Dr. Leonard S. Levy
Industrial Toxicology Unit
Institute of Occupational Health
University of Birmingham
Birmingham, England

Dr. Trent R. Lewis
Environmental and Occupational Toxicologist
Cincinnati, Ohio

Dr. Sarah Liao
EHS Consultants
Hong Kong

Dr. Giuseppe LoJacono
Professor, University of Perugia
Rome, Italy

Dr. Ross Lorimer
The Glasgow Nuffield Hospital
Glasgow, Scotland

Dr. Alonso Armijos Luna
Dean, National University of Loja Medical School
Loja, Ecuador

Frank Lunau
British Occupational Hygiene Society
London, England

Docent Torbjorn Malmfors
Toxicologist
Stockholm, Sweden

Nathan Mantel
Professor, Department of Mathematics and Statistics
The American University
Washington, D.C.

Dr. Luigi Manzo
Professor, Universita Degli Studi Di Pavia
Pavia, Italy

Dr. Aly Massoud
Professor, Department of Occupational Hygiene
University of Ainsham, Annassia
Cairo, Egypt

Milton Meckler, P.E.
Meckler Engineers Group
Encino, California

Dr. Rodrigo Quintero Molina
Vice President, Latin American Federation of Geriatrics and Gerontology
Caracas, Venezuela

Dr. Demetrios Moschandreas
ITT Research Institute
Chicago, Illinois

Dr. Georg S. Neurath
Chemist and Pharmacologist
Hamburg, West Germany

Dr. Dennis Paustenbach
McLaren Environmental Engineering
ChemRisk Division
Alameda, California

Dr. Roger Perry
Professor, Public Health Engineering
Department of Civil Engineering
Imperial College
London, England

Dr. Jack E. Peterson
Peterson Associates
Brookfield, Wisconsin

Dr. A. Poole
Toxicologist
Dow Corporation
Midland, Michigan

Frank Powell
Director of Engineering
National Energy Management Institute
Alexandria, Virginia

Dr. Mark J. Reasor
Professor of Pharmacology and Toxicology
West Virginia University Medical Center
Morgantown, West Virginia

Dr. Benito R. Reverente, Jr.
Philippine Refining Company, Inc.
Manila, Philippines

Gray Robertson
President, Healthy Buildings International, Inc.
Fairfax, Virginia

Dr. Francis J. C. Roe
Toxicologist
London, England

Dr. Jerome K. Roth
President, The Center for Air Quality
Sharon, Connecticut

Dr. Sorell Schwartz
Professor, Georgetown Medical School
Washington, D.C.

Dr. Jarnail Singh
Professor of Environmental Toxicology
Stillman College
Tuscaloosa, Alabama

Dr. John M. Sneddon
School of Pharmacy
Sunderland, England

Dr. Thomas Barry Starr
Environ, Inc.
Washington, D.C.

Dr. C.E. Steele
Reproductive Toxicology
Nice, France

Frank Sullivan
Division of Pharmacology
Guy's Hospital Medical College
London, England

Dr. Hugh Thomas
Middlewood Hospital
Sheffield, England

Professor Alain Viala
Professor of Toxicology
University of Marseilles
Marseilles, France

Dr. Rodrigo Alban Villalba
Professor of Otolaryngology
Central University of Quito
Quito, Ecuador

Dr. Peter Voytek
Clement & Associates
Fairfax, Virginia

Dr. David A. Weeks
General Practice
Boise, Idaho

Dr. Max Weetman
Department of Pharmacology
School of Pharmacy, Sunderland Polytechnic
Sunderland, Tyne, and Wear, England

Dr. Lawrence M. Wexler
Director, Epidemiology Consulting Group and Adjunct Professor of Community and Preventive Medicine
New York Medical College
Valhalla, New York

Dr. Philip Witorsch
Clinical Professor of Medicine
The George Washington University School of Medicine and Health Sciences
Washington, D.C.

Dr. Raphael J. Witorsch
Professor of Physiology
Medical College of Virginia
Virginia Commonwealth University
Richmond, Virginia

Dr. Joseph M. Wu
Professor of Biochemistry and Molecular Biology
New York Medical College
Valhalla, New York

Jocelyn A. S. Wyatt, P. Eng.
Goodfellow Consultants, Inc.
Mississauga, Ontario

Opening Remarks

Donald J. Ecobichon, Ph.D.
Department of Pharmacology and Therapeutics
McGill University

On behalf of McGill University and the Department of Pharmacology and Therapeutics, I welcome you to this international symposium on environmental tobacco smoke. Undoubtedly, as has happened in the past, this meeting will become known by the venue and will become either the McGill meeting or the Montreal meeting, in much the same way as there has been a Vienna meeting, a London meeting and a Tokyo meeting.

I also welcome you to my city, Montreal, and to my university. The program committee has designed a full two days of scientific discussion, leaving you not very much free time. Nevertheless, I hope that you will obtain some appreciation of the city and its delights, the scenic mountain behind us here, which is the best place for a panoramic view of the city, the St. Lawrence River and the surrounding countryside.

Environmental tobacco smoke ("ETS") is a controversial subject of current concern to governments at all levels of jurisdiction, health scientists, the public, ventilation engineers and a number of other people. The flames of the ETS controversy are fed by real or perceived concerns, distrust of studies published in the literature, frustrations over the inconclusiveness or ambiguity of many of the studies and the biases that many people appear to have brought to the study of ETS.

Each year the number of studies relating to ETS is voluminous, as you know. One can read almost anything into some of them, focusing on selected aspects to develop almost any hypothesis of interest. The difficulty in conducting research on ETS is apparent to anyone who has attempted a characterization of the "toxicant" or an estimation of exposure, or has conducted an ETS epidemiological study.

I was recently introduced to the term "legislative toxicology" as pertaining to a toxicity data base that could be used to drive policy decisions. Few other than those who have labored in this field appreciate the fact that in assessing the possible health implications of ETS, one is working at the bottom of a dose effect curve, focusing on a substance that is both highly diluted and very poorly defined. ETS is, of course, a complex mixture whose biological effects can be quantified, if at all, only with great difficulty given the relatively insensitive physiological and biochemical techniques at hand.

Lack of control over any one of these parameters can lead to great variability in study results. With all of these problems present simultaneously, the results of ETS studies have been thus far wide open to misinterpretation and criticism. Certainly, the information currently available on ETS is not the type of toxicity data base that has been used in the past or that one could feel comfortable using in the future as a foundation for policy decisions.

Periodically it is important to step back and review the published studies, to assess the knowledge that has been acquired and to explore avenues for future research. Over the next two days, our opening speakers and discussion panels will address the problems of ETS characterization, estimation of exposure and adverse health effects issues, including cancers, reproductive effects, cardiovascular disease and respiratory effects in both children and adults.

While McGill University is pleased to sponsor this symposium, the McGill Administration wishes to make clear that it does not endorse any comments, statements or opinions presented at the meeting or appearing in the publication that will arise out of this meeting. However, it does support this forum as an important opportunity for an exchange of ideas, research results and hypotheses. The hope of the conference co-organizers, Professor Joseph Wu of New York Medical College and myself, as well as of McGill University, is that this meeting will improve our understanding of any role that ETS may play with respect to human health.

Part I

1

The Chemical Characterization of Environmental Tobacco Smoke

Delbert J. Eatough, Ph.D. with
Lee D. Hansen, Ph.D. and Edwin A. Lewis, Ph.D.
Chemistry Department, Brigham Young University

I. Summary

A detailed characterization of environmental tobacco smoke ("ETS") is needed in order to understand at least four areas which are important to the proper evaluation of the impact of smoking on the nonsmoker in indoor environments:

1. identification of the chemical compounds to which the nonsmoker is exposed;
2. determination of changes in the chemical composition and in the gas-particulate phase distribution of ETS with time in the indoor environment;
3. identification of substances that may be used to estimate the exposure of the nonsmoker to ETS in the indoor environment; and
4. risk assessment of disease and irritant exacerbations associated with exposure of the nonsmoker to ETS.

The first two areas are reviewed in this paper. The last two are beyond the scope of this review and will be covered in other presentations prepared for the symposium.

Chemical Composition of Fresh ETS. ETS consists of sidestream smoke generated by a burning cigarette and mainstream smoke exhaled by the smoker. The major contribution to ETS is from the sidestream smoke. Sidestream and mainstream smoke are qualitatively similar. However, significant quantitative differences exist between the two sources. These difference are reviewed. As ETS emissions are introduced into an indoor environment, substantial changes in the gas-particulate phase distribution of the chemical species occur. Information on the particle size distribution of ETS and on the chemical phase distribution of specific compounds in ETS is reviewed.

The Effect of Aging on the Chemical Composition of ETS. As ETS is emitted into an indoor environment, diluted, recirculated within and vented from the indoor environment, changes occur in both its chemical composition and the distribution of compounds between the gaseous and the particulate phases. These changes may be due to chemical reactions and changes in phase distribution, and they may result from differences in the rate at which various constituents are deposited to surfaces of the environment. Data related to all of these processes are reviewed.

II. The Composition of Environmental Tobacco Smoke

A. Comparison of Mainstream and Sidestream Tobacco Smoke

Chemical characterization of ETS has mainly been limited to comparison of the concentrations of organic (DHHS 1986, NAS 1986, Guerin 1987, Sakuma 1984a,b, 1983, Klus 1982) and inorganic (Jenkins 1982a,b) constituents in particles of tobacco smoke condensate and total sidestream tobacco smoke; determination of the main inorganic gases such as CO_2, CO, NH_3, HCN, NO and $HN0_2$ (Guerin 1987, DHHS 1986, NAS 1986, Eatough 1988a, Rickert 1984, Browne 1980); and determination of the principal organic compounds present in ETS in chambers (Benner 1989, Eatough 1989a, 1989b, Eudy 1986, Heavner 1986, Thome 1986, Löfroth 1989) and indoor environments where ETS is present (Eatough 1989b, 1987a, Ogden 1988a,b, Tang 1989a,b, Lewis 1988, Hoffmann 1987b, Kirk 1988, Klus 1987, Vu Duc 1987).

The chemical composition of ETS has been extensively discussed in reviews by the Surgeon General (DHHS 1986) and the National Research Council (NAS 1986). Newer data have been discussed in recent reviews (Eatough 1989c, Guerin 1987, Reasor 1987) and in a recent IARC Monograph (O'Neill 1987a,b). Included in the IARC Monograph and other publications is a review of the combustion conditions associated with the formation of both mainstream and sidestream tobacco smoke (Guerin 1987a, Baker 1980). The major differences between mainstream and sidestream tobacco smoke arise from the lower combustion temperatures associated with the formation of sidestream tobacco smoke (Guerin 1987a, Baker 1980), leading to an increase in the amounts of distillation products and a decrease in the amounts of combustion products. Sidestream smoke is more alkaline than mainstream smoke (Brunnemann 1974). This alkalinity results from the increased amounts of N-containing bases present as distillation products. The combustion zone of mainstream smoke is more oxygen deficient than the combustion zone of sidestream smoke and, as a result, the CO_2/CO ratios are higher for sidestream smoke than for mainstream smoke.

Concentrations of constituents of fresh sidestream tobacco smoke and the ratios of these constituents in sidestream to mainstream smoke are given in Table 1–1. In his recent review of sidestream cigarette emission measurements (Guerin 1987a), Guerin estimated the expected composition of ETS based on the data found in the National Research Council review (NAS 1986). These estimates are included in parentheses in Table 1–1. In general, the data from the NAS review lead to somewhat higher estimates of emissions than are actually observed. This is because the ranges of quantities of material found in sidestream tobacco smoke estimated from data in the National Research Council review are controlled by the variability in mainstream smoke emissions. A similar variability does not exist for sidestream smoke constituents. The amounts of most constituents in sidestream tobacco smoke are little affected by brand, tobacco moisture content, or mainstream combustion parameters (Guerin 1987a). As a result, total sidestream smoke emissions should be predictable from information on the number of cigarettes smoked. Also, since sidestream tobacco smoke is responsible for most of the ETS in indoor environments, ETS emissions in an indoor environment are also predictable.

The data given in Table 1–1 include results from both studies of concentrated sidestream tobacco smoke generated in small generation and collection devices (Guerin 1987a) and diluted sidestream tobacco smoke in larger chambers (e.g., Löfroth 1989, Eatough 1989a,b, 1986, Benner 1989, Heavner 1986, Eudy 1986, Thome 1986, Klus 1987, Vu Duc 1987). The amounts of any component of sidestream tobacco smoke measured in these different devices are in general agreement (Table 1–1). In some cases, however, rapid and selective removal of some ETS constituents in some chamber experiments results in erroneously low emission rates (see Section II.C.). The most serious disagreement is in the results reported for NH_3, where earlier studies give much higher concentrations than more recent studies.

While the compounds listed as gases in Table 1–1 are expected to be present only as gases in ETS, the distribution of compounds between gases and particles for most of the semi-volatile organic compounds is not well known. Information available on the gas versus particulate phase distribution of semi-volatile organic compounds is given in Section II.B.

Particular mention should be made of nicotine. While nicotine is primarily in the particulate phase in sidestream tobacco smoke generated in small combustion devices (Guerin 1987a), it is primarily in the gas phase in diluted sidestream tobacco smoke in chambers (Caka 1989a,b). The equilibration from the particulate to the gas phase is very rapid (Eudy 1986, Eatough 1989a, Tang 1988a,b). The more alkaline pH of sidestream tobacco smoke (Brunnemann 1974) may be responsible for the rapid displacement of the non-protonated nicotine from the particles (Guerin 1987a).

Table 1–1
Reported and Calculated (Guerin 1987, Calculated from Data in DHHS 1987) Emissions for Sidestream Environmental Tobacco Smoke and Corresponding Sidestream to Mainstream Emission Ratios

Chemical Class	*Compound*	*Sidestream Yield µg/Cigarette*	*SS/MS*	*Reference*
Gases	Carbon monoxide, mg	(1.2 – 65	2.5)	Guerin 1987
		69 – 75		Rawbone 1987
		27 – 37	2.1 – 15	Adams 1987
		67		Löfroth 1989
		56		Eatough 198
		48 – 54		Heavner 198
		40 – 67	2.6 – 21	Rickert 1984
		46 – 61	2.5 – 4.7	Klus 1982
		49 – 63	2.7 – 23	Browne 1980
				Johnson 197
	Carbon dioxide, mg	(81 – 640	8.1)	Guerin 1987
		370 – 570	9.8 – 35	Adams 1987
		450 – 760	8.1 – 11	Klus 1982
				Browne 1980
				Johnson 197
	Nitrogen oxides, mg	(0.1 – 3.5	4.7 – 5.8)	Guerin 1987
		2.2 – 2.6		Eatough 198
		2.0		Löfroth 1989
		1.4 – 2.0		Heavner 198
		1.6 – 2.0	4.7 – 5.8	Klus 1982
		1.8 – 4.4	4.3– 9.9	Norman 198
	Nitrogen dioxide, mg	0.2 – 0.3		Eatough 198
	Ammonia, mg	(0.4 – 9.5	44 – 73)	Guerin 1987
		0.2 – 0.9	5.9 – 46	Adams 1987
		0.8 – 1.0		Eatough 198
		5.2 – 9.4	37 – 63	Sakuma 198
		5.3 – 8.5	110 –170	Klus 1982
		5.1 – 5.8	44 – 73	Brunnemann 1975
				Johnson 197
	Formaldehyde, mg	(1.0 – 4.6	51)	Guerin 1987
		2.0		Löfroth 1989
		1.5	51	Klus 1982
	Acetone, mg	1.0	4	Klus 1982
	Acetonitrile, mg	0.6 – 1.0	3.9 – 5.4	Klus 1982

Table 1–1 continued

Chemical Class	Compound	Sidestream Yield µg/Cigarette	SS/MS	Reference
	Acrolein, mg	(0.1 – 1.7	12)	Guerin 1987
		0.56		Löfroth 1989
		0.92	12	Klus 1982
	Ethene, mg	1.2		Löfroth 1989
		2.0 – 2.4		Persson 1988
	Propene, mg	1.3		Löfroth, 1989
	Isoprene, mg	3.1		Löfroth 1989
	1,3-Butadiene, mg	0.4		Löfroth 1989
	Nitrous acid	370 – 680		Eatough 1989
	Nitric acid	3 – 47		Eatough 1989
	Methylamine	74 – 184	4.2 – 6.4	Sakuma 1984a
	Dimethylamine	29 – 51	3.7 – 5.1	Sakuma 1984a
	Isopropylamine	10 – 14	4.5 – 7.0	Sakuma 1984a
	Hydrogen cyanide	(48 – 203	0.17– 0.37)	Guerin 1987
		14 – 17	0.06– 0.14	Klus 1982
		53– 125	0.22– 0.49	Norman 1983
	Particles Total mass, mg	(0.1 – 76	1.3 – 1.9)	Guerin 1987
		29 – 33		Rawbone 1987
		24 – 64	1.3 – 1.9	Guerin 1989
		14 – 24	1.1 – 17	Adams 1987
		10		Löfroth 1989
		6 – 11		Eatough 1989
		9 – 10		Heavner 1986
		16 – 36	0.9 – 14	Rickert 1984
		11 – 19	0.6 – 2.1	Klus 1982
		20 – 23	0.4 – 1.8	Browne 1980
Bases	Nictone, mg	(0.2 – 7.6	2.6 – 3.3)	Guerin 1987
		4.9		Rawbone 1987
		3.1 – 6.1		Eatough 1989
		3.3		Löfroth 1989
		2.6 – 7.6	2.6 – 3.3	Guerin 1989

Table 1–1 continued

Chemical Class	*Compound*	*Sidestream Yield µg/Cigarette*	*SS/MS*	*Reference*
		3.2 – 4.6	2.3 – 21	Adams 1987
		2.5 – 3.0		Thome, Eudy
		3.5 – 6.6	1.4 – 2.1	Sakuma 1984b
		3.3 – 5.8	1.3 – 1.8	Sakuma 1984a
		2.6 – 6.1	2.4 – 22	Rickert 1984
		3.9 – 4.3	2.1 – 3.2	Klus 1982
		5.9 – 7.0	3.0 – 12	Browne 1980
				Cornell 1978
	Myosmine	73 – 220	4.0 – 7.5	Sakuma 1984a
		107 – 161		Eatough 1989
	Nicotyrine	93 – 260	4.7 – 7.9	Sakuma 1984b
		49 – 210	8.4 – 14	Sakuma 1984
		32		Eatough 1989
	Cotinine	15 – 39		Eatough 1989
	Pyridine	190 – 260	10. – 13	Sakuma 1984b
		160 – 230	7.3 – 10.8	Sakuma 1984a
		176 – 205		Eatough 1989
		290		Thome 1986
		340 –3400	5 – 13	Klus 1982
	3-Hydroxypyridine	160 – 190	1.5 – 1.7	Sakuma 1984b
		150 – 170	0.8 – 1.2	Sakuma 1984a
	Analine	(3 – 36	30)	Guerin 1987
		11	30	Klus 1982
	2-Picoline	90 – 170	5.2 – 10	Sakuma 1984
		123 – 200	4.4 – 6.5	Sakuma 1984
		130 –1090	6 – 21	Klus 1982
	2,4-Lutidine	37 – 75	5.2 – 5.8	Sakuma 1984
	Pyrrole	140 – 270	9.0 – 14	Sakuma 1984
	N-Methylpyrrolidine	25 – 33	5.4 – 8.9	Sakuma 1984
	Pyrrolidine	23 – 33	1.6 – 2.5	Sakuma 1984
	Indole	33 – 109	2.1 – 3.4	Sakuma 1984
	3-Vinylpyridine	260 – 420	15 – 22	Sakuma 1984
		330 – 450	24 – 34	Sakuma 1984
		261 – 462		Eatough 1989
	2-Vinylpyridine	31 – 50		Eatough 1989

able 1–1 continued

hemical lass	Compound	Sidestream Yield µg/Cigarette	SS/MS	Reference
	3-Ethylpyridine	21 – 36	4.7 – 7.2	Sakuma 1984b
		21 – 37	6.9 – 13	Sakuma 1984a
		71 – 960	7 – 67	Klus 1982
	2,3-Bipyridyl	20 – 73	2.0 – 3.3	Sakuma 1984a
	2-Acetylpyridine	27 – 37	6.8 – 9.7	Sakuma 1984a
	3-Cyanopyridine	24 – 64	10. – 17	Sakuma 1984a
	Quinoline	18	11	Klus 1982
	Isoquinoline	5 – 8	2.5 – 4.7	Sakuma 1984a
	Iosamylamine	13 – 21	3.6 – 5.0	Sakuma 1984a
	n-Amylamine	18 – 34	2.8 – 3.8	Sakuma 1984a
	2-Naphthylamine	(0.02– 1.1	39)	Guerin 1987
	4-Aminobiphenyl	(0.06– 0.16	31)	Guerin 1987
	Acetamide	86 – 156	0.8 – 1.5	Sakuma 1984b
nitroso	N-nitrosonornicotine	(0.02– 18	1 – 5)	Guerin 1987
ines		0.19– 0.9	0.7 – 5.1	Adams 1987
		0.2 – 6.1	0.2 – 7	Klus 1982
		0.11– 0.39	0.5 – 1.9	Brunnemann 1983
	N-nitrosodimethyl-amine	(0.04– 149	10 –830)	Guerin 1987
		0.6 – 0.7	24 –167	Adams 1987
		0.14– 1.0		Hoffmann 1987b
		0.46– 1.9	70 –281	Brunnemann 1983
		0.7 – 1.0	19 –160	Klus 1982
				Brunnemann 1980
		0.21– 0.55	37 –310	Rühl 1980
	4-(Methylnitrosamine) -1-(3-pyridyl)-1-butanone	0.39– 1.4	3.4 – 22	Adams 1987
		0.19– 0.8	0.2 – 8	Klus 1982
		0.20– 0.54	1.4 – 7.1	Brunnemann 1983

Table 1–1 continued

Chemical Class	*Compound*	*Sidestream Yield µg/Cigarette*	*SS/MS*	*Reference*
	N-nitrosopyrrolidine	0.12– 0.23	1.8 – 18	Adams 1987
		0.01– 0.70		Hoffmann 1987b
		0.21– 0.38	9 – 25	Klus 1982
		0.28– 0.70	17 –122	Rühl 1980
		0.08– 0.50	3.2 – 2.3	Brunnemann 1983
Phenols/ alcohols	Phenol	(52 – 390	2.6)	Guerin 1987
		69 – 241	1.8 – 2.1	Sakuma 1983a
		104 –290	1.8 – 2.2	Sakuma 1984b
				Cornell 1978
	o-Cresol	14 – 18	1.1 – 1.3	Sakuma 1983a
	m-Cresol	12 – 24	1.2 – 1.5	Sakuma 1983a
		18 – 34	1.0 – 1.5	Sakuma 1984b
	p-Cresol	30 – 46	1.0 – 1.2	Sakuma 1983a
		32 – 59	1.0 – 1.5	Sakuma 1984b
	4-Vinylphenol	25 – 57	1.1 – 1.5	Sakuma 1984b
	Guaiacol	8 – 21	1.3 – 1.7	Sakuma 1983a
	2,6-Xylenol	8 – 21	1.0 – 1.3	Sakuma 1983a
	p-Vinylphenol	21 – 45	0.8 – 1.0	Sakuma 1983a
	Catechol	(28 – 196	0.7)	Guerin 1987
		180 – 292	0.7 – 0.9	Sakuma 1983a
		58 – 117	1.3 – 13	Adams 1987
	4-Methylcatechol	25 – 55	0.7 – 0.9	Sakuma 1983a
	3-Methylcatechol	24 – 47	0.7 – 0.8	Sakuma 1983a
	4-Vinylguaiacol	24 – 33	0.8 – 1.0	Sakuma 1983a
	4-Ethylcatechol	19 – 68	0.5 – 0.7	Sakuma 1983
	4-Vinylcatechol	7 – 41	0.4 – 0.4	Sakuma 1983
	Hydroquinone	91 – 285	0.7 – 1.0	Sakuma 1983
	Methylhydroquinone	21 – 41	0.8 – 1.1	Sakuma 1983
	Solanesol	210 – 280		Benner 1989
		98 – 168		Tang 1989
		200 – 400		Ogden 1988a,b

Table 1–1 continued

Chemical Class	*Compound*	*Sidestream Yield µg/Cigarette*	*SS/MS*	*Reference*
	Fufuryl alcohol	73 – 283	3.0 – 4.8	Sakuma 1984b
	2-Hydroxy-3-methyl-2-cyclopentenone	24 – 30	6.0 – 10	Sakuma 1984b
ldehydes/	2-Furaldehyde	29 – 290	4.9 – 7.4	Sakuma 1984b
	5-Methyl-2-furaldehyde	20 – 127	3.1 – 4.3	Sakuma 1984b
etones	2-Cyclopentenone	70 – 103	2.9 – 3.8	Sakuma 1984b
	2-Methyl-2-cyclopentenone	49 – 95	2.2 – 5.5	Sakuma 1984b
	2,3,-Dimethyl-2-cyclopentenone	21 – 39	1.6 – 2.9	Sakuma 1984b
	?-Butrolactone	40 – 103	3.6 – 5.0	Sakuma 1984b
cids	Formic acid	340 – 690	1.4 – 1.6	Sakuma 1983a
	Acetic acid	640 –2190	1.9 – 3.9	Sakuma 1983a
		695 –1150	2.0 – 2.4	Sakuma 1984b
	3-Methylvaleric acid	20 – 380	0.8 – 1.0	Sakuma 1983a
	Lactic acid	45 – 160	0.5 – 0.7	Sakuma 1983a
	Glycolic acid	35 – 77	0.6 – 1.0	Sakuma 1983a
	Levulinic acid	25 – 43	0.8 – 1.0	Sakuma 1983a
	2-Furoic acid	25 – 60	0.5 – 0.7	Sakuma 1983a
	3-Hydroxypropionic	1 – 25	0.5 – 0.8	Sakuma 1983a
	Benzoic acid	12 – 23	0.7 – 1.0	Sakuma 1983a
	Phenylacetic acid	11 – 30	0.6 – 0.8	Sakuma 1983a
	Succinic acid	65 – 70	0.4 – 0.6	Sakuma 1983a
	Methylsuccinic acid	1 – 13	0.3 – 0.5	Sakuma 1983a
	Glutaric acid	6 – 18	0.3 – 0.5	Sakuma 1983a
	m-Hydroxybenzoic	3 – 15	0.2 0.6	Sakuma 1983a
kanes	n-Hentriacontane			Löfroth 1989
kenes	Limonene	63 – 400	4.2 – 12	Sakuma 1984b
	Neophytadiene	70 – 420	1.1 – 1.8	Sakuma 1984b

Table 1–1 continued

Chemical Class	*Compound*	*Sidestream Yield µg/Cigarette*	*SS/MS*	*Reference*
PAH	Naphthalene	(45	16)	Guerin 1987
	Phenanthrene	3.0 – 5.0		Eatough 198
		2.3	30	Grimmer 198
		0.06	2.1	Klus 1982
	Anthracene	0.71	30	Grimmer 198
	Fluoranthene	0.69	11	Grimmer 198
	Pyrene	0.4 – 1.2		Eatough 198
		0.47	11	Grimmer 198
		0.06	1.9	Klus 1982
	Benzo(a)pyrene	(0.02– 0.14	2.7 – 3.4)	Guerin 1987
		0.04– 0.07	2.6 – 20	Adams 1987
		0.10	9.4	Grimmer 198
		0.03	2.1	Klus 1982
	Benzo(e)pyrene	0.08	11	Grimmer 198
	Indeno(1,2,3-cd) pyrene	0.05	6.1	Grimmer 198
	Benzo(ghi)perylene	0.04	5.7	Grimmer 198
Sterols/	Cholesterol	4.1 – 6.7		Benner 1989
Sterenes	Stigmasterol	5.0 – 16		Benner 1989
	Campesterol	3.7 – 8.1		Benner 1989
	B-Sitosterol	1.0 – 15		Benner 1989
	24-MeC-3,5-diene[a]	0.4 – 4.0		Benner 1989
	24-EtC-3,5,22-triene[b]	3.0 – 9.3		Benner 1989

[a]MeC = Methylcholesta.
[b]EtC = Ethylcholesta.

Differences in the total mass of particles in sidestream emissions are found in studies using a small combustion and collection device as compared to studies using an environmental chamber (Table 1–1). The chamber studies give emission values from 6 to 11 mg particles/cigarette, while the other studies give values greater than 11 mg/cigarette. The difference cannot be accounted for by selective deposition of particles in the chamber experiments, as the data were obtained immediately after combustion of the cigarette (Benner 1989, Heavner 1986, Löfroth 1989). The difference is probably caused by losses of material from the particles as the smoke is diluted. Many of the organic constituents of sidestream tobacco smoke are volatile. Because dilution occurs in the real world, similar losses would be expected in indoor environments. This review assumes that this is the case and that the amount of particulate matter in ETS is about 10 mg per cigarette.

If the difference in the amount of particulate matter observed in the two types of experiments (larger chamber versus small combustion apparatus) is due to volatilization of organic compounds as the smoke is diluted, then the data in Table 1–1 suggest that about one-half of the generated sidestream particle mass is rapidly lost to the gas phase during dilution in indoor environments. Gas phase hydrocarbon measurements (Eatough 1989a) and the results of radiotracer labeled experiments (Pritchard 1989) are consistent with this hypothesis.

The existence of large amounts of gas phase hydrocarbons which can readily condense back to particulate phase material has also been suggested by chamber experiments involving UV radiation of sidestream ETS (Eatough 1989a). The concentration of particles in the irradiated sidestream smoke doubles in less than one hour as a result of chemistry induced by the ultraviolet radiation. This includes the movement of most of the gas phase nicotine back to the particulate state (Benner 1989, Eatough 1989a). Comparable chemistry apparently occurs in environments with unvented combustion heaters. The gas phase compounds responsible for this chemistry are unknown. Identification of gas phase semi-volatile organic compounds in ETS may also help determine which species are responsible for sensory irritation in sensitive individuals (Cain 1987, 1983, Weber 1984, 1980).

B. Gas-Particulate Phase Distribution of Some Compounds in Environmental Tobacco Smoke

Little is known about the distribution of organic compounds between the gas and particulate phases of ETS (NAS 1986, Guerin 1987a, Eatough 1989a,b, 1987b, Eudy 1986). Recent studies have shown that most of the volatile nitrogen-containing compounds such as nicotine, myosmine and pyridine are predominantly present in the gas phase of ETS (Eatough 1989a, 1989b, 1987a, 1987b, 1986, Eudy 1986, Thome 1986). Acrolein, formaldehyde and acetaldehyde are compounds of suspected toxicological importance which are also present in the gas phase (DHHS 1986, NAS 1986). The distribution of many mutagenic and/or toxic compounds, such as the N-nitrosamines, between the gas and particulate phases of ETS is presently not known (NAS 1986). Work recently completed in our laboratory has obtained chemical characterization data for both the gas and particulate phases of ETS in a Teflon chamber (Benner 1989, Eatough 1989a, 1987a). These studies indicate that, in addition to nicotine, NH_3, HNO_2, HNO_3, CH_3COOH, nicotyrine, myosmine, pyridine and alkyl pyridine compounds are also present only or predominantly in the gas phase. The identification of the gas-particle phase distribution of organic compounds of toxicological interest is an area of needed research.

C. Particle Size Distribution of Sidestream Tobacco Smoke

1. Particle and Mass Size Distribution of Sidestream Tobacco Smoke. Figure 1–1 shows typical particle size and mass distribution histograms for sidestream tobacco smoke generated by combustion of four cigarettes in a static 30 m^3 Teflon chamber (Benner 1989). The data shown in Figure 1–1 were obtained using a TSI Differential Mobility Particle Sizer (DMPS). The number and mass median diameters determined immediately after cigarette combustion were 0.107 and 0.255 m, respectively. As shown in Figure 1–1, the number median diameter shifted from 0.107 to 0.221 m over the 4-hour experimental period, while the mass median diameter shifted from 0.255 to 0.340 μm.

Similar results for the particle size distribution of fresh sidestream smoke have been reported in several studies. Median diameters of 0.15 μm using a "conifuge" (Keith 1960), 0.10 m determined by light scattering (Okada 1977), 0.10 μm determined with a DMPS (Ingebrethsen 1986), and 0.32 μm using a SPART (Hiller 1982) have been reported. The SPART measurements appear to be high. The other values are all in reasonable agreement. Mass median diameters determined using an impacter with piezo crystal collection stages (W. Chaing, California Measurements, unpublished results) and a DMPS unit (Ingebrethsen 1986), 0.23 μm and 0.20 μm, respectively, are also in agreement with the results shown in Figure 1–1. Mass median diameter of fresh sidestream tobacco smoke reported using a SPART (Hiller 1982), 0.41 μm, is higher than the other reported value and would appear to be in error.

2. Changes in Total Particle Number, Total Mass and Total Gas Phase Hydrocarbons with ETS Aging. The changes expected to occur in ETS during aging in an indoor environment can be illustrated with data from experiments conducted in a static Teflon chamber (Benner 1989). Figure 1–2 shows how particle number (as determined with a CNC and also with a CNC/DMPS unit) and total mass concentrations change with time at two different concentrations of ETS (Benner 1989). For all curves, lighting of the cigarettes is indicated by the initial large increase in particles/cm^3 and μg/m^3. The data in Figures 1–2A and 1–2B are for experiments where two and four cigarettes, respectively, were burned in a 30 m^3 Teflon chamber. The rate of decrease in particle concentration is fairly constant in both Figure 1–2A (38 ± 10% per hour) and Figure 1–2B (60 ± 18% per hour).

The particulate mass concentration does not decrease as rapidly as the

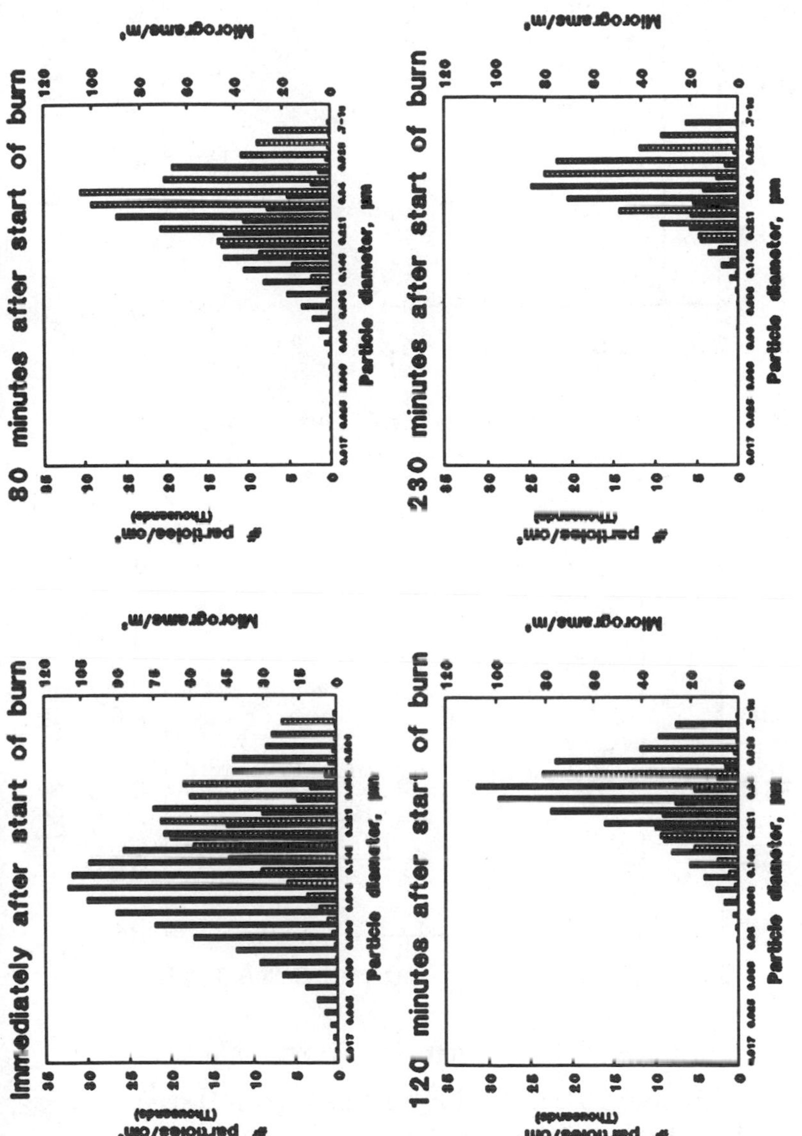

Figure 1–1. Change in Particle Size, Solid Bars, and Mass Distribution, Hatched Bars (0.015 to 0.75 μm DMPS Size Ranges) of Environmental Tobacco Smoke Over a 4-Hour Period.

Source: Benner 1989.

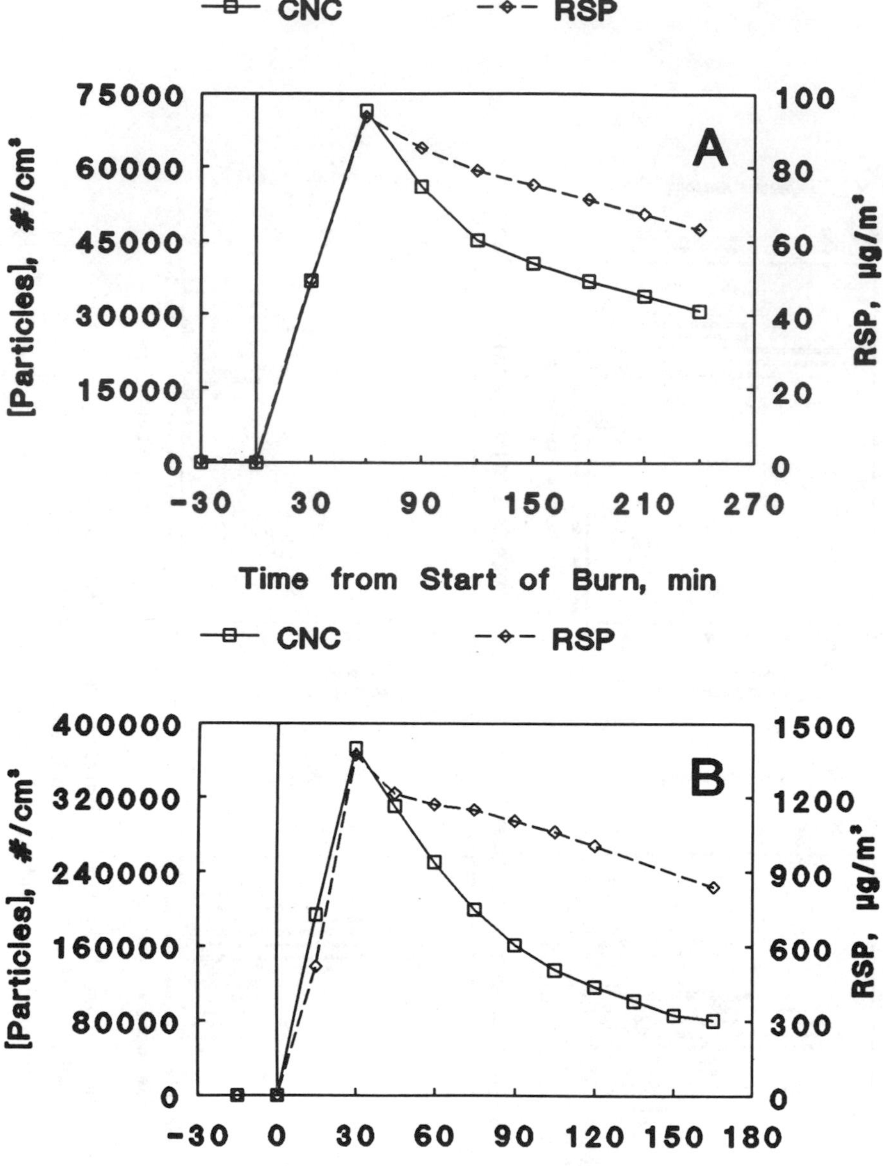

Figure 1–2. Change with Time in Total Particulate Mass as Determined by a Piezo Balance and in Total Particulate Number as Determined by a CNC Instrument for Two Separate Experiments.

Source: Benner 1989.

number concentration (Figure 1–2). The more rapid decrease in the number concentration results from the rapid decrease in the number of particles smaller than 0.2 μm diameter (Figure 1–1). The decrease in the mass concentration is not as rapid as the decrease in number concentration because the majority of the mass is associated with particles larger than 0.2 μm. The mass concentration of particles >0.2 μm actually increases due to the coagulation of smaller particles (Figure 1–1) during most of the experiment. This same increase in the number of larger particles was also seen in the optical counter data (Figure 1–3). The calculated mass distribution indicates that about 95% of the total mass was composed of particles smaller than 0.7 μm diameter, with the remaining mass in 0.7 to 1 μm diameter particles.

The particulate mass decays to 67% of the maximum value after 3 hours (Figure 1–2A) (combustion of 2 cigarettes), and to 62% of the maximum after 2.6 hours, (Figure 1–2B) (combustion of 4 cigarettes). These data indicate the rate of loss of particulate mass for ETS is independent of the concentration. Similarly, Eudy et al. (1986) found the particulate mass of ETS in a stainless steel chamber decreased to 65–70% of the maximum after 2 hours of ETS aging. The total decrease of particulate mass due to both evaporation and particle wall loss during the experiment illustrated in Figure 1–3 is 0.5 mg/m^3. Loss of particulate mass in the chamber is due about equally to an increase in gas phase organic compounds and to loss of particles to the walls of the chamber (Figure 1–3) (Benner 1989).

Loss of total particulate mass in Figures 1–1 and 1–2 is accompanied by an increase in total gas phase hydrocarbons (Figure 3). Nicotine is found mainly in the gas phase very soon after combustion of the cigarettes (Benner 1989, Tang 1988a,b). The more slowly volatilized ETS compounds must have a lower effective vapor pressure than nicotine. Assuming the average molecular weight of the slowly volatilized compounds to be 200 g/mol, the data in Figure 1–3 indicate that the increase in gas phase hydrocarbons during the three hours of the experiment is associated with the loss of about 0.2 mg/m^3 of particles.

To summarize, previously reported data indicate that particle coagulation and evaporation of semi-volatile compounds from particles are major processes during the aging of ETS. Evaporation accounted for nearly half of the observed total change in mass during the experiment illustrated in Figure 3 (Benner 1989). Similar results have been reported in other chamber studies (Ingebrethsen 1986, Vu Duc 1987).

D. Mutagenic Compounds in Environmental Tobacco Smoke

The mutagenic and carcinogenic compounds present in environmental tobacco smoke have been the subject of several reviews (DHHS 1986, NAS

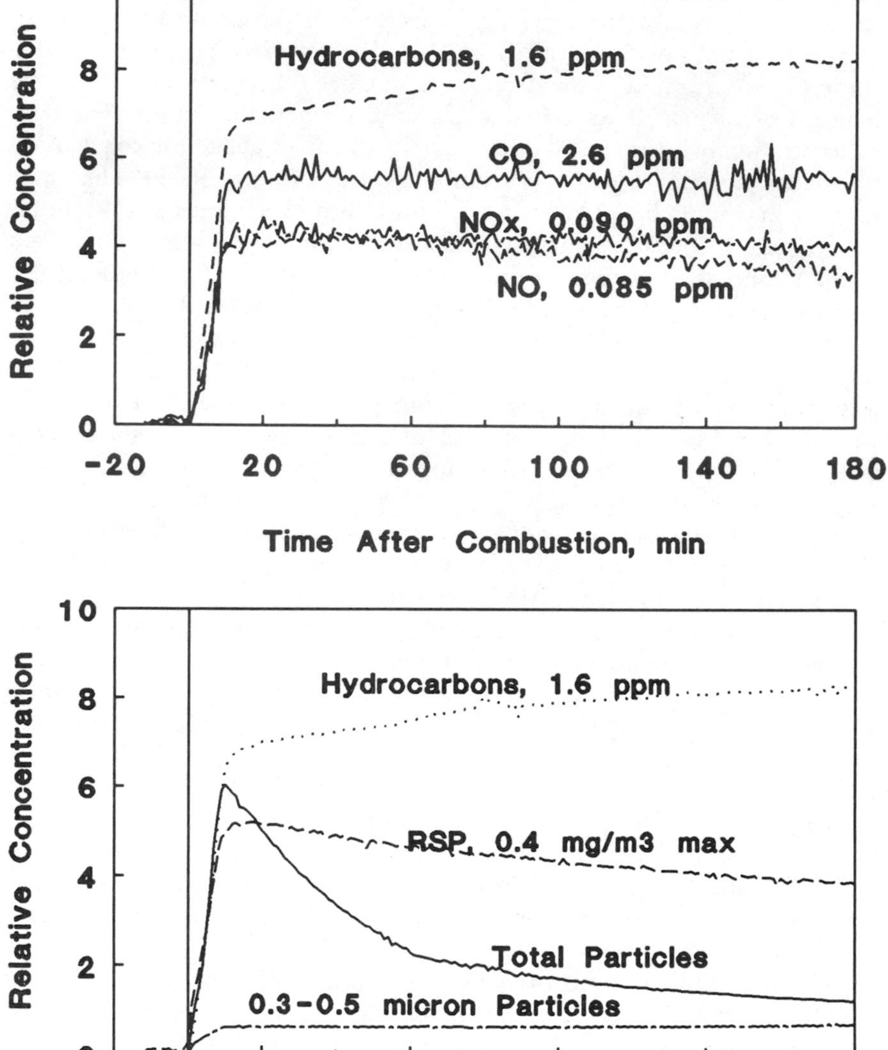

Figure 1–3. Change in Gas Phase Hydrocarbons, CO, NO_x, NO, RSP, Total Particles, and 0.3–0.5 μm Particles with Time in a Teflon Chamber after Combustion of Four Cigarettes.

Source: Benner 1989.

1986, Aviado 1988, Adams 1987, O'Neill 1987b). The yield of many of the potentially carcinogenic compounds is higher in sidestream smoke than in mainstream smoke (see Table 1-1). The amount of these compounds in equivalent amounts of environmental tobacco smoke will probably be little affected by smokers shifting to cigarettes with less of these species in mainstream smoke (Adams 1987, Sonnenfeld 1987).

Extensive data are available on the identities of mutagenic compounds in tobacco smoke condensate (DeMarini 1983). However, there have been few reports on the identities of mutagens in ETS particles (Bos 1984, Husgafvel-Pursiainen 1986, Lewtas 1987b, Löfroth 1989, 1988, 1986, 1983, Ong 1984). Also little information is available on mutagens in the gas phase of ETS (Wesolowski 1986, Ong 1984, Sexton 1985) although gas phase compounds appear to play a significant role in determining the cytotoxicity of ETS (Sonnenfeld 1987, 1985). Several studies have shown that the relative amounts of many of the toxic and mutagenic compounds are higher in ETS than in tobacco smoke condensate (DHHS 1986, NAS 1986). The major classes of potentially mutagenic compounds for which data exist are the N-nitrosamines (Adams 1987, Brunnemann 1987, 1980, Hoffmann 1987b, Klus 1982, Stehlik 1982, Rhl 1980), aldehydes (NAS 1986, Löfroth 1989, Klus 1982) and unsaturated aliphatic hydrocarbons (Löfroth 1989, Persson 1988) (see Table 1–1).

Current data suggest the mutagenicity of ETS particles to be comparable to or less than that of tobacco smoke condensate and other important classes of environmental pollutants such as ambient particulate matter, emissions from home cooking, coke or wood burning emissions and diesel exhaust (Albert 1983, Alfheim 1983, Austin 1985, Chrisp 1980, Hughes 1980, Lewtas 1981, Lioy 1985, Pitts 1985, Williams 1985). However, ETS appears to be the main contributor to mutagenicity of particles in indoor environments where smoking is present (Lewtas 1987a,b, Löfroth 1989, 1988, 1983, McCurdy 1987). This observation is consistent with the observation that smoking frequently leads to significantly increased concentrations of indoor particulate matter (Eatough 1989b, Kirk 1988, Spengler 1985). Exposure to ETS has also been claimed to result in the excretion of mutagens in the urine of nonsmokers (Bos 1983, Sasson 1985, Scherer 1987). This latter observation, however, is tentative at present (DHHS 1986, NAS 1986) and is, in any event, of uncertain significance.

The recent development of microsuspension assay techniques (Kado 1983) and techniques for mutagenic studies of vapors (Cupitt 1988, 1987, Kleindienst 1985, Shepson 1985, Wang 1985, Wesolowski 1986) allows the determination of the mutagenicity of samples where only a limited amount of material can be easily obtained for study, such as studies of indoor air or constituents in environmental chambers.

Several investigators have reported on the mutagenicity of ETS particles using a variety of Salmonella tester strains (Lewtas 1987a,b, Löfroth 1989, 1988, 1986, 1983, Husgafvel-Pursiainen 1986, McCurdy 1987, Wesolowski 1986). Two investigators (Löfroth 1986, Williams 1985) have shown that most of the mutagenicity in ETS particles is found in the chemical fraction containing heterocyclic nitrogen bases and that the mutagenicity of the PAH or nitro-PAH fractions is less than that observed from other sources such as diesel exhaust (Williams 1985, Pitts 1985) or wood smoke (Kamens 1984, 1985).

Kamens et al. (1985) have shown that nitrated mutagenic compounds are rapidly formed in wood smoke in the presence of O_3 and NO_2 and recent studies have shown a large increase in gas phase mutagenicity as a result of this wood smoke chemistry (Cupitt 1988, 1987). ETS contains significant quantities of HNO_2(g) and HNO_3(g) (Eatough 1989a, 1988a), which could also result in the formation of nitrated organic compounds. No data on the mutagenicity of ETS under various aging conditions are yet available. Nitration reactions may also be important in the formation of N-nitrosamines. It is not known if the N-nitrosamines are present in the gas or the particle phase of ETS (DHHS 1986, NAS 1986). The presence of free radicals in ETS (Church 1985, Halpern 1985, Pryor 1986) can be expected to promote such nitration chemistry. Increases in nitrated compounds in aged ETS have been documented (Eatough 1989a, 1988a, Tang 1989a). Data obtained on the rate of loss of NO and NO_x from ETS in an experimental laboratory indicate that NO in ETS is converted to unknown organic species (Tang 1989a). This chemistry may be driven by oxidants that are introduced into the indoor atmosphere from ambient sources (Tang 1989a). The gas and particulate phase compounds formed have not been identified.

Wesolowski et al. (1986) have reported preliminary data on the mutagenicity of both the particulate and gas phases of aged ETS. The response of Salmonella TA98 and TA98NR both with and without activation to extracts of collected particulate matter was determined. The results suggest the presence of nitroarenes in the sample and indicate that these compounds may be principal mutagens in aged ETS. No chemical class fractionation was done in this study but the mutagenicity of the gas phase was estimated by exposure of plates with Salmonella TA98 and TA100 (with and without activation) to the vapor phase of ETS. Techniques have been reported for the quantification of vapor phase exposure mutagenicity tests (Cupitt 1988, 1987, Kleindienst 1985) but were not used in the study by Wesolowski and coworkers. However, recent results on mutagens in the gas phase of wood smoke (Cupitt 1988, 1987) suggest that the results of Wesolowski et al. (1986) should be close to quantitative.

The results from the Wesolowski study (1986) indicate that the mutagenicity of the vapor phase is greater than that of the particulate phase of ETS and that the types of mutagens present are different for the two phases. This is consistent with recent studies on the mutagenicity of wood smoke (Cupitt 1988, 1987), which indicate a greater than ten-fold increase in the mutagenicity of the gas phase as the emissions age. The compounds responsible for this increase in mutagenicity have not yet been identified. The gas phase mutagens that form in wood smoke appear to result from the reaction of nitrogen oxides with organic compounds, and the mutagens are very labile. For example, the compounds will not survive collection and analysis by GC techniques (Cupitt 1988). It is probable that similar compounds form in ETS.

III. Changes during the Aging of Environmental Tobacco Smoke in an Indoor Environment

A. Changes Due to Deposition

As outlined in Section II, ETS is a complex mixture of gas and particulate phase compounds. During aging of ETS in an indoor environment, changes will occur in the chemical composition. Just as seen in chamber studies, these changes will include coagulation of particles which will alter the particle size distribution (see Section II.C.1.), changes in the gas/particle distribution of semi-volatile compounds (Eatough 1989a), and chemical changes due to reactions (Benner 1989, Eatough 1989a, Tang 1989a,b, 1988a,b). In addition, the chemical composition of ETS may be altered during aging in an indoor environment because of differences in the removal rate of various constituents as the ETS is aged (Lewis 1988, Eatough 1987b, Tang 1989a, Thompson 1989).

Many gas phase components of ETS have been shown to be rapidly removed in indoor environments. Several studies have shown the removal rate for gas phase nicotine and other basic nitrogen compounds to be much faster than the removal rates for particles or non-reactive gases such as CO (Lewis 1988, Eatough 1989b,c, 1987a, Thome 1986, Löfroth 1989, Tang 1989a, 1988a,b, Thompson 1989). The relative removal rates may depend on local environmental factors such as wall coverings, furnishings, presence or absence of people, air flow, etc. Thus, ETS will be a constantly changing mixture due to loss of material as a result of adsorption or decomposition and due to changes in gas/particulate phase equilibria for volatile species.

The changes in ETS composition over time complicate the assessment of health effects associated with exposure, and may preclude accurate measurement of human exposure to specific compounds without actual measurement of the compounds of interest. Because of the rapid removal of nicotine from indoor environments, the use of nicotine as a tracer and of nicotine and its metabolites, cotinine and 3-hydroxycotinine, as biological markers for determining exposure to ETS has been questioned (Eatough 1989b,c, Thompson 1989). The measurement of gas phase nicotine or even total nicotine may underestimate exposure to the particulate phase and possibly other components of ETS.

The changes that occur can be illustrated with data recently obtained in a simulated indoor environment (Lewis 1988, Tang 1989a).

Results of experiments with the laboratory sealed, no air circulation and no exchange with outside air are illustrated by the data shown in Figure 1–4. In Figure 1–4 the concentrations of the various species have been normalized to the concentration just after smoking of the cigarettes. The composition of ETS immediately after the combustion of the cigarettes is comparable to composition data determined in Teflon chamber experiments (Benner 1989, Eatough 1989a,b) (Table 1–2). The relative composition as a function of number of cigarettes smoked was constant. The effective air ex-

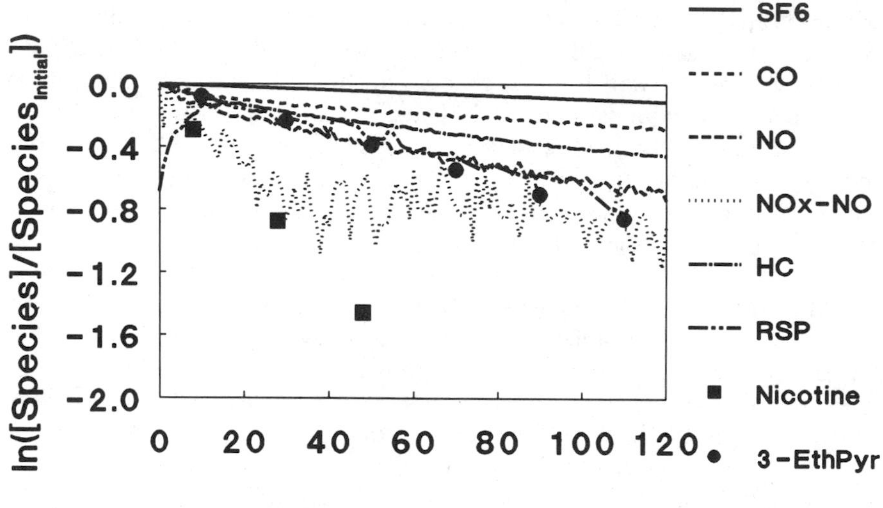

Figure 1–4. Change in the ln of the Ratio of the Concentration of Various Constituents of Environmental Tobacco Smoke to the Concentration at Time Zero versus Time after Combustion of 4 Cigarettes in a Sealed Experimental Indoor Laboratory with No Air Recirculation.

Source: Tang 1989a.

able 1–2
as and Particulate Phase Compounds Potentially Useful as Tracers for nvironmental Tobacco Smoke

hemical lass	*Class wt% of Particle*	*Examples of Identified Compounds*	*µMol Compound/ Mol CO Gas Phase*	*Particles*	*% Compound in Gas Phase*
articles				4.22 ± 0.82g/mol CO	
utagenicity				6.47 ± 1.15revertants/µg	
kanes/	3.6 ± 0.5	Phytadiene	-----a	138 ± 13	-----
kenes		n-Hentriacontane	-----	93 ± 29	-----
		1,3-Butadiene	3100 ± 850	-----	100
		Isoprene	19200 ± 5600	-----	100
		Solanesol	-----	219 ± 43	0
ases	10.9 ± 1.2	Nicotine	12500 ± 3600	393 ± 150	98.3 ± 1.4
		Myosmine	375 ± 38	14.7 ± 1.7	96.1 ± 10.9
		Nicotyrine	16 ± 6	10.6 ± 3.3	60 ± 20
		Cotinine	18.2 ± 9.4	17.7 ± 7.0	54.6 ± 12.8
		Pyridine	1180 ± 72	< 5	100
		3-Ethenylpyridine	1370 ± 460	< 5	100
		2-Ethenylpyridine	207 ± 36	< 5	100
erols	0.5 ± 0.1	Campesterol	-----	6.4 ± 2.4	0
		Stigmasterol	-----	12.1 ± 6.5	0
		B-Sitosterol	-----	9.1 ± 7.5	0
		Cholesterol	-----	5.9 ± 1.3	0
erenesb	0.4 ± 0.3	24-MeC-3,5-dien	-----	8.8 ± 8.5	0
		24-EtC-3,5,22-trien	-----	6.8 ± 3.4	0
AH	<0.1	Pyrene	-----	0.02 ± 0.01	-----
		Phenanthrene	-----	0.11 ± 0.02	-----
organic	-----	NO	36700 ± 3200	0	100
		NO_2	2520 ± 430	0	44 ± 24
		HNO_3	96 ± 127	92 ± 55	98.7 ± 1.0
		HNO_2	4650 ± 1300	54 ± 40	
		SO_2 + Sulfate	71 ± 52	71 ± 40	49 ± 23
		NH_3	51900 ± 5400	155 ± 34	99.6 ± 0.2
		Potassium	0	840 ± 150	0
		Calcium	0	340 ± 100	0

urces: Benner 1989, Eatough 1989a,b, Löfroth 1989, Ogden 1988a,b, Thompson 1989.
--- = not determined.
leC and EtC = Methylcholesta and Ethylcholesta.

change rates for the decrease with time in the concentrations of the various constituents in the sealed laboratory (Tang 1989a) increase in the order,

$$SF_6 < \text{CO}, NO_x\text{-NO} < \text{HC} < \text{NO} < \text{RSP, 3-ethenylpyridine} < \text{nicotine.}$$

The initial decay rates of both NO and NO_x-NO are very rapid for the first 10 to 30 minutes (see Figure 1–4), then slow to the extent that their overall decay rates are in the order given above. This suggests reaction of the nitrogen oxides with the furnishings of the laboratory or with components of the ambient air (e.g., ozone) produces non-volatile products (Eatough 1988a, Pitts 1988).

Results of an experiment with air exchange with the ambient air after combustion of four cigarettes are given in Figure 1–5. For these data, the rate of loss of the various species measured increases in the order,

$$NO_x\text{-NO} < SF_6, \text{CO} < \text{HC} < \text{NO , RSP, 3-ethenylpyridine} < \text{nicotine.}$$

This is the same order as seen in the experiments without air recirculation except that the NO_x-NO species appear more stable. That NO_x-NO decays more slowly than SF_6 (Figure 1–5) indicates post-combustion conversion of NO to oxidized species as additional outside air is brought into the laboratory. The apparent decrease in the rate of disappearance of CO with time (Figure 1–5) results from the fact that the outside air contains measurable CO and the concentration of CO in the chamber decays to this value and not to zero. The background concentrations of all other species are negligible. Data obtained with sequential smoking of cigarettes in the experimental laboratory give comparable rates of disappearance of the various species (Tang 1989a).

In all experiments, nicotine was the ETS compound most rapidly removed from the indoor environment. As a result, the relative amount of nicotine compared to these species decreases as the ETS ages. This result is consistent with previous reports suggesting that RSP and 3-ethenylpyridine behave similarly in indoor environments but that nicotine is removed at a much faster rate than these species (Benner 1989, Eatough 1989b,c, Thompson 1989). The data also suggest that NO from ETS is converted to other products in indoor environments. The conversion possibly involves reaction with oxidants from the ambient air. This may account, at least in part, for the production of nitric and nitrous acids in indoor environments in the presence of ETS (Eatough 1988a, Pitts 1988).

Several studies in controlled indoor environments have shown that nicotine is removed much faster than are CO, RSP, NO, gas phase hydrocarbons or specific particulate phase compounds (Baker 1988, Lewis 1988, Thome 1986, Tang 1989a, Thompson 1989). The importance of these laboratory

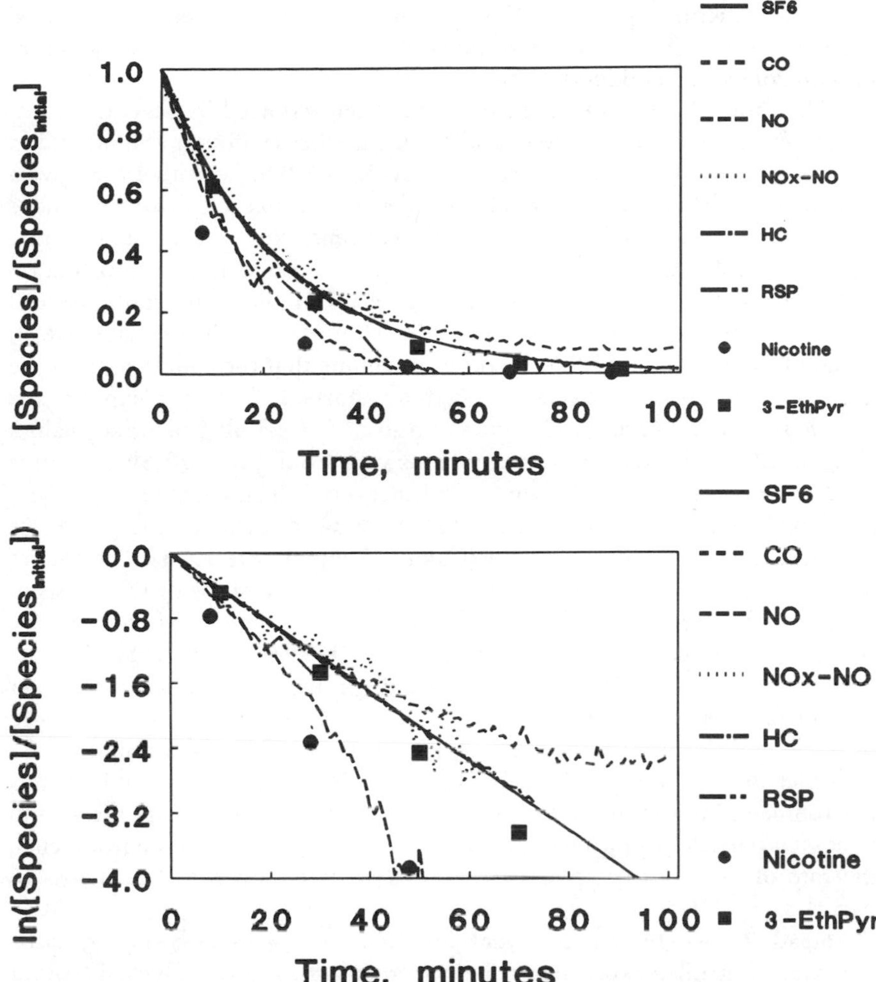

Figure 1–5. Change in the Ratio of the Concentration (A) and ln of the Concentration (B) of Various Constituents of Environmental Tobacco Smoke to the Concentration at Time Zero versus Time after Combustion of Cigarettes in the Laboratory with Both Air Recirculation and Air Exchange with the Ambient.

Source: Tang 1989a.

observations with respect to ETS in typical indoor environments is best illustrated by comparing the concentrations of nicotine to fine particulate matter in both controlled and indoor atmospheres.

The ratio of RSP to total nicotine has been reported by several investigators. Experiments conducted in a Teflon chamber (Eatough 1989a) and in chambers with high ventilation rates (Thompson 1989, Löfroth 1989) give a ratio of 2–3 g RSP/g nicotine in diluted sidestream tobacco smoke. Data have been reported as a function of time for the concentration of particles resulting from the combustion of one cigarette and the concentration of nicotine resulting from the combustion of two cigarettes in the same stainless steel chamber at different times (Heavner 1986, Thome 1986). These data give an initial ratio of about 3 g RSP/g nicotine, assuming that the concentrations are linearly related to the number of cigarettes burned. Chamber experiments reported by Badre et al. (1978) give a ratio of 3.8 g RSP/g nicotine. Values determined in sidestream smoke emissions vary from 2 to 6 g RSP/g nicotine (Guerin 1987, Klus 1982, Sakuma 1984, Rickert 1984), with the higher values probably resulting from partial loss of some nicotine to the gas phase during sample collection on a filter (Caka 1989a,b, Badre 1978). The studies of ETS conducted in non-Teflon chambers give higher ratios of RSP to nicotine, probably because of the more rapid removal of gas phase nicotine by chamber components (Badre 1978, Eatough 1989b, Lewis 1988, Thome 1986, Tang 1989a, Thompson 1989). Results from decay studies in chamber or controlled environment experiments are shown in Figure 1–6. The ratio of nicotine/RSP increases slightly with time in experiments conducted in a Teflon chamber (Benner 1989), because gas phase nicotine is stable in this environment, but the concentration of particles decreases by evaporation and by loss of particles to the chamber walls. In all the other study environments, the rate of decay of gas phase nicotine is greater than the rate of loss of particles.

Steady-state experiments in ventilated chambers with individuals present or in well-controlled experimental indoor environments give values of around 10 to 15 g RSP/g nicotine (Hammond 1987a,b, Lewis 1988, Lewtas 1987b, Löfroth 1989, Piade 1988, Tang 1989a). This ratio is larger than that which would be seen if people (and the accompanying absorptive surfaces) were not present. For example, in studies in the chamber at the U.S. Environmental Protection Agency (Löfroth 1989), the ratio of RSP to nicotine when the chamber had people in it was 13 g RSP/g nicotine. In the empty chamber, the ratio was determined to be 3.0 g RSP/g nicotine, a ratio consistent with the value obtained for sidestream smoke (Guerin 1987, Klus 1982, Sakuma 1984, Rickert 1984) and in inert chambers (Badre 1978, Benner 1989, Eatough 1989a, Thompson 1989).

Nicotine has been suggested as a tracer of ETS particles in indoor environments. However, experiments conducted in indoor environments indicate

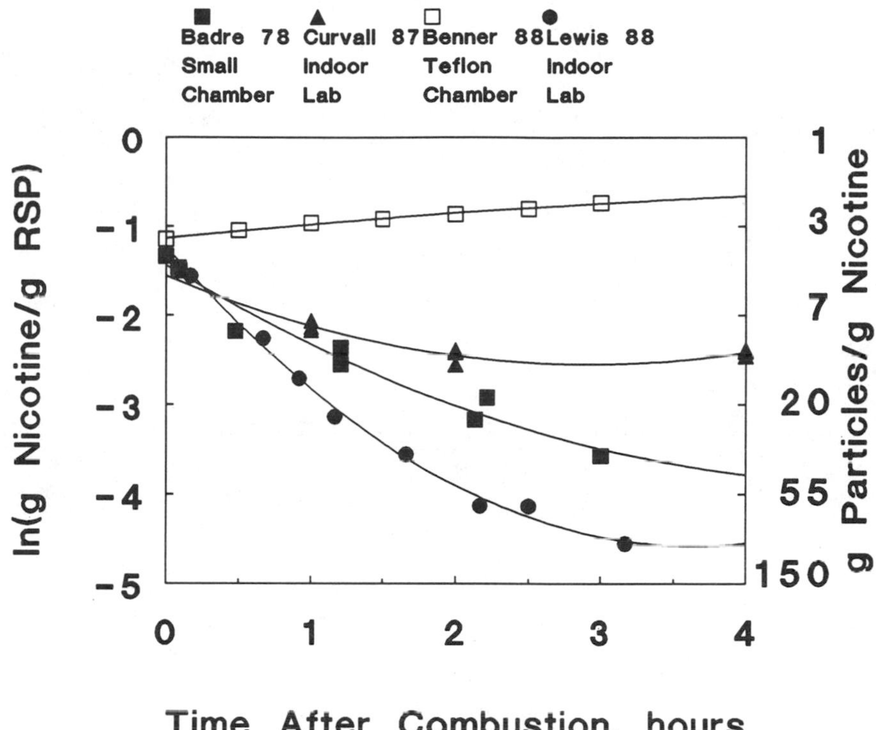

Figure 1–6. Change in the Ratio of Nicotine to RSP with Time in Chamber and Controlled Indoor Experiments.

Source: Eatough 1989c.

that the observed ratio of particles to nicotine in atmospheres dominated by smoking varies from 3 to 80 g RSP/g nicotine (Eatough 1989b, Klus 1987, Eudy 1987, Hammond 1987a, McCarthy 1987, McCurdy 1987, Miesner 1988, Muramatsu 1984, Thompson 1989) (Figure 1–7). The ratio generally increases with increased residence time and/or decreased total nicotine concentrations. Studies by McCurdy et al. (1987) in a bingo parlor indicate that the mass ratio of particles to nicotine was fairly constant at 6.5 ± 0.9 g RSP/g nicotine for nicotine concentrations of 14 to 27 μg/m3. In contrast, the ratio was variable in a casino with lower concentrations of nicotine, 2 to 7 g/m3. Ratios from 14 to 54 were found, with an average value of 25 ± 11 g RSP/g nicotine. The ratio tended to increase with decreasing nicotine concentrations (Figure 1–7). Eudy et al. (1987) have reported ratios of 9 to 33 g RSP/g nicotine in samples collected in occupied restaurants with low concentrations of nicotine, with a similar trend of the ratio with nicotine concentra-

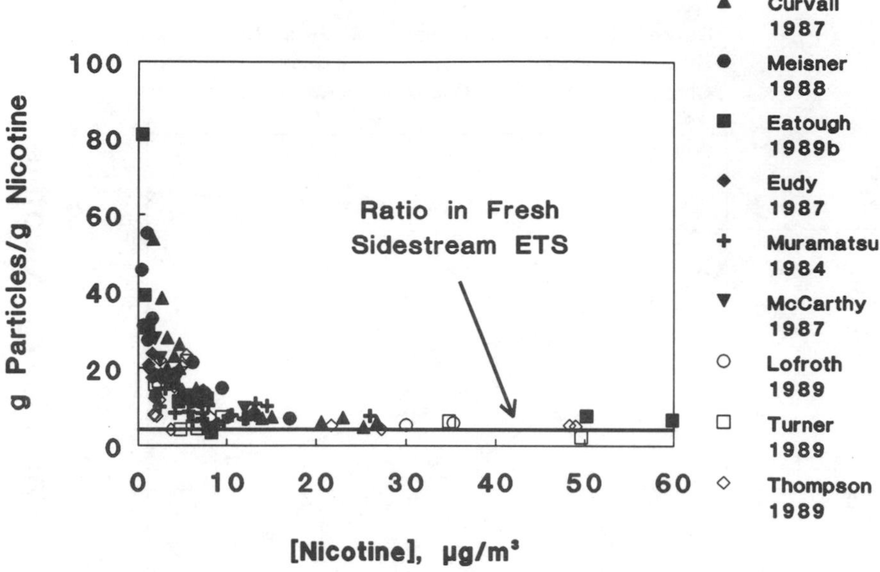

Figure 1–7. Ratio of RSP to Nicotine as a Function of Nicotine Concentration in Indoor Environments.

Sources: Eatough 1989c, Thompson 1989.

Note: The concentration of nicotine on the abscissa is divided by 2 for the open data points.

tion. The same trends have been seen (Eatough 1989b, Miesner 1988, Turner 1988, Thompson 1989) for samples collected in a variety of homes and offices with nicotine concentrations varying from 0.3 to 10 μg/m3 (Figure 1–7).

The ratios found in a disco, bar or office with much higher concentrations of nicotine were comparable to those seen in a Teflon chamber (Eatough 1989a, Löfroth 1989, Turner 1988, Thompson 1989). Muramatsu et al. (1984) reported the ratio of particles to nicotine for samples collected during a single working day in a ventilated office. The ratio measured was fairly constant, 8.3 ± 2.0 g RSP/g nicotine, with nicotine concentrations varying from 2 to 26 μg/m^3 (Figure 1–3). McCarthy et al. (1987) have determined the concentrations of particulate matter and of total nicotine in a wide variety of homes. They only reported average, median and high concentrations for the 68 homes studied. The g RSP/g nicotine and nicotine concentration calculated from these values are shown in Figure 1–7.

The combined results of the various studies reported to date (Figure 1–7) indicate that the ratio of particles to nicotine is constant at about 4–10 g RSP/g nicotine for concentrations of nicotine greater than about 10 μg/m^3.

This value is consistent with that reported in experimental chambers (Curvall 1987, Goldstein 1987, Lewtas 1987b, Löfroth 1989, Thompson 1989). At lower concentrations of nicotine, however, the ratio is much more variable, and probably depends on the ventilation conditions and materials in a given environment. The data in Figure 1–7 suggest that the variability in the ratio of particles to nicotine is about a factor of ten for most indoor environments where smoking is present. The results given in Figures 1–6 and 1–7 suggest that gas phase nicotine (or total nicotine) is not a good marker of the particulate phase of ETS due to its rapid removal from indoor environments.

The results given in Figure 1–7 overemphasize the variability in the ratio of RSP from ETS to nicotine due to the increasing importance of particulate matter from other sources at low concentrations of airborne nicotine. Data on concentrations of nicotine and UV-PM, which is believed to be indicative of the RSP originating from ETS (Carson 1988), provide an additional way to examine the relationship between nicotine and ETS RSP. The ratio of UV-PM to nicotine increases as the concentration of nicotine decreases (Eatough 1989c). The lower limit of the mass ratio of UV-PM to nicotine is about 2. This ratio is consistent with that expected from studies of sidestream tobacco smoke.

Linear regression of UV-PM against nicotine for the data reported by Carson (Carson 1988, Eatough 1989c) gives, $r^2 = 0.504$, a slope of 3.6 ± 0.7 g UV-PM/g nicotine with an intercept of 47 ± 57 μg UV-PM/m^3. The summary of a large data set from an aircraft passenger cabin air quality study (Oldaker 1989a) reports that, at high concentrations of nicotine, the mass ratio of UV-PM to nicotine was 2.6 and 3.6 for the smoking and nonsmoking sections. In indoor environments (Carson 1988), the ratio of UV-PM to nicotine varies from a low of about 2 to a high of about 10 at low nicotine concentrations (Eatough 1989c). Comparison of the data in Figure 1–7, based on total RSP measurements, with the results of the study based on UV-PM measurements (Eatough 1989c) suggests that at low nicotine concentrations from 50% to less than 25% of the RSP present in indoor environments where smoking occurs may come from ETS.

McCurdy, et al. (1987) have reported on the simultaneous determination of the mutagenicity of particulate matter, concentrations of RSP and concentrations of nicotine in a bingo parlor and in a casino, Figure 8. The linear regression of revertants vs RSP, $r^2 = 0.61$, gives a slope of 0.12 ± 0.03 μg RSP/revertant with a positive intercept. These data could then be interpreted to be due to a background of non-mutagenic particulate matter with increasing mutagenicity of the particulate matter as the concentration of ETS RSP increases. The mutagenicity of the RSP determined using a microassay with TA98 tester strain and added S9 is about 8 revertants/μg RSP. This value agrees with the mutagenicity of ETS determined in chamber studies (Lewtas 1987b, Löfroth 1989). In contrast, comparison of the mutagenicity and nic-

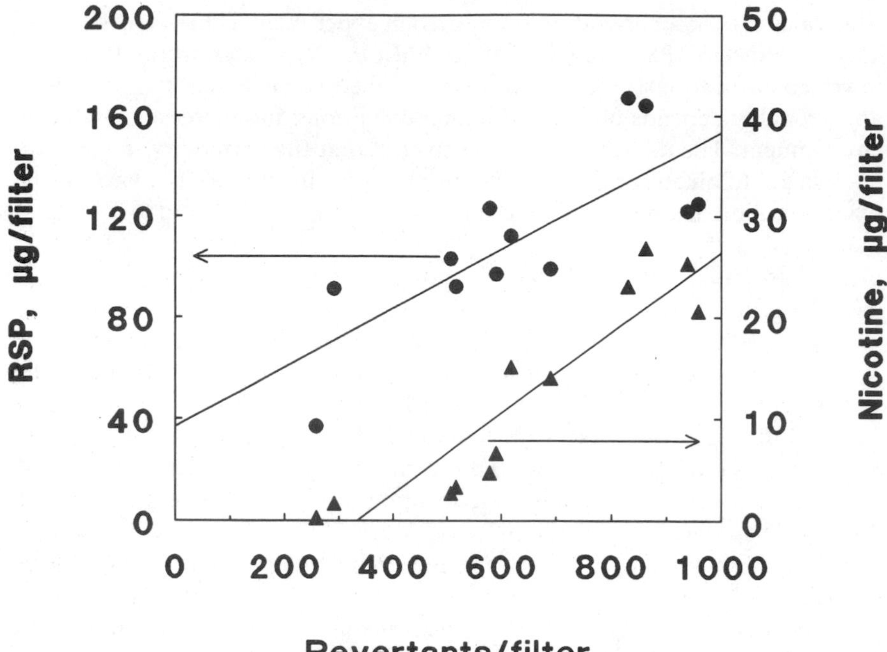

Figure 1–8. Plot of Revertants/Filter versus Concentrations of RSP and Nicotine for Samples Collected in a Casino or a Bingo Parlor.

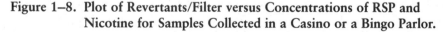

Source: McCurdy 1987, from Eatough 1989c.

otine data, Figure 8, leads to the conclusion that there is measurable background mutagenicity when no nicotine is present and that the increase in mutagenicity with increasing nicotine concentration is about 25 revertants/µg nicotine, a value smaller than expected from chamber studies. The differences between the two interpretations of the data is due to the more rapid removal of nicotine from the casino, as compared to the RSP, e.g., see Figure 7.

B. Changes Due to Chemistry

A few studies report changes in the chemical composition of ETS as it ages in an indoor environment. In the absence of external oxidizing agents or UV light, NO in ETS is only very slowly converted to NO_2, HNO_2 and possible organic nitrogen-oxide compounds (Benner 1989). In the presence of a strong UV light source, this conversion is rapid (Benner 1989). In addition, under these extreme conditions, the photochemistry leads to doubling of total particulate matter, less gas phase basic compounds, loss of solanesol, and photochemical alterations in the nitrogen-containing bases of ETS (Benner 1989, Tang 1989b, 1988a,b). The exact chemical reactions taking place are not known. Under more realistic conditions where some oxidants are introduced into an indoor environment from the ambient air (Tang 1989a), the same reactions appear to occur but at a greatly reduced rate (see Section III.A). The possible significance of such chemistry with respect to the toxicological properties of ETS is discussed in Section II.D.

IV. Recommended Future Research

The following questions need to be answered by future research:

1. How does the chemical composition of ETS vary under different smoking conditions?
2. What chemical and physical changes occur in ETS as it ages in a variety of indoor environments?
3. What particulate and gas phase components of ETS are of importance with respect to potential health and irritant effects on the nonsmoker?
4. What compounds and/or ETS components may be used as tracers of the particles of ETS?
5. For what gas phase compounds in ETS are exposure assessment data needed, and what tracers may be used to assess that exposure?
6. Can a reliable biomarker be developed for determining exposure to ETS?

References

Adams, J.D., K.J. O'Mara-Adams and D. Hoffmann (1987). Toxic and carcinogenic agents in undiluted mainstream smoke and sidestream smoke of different types of cigarettes. *Carcinogenesis* 8: 729–731.

Albert, R.E. (1983). Comparative carcinogenic potencies of particulates from diesel engine exhausts, coke oven emissions, roofing tar aerosols and cigarette smoke. *Environ. Health Perspectives* 47: 339–341.

Alfheim, I., and T. Ramdahl (1984). Contribution of wood combustion to indoor air pollution as measured by mutagenicity in salmonella and polycyclic aromatic hydrocarbon concentration. *Environ. Mutagenesis* 6: 121–130.

Alfheim, I., G. Löfroth and M. Moller (1983). Bioassay of Extracts of Ambient Particulate Matter. *Environ. Health Perspectives* 47: 227–238.

Austin, A.C., L.D. Claxton and J. Lewtas (1985). Mutagenicity of the fractionated organic emissions from diesel, cigarette smoke condensate, coke oven and roofing tar in the ames assay. *Environ. Mutagen* 7: 471–487.

Aviado, D.M. (1987). Suspected pulmonary carcinogens in environmental tobacco smoke. *Indoor and Ambient Air Quality,* Perry R. and Kirk P.W., eds., Selper Ltd., London, pp 141–146.

Badre, R., R. Guillerm, N. Abran, M. Bourdin and C. Dumas (1978). Pollution atmosphe'rique par le fume'e de tabac. *Annal. Pharm. Franc.* 36: 443–452.

Baker, R.R. (1980). Mechanisms of smoke formation and delivery. *Recent Adv. Tob. Sci.* 6: 184–224.

Baker, R.R., P.D. Case and N.D. Warren (1988). The build-up and decay of environmental tobacco smoke constituents as a function of room conditions. *Indoor and Ambient Air Quality,* Perry R and P.W. Kirk, eds., Selper Ltd., London, pp 121–130.

Benner, C.L., J.M. Bayona, M.L. Lee, E.A. Lewis, L.D. Hansen, N.L. Eatough and D.J. Eatough (1989). The chemical composition of environmental tobacco smoke. II. Particulate-Phase Compounds." *Environ. Sci. Tech.* 23: 688–699.

Bos, R.P. and P.Th. Henderson (1984). Genotoxic risk of passive smoking. *Rev. Environ. Health,* IV, No. 2, 161–178.

Bos, R.P., J.L.G. Theuws and P.Th. Henderson (1983). Excretion of mutagens in human urine after passive smoking. *Cancer Lett.* 19: 85–90.

Browne, C.L., K.H. Keith, and R.E. Allen (1980). The effect of filter ventilation on the yield and composition of mainstream and sidestream smokes. *Beit, Tabakforsch. Int.* 10: 81–90.

Brunnemann, K.D., L. Genoble and D. Hoffmann (1987). Identification and analysis of a new tobacco-specific N-Nitrosamine, 4-(methylnitrosamino)-4-(3-pyridyl)-1-butanol." *Carcinogenesis* 8: 465–469.

Brunnemann, K.D., J. Masoryk and D. Hoffmann (1983). Role of stems in the formation of N-nitrosamines in tobacco and cigarette mainstream and sidestream smoke. *J. Agric. Food Chem.* 31: 1221–1224.

Brunnemann, K.D., W. Fink and F. Moser (1980). Analysis of volatile N-nitrosamines in mainstream and sidestream smoke from cigarettes by GLC-TEH. *Oncology* 37: 217–222.

Brunnemann, K.D. and D. Hoffmann (1975). Chemical studies on tobacco smoke - XXXIV. Gas chromatographic determination of ammonia in cigarette and cigar smoke. *J. Chromatogr.* 13: 159–163.

Brunnemann, K.D. and D. Hoffmann (1974). The pH of tobacco smoke. *Food Cosmetics Toxicol* 12: 115–124.

Cain, W.S., T. Tosun, L.-C. See and B. Leaderer (1987). Environmental tobacco smoke: sensory reactions of occupants. *Atmospheric Environment* 21: 347–353.

Cain, W.W., B.P. Leaderer, R. Isseroff, L.G. Berglund, R.J. Huey, E.D. Lipsitt and D. Perlman (1983). Ventilation requirements in buildings—I. Control of occupancy odor and tobacco smoke odor. *Atmospheric Environment* 6: 1183–1197.

Caka, F.M., D.J. Eatough, E.A. Lewis, H. Tang, S.K. Hammond, B.P. Leaderer, P. Koutrakis, J.D. Spengler, A. Fasano, M.W. Ogden and J. Lewtas (1989a). An intercomparison of sampling techniques for nicotine in indoor environments. *Environ. Sci. Technol.,* in press.

Caka, F.M., D.J. Eatough, E.A. Lewis, H. Tang, S.K. Hammond, B.P. Leaderer, P. Koutrakis, J.D. Spengler, A. Fasano, M.W. Ogden and J. Lewtas (1989b). A comparison study of sampling techniques for nicotine in indoor environments. Proceedings, AWMA/EPA Symposium on the Measurement of Toxic and Related Air Pollutants, Air and Waste Management Association, in press.

Carson, J.R. and C.A. Erikson (1988). Results from survey of environmental tobacco smoke in offices in Ottawa, Ontario. *Environ. Tech. Letters* 9: 501–508.

Chrisp, C.E. and G.L. Fisher (1980). Mutagenicity of airborne particles. *Mutat. Res.* 76: 143–164.

Church, D.F. and W.A. Pryor (1985). Free radical chemistry of cigarette smoke and its toxicological implications. *Env. Health Perspectives* 64: 111.

Cornell, A., W. Cartwright and V. Olender (1978). Sidestream/mainstream (SS/MS) distribution ratios of steam volatile phenols in cigarette and cigar smoke. Tobacco Chemists Research Conference Paper No. 43, Montreal, Canada.

Cupitt, L.T., L.D. Claxton, P.B. Shepson and T.E. Kleindienst (1987). IACP emissions: Transformations and fate. Proceedings, EPA/APCA Symposium on Measurement of Toxic and Related Air Pollutants. Air Pollution Control Association, 597–604.

Cupitt, L.T., L.D. Claxton, T.E. Kleindienst, D.F. Smith and P.B. Shepson (1988). Transformation of Boise sources: The Production and distribution of mutagenic compounds in wood smoke and auto exhaust. Proceedings, EPA/APCA Symposium on Measurement of Toxic and Related Pollutants, Air Pollution Control Association, 975–989.

Curvall, M., E. Kazemi-Vala, C.R. Enzell, L. Olander and J. Johansson (1987). Inhaled amount of tobacco smoke during passive smoking. Indoor Air '87, Proceedings of the Fourth International Conference on Indoor Air Quality and Climate, Berlin (West), 17–21 August 1987, B. Seifert, H. Esdorn, M. Fischer, H. Ruden, J. Wegner, Eds., Institute for Water, Soil and Air Hygiene, Vol. 2: 57–60.

DeMarini, D.M. (1983). Genotoxicity of tobacco smoke and tobacco smoke condensate. *Mutat. Res.* 114: 59–89.

DHHS (1986). The health consequences of involuntary smoking, A Report of the Surgeon General, U.S. Department of Health and Human Services, 332 pp.

Eatough, D.J., C.L. Benner, J.M. Bayona, F.M. Caka, G. Richards, J.D. Lamb, E.A. Lewis and L.D. Hansen (1989a). The chemical composition of environmental tobacco smoke. I. Gas phase acids and bases. *Environ. Sci. Technol.* 23: 679–687.

Eatough, D.J., C.L. Benner, H. Tang, V. Landon, G. Richards, F.M. Caka, J. Crawford, E.A. Lewis., L.D. Hansen and N.L. Eatough (1989b). The chemical composition of environmental tobacco smoke. III. Identification of conservative tracers of environmental tobacco smoke. *Environ. Inter.* 18: 19–28.

Eatough, D.J., L.D. Hansen and E.A. Lewis (1989c). Methods for assessing exposure to environmental tobacco smoke. APCA Specialty Conference, Niagara Falls, NY, October 1988, pp 183–200.

Eatough, D.J., C. Benner, R.L. Mooney, D. Bartholomew, D.S. Steiner, L.D. Hansen, J.D. Lamb and E.A. Lewis (1986). Gas and particle phase nicotine in environmental tobacco smoke. Proceedings, 79th Annual Meeting of the Air Pollut. Contr. Assoc. Paper 86–68.5, 22–27 June, Minneapolis, MN.

Eatough, D.J., L. Lewis, J.D. Lamb, J. Crawford, E.A. Lewis, L.D. Hansen and N.L. Eatough (1988a). Nitric and nitrous acids in environmental tobacco smoke. Proceedings of the 1988 EPA/APCA Symposium on Measurement of Toxic and Related Air Pollutants, pp 104–112.

Eatough, D.J., C.L. Benner, J.M. Bayona, F.M. Caka, R.L. Mooney, J.D. Lamb, M.L. Lee, E.A. Lewis, L.D. Hansen and N.L. Eatough (1987a). Identification of conservative tracers of environmental tobacco smoke. Indoor Air '87, Proceedings of the Fourth International Conference on Indoor Air Quality and Climate, Berlin (West), Seifert B., H. Esdorn, M. Fischer, H. Ruden, J. Wegner, Eds., Institute for Water, Soil and Air Hygiene, Vol. 2, 3–7.

Eatough, D.J., C.L. Benner, J.M. Bayona, F.M. Caka, H. Tang, L. Lewis, J.D. Lamb, M.L. Lee, E.A. Lewis and L.D. Hansen (1987b). Sampling for gas and particle phase nicotine in environmental tobacco smoke with a diffusion denuder and a passive sampler. Proceedings, EPA/APCA Symposium on Measurement of Toxic and Related Air Pollutants. Air Pollution Control Association, pp. 132–139.

Eudy, L.W., F.A. Thome, D.K. Heavner, C.R. Green and B.J. Ingebrethsen (1986). Studies on the vapor-particulate phase distribution of environmental nicotine by selective trapping and detection methods. Paper 86–38.7, Proceedings of the 79th Annual Meeting of the Air Pollution Control Association. Minneapolis, MN.

Goldstein, G.M., A. Collier, R. Etzel, J. Lewtas and N. Haley (1987). Elimination of urinary cotinine in children exposed to known levels of sidestream cigarette smoke. Indoor Air '87, Proceedings of the Fourth International Conference on Indoor Air Quality and Climate, Berlin (West), 17–21 August 1987, B. Seifert, H. Esdorn, M. Fischer, H. Ruden, J. Wegner, Eds., Institute for Water, Soil and Air Hygiene, Vol 2, 61–67.

Grimmer, G., Naujack K.-W. and Dettbarn G. (1987). Gas chromatographic determination of polycyclic aromatic hydrocarbons, aza-arenes, aromatic amiens in the particle and vapor phase of mainstream and sidestream smoke of cigarettes. *Toxicology Letters* 35: 117–124.

Guerin, M. R., C.E. Higgins and R.A. Jenkins (1987a). Measuring environmental emissions from tobacco combustion: sidestream cigarette smoke literature review. *Atmos. Environ.* 21: 291–297.

Halpern, A. and Knieper J. (1985) "Spin-Trapping of Radicals in Gas-Phase Cigarette Smoke." *Z. Naturforsch* 40b: 850.

Hammond, S.K. and J. Coghlin (1987a). Field study of passive smoking exposure with passive sampler. Indoor Air '87, Proceedings of the Fourth International Conference on Indoor Air Quality and Climate, Berlin (West), 17–21 August 1987, B. Seifert, H. Esdorn, M. Fischer, H. Ruden, J. Wegner, Eds., Institute for Water, Soil and Air Hygiene, Vol. 2, 131–136.

Hammond, S.K., B.P. Leaderer, A.C. Roche and M. Schenker (1987b). Collection and analysis of nicotine as a marker for environmental tobacco smoke. *Atmos. Environ.* 21: 457–462.

Heavner, D.L., F.A. Thome, L.W. Eudy, B.J. Ingebrethsen and C.R. Green (1986). A test chamber and instrumentation for the analysis of selected environmental tobacco smoke (ETS) components. Paper 86–37.9, Proceedings of the 79th Annual Meeting of the Air Pollution Control Association. Minneapolis, Minnesota.

Hiller, F.D., K.T. McCusker, M.K. Mazumder, J.D. Wilson and R.C. Bone (1982). Deposition of sidestream cigarette smoke in the human respiratory tract. *Am. Rev. Respir. Dis.* 125: 406–408.

Hoffmann, D., J.D. Adams and K.D. Brunnemann (1987b). A critical look at N-nitrosamines in environmental tobacco smoke. *Toxicology Letters* 35: 1–8.

Hughes, T.J., E. Pellizzari, L. Little, C. Sparacino and A. Kolber (1980). Ambient air pollutants: collection, chemical characterization and mutagenicity testing. *Mutat. Res.* 76: 51–83.

Husgafvel-Pursiainen, K., M. Sorsa, M. Moller and C. Benestad (1986). Genotoxicity and polynuclear aromatic hydrocarbon analysis of environmental tobacco smoke samples from restaurants. *Mutagenesis,* 1: 287–292.

Ingebrethsen, B.J. (1986). Aerosol Studies of Cigarette Smoke. TCRC, Knoxville, TN, October 13–16, 1986.

Jenkins, R.A., C.V. Thompson, and C.E. Higgins (1988). Development and application of a thermal description based method for the determination of nicotine in indoor environments. *Indoor and Ambient Air Quality,* (R. Perry and P.W. Kirk, eds.), Selper Ltd., London, pp. 551–565.

Jenkins, R.W. Jr., R.H. Newman, G.F. Lester, A.F. Frisch and T.G. Williamson (1982a). Neutron activation analysis in tobacco and cigarette smoke studies: the halogens. *Beit. Tabakforsch.* 11: 195–202.

Jenkins, R.W. Jr., B.W. Francis, H. Flachsbart, W. Stober, J.R. Tucci and T.G. Williamson (1982b). Inorganic composition of mainstream tobacco smoke as a function of aerodynamic particle Size. *J. Aerosol Sci.* 13: 459–468.

Johnson, W.R., R.W. Hale, J.W. Nedlock, H.J. Grubbs, and O.H. Powell. (1973). The distribution of products between mainstream and sidestream smoke. *Tob. Sci.* 17: 141–144.

Kado, N.Y., D. Langley and E. Eisenstadt (1983). A simple modification of the salmonella liquid-incubation assay: increased sensitivity for detecting mutagens in human urine. *Mutat. Res.* 121: 25–32.

Kamens, R.M., D.A. Bell, A. Dietrich, J.M. Perry, R.G. Goodman, L.D. Claxton, S. Tejada (1985). Mutagenic transformations of dilute wood smoke systems in the presence of ozone and nitrogen dioxide. Analysis of selected high-pressure liquid chromatography fractions from wood smoke particle extracts. *Environ. Sci. Technol.* 19: 63–69.

Kamens, R.M., G.D. Rives, J.M. Perry, D.A. Bell, R.F. Paylor, Jr., R.G. Goodman and L.D. Claxton (1984). Mutagenic changes in dilute wood smoke as it ages and reacts with ozone and nitrogen dioxide: An outdoor chamber study. *Environ. Sci. Technol.* 18: 523–530.

Keith, C.H., J.C. Derrick (1960). Measurement of the particle size distribution and concentration of cigarette smoke by the "conifuge." *J. Colloid Sci.* 15: 340–356.

Kirk, P.W.W., M. Hunter, S.O. Baek, J.N. Lester and R. Perry (1988). Environmental tobacco smoke in indoor air. *Indoor and Ambient Air Quality,* R. Perry and P.W. Kirk, eds., Selper Ltd., London, pp 99–112.

Kleindienst, T.E., P.B. Shepson, E.O. Edney, L.T. Cupitt and L.D. Claxton (1985). The mutagenic activity of the products of propylene photo-oxidation. *Environ. Sci. Technol.* 19: 620–627.

Klus, H. and H. Begutter (1987). Environmental tobacco smoke in real life situations. Indoor Air '87, Proceedings of the Fourth International Conference on Indoor Air Quality and Climate, Berlin (West), B. Seifert, H. Esdorn, M. Fischer, H. Ruden, J. Wegner, Eds., Institute for Water, Soil and Air Hygiene, Vol. 2, 137–141.

Klus, H. and H. Kuhn (1982). Verteilung verschiendener tabakrauchbestandteile auf haupt and nebenstromrauch. *Beit. Tabakforsch. Int.* 11: 229–265.

Lewis, E.A., H. Tang, J.W. Crawford, L.D. Hansen and D.J. Eatough (1988). Laboratory for the study of environmental tobacco smoke components. Proceedings, 81st Annual Meeting of the Air Pollution Control Association, Paper 88–76.7, Dallas, TX.

Lewtas, J. (1989). Genotoxicity of complex mixtures: strategies for the identification and comparative assessment of airborne mutagens and carcinogens from combustion sources. *Fundamental Appl. Tox.* 10: 571–589.

Lewtas, J., S. Goto, K. Williams, J.C. Chuang, B.A. Petersen and N.K. Wilson (1987a). The mutagenicity of indoor air particles in a residential pilot field study. *Atmos. Environ.* 21: 443–449.

Lewtas, J., K. Williams, G. Löfroth, K. Hammond and B. Leaderer (1987b). Environmental tobacco smoke: mutagenic emission rates and their relationship to other emission factors. Indoor Air '87, Proceedings of the Fourth International Conference on Indoor Air Quality and Climate, Berlin (West), B. Seifert, H. Esdorn, M. Fischer, H. Ruden, J. Wegner, Eds., Institute for Water, Soil and Air Hygiene, Vol. 2, 8–12.

Lewtas, J., R.L. Bradow, R.H. Jungers, B.D. Harris, R.B. Zweidinger, K.M. Cushing, B.E. Gill and R.E. Albert (1981). Mutagenic and carcinogenic potency of extracts of diesel and related environmental emissions: Study design, sample generation, collection, and preparation. *Environ. Int.* 5: 383–387.

Lioy, P.J., M. Avdenko, B. Harkov, T. Atherholt and J.M. Daisey (1985). A pilot indoor-outdoor study of organic particulate matter and particulate mutagenicity. *JAPCA* 35: 653–657.

Löfroth, G., R.M. Burton, L. Forehand, S.K. Hammond, R.L.Sella, R.B. Zwerdinger and J. Lewtas (1989). Characterization of environmental tobacco smoke. *Env. Sci. Tech.*, in press.

Löfroth, G., P.I. Ling, E. Agurell (1988). Public exposure to environmental tobacco smoke. *Mut. Res.* 202: 103–110.

Löfroth, G. and G. Lazaridis (1986). Environmental tobacco smoke: Comparative characterization by mutagenicity assays of sidestream and mainstream cigarette smoke. *Environ. Mutagenesis* 8: 693–704.

Löfroth, G., L. Nilsson and I. Alfheim (1983). Passive smoking and urban air pollution: Salmonella/microsome mutagenicity assay of simultaneously collected indoor and outdoor particulate matter. Short-Term Bioassays in the Analysis of Complex Environmental Mixtures, III, S. Waters, et al., eds., Plenum, New York, 515–525.

McCarthy, J., J. Spengler, B-H. Chang, D. Coultas and J. Samet (1987). A personal monitoring study to assess exposure to environmental tobacco smoke. Indoor Air '87, Proceedings of the Fourth International Conference on Indoor Air Quality and Climate, Berlin (West), 17–21 August 1987, B. Seifert, H. Esdorn, M. Fischer, H. Ruden, J. Wegner, Eds., Institute for Water, Soil and Air Hygiene, Vol. 2, 142–146.

McCurdy, S.A., N.Y. Kado, M.B. Schenker, S.K. Hammond and N.L. Benowitz (1987). Measurement of personal exposure to mutagens in environmental tobacco smoke. Indoor Air '87, Proceedings of the Fourth International Conference on Indoor Air Quality and Climate, Berlin (West), B. Seifert, H. Esdorn, M. Fischer, H. Ruden, J. Wegner, Eds., Institute for Water, Soil and Air Hygiene, Vol. 2, 91–96.

Meisner, E.A., S.N. Rudnick, F.-C. Hu, J.D. Spengler, L. Preller, H. Ozkaynak and W. Nelson (1988). Aerosol and ETS sampling in public facilities and offices. Proceedings of the Annual Meeting of the Air Pollution Control Association, Paper 88–76. Dallas TX.

Muramatsu, M., S. Umemura, T. Okada and H. Tomita (1984). Estimation of personal exposure to tobacco smoke with a newly developed nicotine personal monitor. *Environ. Res.* 35: 218–227.

NAS (1986). *Environmental tobacco smoke. Measuring exposure and assessing health effects.* National Research Council, National Academy Press, Washington, 337 pp.

Norman, V., A.M. Ihrig, T.M. Larson and B.L. Moss (1983) "The effect of nitrogenous blend components on NO/NO_2 and HCN levels in mainstream and sidestream smoke." *Bietr. Tabakforsch.* 12: 55–62.

O'Neill, I. and E. Riboli (1987a). IARC approaches to monitoring exposure of passive smoking. *Toxicology Letters,* 35: 29–33.

O'Neill, I.K, K.D. Brunnemann, B. Doden and D. Hoffmann, eds. (1987b). Environmental carcinogens methods of analysis and exposure measurement, IARC Scientific Publications No. 81. International Agency for Research on Cancer, Oxford University Press, Lyon.

Ogden, M.W. and K.C. Maiolo (1988a). Collection and analysis of solanesol as a tracer of environmental tobacco smoke. Indoor and Ambient Air Quality, R. Perry and P.W. Kirk, eds., Selper Ltd., London, pp 77–88.

Ogden, M.W. and K.C.Maiolo (1988b). Gas chromatographic determination of solanesol in environmental tobacco smoke. *J. High Res. Chrom. & Chrom. Commun.* 11: 341–343.

Okada, T., Y. Ishizu and K. Matsunuma (1977). Determination of particle size distribution and concentration of cigarette smoke by a light scattering method. *Beitr. Tabakforsch* 9: 153–160.

Oldaker, G.B. III, M.W. Stancill and F.C. Conrad Jr. (1989a) Estimation of Effect of Environmental Tobacco Smoke on Air Quality within Passenger Cabins of Commercial Aircraft. II. *Environ. Sci. Technol.,* in press.

Ong, T., J. Stewart and W.Z. Whong (1984). A simple in situ mutagenicity test system for detection of mutagenic air pollutants. *Mutat. Res.* 139: 177–181.

Piade, J.J., C. Gerber and W. Fink (1988). Assessment of ETS impact on office air quality, Part 2. Indoor and Ambient Air Quality, R. Perry and P.W. Kirk, eds., Selper Ltd., London, pp 594–601.

Pitts, J.N., Jr., H.W. Breemann, E.C. Tuazon, M. Green, W.D. Long and A.M. Winer (1989). Time-resolved identifications and measurement of indoor air pollutants by spectroscopic techniques: gaseous nitrous acid, methanol, formaldehyde and formic acid. *JAPCA* 39: 1344–1347.

Pitts, J.N. Jr., J.A. Sweetman, W. Harger, D.R. Fitz, H.R. Paur and A.M. Winer (1985). Diurnal mutagenicity of airborne particulate organic matter adjacent to a heavily traveled West Los Angeles freeway. *JAPCA* 35: 638–643.

Pritchard, J.N., A. Black and J.J. McAughey (1989). The physical behaviour of sidestream tobacco smoke under ambient conditions. Submitted.

Pryor, W.A. (1986). Oxy-radicals and related species: their formation, lifetimes, and reactions. *Annu. Rev. Physiol.* 48: 657–667.

Rawbone, R.G., W. Burns and R.A. Patrick (1987). The measurement of environmental tobacco smoke particulates. *Toxicology Letters* 35: 125–129.

Reasor, M.J. (1987). The composition and dynamics of environmental tobacco smoke. *Journal of Environmental Health* 50: 20–24.

Rickert, W.S., J.C. Robinson and N. Collishaw (1984). Yields of tar, nicotine and carbon monoxide in the sidestream smoke from 15 brands of canadian cigarettes. *Amer. J. Public Health* 74: 228–231.

Rühl, C., J.D. Adams and D. Hoffmann (1980). Chemical studies on tobacco smoke-LXVI. Comparative assessment of volatile and tobacco-specific N-nitrosamines in the smoke of selected cigarettes from the U.S.A., West Germany and France. *J. Anal. Toxicol.* 4: 225–259.

Sakuma, H., M. Kusama, K. Yamaguchi, T. Matsuki and S. Sugawara (1984a). The distribution of cigarette smoke components between mainstream and sidestream smoke. II. Bases. *Beit. Tabakfors. Int.* 12: 199–209.

Sakuma, H., M. Kusama, K. Yamaguchi and S. Sugawara (1984b). The distribution of cigarette smoke components between mainstream and sidestream smoke. III. Middle and higher boiling components. *Beit. Tabakfors. Int.* 12: 251–258.

Sakuma, H., M. Kusama, S. Munakata, T. Obsumi and S. Sugawara (1983). The distribution of cigarette smoke components between mainstream and sidestream smoke. I. Acidic components. *Beit. Tabakfors. Int.* 12: 63–71.

Sasson, I.M., D.T. Coleman, E.J. LaVoie, D. Hoffmann and E.L. Wynder (1985). Mutagens in human urine: effects of cigarette smoking and diet. *Mutation Research* 158: 149–157.

Scherer, G., K. Westphal, I. Hoepfner and F. Adlkofer (1987). Biomonitoring of exposure to potentially mutagenic substances from environmental tobacco smoke (ETS). Indoor Air '87, Proceedings of the Fourth International Conference on Indoor Air Quality and Climate, Berlin (West), B. Seifert, H. Esdorn, M. Fischer, H. Ruden, J. Wegner, Eds., Institute for Water, Soil and Air Hygiene, Vol. 2, 109–114.

Sexton, K., L.M. Webber, S.B. Hayward and R.G. Sextro (1985). Characterization of particle composition, organic vapor constituents, and mutagenicity of indoor air pollutant emissions. Paper 85–30B.6, Proceedings of the 78th Annual Meeting of the Air Pollution Control Association. Detroit, Michigan.

Shepson, P.B., T.E. Kleindienst, E.O. Edney, G.R. Namie, J.H. Pittman, L.T. Cupitt and L.D. Claxton (1985). The mutagenic activity of irradiated toluene/NO_x/H_2O/air mixtures. *Environ. Sci. Technol.* 19: 249–255.

Sonnenfeld, G. and Wilson D.M. (1987). The Effect of Smoke Age and Dilution on the Cytotoxicity of Sidestream (Passive) Smoke. *Toxicology Letters* 35: 89–94.

Sonnenfeld, G., R.B. Griffith and R.W. Hudgens (1985). The effect of smoke generation and manipulation variable on the cytotoxicity of mainstream and sidestream cigarette smoke to monolayer cultures of L-929 cells. *Arch. Toxicol.* 58: 120–122.

Spengler, J.D., R.D. Treitman, T.D. Testeson, D.T. Mage and M.L. Soczek (1985). Personal exposures to respirable particulates and implications for air pollution epidemiology. *Environ. Sci. Tech.* 19: 700–707.

Stehlik, G., O. Richter and H. Altmann (1982). Concentration of dimethyl-nitrosamine in the air of smoke-filled rooms. *Ecotoxicology and Environmental Safety* 6: 495–500.

Tang, H., D.J. Eatough, E.A. Lewis, L.D. Hansen, K. Gunther, D. Belnap and J. Crawford (1989a). The generation and decay of environmental tobacco smoke constituents in an indoor environment. Proceedings, EPA/AWMA Symposium on the Determination of Toxic and Related Air Pollutants, Air and Waste Management Association, in press.

Tang, H., G. Richards, M.L. Lee, E.A. Lewis, L.D. Hansen and D.J. Eatough (1989b). Solanesol—A tracer for environmental tobacco smoke. *Env. Sci. Tech.*, Submitted.

Tang, H., G. Richards, K. Gunther, J. Crawford, M.L. Lee, E.D. Lewis and D.J. Eatough (1988a). Determination of gas phase nicotine and 3-ethenylpyridine, and particulate phase nicotine in environmental tobacco smoke with a collection bed -capillary gas chromatography system, *High Resol. Chromatogr. and Chromatogr. Commun.* 11: 775–782.

Tang, H., C.L. Benner, G.H. Richard, M.L. Lee, E.A. Lewis, L.D. Hansen and D.J. Eatough (1988b). Monitoring of environmental tobacco smoke with a sorbent bed-capillary gas chromatograph system. *International Journal Environ. Anal. Chem.* 33: 197–208.

Thome, F.A., D.L. Heavner, B.J. Ingebrethsen, L.W. Eudy and C.R. Green (1986). Environmental tobacco smoke monitoring with an atmospheric pressure chemical ionization mass spectrometer/mass spectrometer coupled to a test chamber. Proceedings, 79th Annual Meeting of the Air Pollution Control Association. Paper 86–37.6, 23–27 June, Minneapolis, MN.

Thompson, C.V., R.A. Jenkins and C.E. Higgins (1989). A thermal desorption method for the determination of nicotine in indoor environments. *Environ. Sci. Technol* 23: 429–435.

Turner, S. (1988). Environmental tobacco smoke and smoking policies. Proceedings of the APCA Specialty Conference, Combustion Processes and The Quality of the Indoor Environment, Niagara Falls, September, in press.

Vu Duc, T. and C.K. Huynh (1987). Sidestream tobacco smoke constituents in indoor air modelled in an experimental chamber. Indoor Air '87, Proceedings of the Fourth International Conference on Indoor Air Quality and Climate, Berlin (West), B. Seifert, H. Esdorn, M. Fischer, H. Ruden, J. Wegner, Eds., Institute for Water, Soil and Air Hygiene, Vol. 2, 170–174.

Vu Duc, T. and C.K. Huynh (1986). Deposition rates of sidestream tobacco smoke particles in an experimentl chamber. *Toxicology Letters* 35: 59–65.

Wang, Y.Y., L.M. Webber, C.P. Flessel, K. Chang and K. Sexton (1985). Detection of mutagens in particle and vapor emissions from major indoor sources. Proceedings of the 78th Annual Meeting of the Air Pollution Control Association, Detroit, Michigan.

Weber, A. and T. Fischer (1980). Passive smoking at work. *Int. Arch. Occup. Environ. Health* 47: 209–221.

Weber, A. (1984). Acute effects of environmental tobacco smoke. *Eur. J. Resp. Dis.* (Supplement 133) 68: 98–108.

Wesolowski, J.J., Y.Y. Wang, C.V. Hanson, R. Haas, P. Flessel, and S. Hayward (1986). Indoor air quality measurements: Emerging technologies. Proceedings of the EPA/APCA Symposium on Measurement of Toxic Air Pollutants, EPA, 1–1.

Williams, K., and J. Lewtas (1985). Metabolic activation of organic extracts from diesel, coke oven, roofing tar, and cigarette smoke emissions in the ames assay. *Environ. Mutagenesis* 7: 489–500.

2
Panel Discussion on Chemical Characterization

Donald Ecobichon: I would ask the discussants for this presentation, Dr. Feuer, Dr. Gorrod, Dr. Neurath, Dr. Perry and Dr. Reasor, to come to the podium. While they are doing that, let me explain our format for this and the following panels.

Following each opening presentation, we will have a panel discussion. Each panelist will make a five or six minute presentation commenting on the opening presentation. This will be followed by an open discussion involving the panelists as well as the scientists in the audience. I would ask that you use the microphones. For future speakers, would you please remain close to the microphone because our translators can't translate silence. If someone needs overheads changed, we will do that for you.

Our first discussant is Dr. Feuer.

Dr. Feuer: In my comments I should like to discuss the importance of ETS characterization as it relates to the possible health effects of ETS. I should like to emphasize four points:

First, ETS is only one of many air pollutants, and it is the contribution of all pollutants that will determine the level of exposure to any particular chemical constituent. Dr. Eatough's work characterizing the components of ETS present in air is very important, but we must not forget that many of these components have other sources. Indeed, air pollutants other than ETS may be far more significant in terms of any possible health effects.

When we are talking about health risks we have to consider some of the many particles which are present in the air and not derived from ETS. These particles include dust particles produced by heaters, wood and coal stoves and outside air, and may contain toxic trace metals; carbon monoxide; carbon dioxide from heaters and so on; ozone; nitrogen dioxide; radon; radon daughters; volatile organic compounds; fluorinated hydrocarbons; herbicides; insecticides; and many other substances, including infectious, allergenic, or irritating biologic materials, such as bacteria, fungi, viruses, pollens and so on. I should like to emphasize that measuring ETS composition alone does not provide a clear view of the health risks of indoor pollutants.

The second point I should like to raise is that there are many sources in our environment that produce chemicals identical to those present in ETS. These sources must be considered in any investigation into the possible adverse health effects of ETS.

I'll mention just a few examples. Combustion of gas during cooking and the burning of pilot lights release nitrogen oxides, nitrogen dioxides, carbon monoxide, carbon dioxide, etc. Carbon monoxide is produced by many sources in the home, office and other environments. Emissions from fireplaces and vehicles in attached garages increase indoor carbon monoxide levels.

Formaldehyde is produced by several sources in the home and office, including insulation, furniture, carpets, carbonless copy papers, etc. Radon and radon daughters, which are decay products of uranium and radium, are present in all rocks and soils, although at varying concentrations. Woodburning stoves and fireplaces emit carbon monoxide, particles and polycyclic aromatic hydrocarbons. Polycyclic aromatic hydrocarbons are also generated by automobiles, generators, barbecues and so on. Many other compounds also pollute our air, water and food. Nitrite and amines are present in many food stuffs as constituents of preservatives. Acrolein is formed by burning of fat products or in atmospheric reactions between ozone and gasoline vapors.

The third point I want to make is that the interaction of pollutants could be a source of concern. However, at present we don't know much about chemical interactions in complex mixtures. More studies are necessary to evaluate whether known ETS components have interactive effects.

Finally, I should like to raise the importance of measuring so-called stable compounds like vinylpyridine, isoprene and solanesol in assessing the health effects of ETS exposure. We can praise the very comprehensive studies of Dr. Eatough and his associates establishing measures for the true quantity of ETS in air. However, even if the determination of the level of inactive components may reflect very accurately the amount of ETS in the air, measurement of the levels of vinylpyridine or solanesol cannot give an accurate picture of the possible health effects of ETS. The active ingredients decay, and there is no reason to expect that measurement of the concentration of stable but inactive components will indicate much if anything about the possible health effects of the active ingredients. Moreover, solanesol and other inactive compounds may derive from other sources, like tomatoes and potatoes, and it is possible that when we metabolize these foodstuffs they produce solanesol endogenously. Thus, the levels of inactive compounds may be questionable markers for active ETS components.

In summary, measuring the level of a known inactive ETS component only confirms that ETS is present in the air. It doesn't provide evidence of any ETS-related health effects.

John Gorrod: I think one shouldn't underestimate the value of Dr. Eatough's paper. It is a very good review of our current knowledge. It emphasizes the importance of developing and being able to substantiate very specific and sensitive analytical methods; one of our problems is that we've been lacking analytical methods of sufficient sensitivity. By the end of his talk, I felt that he'd really stated the problem rather than the answer, and I do not mean that in a derogatory way at all.

I think what his talk forces us to consider is what we are trying to do in characterizing ETS. Presumably we're looking for a biomarker of exposure. I am worried, however, that, in the search, we don't latch on to one thing and give it, as it were, scientific credibility when in fact it is non-scientific. I say this because of the tremendous variation in the composition of tobacco. What you do with tobacco varies—some people chew it, some use it as snuff, and others smoke it. If you smoke it, there are differences in combustion temperature, puff frequency, volume and so forth. In addition mainstream smoke is taken in and expelled before it becomes ETS. What I'm suggesting is that ETS is the end product of many complicated variables, and any onze measurement or even any twenty measurements may still give us a very misleading picture. That worries me as a scientist. I believe that, at the present time, one has to say that the measurement of any individual component of ETS is purely a measure or a marker of that component and nothing else.

Dr. Feuer mentioned the many sources of some components found in ETS. I'm worried, as indeed was Dr. Eatough, that the large number of natural volatile components could give rise to misleading results in attempts to measure ETS. For example, di and trimethylamine are the end products of amino acid metabolism, so urine contains a fair amount of these amines. Now, it would be very silly of us to measure the levels of trimethylamine in urine or in air and then claim that this concentration could be extrapolated as a measure of ETS. The same arguments apply to numerous other non-tobacco specific compounds.

Another thing that I thought was brought out very nicely was the variation in chemical reactivity. We know very little about these things, and even those of us with a slight chemical knowledge are amazed at the complexity of ETS. With hundreds of compounds present we have an extremely difficult task in characterizing the components which are being formed, rather than those that have already formed, reacted and disappeared. This problem is actually made worse when we consider that biological reactivity and chemical reactivity do not always go hand in hand.

I was delighted that the minor tobacco alkaloids were mentioned, but again I am wary of extrapolation from their presence or concentrations. Nicotine is well studied, but when you come to components like myosmine, ni cotyrine, and anabasine, these are very poorly understood. Their chemical reactivity varies tremendously. In some cases they are saturated compounds with very little reactivity and at other times they're extremely reactive compounds. Beautiful work by Crooks and Castagnoli in the United States has shown very big differences in the biological reactivity of some of these compounds. One thing we must never do is to talk about cotinine as though it were nicotine. Cotinine and nicotine are two entirely different chemicals having virtually nothing in common, and the use of the expression "nicotine analogue" is very misleading.

Georg Neurath: I'd like to comment on some aspects of ventilation and its importance for ETS. In our laboratory we ran a standard experiment as a base for ETS studies. We have a room of thirty-five cubic metres, which purportedly was not ventilated. Three smokers smoked one cigarette every thirty minutes, to a total of eighteen cigarettes. In another experiment, we used a very old-fashioned method of ventilation. We opened a window every fifteen minutes after the smoking of the cigarettes for a period of three minutes. We call it "shock ventilation" (Figures 2–1 and 2–2). In these experiments, we saw that the concentrations of the continuously measured components came down to about ten to twenty percent of the original concentrations when we ventilate. The attached figures show this. This result suggests, of course, that ventilation can have a highly significant effect on concentrations and, in theory and maybe in fact, any possible health effects.

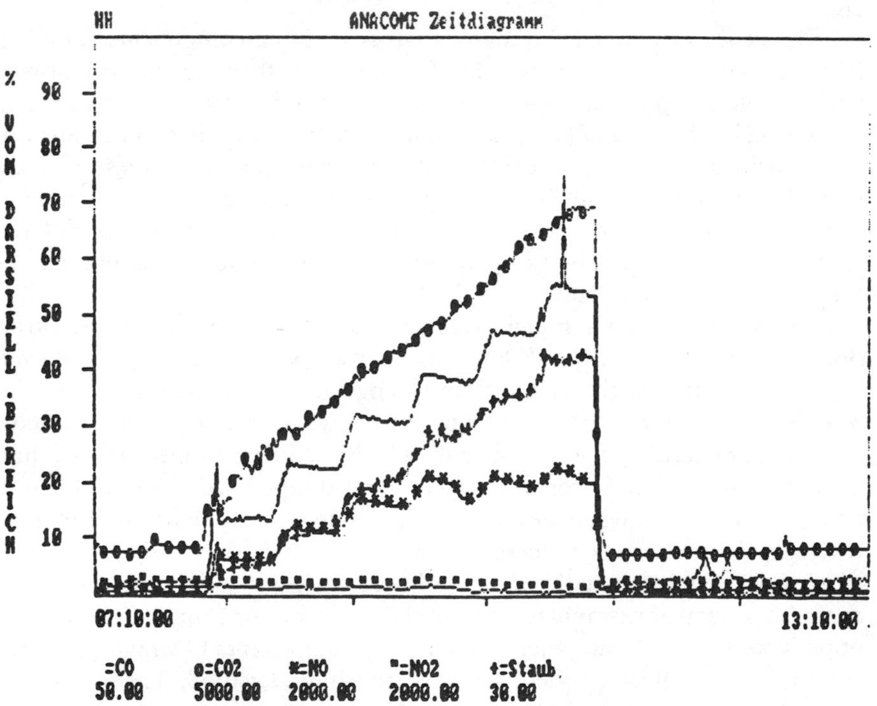

Figure 2–1. Indoor Air: ETS Study.

Note: Continuous measurements: 3 smokers, 1 cigarette every 30 min, total of 18 room 35 m', no ventilation, air circulation.

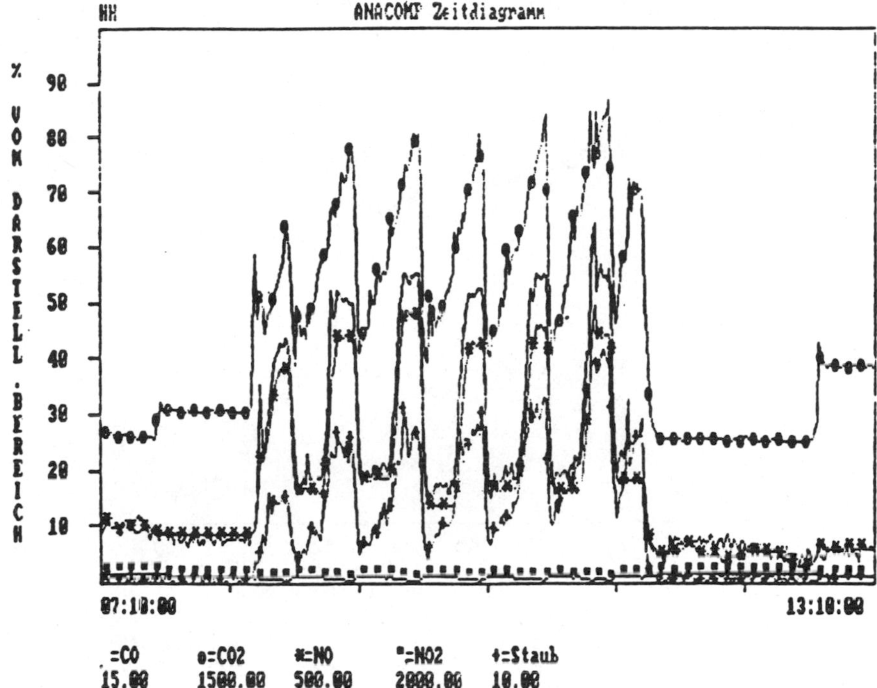

Figure 2–2. Indoor Air: ETS Study.

Note: Continous measurements, shock ventilation: 3 smokers, 1 cigarette every 30 min, every 30 + 15 min: shock ventilation 1.5 m', 3 min.

In general, we can measure ventilation effects very easily. We use Frigen—which is CCl_2F_2—as a tracer. Figure 2–3 shows that Frigen and carbon monoxide decay at quite similar rates. This fact allows us easily to follow the effects of ventilation during ETS measurements.

Roger Perry: I would like to compliment Dr. Eatough on an excellent paper. He certainly gave us a comprehensive overview of the very complex chemistry of ETS, its mode of production, its chemical change and its dispersion.

Much of the work that he presented dealing with chemical interaction related to chamber experiments; of particular interest was the NO-NO_2 balance and its interrelation with the other complex chemical reactions. I agree with Dr. Eatough that we need to know more about ETS and the way in which different compounds are formed and the potential way in which these will act as irritants or otherwise in the indoor air environment. I do feel, however, that in the real world, away from the exposure chamber, the contribution to the NO balance will be significant from other sources. Indeed,

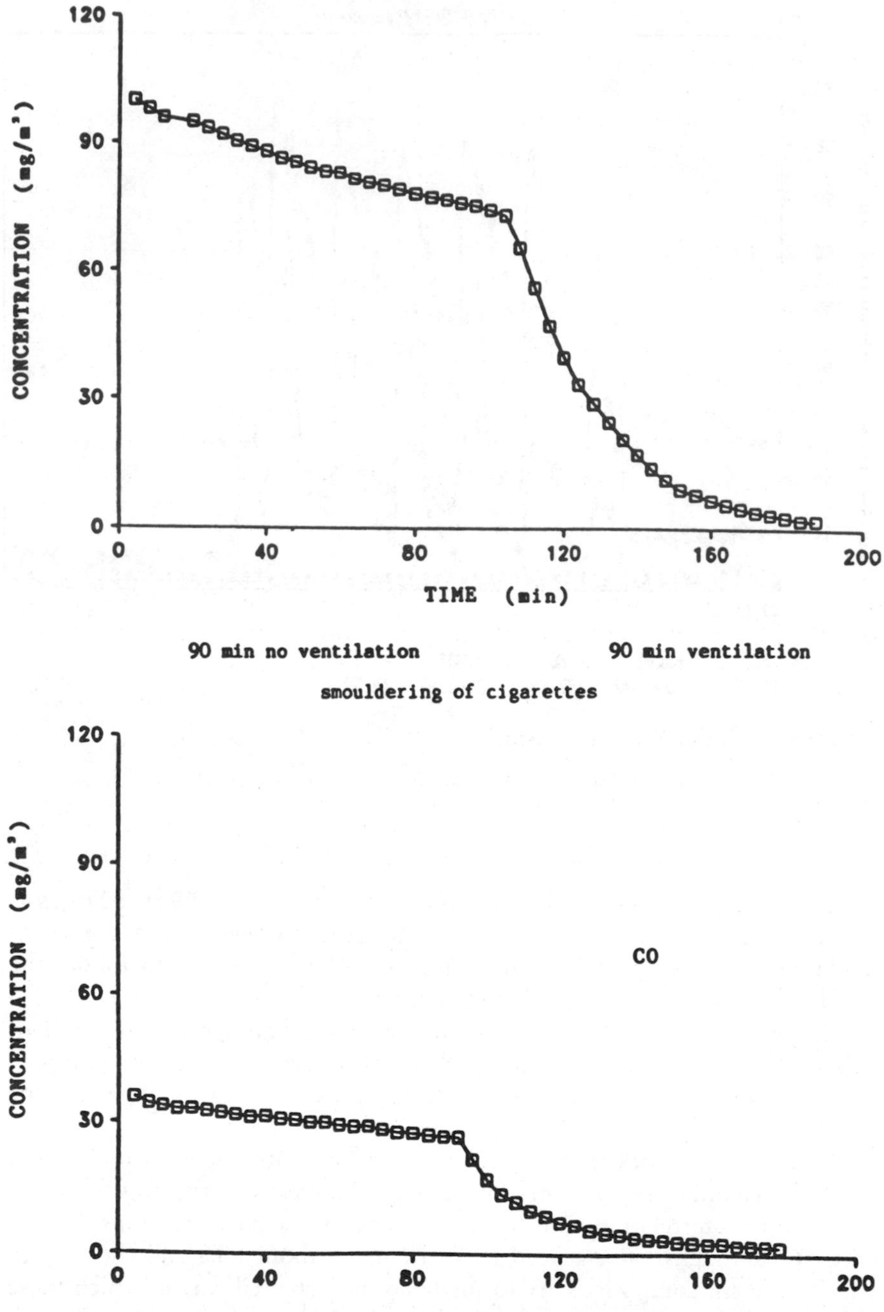

Figure 2–3. Indoor Air: ETS Study. Continuous Ventilation Measurements by Means of Frigen. Decay of Frigen and CO.

in looking at the exposure situation, I feel that the need for additional research is demonstrated by the way in which ETS has been looked at in isolation and not in the presence of many of the other pollutants from other sources that are found in indoor air.

In much of the recent work that we have been undertaking in London, CO levels in indoor air clearly demonstrate the contribution of vehicle emissions and other complex sources of combustion. I do wonder, therefore, in the work that Dr. Eatough has done, about his opinion as to the influence of NO from other sources as a contributor to the formation of many of the compounds that he has identified.

This sort of chemistry is also complicated by our lack of knowledge of the combustion and the products of combustion from other sources. Vapor emissions, as you know, are characterized by general analytical parameters such as total hydrocarbons, CO and NO_2. Little attention has been paid to monitoring specific hydrocarbons either in street air or in the indoor air scene.

In my view, in the majority of the world, it is these sources of combustion and their interactive chemistry with the products of tobacco smoke that represent the real exposure situation and the problems that need to be quantified in a much more detailed way.

Many of the other points I would have made have already been made, but I do feel that Dr. Eatough's paper represents a very comprehensive overview of the complexities of this chemistry, and I compliment him on his work.

Mark Reasor: The question of composition really involves two separate considerations. One is the availability of a marker or markers to assess in some manner, either qualitatively or quantitatively, the presence of ETS in an environment. Dr. Eatough certainly has made significant inroads in doing that, and clearly the analytical methodology is available for those types of measurements to be made.

But secondly, and perhaps more importantly, is once that's been done, how do we take that information and assess the possible health effects of ETS or ETS components? In particular, I think it's important that compounds that have health relevance be measured in either the laboratory setting or the ambient setting, and I would like—hopefully, after I finish speaking—Dr. Eatough to comment on this a little bit more.

For example, what about the nitrosamines? This is a very important class of compounds that is mentioned in the literature quite frequently with respect to sidestream smoke emissions. We didn't see any data related to the volatile nitrosamines, nor the tobacco-specific nitrosamines. The question is are they not there in an ambient condition, or are they not there in sufficient quantities to measure, or is the analytic methodology not available? I think it's very important that we try to find compounds that have health relevance in trying to assess the health effects due to the chemical composition.

Also, now that the baseline data have been produced, it is important that measurements take place in the ambient condition. It's very important to go out into the real world environment, into restaurants, into office buildings, into malls and other places, and do the same type of analysis, and see if we can differentiate between background levels that are not emissions from tobacco sources and tobacco-source emissions. I think it will give us a very important piece of information and get us closer to understanding the significance of ETS exposure.

Also, for some specific aspects, I think it's important that the size of the particles associated with ETS be characterized and the relevance of those particle sizes to actual pulmonary retention be examined more carefully. We know that ETS particles are in the respirable range, but what percent deposition and retention should we expect for particles in that range, and particles in the ambient environment? Because there are a lot of particles in an environment that might be respirable, we need to know what fraction of those particles would be retained in the lungs in order to have a better idea of the health significance of respirable particles.

In the area of airborne mutagens, I think it's important to try to assess their biological significance. In these studies you draw large volumes of air into some sort of sampling device, with the result that you have a very concentrated material on a filter that is extracted and concentrated even further and put into a bacterial assay. Is that something that we really need to be concerned about? Efforts need to be directed to try to answer that question.

Donald Ecobichon: Thank you very much.

We're running a little short of time. I'm sure Dr. Eatough has all those pertinent questions written down. I don't know if you want to respond to any one of them in particular.

Delbert Eatough: Just a comment in connection with the nitrosamines, because it raises an interesting point to think about in terms of some weaknesses in our knowledge of chemistry. There is very little data on nitrosamines in indoor environments. There is much more data on nitrosamines in tobacco smoke. It is impossible, I think, to really draw any conclusions about what's happening to nitrosamines from the data that currently exist. One of the real problems is that, in all the data sets that exist, nitrosamines have been measured in environments where smoking occurred. There's no question that environmental tobacco smoke was there, but there is insufficient information to make any kind of source attribution conclusions from data sets that currently exist.

To me, one of the unknown and intriguing questions is what is the reactivity of the organic phase of environmental tobacco smoke, and what is known about the chemistry, for example, of wood smoke. There's got to be NO_2-organic chemistry that's going on, whether that NO_2 came from environmental tobacco smoke or from other sources, and to some extent the presence of other sources may only increase the extent to which that kind of chemistry goes on. You're going to form nitrated compounds. Some of those may be nitrosamines, but also some of those will be compounds that we possibly ought to be worrying about whether they're nitrosamines or not. That's a completely unknown area, so far as I know.

Roger Perry: Do you think, then, that all the work that we've done on characterizing ETS by carbon monoxide and nicotine is really a waste of time?

Delbert Eatough: Well, I've been very critical of both of those substances as tracers. The more data that we generate the more we see that as a tracer nicotine has some very serious shortcomings. I think the data are clear that carbon monoxide is dominated by other sources in indoor environments. You obviously can't tell anything about ETS exposure from a carbon monoxide measurement. I think that's very clear.

Donald Ecobichon: We'll accept two quick questions or comments from the floor. Dr. Neurath, your comment first, and then you, sir.

Georg Neurath: Just a comment on the question of Dr. Perry as to NO_2 and ETS. If we open a window, we normally find higher values of NO_2 in our room than after closing the window and smoking. You can block the NO_2 from outside, and NO_2 levels decrease during the smoking experiment but rise after opening the window again. This is another example of interferences from external sources.

Donald Ecobichon: Sir, could you identify yourself?

John Dilley: John Dilley, occupational physician, UK. I'm most interested to hear the view of the panel on the probability of identifying in the foreseeable future a valid biological marker for exposure to ETS at work.

Donald Ecobichon: Would one of you like to tackle that question?

John Gorrod: If you want a short answer, I'd say it was virtually impossible.

The work that has been presented this morning has clearly shown that there are ways of going forward, and it's important to keep an open mind on all of these things. What worries me is that people, because of various pressures, forge ahead on one line of inquiry only. Now, that is not the correct way of doing things, and I would suggest that it is a very wrong approach.

All I'm saying is that at the moment and over the next five years much greater effort has got to be put into developing sensitive and specific analytical methods for these compounds and applying them to ETS. It is tremendously important to keep people's minds open about the other factors that can influence results.

Gary Flamm: I would like to comment on Dr. Eatough's discussion of mutagenicity in connection with ETS. I'm concerned that there was no real discussion of the probable quantitative meaning of the mutagenicity studies in terms of human health. The job of taking mutagenicity data in bacteria and relating it to human health risk is not simple and, at a minimum, requires substantial analysis.

One point that should be made, in this regard, is that the Salmonella test will overstate the potency in mammals of some mutagens such as the nitro-organic compounds while it will understate the potency of other mutagens. Consequently, conclusions based on potency changes, as measured by the Salmonella test, need to be examined very carefully before determining their health significance to humans. The other aspect that I find troubling is that nothing was said about what the findings mean from a quantitative risk point of view. If, as may be the case, it is impossible to state what these positive findings mean quantitatively, it would be worthwhile to so state and explain why it is impossible to assess health risks from these findings. The mutagen content of ETS may be thousands of times less than that of a single charcoal broiled steak. Were that the case, the mutagenicity findings would not appear very important from a quantitative point of view. It is necessary, therefore, that the findings be placed in proper context.

As the matter now stands, one is led to conclude that the mutagenicity findings imply that ETS poses a health risk to those who inhale such smoke. However, without addressing the points I have mentioned, such conclusions would be unjustified and inappropriate.

Donald Ecobichon: I think I'll use the Chairman's prerogative to close the discussion at this point. If you have burning questions, find these people during the break.

Part II

3
Assessing Exposures to Environmental Tobacco Smoke

Howard D. Goodfellow, Ph.D.,
with S. Eyre, M.H.Sc., and
J.A.S. Wyatt, P.Eng.
Goodfellow Consultants Inc.

I. Introduction

Accurate assessments of exposure are fundamental to any credible epidemiological study of the health effects of environmental tobacco smoke ("ETS"). Measuring exposure to ETS is a complicated task, made difficult by the complex nature of ETS itself. As the previous panel has discussed, ETS is not a single substance. Rather, it is a diverse and dynamic mixture consisting of several thousand constituents. Some of these constituents may serve as surrogates for the ETS mixture as a whole or for potentially significant portions of the mixture. However, accurate detection of even these surrogates is often difficult because many are present in extremely low concentrations in air. Further, many substances found in ETS also emanate from other indoor sources, such as building materials and furnishings, cooking and heating fuels, aerosol propellants and cleaning compounds. Thus, there are substantial problems in attempting to trace the existence of these substances back to ETS. Finally, the physical and chemical complexity of ETS is increased by its propensity to change over very brief periods of time. Such change can occur as a result of reactions among constituents or between these constituents and other surfaces or chemical sources. This dynamic quality further complicates the measurement of ETS.

Given these difficulties, it is not surprising that there is no universally accepted and standardized method to quantify the exposure of an individual to ETS. A large number of studies have based estimates of exposure on retrospective data obtained from questionnaires. But problems of recall and bias associated with these subjective responses have led investigators to search for a more objective method for measuring exposure.

Investigators have utilized two such methods. The first is to measure levels of ETS constituents in blood, urine or saliva (i.e., biological monitoring). The second is to measure levels of ETS constituents in samples of air collected at a fixed sampling location or in the breathing zone. The prospects and problems of the former approach will be addressed by Dr. Reasor. Issues involved with the latter approach will be examined here.

Thus, this paper will first discuss a variety of sampling strategies that have been used to measure ETS. Next, the paper reviews several of the airborne markers that have been tracked as surrogates for ETS and assesses their relative merit. Third, the paper briefly summarizes results from several field studies focusing on ETS. Finally, the paper provides some concluding observations and recommendations for further work in this area.

II. Discussion

A. Methods of Measuring Exposure

1. Sampling Strategies. Grab or spot sampling is one method for determining indoor air pollutant concentrations. As its name suggests, grab sampling allows an investigator to analyze a small amount of air collected over a brief period of time. Gases or vapour samples are taken by filling an impervious container (e.g., flask or bag) with air. Once the sample has been collected, the container must be sealed to prevent sample loss or contamination. Samples are then sent to a laboratory for analysis.

Grab sampling is a useful technique for measuring airborne contaminants that vary in concentration with respect to time and location (Report of WHO meeting, Nördlingen, 1982). It can therefore be helpful in obtaining information on when peak concentrations are present. However, because of the brief sampling duration (usually less than five minutes), grab samples are rarely used to estimate an eight hour average concentration. Further, because of the brief sampling duration and subsequently the small volume of air sampled, the analytical equipment used must be capable of low limits of detection.

Another method for determining indoor air pollutant concentrations is time-integrated sampling. This technique consists of one or more samples taken in series, with the sampling duration varying from 15 minutes to eight hours depending on what is being evaluated. Integrated air sampling is often used to determine a worker's eight-hour time weighted average exposure to a chemical. It is also recommended if the concentration of the particular material varies significantly during the work shift or if a large sample volume is necessary to satisfy the sensitivity requirements of the analytical method (National Safety Council 1988). Time-integrated samples are also useful for contaminants whose effects are proportional to a long-term average of the concentration, (i.e., a linear response) (Report of WHO meeting, Nördlingen, 1982).

Time-integrated samples are collected by drawing a known volume of air through some form of collection media using a battery-powered pump. Most pumps can be categorized by the amount of air they pull through the sampling system per unit of time (i.e., low flow, high flow or dual range). In order to establish reliable concentrations of airborne constituents, an accurate measurement of the flow rate and sampling duration is required. The flow rate must be calibrated to provide this information. As in grab sampling, the collected contaminant requires some form of laboratory analysis subsequent to collection.

A disadvantage with time-integrated sampling is that there frequently is a substantial delay between sample collection and analysis. Delays can lead to sample loss by chemical reactions or light-induced decomposition. Delays can also prevent the inclusion of the data as real-time information in time-dependent pollutant behavior studies.

2. Sampling Devices. Two types of sampling devices worthy of particular attention are passive monitors and direct reading instruments (DRIs). Passive monitors or samplers are becoming increasingly popular for monitoring gases and vapours and have been developed for a wide variety of air pollutants. Passive monitors do not require the use of a pump; "they are easy to use, have no moving parts to maintain, are small, lightweight and inexpensive, and can be used relatively unattended." (National Safety Council 1988).

There are two types of passive systems: diffusion and reactive. The first system utilizes the principle of passive diffusion, in which contaminants are absorbed onto a collection medium. This method is used for organic vapours, which can be collected using activated charcoal as the collection medium. The second system is used for sampling reactive gases (e.g., SO_2, NO_2). Instead of being passively collected, the contaminant is reacted with a chemical coating on the collection surface of the monitor.

A DRI is "a device in which sampling and analysis are carried out within the instrument and the required information is read directly from an indicator." (National Safety Council 1988). DRIs offer real-time analysis of data, as opposed to integrated data. An advantage of this approach is the ability to obtain information concerning peak concentrations. Moreover, DRIs can be connected to data loggers so that information can easily be collected over extended periods. The principal disadvantages of "continuous monitoring equipment are that it is bulky, expensive to operate and relatively labor- intensive. Maintenance, adjustment and calibration, as well as readings, also require considerable effort." (WHO 1982)

3. Sampler Location. Sampler location is an issue that should be considered when assessing exposure. Samplers can be located near a person's breathing zone or at a fixed site in an area where exposure is likely to occur. However, as studies have indicated, area samples may be less desirable when estimating personal exposures (Ott 1985; Spangler et al. 1981).

Monitoring systems have been developed that are small and portable enough to be carried with an individual during daily activities (Turner et al. 1979). These devices allow investigators to measure personal exposure throughout an entire day. However, this requires voluntary participation and may increase awareness and ultimately affect occupant behavior and outcome (Oldaker 1989).

Further, the use of a long-term integrated personal monitor may be inappropriate for ETS because some of the constituents of ETS such as nicotine break down or change over time. Loss of volatile materials from the sampling media may result in an inaccurate assessment of exposure (Dinardi).

B. Markers for ETS

As mentioned previously, investigators rely on tracers or surrogates in measuring exposure to ETS. These findings are then related to the ETS mixture as a whole. As summarized by the National Research Council (1986), important criteria for a suitable tracer are that it should be:

- unique or nearly unique to ETS;
- present in sufficient quantity that concentrations can be easily detected in air, even at low smoking rates;
- characterized by similar emission rates for a variety of tobacco products; and
- in a fairly constant ratio to the contaminants of interest (e.g., suspended particulates) under a range of environmental conditions encountered and for a variety of tobacco products.

As discussed below, no single parameter has met all of these criteria and none have been universally accepted (Muramatsu et al. 1987). A more promising approach may be to measure simultaneously several tracers, ETS specific and non-specific, in the vapour and particulate phases, in an attempt to determine the exposure relative to each phase and to ETS as a whole. It is important that the monitoring methods for ETS be standardized (O'Neill and Riboli 1987), so that information can be integrated and the results of multiple studies can be compared with reasonable assurance.

1. Carbon Monoxide (CO). Carbon monoxide is a commonly used surrogate for ETS. In the studies reviewed by the author, CO was used as the tracer 35% of the time. The frequency of its use is a likely result of the readily available techniques for measuring CO concentrations in air. DRIs that operate on electrochemical oxidation and non-dispersive infrared detection are the most common.

The primary problem with using carbon monoxide as a tracer of ETS is that it is not tobacco-specific. Cooking, heating, automobiles and numerous other combustion processes generate carbon monoxide in quantities significantly greater than ETS. Using CO as a tracer, therefore, generally will produce an overestimate of exposure to ETS.

2. Particulate Matter. Another parameter that has been used to estimate exposure to ETS is the concentration of particulate matter in the atmosphere (NAS 1986). Of particular relevance are respirable suspended particulates (RSP), which are those particles in the size range that permits them to penetrate deeply into the lungs upon inhalation.

Particulates can be collected using filters, impactors, impingers, electronic precipitators and cyclones. Several of these methods are used in the front of a sampling train and perform a size selection function. Although DRIs are available for measuring particulate matter, they lack suitable calibration standards and there are accuracy and maintenance difficulties. The piezobalance, for example, has been reported to have an error of 10–15%. (Sterling and Dimich 1982).

Particulate matter has been used as a tracer of ETS in 30% of the studies reviewed. As with CO, a major drawback is its lack of specificity. The many non-ETS sources of particulates in indoor environments, both from combustion and other activities, make it difficult to determine the contribution to particulate levels from ETS alone. Correction for other sources by determination of background levels is therefore necessary to avoid overestimation (DiNardi).

Particulate levels should be studied with respect to occupancy factors and room characteristics. Much of the scientific literature is notable for its lack of consistency in these parameters. Some studies (Leaderer et al. 1984; Baker et al. 1988) report that higher occupancy results in a decrease in particulate matter due to adsorption onto surfaces, whereas the opposite might be expected. (First 1984).

An accepted definition of RSP is also required. RSP and total particulate matter (TPM) are often used interchangeably in the literature. In the studies reviewed, the cutoff point for RSP has varied between 2.5 and 10 μm. A separate definition for ETS-derived RSP may be desirable. Leaderer reported that 98% of ETS particulates were between 0.05 and 1.0 m (Leader et al. 1984). Another study by Klus et al. (1985) demonstrated that ETS-derived RSP falls into the 0.25 to 0.45 μm range.

3. Nitrogen Oxides. Nitrogen oxides have been used as a tracer for ETS in 5% of the studies reviewed by the author. These can be measured using active or passive time-integrated techniques, as well as DRIs. The current method of choice is chemiluminescence monitoring. Although an extremely sensitive and accurate method, chemiluminescent monitoring suffers from potential interferences and is hampered by the limited portability of the DRI. Nitrogen oxides are also not ETS-specific and may, therefore, lead to overestimates of exposure.

4. Nicotine. The use of nicotine to determine ETS exposure has particular appeal since nicotine is one of the few airborne compounds that is unique or largely unique to tobacco. Nicotine was used as a tracer for ETS in about 20% of the studies reviewed by the author. Several types of active and passive time-integrated methods have been developed for nicotine collection and analysis (Sterling 1988; Hammond et al. 1987; Williams et al. 1985; Muramatsu et al. 1987; Hammond and Leader 1987; Eudy et al. 1986; Levin 1989).

Recent nicotine characterization research (Ogden and Maiolo 1988) has shown that 90% of the nicotine in ETS is in the vapour phase, not the particulate phase as was previously thought. These results suggest that nicotine should not be used as a tracer for the particulate phase of ETS.

Although nicotine is largely specific to tobacco smoke, its rapid decay rate and high volatility make it a less than ideal marker for ETS (Editorial 1989). Of seven tracers studied by Baker et al. (1988), nicotine was found to have the fastest decay rate and, correspondingly, the shortest half life. The order of half lives was reported as follows: $NO_2 > CO = CO_2 > NO = THC > TPM >$ nicotine. Muramatsu (1987) confirmed that ambient nicotine concentrations decrease rapidly in comparison to other ETS constituents.

5. Mutagenic Tracers. Mutagenic tracers have been used in approximately 10% of the studies reviewed. There are many sources of mutagens in the environment. Several mutagenic compounds have been isolated in ETS (Proctor 1988).

Volatile nitrosamines (VNAs) and polycyclic aromatic hydrocarbons (PAHs) have been used as tracers. Unlike PAHs, several of the nitrosamines are derived from the thermal decomposition of tobacco alkaloids, making them tobacco-specific. However, the analysis of these compounds in ETS tends to be fairly complicated because they are present in extremely low concentrations. Several studies (Eatough et al. 1988; Husgafvel-Pursiainen et al. 1986) have looked at particulate phase mutagens. These studies have attempted to determine the mutagenicity of the entire particulate phase of ETS, rather than to identify individual mutagenic components.

Although the majority of mutagenic agents in ETS are found in the particulate phase (WHO 1985), the gaseous or vapour phase also contains several mutagenic components. The mutagenicity of the entire vapour phase has not yet been adequately investigated.

Identification of the individual components of ETS can be accomplished using multi-component chromatographic profiling techniques. In this method, the components are visualized on a chromatogram that can be likened to a fingerprint of the smoke compositional pattern (Jenkins and Guerin 1984). This technique is especially useful because it permits the measurement of several analytes at once. By providing synergistic information, it allows a more accurate estimation of ETS contribution than does the measurement of a single analyte (Proctor 1988). The combination of particulate and vapour phase mutagenicity measurements and multicomponent chromatographic techniques may yield useful information on the synergistic action of ETS components.

6. Solanesol. Solanesol is a tobacco-specific compound found in the particulate phase of ETS. Solanesol comprises 2–3% by weight of RSP attributable to ETS (Ogden and Maiolo 1988). Because of its high molecular weight and low volatility, solanesol maintains its equilibrium between vapour and particulate phases. The relationship between solanesol and ETS as a whole, however, has not been sufficiently explored.

C. *Field Survey Results*

Scientists are still gathering basic data about ETS exposure. Much of the data collected in the 1970s and early to mid-1980s are of dubious scientific validity. For example, many of these earlier studies were based on measurements of only carbon monoxide or RSP. The problems associated with relying on these constituents as surrogates are now well documented.

Field studies that have been conducted to date can be classified as: (1) single component investigations; (2) multi-component investigations and surveys; or (3) surveys using a portable air sampling system (PASS). Table 1 identifies the researchers who have reported field survey data for ETS based on the different sampling techniques.

1. Single Component Investigations. Airborne dust concentrations measured by Skov et al. (1987) ranged from 86 to 382 μg/m³, with an average of 201 μg/m³ for 14 buildings. Although the report implies that smoking was permitted in the buildings investigated, no data regarding smoking rates were provided; thus, the results cannot be interpreted from the standpoint of ETS exposure.

Nicotine levels have been measured by several researchers to estimate ETS exposure. The results all showed very low exposures (Muramatsu et al. 1984; 1987). Average nicotine concentrations in three offices ranged from 5.9 to 19.8 μg/m³. Hammond et al. (1987) reported nicotine concentrations

Table 3–1
Size of Partial Sample for Top 10% of Exposed Individuals with 0.90 Confidence

Size of Group	*Number of Required Samples*
8	7
9	8
10	9
11–12	10
13–14	11
15–17	12
18–20	13
21–4	14
25–29	15
30–37	16
38–49	17
50	18

ranging from 3.1 to 48.0 μg/m³ for personal samples collected by four office workers. The average nicotine concentration reported was 19.0 μm/m³. To express the relative meaning of nicotine levels, the "cigarette equivalent" measure is sometimes used. This is somewhat subjective; however, the aforementioned levels correspond to approximately 0.0145 to 0.089 cigarettes per day that a non-smoker would be exposed to (Robertson 1989). Reported exposure to ETS particulate matter ranged from 45 to 132 μm/m³.

2. Multicomponent Investigations and Surveys. Sterling et al. (1987) reported measurements of nicotine, carbon monoxide and RSP in offices. For 10 samples collected in offices where smoking was permitted, they found nicotine concentrations ranging from none detected to 53.01 μg/m³ with a median concentration of 8.5 μg/m³. Concentrations of respirable suspended particles from 81 measurements ranged from none detected to 700 μg/m³ with a median of 38 μg/m³. For offices in which smoking was prohibited (and, consequently, in which measurements of nicotine were not made), 20 measurements of RSP yielded concentrations ranging from 14 to 320 μg/m³ with a median of 38 μg/m³.

Miesner et al. (1988) surveyed ETS in 12 offices of five buildings by measuring nicotine and RSP. Nicotine concentrations in offices in which smoking was permitted ranged from none detected to 4.3 μg/m³; corresponding concentrations of RSP ranged from 16.2 to 80.0 μg/m³. Average concentrations of nicotine and RSP were 1.2 and 35.8 μg/m³, respectively. For offices where smoking was prohibited, nicotine concentrations ranged from none detected to 0.4 μg/m³ with an average concentration of 0.05 μg/m³; concentrations of RSP ranged from 11.1 to 18.2 μg/m³, with an average of 15.1 μg/m³.

Turner (1988) reported results from measurements of RSP, carbon monoxide and nicotine for eight offices located in Australia, the United Kingdom and the United States. RSP concentrations ranged from 20 to 120 μg/m³; concentrations of carbon monoxide, from 2.5 to 4.0 parts per million; and concentrations of nicotine, from below 0.80 to 34.8 μg/m³.

Kirk et al. (1988) reported results from a 30-week survey of ETS in "work" environments in the United Kingdom. They measured a mean nicotine concentration of 14 μg/m³ in work environments where smoking occurred, a value that they recognized as a likely overestimate of ETS exposure. This concentration is contrasted with a mean value of 9 μg/m³ (also a likely overestimate) for work environments where smoking did not occur. Mean concentrations of carbon monoxide for the two work categories were both low and not significantly different. For smoking environments, the mean was 2.2 parts per million, and for non-smoking environments, 2.1 parts per million.

In a limited follow-up study, Kirk et al. (1988) reported results from four offices, two nonsmoking and two smoking. In the nonsmoking offices, concentrations of RSP were 77 and 46 μg/m³; nicotine concentrations were 1.2 and 0.8 μg/m³. In the smoking offices, RSP concentrations were 120 and 117 μg/m³; corresponding nicotine concentrations were 5.7 and 3.3 μg/m³.

3. Portable Air Sampling System (PASS) Surveys. The greatest number of data have been gathered through the use of the portable air sampling system (PASS), a specially outfitted briefcase that can be used unobtrusively to measure nicotine, RSP and CO in indoor environments. Carson and Erikson (1988) reported results of nicotine, ultraviolate particulate matter (UV-PM) and CO from a survey of 31 offices in Ottawa, Ontario. Because of analytical problems, measures of RSP were not reported. Nicotine concentrations ranged from less than 1.2 μg/m³ to 69.7 μg/m³ with an average concentration of 12.0 μg/m³. In computing this average, the authors excluded results that were below the limit of detection as well as results made when smoking was not visually observed. Concentrations of UV-PM, which focus on the RSP fraction most likely attributable to ETS, ranged from 6 to 426 μg/m³ and averaged 44 μg/m³. Indoor CO concentrations did not differ substantially from outdoor concentrations. CO was therefore found to be an inadequate indicator of ETS exposure.

Results from several PASS surveys were analyzed by Crouse et al. (1988). The geometric mean concentrations for nicotine, ultraviolet particulate matter, and RSP were 4.4, 34, and 124 $\mu g/m^3$, respectively.

III. Conclusions and Recommendations for Future Research

Although numerous studies have attempted to measure ETS exposure through the use of one or more surrogates for ETS, this approach has achieved little success so far. As Repace concluded, after reviewing 50 indoor air quality studies, "few . . . have recorded sufficient information to enable observed concentrations to be related to the parameters of smoking and ventilation." (Repace 1987). A major cause of this failure is the lack of standardized monitoring methods for ETS. (O'Neill and Riboli 1987). A common approach to design is essential when comparing studies. Another problem is that many studies fail to address or control for the weaknesses associated with relying on particular surrogates/tracers for ETS.

While standardized instrumentation is available for a number of gases, vapours and suspended particulates, further research on instrument calibration, standards of measurement and the applicability of data loggers in combination with DRIs is needed to ensure comparability of results. Investigators should provide data concerning type, model, range, efficiency, sensitivity and the flow rate of relevant sampling devices in order for a common method of analysis to emerge.

In addition, there has been little investigation into alternate sources (internal and external) and background levels of ETS markers. The estimation of ETS concentrations using surrogates must include corrections for alternate contaminant sources by determining background levels to avoid overestimation.

Further, there has been a consistent lack of information on the sampling environment, i.e., the effect of furniture, carpeting, draperies and density of occupation on ETS concentrations. Similar gaps in information appear with respect to building characteristics such as ventilation system descriptions, rates and parameters, supply rates, exhaust rates, fresh air makeup, location and type of diffusers, ventilation effectiveness, etc. In the future, these considerations should be taken into account to strengthen the validity of the data collected.

Many of the studies reviewed by the author failed to meet two basic criteria with respect to statistical methods at the experimental design stage. First, the studies did not select a subgroup of adequate size that high exposures would be detected if they were present (refer to Table 3–2). Second, investigators failed to select sampling locations or individuals at random.

Table 3–2
Summary of Pertinent Sampling Techniques

Single Components	*Multi Components*	*Portable Air Sampling System*
Skov et al. (1987)	Sterling et al (1987)	Oldaker et al. (1988)
Muramatsu et al (1988)	Meissener et al (1988)	
Hammond et al. (1987)	Bayer and Black	Carson et al. (1988)
Hammond et al. (1988)	Turner (1988)	
	Kirk (1988)	Crouse et al. (1988)

Random selection is used when employees are involved in work operations with identical exposure potential and the air in the work area is well mixed. In these cases it is not possible to select a maximum risk employee. The method minimizes the sampling burden while obtaining a high probability of sampling a high risk employee (NIOSH 1977). Until these and other deficiencies are addressed, efforts at assessing exposure to ETS based on airborne markers will have to be interpreted with some caution.

Problems also exist with respect to the use of particulate markers. If nicotine is to be used as a tracer for ETS, it should be used as a tracer for the vapour phase. Further work is needed to establish the relationship between nicotine in the vapour phase and particulate phase tracers such as RSP.

An accepted definition for RSP is lacking in the literature reviewed. As mentioned previously, the cutoff point for RSP was observed to vary between 2.5 and 10 μm. Before further studies are undertaken using RSP measurements, this issue should be addressed.

As for mutagenic tracers, the mutagenicity of the entire vapour phase should be determined due to the physical difference between the vapour and particulate states. The overall mutagenicity of ETS is important in determining the synergistic action of unknown components. The use of multicomponent chromatographic techniques may yield useful information in this area.

There are two avenues of research regarding solanesol. The first should address the issue of solanesol's effect on human health, if any. Second, more research is required to determine the relationship between solanesol and ETS as a whole to establish its validity as a marker.

Multi-component studies offer a greater possibility of success than single components ones. Measuring several tracers simultaneously, both ETS-specific and non-specific and in the vapour and particulate phases, will go far toward eliminating the deficiencies associated with the use of single markers. Finally, there is a definite need to standardize both sampling methodology and certain experimental design parameters so that the results of multiple studies can be compared with reasonable assurance.

References

Aviado, D. (1984). Carbon monoxide as an index of environmental tobacco smoke exposure. *Eur. J. Resp. Dis.* 65:47–60.

Baker, S. et al. (1985). Exposure to indoor air pollutants and their health effects. *Report on Annual Meeting of Am. Assoc. for Advancement of Sciences.* Los Angeles, Ca.

Baker, R. and S. Colome (1988). The build-up and decay of environmental tobacco smoke constituents as a function of room conditions. *Proc. Indoor Amb. Air Qual. Conf.* London.

Bayer, C. et al. (1988). IAQ (indoor air quality) evaluation of three office buildings. *ASHRAE J.* 30:48–53.

Bell, S. et al. (1983). Indoor air quality in office buildings. *Occupational Health in Ontario* 4(3).

Bridge, D. et al. (1972). Contribution to the assessment of exposure of nonsmokers to air pollution from cigarette and cigar smoke in occupied spaces. *Envir. Res.* 5:192–209.

Cain, W. et al. (1987). Environmental tobacco smoke: sensory reactions of occupants. *Atmospheric Envir.* 21(2):347–353.

Cain, W. et al. (1983). Ventilation requirements in buildings. *Atmospheric Envir.* 17(6):1183–1197.

Cain, W. et al. (1982). Ventilation requirements in occupied spaces during smoking and nonsmoking occupancy. *Envir. Int'l* 8:505–514.

Carson, J. et al. (1988). Results from surveys of environmental tobacco smoke in offices in Ottawa, Ontario. *Envir. Tech. Lett.* 9:501–508.

Claxton, L. et al. (1989). Genotoxic assessment of environmental tobacco smoke using bacterial bioassays. *Mutation Res.* 222:81–99.

Cortese, A. et al. (1976). Ability of fixed monitoring stations to represent personal carbon monoxide exposure. *J. A.P.C.A.* 26(12):1144–1150.

Cortese, A. et al. (1985). Performance of aerodynamic particle sizer. *Aerosol & Tech.* 4(1):9–98.

Coultas, D. et al. (1987). Reliability and validity of questionnaire assessment of involuntary tobacco smoke exposure. *Proc. 4th Int'l Conf. Indoor Air Qual. and Climate.* West Berlin 2:121–125.

Crouse, W. et al. (1988). Results from a survey of environmental tobacco smoke (ETS) in restaurants. Presented at APCA Int'l Speciality Conf., Niagara Falls, NY.

DiNardi, S. (Unpublished). Conceptual considerations for monitoring exposure to environmental tobacco smoke. Univ. Mass., Amherst.

DiNardi, S. (Unpublished). Exposure assessment for respirable suspended particles from environmental tobacco smoke in the indoor environment. Univ. Mass., Amherst.

Dube, M. et al. (1982). Methods of collection of smoke for analytical purposes. *Rec. Adv. Tub. Sci.* 8:42–102.

Eatough, D. et al. (1988). Assessing exposure to environmental tobacco smoke. *Proc. Indoor Amb. Air Qual. Conf.*, London.

Editorial (1989). Environmental tobacco smoke in the context of indoor air quality. *Human Toxicol.* 8:3–4.

Eudy, L. (1986). Studies on the vapor-particulate phase distribution of environmental nicotine by selective trapping and detection methods. Presentation at 79th Annual Meeting of APCA, Minneapolis, Minn.

First, M. (1984). Constituents of sidestream and mainstream tobacco smoke and markers to quantify exposure to them. *Proc. of 7th Life Sci. Symposium*. Knoxville, Tenn.

Hammond, S. et al. (1987). Collection and analysis of nicotine as a marker for environmental tobacco smoke. *Atmospheric Envir.* 21:457–462.

Hammond, S. et al. (1987). Field study of passive smoking exposure with passive sampler. *Proc. 4th Int'l Conf. Indoor Air Qual. & Climate,* West Berlin 2:131–136.

Hammond, S. et al. (1988). Markers of exposure to diesel exhaust and cigarette smoke in railroad workers. *Am. Ind. Hygiene Assoc. J.* 49:516–522.

Hammond, S. et al. (1987). A diffusion monitor to measure exposure to passive smoking. *Envir. Sci. Tech.* 21(5):494–497.

Hinds, W. et al. (1975). Concentrations of nicotine and tobacco smoke in public places. *N. Engl. J. M.* 292:16.

Hugod, C. et al. (1978). Exposure of passive smokers to tobacco smoke constituents. *Int'l Arch. Occup. Envir. Health* 41:21–29.

Husgafvel-Pursiainen, K. (1986). Genotoxicity and polynuclear aromatic hydrocarbon analysis of environmental tobacco smoke samples from restaurants. *Mutagenesis* 4:287–292.

Indoor air pollutants: exposure and health effects (1982). Report on WHO meeting, Nördlingen.

Jarvis, M. et al. (1983). Absorption of nicotine and carbon monoxide from passive smoking under natural conditions of exposure. *Thorax* 38:829–833.

Jenkins, R. et al. (1984). Analytical chemical methods for the detection of environmental tobacco smoke constituents. *Eur. J. Respir. Dis.* 133:33–46.

Jenkins, R. et al. (1987). General analytical considerations for the sampling of tobacco smoke in indoor air. *IARC Sci. Pub.* 9(81):105–113.

Kabat, G. et al. (1986). Patterns of exposure to environmental tobacco smoke in a group of hospitalized patients. 79th Annual Meeting, APCA, Minneapolis, Minn.

Kirk, P. et al. (1988). Environmental tobacco smoke in indoor air. *Proc. Indoor Amb. Air Qual. Conf.*, London.

Kirk, P. et al. (1988). Environmental tobacco smoke in public places. Presented at Symposium on Environment and Heritage, Hong Kong.

Klus, H. et al. (1985). Indoor air pollution due to tobacco smoke under real conditions, preliminary results. *Tokai J. Exp. Clin. Med.* 10(4):331–340.

Leaderer, B. et al. (1984). Ventilation requirements in buildings. *Atmospheric Envir.* 18(1).

Levin, H (1989). *Indoor air quality update* 2(2).

Ling, P. et al. (1987). Mutagenic determination of passive smoking. *Toxicol. Lett.* 35:147–151.

Mattson, M. et al. (1989). Passive smoking on commercial airline flights. *JAMA* 261(6).

Miesner, E. (1988). Aerosol and ETS sampling in public facilities and offices. Presented at 81st Annual Meeting of APCA, Dallas, Tx.

Muramatsu, M. et al. (1987). Estimation of personal exposure to ambient nicotine in daily environment. *Int'l Arch. Occup. Envir. Health* 49:545–550.

Muramatsu, M. et al. (1984). Estimation of personal exposure to tobacco smoke with a newly developed nicotine personal monitor. *Envir. Res.* 35:218–227.

Nagda, N. et al. (1985). Characterization and abatement of indoor pollutants. Presentation at 78th Annual Meeting of APCA, Detroit, Mich.

National Research Council (1986). *Environmental tobacco smoke: measuring exposures and assessing health effects*. National Academy Press.

Nystrom, C. et al. (unpublished). Assessing the impact of environmental tobacco smoke on indoor air quality: current status.

Odgen, M. (1988). Collection and analysis of solanesol as a tracer of environmental tobacco smoke (ETS). *Proc. Indoor Amb. Air Qual. Conf.*, London.

Okada, T. et al. (1974). Determination of particle-size distribution and concentration of cigarette smoke by a light-scattering method. *J. Colloid & Interface Sci.* 48:3.

Oldaker, G. et al. (1988). Portable air sampling system for surveying levels of environmental tobacco smoke in public places. Presented at Symposium on Environment and Heritage, Hong Kong.

Oldaker, G. et al. (1987). Results from surveys of environmental tobacco smoke in offices and restaurants. Int'l Conf. on Indoor Air Qual., Tokyo, Japan.

O'Neill, J. et al. (1987). IARC approaches to monitoring exposure of passive smoking. *Toxicol. Lett.* 35:29–33.

O'Neill, J. et al. (1987). Environmental carcinogens: Methods of analysis and exposure measurement. *Passive Smoking* (IARC).

Ott, W. et al. (1986). Automated data-logging personal exposure monitors for carbon monoxide. *J. A.P.C.A.* 36(8):883–887.

Ott, W. (1985). Total human exposure. *Environmental Science and Technology* 19:880–886.

Ott, W. et al. (1982). Measurement of carbon monoxide concentrations in indoor and outdoor locations using personal exposure monitors. *Envir. Int'l* 8:295–304.

Proctor, C. (1988). The analysis of the contribution of ETS to indoor air. *Envir. Tech. Lett.* 9:553–562.

Pritchard, J. et al. (1988). The physical behaviour of sidestream tobacco smoke under ambient conditions. *Envir. Tech. Lett.* 9:545–552.

Repace, J. (1987). Indoor concentrations of environmental tobacco smoke: models dealing with effects of ventilation and room size. *IARC Sci. Pub. 81, Environmental carcinogens: selected methods of analysis* 9:25–41.

Robinson, D. et al. (1988). Prediction of the buildup and decay of ETS components by mathematical modelling. *Proc. Indoor Amb. Air Qual. Conf.*, London.

Robertson, G. (1989). Testimony in Hearings Before the Subcommittee on Aviation of the House Committee on Public Works and Transportation, 100th Cong., 1st Sess. (June 22, 1989).

Skov, P. et al. (1987). The sick building syndrome in the office environment: the Danish town hall study. *Envir. Int'l* 13:339–349.

Spengler, J. D. et al. (1985). Personal exposures to respirable particulates and implications for air pollution epidemiology. *Envir. Sci. Tech.* 19(8).

Spengler, J.D. et al. (1981). Long-term measurements of respirable sulfates and particles inside and outside the home. *Atmospheric Environment* 15:223–230.

Sterling, T. et al. (1988). Concentrations of nicotine, RSP, CO and CO_2 in nonsmoking areas of offices ventilated by air recirculated from smoke designated areas. *Am. Ind. Hyg. Assoc. J.* 49(9):423–426.

Sterling, D. et al. (1987). Environmental tobacco smoke and indoor air quality in modern office work environments. *J.M.* 29(1):57–62.

Sterling, T. (1988). ETS concentrations under different conditions of ventilation and smoking regulation. *Proc. Indoor Amb. Air Qual. Conf.*, London.

Sterling, T. et al. (1982). Indoor byproduct levels of tobacco smoke: a critical review of the literature. *J. A.P.C.A.* 32(3).

Stolwijk, J. et al. (1984). Experimental considerations in the measurement of exposures to cigarette smoke. *Proc. of 7th Life Sci. Symposium,* Knoxville, Tenn.

Triebig, G. et al. (1984). Indoor air pollution by smoke constituents—a survey. *Prev. Med.* 13:570–581.

Turner, S. (1988). Environmental tobacco smoke and smoking policies. Presented at APCA Int'l Speciality Conf., Niagara Falls, N.Y.

Turner, W. et al. (1979). Design and performance of a reliable personal monitoring system for respirable pariculates. *J. A.P.C.A.* 29(7).

Wallace, L. et al. (1987). Personal, biological and air monitoring for exposure to environmental tobacco smoke. *IARC Sci. Pub. 81, Environmental carcinogins: selected methods of analysis* 9(81):87–103.

Wallace, L. et al. (1987). Exposures of benzene and other volatile compounds from active and passive smoking. *Archives Envir. Health* 42(5).

Williams, D. (1985). Measurements of nicotine in building air as an indicator of tobacco smoke levels. *Envir. Health Persp.* 60:405–410.

4
Biological Markers in Assessing Exposure To Environmental Tobacco Smoke

Mark J. Reasor, Ph.D.
Department of Pharmacology and Toxicology
West Virginia University Health Sciences Center

A controversy now exists regarding the relationship between exposure to environmental tobacco smoke ("ETS") and adverse health effects in humans. A major criticism in the interpretation of the results of health-related studies has been the lack of objective and quantitative measures of exposure to ETS. Many studies that have examined this problem have relied on questionnaires to assess duration and/or intensity of exposure. While questionnaires have the advantage of estimating exposure retrospectively, they are subjective in nature. Problems associated with their use are numerous and include respondent bias, interviewer bias, lack of recall, and subsequent change in smoking status, to name a few (Jarvis 1989). There is broad agreement that an objective, quantitative measure of ETS exposure is required in order to properly evaluate potential health effects.

Biological markers, which are representative of the dose of chemical(s) entering the body, have been used frequently as an objective means of assessing exposure to ETS. These markers are, in effect, surrogates for the ETS mixture as a whole. An effective marker should satisfy the following criteria (Jarvis et al. 1989):

1. It should be tobacco-specific in order to be certain of its origin.
2. It should have a long half-life so that it serves as an index of exposure over an extended period of time.
3. The marker should give a valid indication of the health risks of exposure.
4. Analytical techniques should be available that can reliably and conveniently measure the low levels of the marker present in nonsmokers exposed to ETS.

A number of chemicals and processes have been examined as markers, but no single marker satisfying all the above criteria has been identified. This paper reviews the literature on biological markers for ETS and highlights the conclusions that can be derived from it. The paper then focuses on the information that is lacking in this area and offers suggestions for future research.

I. Nicotine and Cotinine in Biological Fluids

The presence of nicotine or its metabolite, cotinine, in body fluids (blood, urine and saliva) has been used widely to assess exposure of nonsmokers to ETS (Jarvis 1989). Since nicotine is found almost exclusively in tobacco, nicotine and cotinine offer the advantage of being tobacco–specific. Using these markers, it is possible, with few exceptions, to distinguish smokers from nonsmokers. Nicotine has a half-life of 1 to 2 hours in blood and may have a shorter half-life in saliva and is therefore useful in documenting recent exposure. Cotinine, which has a half-life of about 10–20 hours in blood and urine, is more valuable for assessing day to day exposure (Hoffmann et al. 1984; Jarvis 1989). In general, the strongest relationship between self-reported exposure, number of smokers in the home or home air nicotine and a biological marker is with urinary and salivary cotinine (Jarvis 1989). This has been noted with only certain populations (Coultas et al. 1987; Greenberg et al. 1984; Henderson et al. 1989; Jarvis et al. 1984, 1985; Matsukara et al. 1984; Mattson et al. 1989; Pattishall et al. 1985). Jarvis et al. (1987) reported that values for salivary cotinine in adolescents were consistent with parental smoking habits for a period of one year. It is yet to be determined if these relationships exist across the general population. In many cases a certain degree of misclassification of exposure has been observed and must be considered in interpreting the data (Coultas et al. 1987; Henderson et al. 1989).

A problem with the use of blood or salivary nicotine or cotinine is that, often, only single samples are taken. It is virtually impossible to relate a single value to a dynamic process such as ETS exposure. Since urine samples reflect cumulative excretion over a period of time (24 hour samples are used frequently), urinary cotinine values are somewhat less sensitive to the time of exposure represented by the sample. To minimize variability further, values are usually normalized to the concurrent levels of creatinine (a normal urinary constituent that is an index of renal function).

Methodological considerations are important in analyzing urinary cotinine. Both interlaboratory and intralaboratory variation in the absolute values of these markers has been reported, particularly when the values are low as would be observed for nonsmokers (Biber et al. 1987; Letzel et al. 1987). The values are highly susceptible to procedural differences such as the length of time between collection and assay, and the sample size of the urine employed in the assay. Such variations make comparison of values between laboratories difficult even when the same analytical technique is used. Mathematical modeling of nicotine and cotinine as markers for exposure to ETS reveal that nicotine is not an acceptable quantitative marker and, at best, cotinine is only a semiquantitative marker for nicotine exposure (Schwartz et al. 1987; Balter et al. 1988).

The most important limitation with the use of nicotine and cotinine is that they represent exposure only to nicotine in ETS. They cannot be used as surrogates for exposure to other constituents of ETS unless they can be shown to parallel those constituents in behavior in indoor air and in the body. Additionally, they cannot, with any degree of validity, be used to estimate cigarette equivalents or make risk assessments by comparing values in nonsmokers with those in smokers (Jarvis 1989; Russell et al. 1985, 1986; Wigle et al. 1987). For example, a comparision of urinary cotinine levels between smokers and nonsmokers has been used to estimate yearly mortality due to exposure to ETS (Russell et al. 1986). There are several reasons why such an estimation has little scientific validity.

First, active smoking and exposure to ETS represent different exposure situations with regard to nicotine. Nicotine in the mainstream smoke inhaled by active smokers is associated with the particulate phase of the smoke, while nicotine in ETS is principally in the gas phase (Eudy et al. 1985; Tang et al. 1988). Consequently, nicotine or cotinine in body fluids of those exposed to ETS represents exposure to a gas phase component while these values in active smokers represent exposure to a particulate phase component. There is evidence that gas phase and particulate phase components decay at different rates in indoor air (Tang et al. 1988), a factor which will influence the relationship between values in smokers and those exposed to ETS. Second, nicotine is metabolized at a more rapid rate in smokers than in nonsmokers, with the result that the same dose of nicotine will result in different urinary cotinine levels in the two populations (Kyerematen et al., 1982). Clearly, to use nicotine or cotinine values in nonsmokers for comparison to smokers is inappropriate and misleading.

II. Urinary Mutagenicity

As a measure of exposure to ETS, studies have been conducted on the ability of concentrated extracts from the urine of nonsmokers to induce mutations in bacteria using the popular Ames assay (Bos et al. 1983; Mohtashamipuri et al. 1987; Putzrath et al. 1981; Scherer et al. 1987; Sorsa et al. 1985). The rationale behind this approach is that the presence of mutagens in the urine is an indication that the person has been exposed to chemicals that can induce genetic mutations and, theoretically, increase the risk of cancer. In order to interpret the results of such studies properly, it is necessary to consider certain aspects of the experimental design and analysis that have been employed. In that vein, the following points are significant:

1. The conditions of exposure to ETS in laboratory settings have not always been realistic in that the levels of ETS have been much higher than commonly encountered under ambient conditions (Bos et al. 1983; Mohtashamipuri et al. 1987).
2. It is known that diet can markedly influence the mutagencity of urine (Sasson et al. 1985). Possible confounding factors such as diet have not always been controlled for in studies examining the mutagencity of urine following experimental exposure to ETS (Bos et al. 1983).
3. Claims of increased urinary mutagenicity have not always been supported by the data because of the absence of statistical analysis (Mohtashamipuri et al. 1987; Sorsa et al. 1985) or because of misrepresentation of the actual data presented (Sorsa et al. 1985).
4. The putative urinary mutagens have not been identified.
5. The biological significance of low-level mutagencity in urinary concentrates has not been established.

When studies in this area are considered together, there is no compelling evidence that exposure to ETS results in an increase in urinary mutagenicity or that it will be possible to assess exposure to ETS by its use.

III. Adducts

Adducts are products derived from reactions between chemicals and biological material such as DNA and protein. The formation of DNA adducts is reported to be associated with mutagenesis and carcinogenesis (Pelkonen et al. 1980). Consequently, adducts of DNA or adducts of proteins such as hemoglobin have been suggested as predictors of the biological effects of ETS exposure (Belinsky et al. 1986; Hecht et al. 1987; Perera et al. 1987). An advantage of such a marker is the potential to monitor exposure on a more chronic basis than with other markers (e.g., hemoglobin has a lifespan of 120 days). At present, little work has been done in this area relating to ETS exposure. Adducts that have been studied for this purpose include benzo(a)pyrene diol epoxide-1-DNA in white blood cells and 4-aminobiphenyl-hemoglobin (Perera et al., 1987). However, the adducts of benzo(a)pyrene diol epoxide-1-DNA were not stable over a period of 48 hours in either smokers or nonsmokers, indicating that adducts may not be as useful as originally thought. Additionally, neither of the parent compounds is tobacco specific.

A more useful approach would be to have a DNA or protein adduct originating from a tobacco–specific chemical. NNK, a nitrosation product of nicotine, has been shown to form DNA and protein adducts when injected into animals (Hecht and Trushin 1988). Measurement of the O_6-methylguanine and 7-methylguanine moieties occurring in tissues or cells may be useful in assessing exposure to NNK and ETS. Additionally, it has been reported that nicotine is bioactivated to a chemical species that binds macromolecules (Shigenaga et al. 1988). Little information currently exists as to the feasibility of using nicotine-derived adducts to monitor exposure to ETS, making this a promising area for future research.

IV. Breath Analysis

Another reported index of exposure to ETS is the level of volatile organic chemicals in the exhaled breath of nonsmokers (Wallace et al. 1987). Because of the lack of tobacco specificity of the chemicals examined and the very low levels detected, however, there is little evidence that breath analysis will be of any value in assessing exposure to ETS. Other markers that have been used have been less successful in assessing exposure to ETS. These are described briefly below.

One component of ETS is carbon monoxide. The presence of carboxyhemoglobin in the blood is indicative of exposure to carbon monoxide. Carbon monoxide may originate from a number of sources, including internal combustion engines, gas heaters, and stoves. This lack of specifity seriously limits its value as a marker for ETS.

The presence of thiocyanate in body fluids, resulting from cyanide, has also been used as an index of exposure to ETS. This compound, however, also lacks specificity as dietary materials may result in the appearance of thiocyanate in the blood. Additionally, levels of neither carboxyhemoglobin nor thiocyanate change significantly during exposure to ETS under experimental or ambient conditions. Carbon monoxide and thiocyanate therefore are not useful indicators of ETS exposure (Hoffman et al. 1984; Jarvis 1989; Robertson et al. 1987).

Cytogenetic changes (structural chromosomal changes and sister chromatid exchange) (Sorsa et al. 1989; Perera et al. 1987), levels of urinary N-nitrosoproline (Hoffmann et al. 1984), hydroxyproline (Adlkofer et al. 1985) and nicotine-1-'N-oxide (Kyerematen et al. 1982) have all been examined as potential markers for ETS exposure. None, however, appears to change significantly as a result of exposure to ETS.

From the discussion presented, it is evident that existing biological markers for ETS exposure have distinct limitations. Nicotine or cotinine levels in biological fluids can be used to assess exposure to ETS qualitatively. At present, however, there is no reliable way, through the use of biological markers, to assess long term exposure to ETS. Neither is it appropriate to use them to make valid estimates of risk of adverse health effects.

The important question is whether the potential exists for improving this situation. Some approaches have a greater probability of success than others. It is possible, for example, to refine current methods to improve the qualitative assessment of short-term and longer-term ETS exposure using nicotine and cotinine. Standardization of sample processing and analysis should reduce variations among laboratories. The use of other analytical techniques, such as high performance liquid chromatography, may aid in this process. In order to evaluate short-term or longer-term exposure to ETS quantitatively, it is necessary to identify a number of biological markers that are representative of ETS constituents. In any study designed to monitor long-term exposure, subject compliance will undoubtedly be a complication, for which adequate numbers of subjects may compensate. At present there are no markers to monitor long-term exposure to ETS that are relevant for assessing potential health risks, particularly cancer. DNA or protein adducts that are specific for tobacco components offer an opportunity to monitor long-term exposure to ETS qualitatively. Adducts, however, would be of value only if they could be sampled from tissues in which cancer or documented toxicity from ETS exposure has been implicated. It would have to be established that they are specific for that tissue, are involved in causing the toxic or neoplastic event, and are present in the disease that developed there. In any situation where adducts are studied, proper controls must be employed and analytical procedures must be developed to increase the sensitivity of detection.

V. Animal Research

To complement efforts directed toward improving biological markers, the use of laboratory animals should receive increased emphasis. Studies may be conducted under strictly controlled conditions using large numbers of animals in exposure chambers. The levels of ETS can be varied to simulate a wide range of ambient conditions, and the duration of exposure can be of any length desired. For example, it is possible to expose pregnant animals to examine effects on the fetus. Alternatively, exposure may occur for the lifespan of the animal. Urine can be sampled; blood can be collected; amniotic fluid can be analyzed; animals can be sacrificed at prescribed times to measure levels of markers.

As with all animal research in the biomedical sciences, however, such studies have inherent limitations. They will always suffer, for example, from the uncertainty of extrapolation to humans. Nevertheless, important relationships can be examined. Well planned and carefully conducted studies using a number of species will facilitate the extrapolation process. Utilizing improved techniques and methodologies with human biological markers combined with animal-based research, it should be possible to make significant progress towards developing biological markers for ETS that will permit a quantitative assessment of exposure. The goal of achieving estimations of risk of adverse health effects may be more difficult to attain.

References

Adlkofer, F., G. Scherer, U. von Hees, and X. Suenkeler (1985). Urinary hydroxyproline excretion in smokers, non-smokers and passive smokers. *Tokai J. Exp. Clin. Med.* 10:415–425.

Balter, N.J., D.J. Eatough, and S.L. Schwartz (1988). Application of physiological pharmacokinetic modeling to the design of human exposure studies with environmental tobacco smoke. *Proc. Indoor Amb. Air Qual. Conf. London,* pp. 179–188.

Belinsky, S.A., C.M. White, J.A. Boucheron, F.C. Richardson, J.A. Swenberg, and M. Anderson (1986). Accumulation and persistence of DNA adducts in respiratory tissue of rats following multiple administrations of the tobacco specific carcinogen 4-(N-methyl-N-nitrosamino)-1-(3-pyridyl)-1-butanone. *Cancer Res.* 46: 1280–1284.

Biber, A., G. Scherer, I. Hoepfner, F. Adlkofer, W.D. Heller, J.E. Haddow, and G.J. Knight (1987). Determination of nicotine and cotinine in human serum and urine: An interlaboratory study. *Toxicol. Lett.* 35:45–52.

Bos, R.P., J.L.G. Theuws, and P.T. Henderson (1983). Excretion of mutagens in human urine after passive smoking. *Cancer Lett.* 19:85–90.

Coultas, D.B., C.A. Howard, G.T. Peake, B.J. Skipper, and J.M. Samet (1987). Salivary cotinine levels and involuntary tobacco smoke exposure in children and adults in New Mexico. *Am. Rev. Respir. Dis.* 136:305–309.

Eudy, L.W., F.A. Thome, D.L. Heaven, C.R. Green, and B.J. Ingebrethsen (1985). Studies on the vapor-particulate phase distribution of environmental nicotine. Presented at the 39th Tobacco Chemists Research Conference, Montreal, Canada, October 2–5.

Greenberg, R.A., N.J. Haley, R.A. Etzel, and F.A. Loda (1984). Measuring the exposure of infants to tobacco smoke. Nicotine and cotinine in urine and saliva. *New Engl. J. Med.* 310:1075–1078.

Hecht, S.S., S.G. Carmella, N. Trushin, P.G. Foiles, D. Lin, J.M. Rubin, and F.L. Chung (1987). Investigations on the molecular dosimetery of tobacco-specific nitrosamines. *IARC Sci. Publ.* 84:423–429.

Hecht, S.S. and N. Trushin (1988). DNA and hemoglobin alkylation by 4-(methylnitrosamino)-1-(3-pyridyl)-1-butanone and its major metabolite 4-(methylnitrosamino)-1-(3-pyridyl)-1-butanol in F344 rats. *Carcinoginesis* 9:1665–1668.

Henderson, F.W., H.F. Reid, R. Morris, O.L. Wang, P.C. Hu, R.W. Helms, L. Forehand, J. Mumford, J. Lewtas, N.J. Haley, and S.K. Hammond (1989). Home air nicotine levels and urinary cotinine excretion in preschool children. *Am. Rev. Respir. Dis.* 140:190–201.

Hoffmann, D., N.J. Haley, J.D. Adams, and K.D. Brunnemann (1984). Tobacco sidestream smoke: Uptake by nonsmokers. *Prev. Med.* 13:608–617.

Jarvis, M.J. (1989). Application of biochemical intake markers to passive smoking measurement and risk estimation. *Mutation Res.* 222:101–110.

Jarvis, M., H. Tunstall-Pedoe, C. Feyerabend, C. Vesey, and Y. Salloojee (1984). Biochemical markers of smoke absorption and self-reported exposure to passive smoking. *J. Epidem. Commun. Health* 38:335–339.

Jarvis, M.J., M.A.H. Russell, C. Feyerabend, J.R. Eiser, M. Morgan, P. Gammage, and E.M. Gray (1985). Passive exposure to tobacco smoke: saliva cotinine concentrations in a representative population sample of non-smoking schoolchildren. *Brit. Med. J.* 291:927–929.

Jarvis, M.J., A.D. McNeill, M.A.H. Russell, R.J. West, A. Bryant, and C. Feyerabend (1987). Passive smoking in adolescents: One year of stability in the home. *Lancet* i:1324–1325.

Kyerematen, G.A., M.D. Damiano, B.H. Dvorchik, and E.S. Vessell (1982). Smoking-induced changes in nicotine dispostion: Application of a new HPLC assay for nicotine and its metabolites. *Clin. Pharmacol. Ther.* 32:769–780.

Letzel, H., A. Fischer-Brandies, L.C. Johnson, K. Überla, and A. Biber (1987). Measuring problems in estimating the exposure to passive smoking using the excretion of cotinine. *Toxicol. Lett.* 35:35–44.

Matsukura, S., T. Taminato, N. Kitano, Y. Seino, H. Hamada, M. Uchihashi, H. Nakajima, and Y. Hirata (1984). Effects of environmental tobacco smoke on urinary cotinine excretion in nonsmokers. *New Eng. J. Med.* 311:828–832.

Mattson, M.E., G. Boyd, D. Byar, C. Brown, J.F. Callahan, D. Corle, J.W. Cullen, J. Greenblatt, N.J. Haley, S.K. Hammond, J. Lewtas, and W. Reeves (1989). Passive smoking on commercial airline flights. *JAMA* 261, 867–872.

Mohtashamipur, E., G. Muller, K. Norpoth, M. Endrikat, and W. Stucker (1987). Urinary excretion of mutagens in passive smokers. *Toxicol. Lett.* 35:141–146.

Pattishall, E.N., G.L. Strope, R.A. Etzel, R.W. Helms, N.J. Haley, and F.W. Denny (1985). Serum cotinine as a measure of tobacco smoke exposure in children. *Am. J. Dis. Child.* 139:1101–1104.

Pelkonen, O., K. Vahakangas, and D.W. Nebert (1980). Binding of polycyclic aromatic hydrocarbons to DNA: Comparison with mutagenesis and tumorigenesis. *J. Toxicol. Environ. Health* 6:1009–1020.

Perera, F.P., R.M. Santella, D. Brenner, M.C. Poirier, A.A. Munshi, H.K. Fischman, and J. Van Ryzin (1987). DNA adducts, protein adducts and sister chromatid exchange in cigarette smokers and nonsmokers. *J. Nat. Cancer Inst.* 79:449–456.

Putzrath, R.M., D. Langley, and E. Eisenstadt (1981). Analysis of mutagenic activity in cigarette smokers' urine by high performance liquid chromatography. *Mutation Res.* 85:97–108.

Robertson, A.S., P.S. Burge, and B.L. Cockrill (1987). A study of serum thiocyanate concentrations in office workers as a means of validating smoking histories and assessing passive exposure to cigarette smoke. *Brit. J. Indust. Med.* 44:351–354.

Russell, M.A.H., R.J. West, and M.J. Jarvis (1985). Intravenous nicotine simulation of passive smoking to estimate dosage to exposed non-smokers. *Brit. J. Addict.* 80:201–206.

Russell, M.A.H., M.J. Jarvis, and R.J. West (1986). Use of urinary nicotine concentrations to estimate exposure and mortality from passive smoking in non-smokers. *Brit. J. Addict.* 81:275–281.

Sasson, I.M., D.T. Coleman, E.J. LaVoie, D. Hoffmann, and E.L. Wynder (1985). Mutagens in human urine: effects of cigarette smoke and diet. *Mutation Res.* 158:149–157.

Scherer, G., K. Westphal, A. Biber, I. Hoepfner, and F. Adlkofer (1987). Urinary mutagenicity after controlled exposure to environmental tobacco smoke (ETS). *Toxicol. Lett.* 35:135–140.

Schwartz, S.L., R.T. Ball, and P. Witorsch (1987). Mathematical modelling of nicotine and cotinine as biological markers of environmental tobacco smoke exposure. *Toxicol. Lett.* 12:53–58.

Shigenaga, M.K., A.J. Trevor, and N. Castagnoli Jr. (1988). Metabolism-dependent covalent binding of (S)-[5-^{3}H]Nicotine to liver and lung microsomal macromolecules. *Drug Metab. Dispos.* 16:397–402.

Sorsa, M., P. Einisto, K. Husgafvel-Pursiainen, H. Jarventaus, H. Kivisto, Y. Peltonen, T. Tuomi, S. Valkonen, and O. Pelkonen (1985). Passive and active exposure to cigarette smoke in a smoking experiment. *J. Toxicol. Environ. Health* 16:523–534.

Sorsa, M., K. Husgafvel-Pursiainen, H. Jarventaus, K. Koskimies, H. Salo, and H. Vainio (1989). Cytogenetic effects of tobacco smoke exposure among involuntary smokers. *Mutation Res.* 222:111–116.

Tang, H., G. Richards, K. Gunther, J. Crawford, M.L. Lee, E.A. Lewis, and D.J. Eatough (1988). Determination of gas phase nicotine and 3-ethenylpyridine, and particulate phase nicotine in environmental tobacco smoke with a collection bed-capillary gas chromatography system. *J. High Resolution Chrom. Communications* 11:775–782.

Wallace, L., E. Pellizzari, T.D. Hartwell, R. Perritt, and R. Ziegenfus (1987). Exposures to benzene and other volatile compounds from active and passive smoking. *Arch. Eviron. Health* 42:272–279.

Wigle, D.T., N.E. Collishaw, and J. Kirkbride (1987). Exposure of involuntary smokers to toxic components of tobacco smoke. *Can. J. Public Health* 78:151–154.

5
Panel Discussion on Exposure and Dose

Donald Ecobichon: We have a number of discussants for this particular session and I would ask them to come to the front.

Larry Holcomb: First, I'd like to congratulate both speakers. There's not much that I can add to what they have said. I'd like to emphasize a few of the points that they've made.

I think we need to look back at what people are really being exposed to in real life situations, to recognize how difficult it is to measure exposure and determine what that exposure may mean. If you actually calculate absorbed dose to the human from respirable particulate UV-PM data, the absorbed dose of an office worker or a person who spends his entire working hours at a restaurant where there is at least one smoker present is a tar equivalent of less than one cigarette over an entire year of exposure—an entire year, eight hours a day for the whole year.

Trying to understand what that means is indeed very difficult. It's very important that, if we pursue the animal experiments that Dr. Reasor talked about, we design a realistic exposure. The exposures should not be at the maximum tolerable dose, which produces abnormal results because the animal is stressed in many different ways. It's not just stress in the ways you're trying to measure but in a multitude of ways, some near death.

I'd like to suggest some possibilities for future research, though with the caveat that this work will be difficult to perform. First I would suggest the possibility of using two-dimensional gel electrophoresis, where you can identify specific proteins that are subject to change. We then must determine whether realistic concentrations do affect those tissues. You could focus on specific tissues, not just the animal as a whole.

Although nicotine is present in cigarette smoke in the air, it is also present in certain foods. Consumption of these foods may therefore affect dose and nicotine and cotinine concentrations in body fluids. The levels of nicotine in certain foods may be small, but it wouldn't take much consumption to give you the equivalent of a tenth of a cigarette per day. There is a paper that should be out in January or February of 1990—I believe in the Journal of Clinical Epidemiology—that goes into some detail on that.

If you're looking at body fluids, there is a tremendous opportunity for confounding. I think that animal studies are of great value because you can control the conditions very carefully. They need to be done at realistic doses, perhaps between twenty-five to two hundred micrograms of RSPs per cubic meter of air. You may find no effect, but if that's what we find, that's what we find. We're attempting to determine if real life doses have an effect.

Roger Jenkins: Chemical markers of ETS are more applicable to the assessment of exposure. It is generally easier to acquire data on levels of chemical markers, and the findings are usually more applicable to a larger number of individuals. The matrix in which the levels are usually determined, air, is not as difficult to acquire or as complex for analytical measurements as physiological media. The sample size is much less limited than that of physiological fluids. However, the time points over which a sample can be acquired are usually much shorter. Thus, inaccuracies may arise when data acquired over a limited time is extrapolated to an overall exposure. In addition, the presence of sampling and/or analysis equipment may alter the behavior of people present, and thus the amount of smoke which is released to the environment.

Biochemical markers tend to assess the dose that a particular individual receives. Once the biochemistry and metabolism of the marker compound are thoroughly understood, accurate determination of the marker can be extrapolated to dose. Typically, samples acquired from humans represent a longer, more integrated exposure. However, biochemical markers are subject to differences in metabolism, both as groups (smokers tend to metabolize nicotine differently than nonsmokers) and as individuals. Typically, there may be more than one pathway by which the physiological concentration of a specific constituent or metabolite can be reached. Diet and other environmental factors can also influence the amount of the marker present. Samples tend to be more difficult to acquire because they involve interruptions in the daily routines of the individuals providing the samples. Finally, the physical state of the compound is likely to influence the rate of uptake.

Both types of markers can further our understanding of the potential health effects of exposure to ETS. However, it is critical to understand the limitations of each.

Comments on Specific Chemical Markers

Carbon monoxide: CO is likely to be useful only when the presence of other sources is minimized. Large fluctuations in the background levels are likely to occur as a result of certain types of human activity (e.g., cooking, traffic).

Carbon dioxide: Non-dispersive infrared analysis can also be use for ambient air monitoring, and is less subject to interferences. However, CO_2

is not likely to be of much utility for assessing ETS exposure, given the number of other sources and the large fluctuations due to diurnal variations.

Nicotine: ETS exposure has been assessed using adsorption on Tenax-GC resin (Thompson, C.V., R.A. Jenkins and C.E. Higgins (1989). A thermal desorption method for the determination of nicotine in indoor environments, *Environ. Sci. Tech.* 23: 429–435).

Respirable suspended particulates: ETS RSP can also be measured with a tapered element oscillating microbalance (TEOM). The TEOM has an important advantage over the automated piezobalance, in that the material which contributes to the mass loading is collected on a filter attached to the tapered element.

Other potential markers exist. These may not be as unique as nicotine, but they seem less likely to undergo the adsorptive behavior which diminishes the utility of nicotine as a marker. They include:

Isoprene: Higgins and Guerin ("Studies on the Source Apportionment of Volatile Organic Indoor Air Contaminants Due to Cigarette Smoke," presented at the 42nd Tobacco Chemists' Research Conference, Lexington, Kentucky, October 2–5, 1988) have reported this as a potential marker of the vapor phase of ETS. Isoprene arises from the pyrolytic degradation of higher terpenes in the tobacco. It is likely to arise from the combustion of any plant material, such as firewood, but may be appropriate in those environments where such interferences are limited. It can be determined by adsorption on resin cartridges, followed by thermal desorption GC analysis.

Vinyl pyridine: Eatough's group at Brigham Young University has published a number of manuscripts with data suggesting that vinyl pyridine may be a much better marker for the ETS vapor phase than nicotine, since the former is much less subject to absorption on surfaces. It can be determined in much the same manner as nicotine.

Neophytadiene: This is a higher molecular weight terpene which is relatively specific to tobacco. It is usually considered a particulate phase constituent. However, due to the large surface area to volume ratio of the ETS droplets, a significant fraction of ETS neophytadiene is probably distributed into the vapor phase.

n-$C_{31}H_{64}$: This compound, probably a component of the leaf wax of tobacco, appears promising as a marker for the particulate phase of ETS (R.S. Ramsey et al., "The Generation, Sampling and Chromatographic Analysis of Particulate Matter in Dilute Sidestream Tobacco Smoke," Analytical Chimica Acta, submitted, 1989; Taylor and Graham, "Measurement of Filter Selectivity Using a New Reference Compound," presented at the 42nd Tobacco Chemists' Research Conference, Lexington, Kentucky October 2–5, 1988). It may be easier to determine than solanesol.

The entire concept of the utility of a marker compound must be carefully considered. Typically, markers are used because it is easier to trace the marker than the whole of the material whose exposure is being assessed. But the chemical complexity of ETS makes such an approach more difficult. First, because of the impact of dilution, chemical thermodynamic forces act to drive compounds of relatively low volatility into the vapor phase. For example, it is likely that a significant fraction of the benzo(a)pyrene present in ETS is distributed into the vapor phase. Thus, it is critical to make certain that the marker compound is distributed in a manner similar to the material being tracked. Secondly, the reactivity or absorptivity of many of the components of ETS act to reduce the exposure to a level below that which might have been predicted by more stable compounds. For example, using vapor phase isoprene as a marker may seriously overestimate the levels of reactive dimethyl nitrosamine or adsorptive nicotine. Finally, the data base regarding the emissions of sidestream smoke constituents by commercial products into the indoor environment is very limited, making it difficult to know the relationships between marker levels and those of the constituents being tracked.

Because of the political ramifications of ETS and smoking policies, there is a temptation to oversimplify many issues in order that concepts can be communicated with the public and lay press. One such example is the use of the term "cigarette equivalent." This is an attempt to relate ETS exposure—as measured by the concentration of some marker compound—to that of mainstream cigarette smoking. Such an approach is fraught with a number of difficulties.

First, sidestream smoke (SS), the major input term to ETS, is not mainstream smoke (MS). It is generated at a different temperature, air flow, pH, and oxidative conditions. Because of this, the two have different relative compositions. One might use these differences to rationalize nearly any conclusion. For example, because the nitrosamine content is higher in SS than in MS, one might argue that SS is potentially more harmful. However, CO represents a smaller fraction of the total oxides of carbon in SS, therefore, SS may be less harmful. The important point is that while both SS and MS contain the same constituents they are frequently present in much different relative levels. As a result, it is difficult to extrapolate from one to another.

Second, the MS cigarette equivalent is much too dependent on which ETS marker is used to compute the equivalency. For example, consider the typical sales-weighted average cigarette. When smoked under FTC conditions, the cigarette will produce approximately 12 mg "tar," 0.8 mg nicotine, and 12 mg CO. Of course, most human smoking data indicate that individuals tend to generate more smoke than that produced from FTC conditions, which further complicates the comparison. In an environment where smoking is not prohibited, published data suggests that a typical set of conditions which might be encountered would be 4 ug/m^3 nicotine and perhaps CO at a level of 2 ppm (2.2 mg/m^3) above that which would be encountered with no smokers present. If an individual breathes 1 m^3/hour (again, a typical value), the exposure will be 5 μg nicotine, or 0.005 cigarette's worth. In contrast, the CO exposure will be 2.2 mg, or 0.18 cigarette's worth. Thus, there can exist nearly a 40-fold difference in the exposure assessment, depending on the marker chosen. If dimethyl nitrosamine (DMN) would have been selected as a marker (there is as much as 40 × more DMN in SS than MS), against which to compare MS, the computed cigarette equivalents might be in the range of whole numbers of cigarettes per hour. However, it is also important to consider that if a constituent such as nicotine is depleted in the ETS relative some of the other components, then an individual's dose of that component will also be less. Given these considerations, it would seem that the term "cigarette equivalent" is too misleading and simplistic to be used accurately.

It seems likely that the physical state of the constituent in question will affect the fraction of that constituent which is retained in the lung. For example, gas phase compounds with significant water solubility are likely to be retained to a greater extent that those present in particulates. This is due to the much greater diffusion rates of vapor phase molecules across the spaces in the lower airways, relative to those of particles. Modeling done on particulate retention fractions in the respiratory tract (O.G. Rabbe, "Deposition and Clearance of Inhaled Aerosols," DOE Report UCD 472–503, NTIS) indicates 80–25% retention of particles in the 0.005–0.3 micron diameter range. Hiller et al. (1982). Disposition of sidestream cigarette smoke in the human respiratory tract, *Am. Rev. Respir. Dis.* 125: 406–08.) have reported 11% retention of sidestream smoke particulates. Retention of constituents such as CO or NO_x is likely to be near 100%. This suggests a nearly 10-fold range of retention for ETS materials, further complicating the translation of exposure to dose. Given the reactivity and absorptivity of ETS components in real environments, and the differences in uptake of various ETS components, it seems likely that the relative composition of the integrated dose that a person receives will bear little resemblance to the relative composition of material emanating from the smoldering firecone of a cigarette.

An ongoing problem with the use of nicotine as a biomarker has been the ability to account for only a small fraction of the total dose received. For example, the increase in plasma nicotine plus cotinine resulting from the smoking of one cigarette, integrated over an individual's entire blood volume, typically accounts for less than 10% of the known dose (N.J. Haley, D.W.

Sepkovic, D. Hoffmann, and E.L. Wynder (1985). Cigarette smoking as a risk for cardiovascular disease. Compensation with nicotine availability as a single variable *Clin. Pharm. and Therapeutics* 38: 164–70.). Some interesting new information has recently been reported which may aid in accounting for a much greater fraction of the retained dose of nicotine. Previously, most studies examining 24-hour urine samples have focused on nicotine and cotinine to assess smoke exposure. Recently, Curvell et al. ("Urinary Excretion of Nicotine and Its Major Metabolites," presented at the 43rd Tobacco Chemists' Research Conference, Richmond, Va., USA, October 2–5, 1989) reported results indicating that the majority of a nicotine dose is excreted as trans-3-hydroxy cotinine, and that nearly 30% of the nicotine, cotinine, and trans-3-hydroxy cotinine is excreted as conjugates of glucuronic acid. Less than 15% of the total nicotine dose is excreted as free nicotine plus cotinine. In contrast, the newer procedure, which quantifies all six major metabolites, accounts for 80–90% of the total dose. This new data should serve as a reminder that the metabolism of a marker should be fairly well understood before it can be used effectively in dosimetric studies.

Yoon Shin Kim: Dr. Goodfellow's paper provided much valuable information. Studies of this kind basically seek to answer such questions as whether ETS exposure is harmful to health, and what regulatory measures are desirable as a result. These questions have important social consequences, and we need to be sure the methods used to answer them have our fullest confidence.

This paper acknowledges that reports of the presence or absence of tobacco smoke in a given environment obtained from questionnaire responses are one of the methodologies that have been used in the past to measure exposure to ETS. In fact, the use of questionnaires has been the principal research tool for the retrospective evaluation of exposure to ETS. Nevertheless, the relationship between response to these questionnaires and actual past exposure to ETS is difficult to evaluate. However, it can be expected that errors in classifying smokers versus non- and never-smokers by this approach will generally distort the results of ETS studies due to misclassification and other effects.

The studies that have been completed to date on ETS have provided some useful information. However, unfortunately, these are often introduced into public discussion as absolute truths and are used to postulate dangers, relationships, and causalities. As a result, a progressive discrepancy has developed between basic scientific data and practical-clinical experience with respect to exogenous agents and their effects on human health.

In my opinion, all the epidemiological studies carried out so far have lacked an appropriate method to determine the extent of exposure to ETS. I do not think any epidemiological investigation will be performed convincingly in the future until the problem of determining the extent of exposure to ETS has been solved satisfactorily.

As long as there are possible health effects in certain risk groups exposed to ETS, there will continue to be a social problem and a controversy. Therefore, I would like to emphasize the urgent need for international cooperation on research assessing exposure to ETS.

Finally, it is my hope that additional papers and discussions will contribute to clarification of the true situation and ensure objectivity so as to assist the public and research scientists in countries such as those in Asia, where scientists have just begun to be interested in this kind of research.

Sarah Liao: From the papers that we've heard so far, I'm indeed very impressed with the amount of work that has been done on ETS. I think as scientists in this field our ultimate aim is to protect the environment, especially with regard to indoor air. But ETS should not be considered in isolation when we consider indoor pollution.

From the experience we have in Asia, the pollutant agents in our workplace are at levels which are orders of magnitudes higher than ETS. Research should be conducted in these areas in the same manner as research on ETS.

The evaluation of hazards deriving from mixtures of chemicals in the environment is very complicated and hardly accurate most of the time. There is evidence that the presence of one or more chemicals may produce an enhancement of toxicity for another chemical. Evaluation for multiple exposure needs to consider additional factors such as the sequence and temporal exposure of chemicals, the chemical and physical interactions of the individual chemicals, the mutual effects of the different chemicals on absorption, metabolism, pharamacokinetic parameters, target tissue affinities and the possible interrelationship and interactions between toxic parent compounds and active metabolites.

The use of specific bilogical markers for ETS such as nicotine or cotinine may give some indication of absorbed dose considering the reasonable half life of these compounds. However, the use of microbiological revertant techniques is far too non-specific and certainly other agents present in diet would have an overwhelming influence. The use of nitrogen compound specific adducts is also of remote use due to the very low concentration of N-compounds in ETS and the vast quantities of confounding factors in the system.

So, in conclusion, I would like to see a practical approach to ETS and other agents in indoor air pollution, with laboratory studies, risk assessments, and field survey data leading to standard guidelines that can be applied in situations where indoor air pollution can be a real problem, as in Asian countries.

Torbjorn Malmfors: Ladies and gentlemen, having the chance of commenting upon two very nice papers, I will also take the chance to present some new results and some results of my own. But, first, I was challenged by an attempt to try to define the terms "exposure" and "dose."

I think it's important to realize that exposure is an overall term we use for the contact we have with chemicals. We then have to look at what happens when we are exposed to chemicals. A portion of the chemical compound may come into the body, but not all is absorbed. We then have to distinguish between what goes to the target organ and to non-target organs.

Dose is generally used to describe the quantitative dimension of exposure. I think we should distinguish among several dose terms. First is the external dose which could also be called the administered dose. Second is the intermediate dose or the absorbed dose that can be found in the blood. Finally, we will have the internal dose or the effective dose, which goes to the target organ. There, we might be able to identify adducts, which as indicated by Professor Reasor could be a very interesting area for future research.

In order to assess dose, we have to use different methods in different situations. And I will just show you one ongoing study that is trying to analyze nicotine in hair as an indicator of ETS exposure. This is a project led by Professor Nilsen in Norway. Can hair perhaps be used as a cumulative measurement of nicotine exposure over a long time?

A comparison between smokers and nonsmokers shows that the levels of nicotine in hair are, not surprisingly, greater in smokers than in non-smokers. These are brand new results which haven't yet been published, but I thought it would be interesting to present these data regarding a potential new marker, even if it doesn't fulfill all the criteria we heard about.

In order to show that measuring ETS in airplane cabins could be of interest, I'll show you some of the results from a recently published study on SAS DC9s involving the measurement of several parameters. (Malmfors, T., D. Thorburn and A. Westlin (1989). Air quality in passenger cabins of DC-9 and MD-80 aircraft *Environ. Technol. Letters* 10:613–628). We were interested in determining the levels of ETS in business class and tourist class.

What is most interesting is that if you concentrate upon the tourist non-smoking section, the nicotine concentration is relatively high there, almost as high as in the business smoking and tourist smoking class. By statistical evaluation, we have shown that the air is drawn backwards in the airplane and that the boundaries between nonsmoking and smoking sections could function better. Furthermore, you can see that the carbon dioxide concentration is rather high and the relative humidity low. These levels clearly affect passenger comfort. We have concluded that the ventilation in the DC9s, not only in SAS planes, is not very good.

Dr. Demetrios Moschandreas: I assume that the concern is *population* exposures to ETS. I further assume that office and airline exposures constitute only a segment of the population potentially exposed to ETS, a small segment that excludes exposures of children, elderly, infirm (most sensitive groups), housewives, students and other segments of the population. No information was provided by the presentation on population exposure. I assert that the ventilation rate does not, it cannot, generate pollution; it may affect pollutant levels but it does not generate pollution. The factor that determines an individual's exposure to ETS or any other pollutant is the source emission rate. In the paper distributed for review, Dr. Goodfellow and his coauthors assert: In determining indoor air quality "By far the most important factor is building ventilation and air conditioning systems." Obviously the issue needs to be addressed in more detail. I further assert that the ETS research community has not measured population exposure to ETS. Episodic studies have been performed but post-hoc statistical analyses lead to erroneous, conflicting, and/or confusing conclusions. I agree with Dr. Goodfellow and his coauthors that comprehensive studies may lead to many indoor sources that cause complaints by occupants, but I disagree that merely correcting ventilation rates addresses the complex concerns associated with ETS. This issue needs to be addressed in greater depth. I assert that the recommendations for further R&D by Goodfellow et al. should be pursued. But unless properly designed population exposure studies are carried out, the ETS community shall be unable to attain its principle objective: determine the population exposure to ETS.

Researchers in Europe, Japan and the U.S.A. are studying emission rates from building materials, combustion products (including cigarettes) and human activities. The objective is clear: control, i.e., reduce source emission rates. This is a preventive, proactive strategy for reducing exposures to air pollutants. It is based on documented IAQ evidence indicating that source variation can explain observed indoor pollutant concentrations that cannot be explained by variation of the ventilation rate. I welcome the emphasis that Dr. Goodfellow placed on source emission rates during his presentation. One can clearly state that indoor air quality is sensitive to air exchange rate but I do not agree with the premise that indoor air pollution is caused by ventilation. This is not simply an academic curiosity, and an inconsequential difference, the importance of the source in IAQ concerns addresses both complaint and non-complaint buildings, ventilation inadequacies refer mostly to complaint buildings. Dr. Goodfellow's experience is used to point that in many buildings with poor ventilation conditions complaints increase. The question with respect to exposures to ETS is not, however, simply the complaints about buildings; rather, the question is more general: what is the population exposure to ETS? My research team just finished a 2-month monitoring investigation of two healthy buildings. I will focus on one of the buildings because analysis of the second building data base has not progressed sufficiently. The building was selected because over a two-year period its occupants registered only five complaints. This number is to be compared to the large number of environmentally related complaints (over 50) registered by occupants in each of six similar buildings operated by the same management group. Over a month, my associates and I characterized a building for comfort (with surveys of about 65% of the occupants), air quality (including nicotine and particulate matter) and HVAC parameters (efficiency, effectiveness, REI). Preliminarily, both nicotine and particulate matter concentrations were higher in offices with smokers than in offices occupied by no smokers. The point is: in a no-complaint building, with an HVAC system operating at prescribed, by ASHRAE, regulations, smoking led to elevated ETS exposures. Whether the ETS levels are statistically different in smoking and non-smoking areas I do not know at this time, as I do not know whether the increased levels constitute a health hazard, but I can conclude that the presence of a source determines levels of exposure and not just the ventilation rate.

My second point is that population exposures to ETS have not been measured. Surveys of offices provide a biased data base which does not necessarily represent all offices, and exposures estimated from such surveys do not represent population studies. The obvious conclusion is: ETS office exposure studies are anecdotal studies that do not investigate a clearly stated population.

The ETS exposure research community is divided into two groups: (1) the determinists and (2) the skeptics. The determinists use their small data base and make inferences on the population. The skeptics point to the sample size of the determinists, and use statistical tools to document that conclusions of the determinists cannot be substantiated. Unfortunately, most skeptics turn around and use their small data base to assert their own conclusions. I reviewed the airline cabin research in some detail. All published information contributes to an overall picture; unfortunately, none of the publications were sufficiently large to reach general conclusions regarding ETS exposure of the airline cabin population. This assertion should surprise no one, because in-cabin air quality is a function of at least a dozen parameters, resulting in a large range of measured pollutant concentrations. How can any study with a sample size of 10 to 20 provide an inference for the population? Several post-hoc statistical analyses have been performed on the airline ETS data base. Some of them are simply not illuminating, others are good and informative, all are constrained by the limitation of their size and population they sampled. Unfortunately, conclusions from anecdotal studies taken together do not give a solid hint of population exposure, they are all over the range of potential values. If a study has been performed with an experimental design appropriate to support inferences for the air cabin population, the study has not crossed my desk. I assume such a broadly designed study does not exist. I conclude exposure to ETS of the airline cabin population has not been measured.

This brings me to the last of the issues I would like to address: recommendations for further research. The items that Goodfellow and associates suggest for future research should be studied but they constitute one component of what needs to be done. I assert that existing tools must be used to design and carry out a second component: a statistically sound experimental design that will estimate the population exposures to ETS. There are many tools that need to be improved but that should not stop us from undertaking the correct study.

Population exposure to CO, Rn, NO_2, certain VOCs, and to a lesser extent, asbestos, have been estimated successfully. ETS should follow. If we await to improve our monitoring tools, the field will be dominated by episodic research and by results that will not characterize ETS exposure. The sad consequence of such an approach is that important decisions will be made by the regulator without sound scientific input. I recommend a parallel path: in addition to carrying out the recommendations made by Goodfellow et al., a research program based on a series of statistically-designed studies should be implemented to characterize population exposure to ETS. Subject to the uncertainties of the state-of-the-art, the risk analyst needs population exposures, the regulator should require this input, and the consumer is owed this information. We can and should provide it to them.

Roger Perry: Dr. Moschandreas has made many of the points that I wanted to raise.

I am convinced, in going back to Dr. Goodfellow's paper, that we are still in a situation that many of the analytical data lack credibility from the standpoint of adequate calibration. Many of the procedures we use, particularly in unobtrusive sampling procedures, are not sensitive nor specific enough to be able to monitor the components of ETS that we are trying to quantify in the midst of a whole range of other pollutants.

In real exposure situations, we have variable generation rates and many variables in terms of concentrations of materials in incoming air. Buildings in the majority of the world do not resemble a typical ventilated office building in the United States. Exposure is dependent upon many other direct factors, including other sources.

Typically, if we look at the specifications of the equipment frequently used to monitor ETS, its minimum detection limit is one PPM. Its level of accuracy at that point is plus or minus fifty percent. This means that for the majority of indoor situations, where eco-analyzers are used, the data are largely invalid. The instruments are simply not sensitive enough for adequate quantification.

Again, many methods for measuring RSP, and in particular light-scattering techniques, are singularly unsuitable. Although it is possible in a chamber to get good correlations between minirams, the same procedure in the real world, with particulates of different characteristics, given widely varying results.

And so I would endorse much of what Dr. Goodfellow has said, and add that many of the surveys that have been undertaken have lacked adequate perception in their design, with insufficient attention to the specificity and sensitivity of the analytical procedures.

Joseph Wu: Several comments and observations on this important subject matter: as illustrated by our presenters, the literature on the biological monitoring of ETS is inconsistent, disputable and controversial. The interpretations are even more difficult to follow. Many of these problems arise because of conceptual and technical limitations in research design.

However, I would like to suggest that there is another factor which has been generally overlooked, which has to do with the recognition that there are biological rhythms within each one of us. Furthermore, as individuals, the central nervous system plays a very important part in our well-being. It has a profound impact on physiological responses and also on our biological activities.

As an example, I would like to remind everybody that the human lifespan generally is recognized to have an upper limit of between ninety to a hundred years. This has remained essentially unchanged, despite the large advances that have been made in this century in the diagnosis and treatment of diseases. Recent medical advances have not extended the lifespan of the human species, but rather have increased average life expectancy because of the increased ability to recognize and treat diseases.

And also in the scientific field, certainly in the psychological areas, it is recognized that mind has a tremendous impact on matter. I would suggest that this particular factor, which is intuitively evident but scientifically mystifying, should be included in all the future studies dealing with exposure to ETS.

With respect to future research directions, I would like to suggest that the yields of molecular biology techniques be included and integrated into all studies, whether animal, epidemiological, or other studies. For example, molecular biological approaches might be included to probe the expression of certain oncogens that have been shown to be causally related to disease states. These studies should be conducted using the tissues or the organs that are alleged to be at risk from ETS exposure.

Moreover, these exposure assessment strategies should be designed to take into account exposures through multiple routes, and they should integrate the consequences of intermittent, as well as continuous, exposure. They should provide evidence of total risk from multiple sources and to multiple agents. And ideally they should be the type that can distinguish the risk from one source or agent from an unrelated source or agent.

Donald Ecobichon: Thank you. Now, with all that food for thought, some questions or comments.

Peter Lee: I'd like to make a couple of points. One is to ask the panel, and in particular Dr. Malmfors, do we have any good indicator of the relative

ETS exposure of active and passive smokers? This is quite important when one considers the health effect data where, in some cases, it has been claimed that exposure to ETS is related to conditions which are not related to active smoking. If Dr. Malmfors' data on hair can be taken to indicate ETS exposure—which I'm not totally sure it can—that seems to indicate that smokers had enormously more ETS exposure than passive smokers. That's one point.

Second, I wonder if it's taken as religion that a good marker should be tobacco-specific. I don't actually see any logic to this. Suppose the situation is that ETS does have some health effect and this is due to some component that is not tobacco-specific. Surely, it is preferable to have a marker that measures that component. I don't see why one should concentrate wholly on nicotine-based markers and rule everything else out. Dr. Reasor seemed to be saying, we must have tobacco-specific markers. Here are all the markers. We'll throw most of them away. He ends up with nicotine and then, when commenting on nicotine, said, one of the limitations of nicotine is that it doesn't indicate exposure to other toxicants. That seems to be a circular argument.

I think one of the limitations of the data, which no one seems to have alluded to as important, is that we don't have any good studies relating biological markers of tobacco smoke constituents to chronic health effects, even in the active smoking situation. I'm hoping the day will come when someone will publish studies which will actually look at this. Data bases are beginning to develop, but until we have that data, I don't see how we can actually judge whether the markers are of value or not. One's got to know whether they relate to health effects.

Donald Ecobichon: I'll give Dr. Malmfors the first chance, and then maybe Dr. Reasor would like to comment.

Torbjorn Malmfors: I can give a theory for the answer to the first question, and that is, of course, to be able to measure the internal dose in the target organ. That's a simple question. But, first, we must identify the target organ. Secondly, we must identify which compound to measure. And we are far away from that. But let me come back when they talk about risk assessment tomorrow.

Mark Reasor: I think that was an excellent point about tobacco specificity. The main point I was trying to make is that if we want to be able to attribute something to ETS, we need to be able to rule out other sources. If the compound of interest or the marker of interest is tobacco-specific, it enables us to do that more easily. It doesn't mean that it can't be done with a non-tobacco-specific component. It simply means that it's much more difficult. One aspect of animal studies that I think is particularly exciting is that, in the controlled conditions that would exist one need not worry about tobacco specificity, because you're controlling the environment in which the animal exists. Therefore, if benzo(a)pyrene or 4-aminobiphenyl are measured, you know it's coming from tobacco smoke.

So we can eliminate some of that problem in the use of animal studies, but it's a good point that Peter Lee makes. It's a problem we've had all along.

The point I was trying to make was that this would be the best way to do it, but certainly not the only way.

Flemming Kissmeyer: I had a small remark to Dr. Malmfors, too.

You started or ended your small lecture stating that the ventilation in DC-9s was bad. I have read somewhere—I can't give you a reference—that the ventilation in airplanes is excellent. You didn't say much about sampling, but how can you be sure that it's not the flight just before you did the sampling in the business class, in the tourist class? The flight before the sampling could have influenced the nicotine content in the air.

George Feuer: I have just realized that it is better to be on this side of the table. From this point of view, I should like to raise a number of questions. What is essential in the exposure to ETS is what is actually getting into our body. We really should concentrate our attention on components of ETS that are found in the tissues.

Second, in all these studies the population or the various people who were involved were healthy. Yet we have learned that some constituents like nicotine undergo metabolic changes which depend on liver function. Were these people healthy? Were they alcoholics? They are likely to metabolize nicotine at different rates.

Third, we learned that there are hemoglobin adducts. We know that diabetics produce some adducts with sugar. Were these people diabetics or prediabetics? That information is not reported.

Regarding Dr. Wu's reference to biological rhythms, we now know that there are chronological differences in the binding and metabolism of various compounds. These are determined in part by our pineal activity. There are some diseases—for instance, schizophrenia, manic-depression—which are known to be associated with abnormal biorhythms. Again, a question, were any people checked for any mental disease?

We also know that melatonin, one of the major products of the pineal, is an oncogenic agent. People who smoke in the evening, when melatonin production is very high, have greater oncogenic activity than those who smoke during the daytime, when melatonin production is low. Has this been accounted for?

Robert Brown: I want to make two points. One was about the animal experiments which you mentioned.

The first point is that it is now very difficult to do any animal experiments with cigarette smoke, in the UK at least.

Secondly, the problem was mentioned of determining realistic doses of cigarette smoke. Even massive doses of cigarette smoke do not produce very much disease in animals. It's extremely difficult to model what we see in humans in animals. And the condition in humans—conditions we know are associated with active smoking—are found in those areas where the cigarette smoke is deposited, not areas where the absorbed dose is metabolized and transported around in the blood. They're the areas of the large bronchi, large airways, where cigarette smoke is deposited and remains. In cigarette smokers it can be found in cells many years after they quit smoking. There is still evidence of cigarette smoke deposits at those sites.

So I think a lot of the questions about absorption are not really relevant. It's not the absorbed dose but the deposited dose, the stuff that's deposited in the airways that we should consider. And we can get that deposition in animals but we certainly can't model the disease process in animals in any realistic fashion, certainly not in any realistic doses compared with ETS.

So looking for adducts in animals just isn't going to tell us very much about what happens in humans, I'm afraid.

Francis Roe: I'd like to ask Dr. Wu to explain what he has in mind. In our frantic attempts to make some sense out of this complex, evasive subject, we see molecular biology as perhaps offering something. But is it really a sacred cow? I can't really think of any of the studies that have been undertaken and published, particularly by epidemiologists, in which molecular biology techniques would have been useful. It seems to me you have to have a theory first and the chances of that theory being right or useful are pretty small. What sort of molecular biology methods should we use? Should we attach it to all studies? What you do is premised on the theory you have in advance. What's your practical suggestion?

Joseph Wu: Yes, that's a very good question. First, we can measure specific oncogens that have been shown to be correlated with some proliferation of tissues. For example, in some of the studies in which lung cancer or other cancers have been alleged to be related to ETS exposure, we can sample material from these patients and perform in situ hybridization using a CDNA probe directed against specific oncogens. The first place to start is to show that the establishment of the cancer is correlated with the expression of the oncogens. At a minimum, you could establish that the purported etiological agent is there to begin with.

Another possibility is to take air samples from, for example, smoking and nonsmoking sections of buildings. You can take some tissue culture cells and expose them over a long period to the samples. We can measure the expression of any oncogens. Of course, this wouldn't tell you that ETS is the active ingredient. At least, however, it would show that in those cases from smoking sections you have identified oncogenic activity.

Donald Ecobichon: This is the situation where the molecular biologists have the answers but they're really looking for a question.

Robert Brown: What you've just described is simply a far more expensive way of doing the mutation studies using bacterial rotation. You'll study exactly the same events with the tissue cancer cells that you would using bacterial rotation but you'd be spending a lot more money. Molecular biology may be more trendy and certainly far more likely to be supported by grant giving bodies, but it wouldn't tell us anymore about anything.

George Neurath: I wanted to respond to an earlier question on airline quality. There are not a lot of studies in this area. The paper that I wrote last year summarized all the information to date. Malmfors and his colleagues looked at it in their SAS airline study. The showed the need for good ventilation and air distribution and the fact that most aircraft have plenty of fresh air capability. The pilot controls that and he can regulate it depending on whether he's taking off or landing. If you look at the data specifically, as we have, you find that the DC-9-21 had roughly fifteen cubic feet per minute per person. The DC-9-41 had almost twenty, 19.2 or something, and the MD-80 had about twenty-four. You had progressively better air quality as you got better ventilation. What we see, unfortunately, are people trying to save a few dollars by reducing ventilation in aircraft and experiencing the same problems they did in buildings that were sealed. The MD-80 recirculates almost a third, perhaps forty percent of the air now. The result is that you have progressively deteriorating air quality.

John Gorrod: I think there are a lot of data which support the need for continued metabolic studies. Also, with regard to tobacco-specific or non-tobacco-specific markers, I think what one is trying to do here is identify the source of the problem. If by using tobacco-specific markers you can eliminate one area of risk, then that's one job you've done. If you use a non-tobacco-specific marker, the source is problematic. Is it tobacco or is it geraniums? By using tobacco-specific markers, we at least have the chance of clearly isolating the source.

One other comment I would like to add concerns something I earn my living at, so I'm biased. Apart from the route, other areas being explored are genetics and pharmacogenetics. The pharmacogenetics of nicotine show very clearly that some populations cannot metabolize nicotine very well.

William Butler: I have a question for Dr. Reasor. It's related to the point that a marker should be tobacco-specific. I think from an epidemiologic perspective, we need something that goes beyond that because there are two sources of tobacco: direct smoking and ETS exposure. In epidemiologic experiments we're very interested in distinguishing between smokers who report being nonsmokers and true nonsmokers exposed to ETS. When we look at our dose response relationships, the method we use to determine cigarette equivalence—which is admittedly incorrect—is to measure cotinine levels in smokers and nonsmokers. Those two groups have the same level of cotinine or could have the same level of cotinine. It would be useful from an epidemiologic perspective to add a new dimension to these measurements by distinguishing between tobacco from ETS and tobacco from direct smoking. Existing markers such as carbon monoxide and thiocyanate, that are not adequate to distinguish ETS exposure from other exposures might be adequate to distinguish mainstream smoke from ETS. I'd be interested if that is available or whether anybody has looked at that.

Mark Reasor: I agree that would be an interesting distinction to make. From the data that Jarvis and others have published, it appears that carboxyhaemoglobin is a reasonably good indicator. The data show that the population of smokers had about four percent carboxyhaemoglobin and nonsmokers had maybe one percent. The cotinine values apparently are pretty good but it would be useful to address the issue that you raise. I don't quite know how you would do that, however, because I don't think there's anything specific for ETS that's not present in mainstream smoke.

William Butler: It's not that they wouldn't be present but they would be present in different proportions. Carbon monoxide, for example, might be different. Although nicotine is present in both sources, it's present in different degrees. So it would be the relative concentrations of those constituents which might be used to distinguish between these two populations.

Jack Peterson: Dr. Malmfors may have the answer.

The hair data are consistent with the idea that hair may be a good passive sampler for nicotine from ETS; it didn't get there through metabolism. Hair samples would enable us at least to determine environmental exposure to nicotine, for what that may be worth. Smokers are exposed to more ETS than anybody else; the data are consistent with this observation. Has that been checked?

Torbjorn Malmfors: No, Professor Nilssen is trying to find out. They really don't know where the nicotine in the hair comes from. It appears from the data that it's accumulated from outside but I expect everyone would think it's coming from the inside. It's an interesting question.

Frank Sullivan: I'd like to come back to the point that Peter Lee made because I feel that's of very great importance to us. The question is why are we interested in the chemistry of ETS. The whole morning has been devoted to this topic and, although it's an interesting scientific exercise for chemists to try and measure smaller and smaller amounts of materials that are present, I think that those of us who are interested in the biological effects of ETS are more concerned about other things. I'm particularly interested in the reproductive effects of smoking. When we're considering whether ETS has any reproductive toxic effect, one of the most important questions asked by us and also by the regulatory authorities, certainly in the U.K., is whether the effects that have been ascribed to ETS are plausible. The possibility to a large extent depends on the question of the relative doses that people get from direct smoking versus ETS. Three types of data should be accumulated to address this area. First, we want to know the doses of the different components that are absorbed by direct smoking. Second, we want to know the doses for people exposed to ETS. Third, we want to know the background levels of components that one finds normally in people.

One very important component for reproductive effects is carbon monoxide. If people are exposed environmentally to amounts of carbon monoxide, that becomes a very important fact for us to know. As far as direct smoking is concerned, there's a lot of evidence that would suggest that carbon monoxide is an important component. So I really do feel that it is important for the people who are working on the chemistry of ETS not to ignore substances like carbon monoxide, which are of critical importance from the reproductive point of view, just because it's not a very good marker from your point of view. It's very important for us to be able to accumulate data on relative exposures in order to work out whether the effects ascribed really are plausible or not.

Part III

6
Environmental Tobacco Smoke and Cancer: The Epidemiologic Evidence

Maxwell W. Layard, Ph.D
Layard Associates, Mountain View, California

I. Introduction

In this paper, I review the epidemiologic evidence for the effect of exposure to environmental tobacco smoke ("ETS") on cancer incidence in human populations. Most of the available data relate to lung cancer, but a few studies have investigated the incidence of cancer of all sites, or of particular sites other than the lung. A question of obvious importance is whether the collective epidemiologic data adequately satisfy the accepted criteria for the use of epidemiologic evidence in supporting a causal inference. My conclusion is that the currently available data do not support such a judgment.

II. The Role of Epidemiologic Evidence in Drawing Causal Inferences

In assessing whether epidemiologic evidence reflects a casual association between an exposure and a health effect, it is first necessary to consider whether the data demonstrate a statistically significant association, that is, an association which is unlikely to be due to chance. If a statistically significant association has been demonstrated, it is then necessary to assess the validity and weight of the evidence in light of criteria which refer to the epidemiologic studies themselves. The most important of these criteria are:

a. strength of association;
b. consistency of results;
c. demonstration of dose-response relationship;
d. freedom from biases; and
e. control of confounding factors.

However, even after these criteria have been considered, epidemiologic evidence must be corroborated by other types of evidence before it is appropriate to draw a causal inference. The biologic plausibility of an observed association between exposure and health effect must be considered. Considerations of biologic plausibility involve such matters as knowledge of disease mechanisms, coherence with known facts about the natural history of the disease in question, and toxicologic experiments with animals which avoid problems of confounding and bias typically seen in epidemiologic studies.

III. Epidemiologic Studies of Lung Cancer

Reports of 23 epidemiologic studies have been published concerning ETS and the incidence of lung cancer in humans. Twenty of these were retrospective case-control studies and three were prospective cohort studies. These studies are listed in Table 6–1. In nearly all cases, spousal smoking has been used as the index of the exposure of nonsmokers to ETS.

Of the 23 epidemiologic studies of lung cancer and ETS referred to above, five reported statistically significant associations between ETS and lung cancer at the 5% level of significance. The other 18 studies reported relative risks which were not significantly elevated, with 95% confidence intervals encompassing 1.0.

In addition to the reported associations in the individual studies, the National Research Council ("NRC") Committee on Passive Smoking calculated a statistically significant association using a statistical technique known as "meta-analysis." This technique is sometimes employed to combine the results of individual epidemiologic studies, in order to derive a quantitative summarization of data relating to a particular area of investigation. The NRC conducted a meta-analysis of the results of 13 of the 23 studies listed in Table 6–1 (NRC 1986). This calculation produced a combined relative risk of 1.34, which, though small, was statistically significant.

There are several reasons why combining the results of these studies is of doubtful validity. A fundamental consideration in conducting a meta-analysis is whether the published literature is representative of all studies of a particular question. A "publication bias" would result if studies reporting a positive association were more likely to be published than negative studies, and it is possible that such a bias exists in the literature on ETS and lung cancer (Vandenbrouke 1988). Meta-analysis should not be used unless it can reasonably be concluded that the results of the various studies provide comparable estimates of a common quantitative endpoint, in this case, the relative risk of lung cancer among nonsmokers exposed to ETS. Such a conclusion requires that the studies be reasonably comparable with respect to exposure indices, demographic and social characteristics of the study populations, and disease diagnosis, among other factors. In fact, the studies of ETS and lung cancer display substantial diversity in these and other areas. As well as being com-

Table 6–1
Studies of ETS and Lung Cancer in Nonsmokers

Study	*Sex*	*Number of Cases in Exposed Group*	*Relative Risk*	*95% Confidence Interval*
Case-control studies				
Chan and Fung, 1982	F	34	0.75	(0.43, 1.30)
Trichopolous *et al.*, 1983	F	38	2.13*	(1.18, 3.83)
Correa *et al.*, 1983	F	14	2.07	(0.81, 5.26)
	M	2	1.97	(0.38, 10.29)
Kabat and Wynder, 1984	F	13	0.79	(0.25, 2.45)
	M	5	1.00	(0.20, 5.07)
Buffler *et al.*, 1984	F	33	0.80	(0.34, 1.89)
	M	5	0.51	(0.14, 1.80)
Garfinkel *et al.*, 1985	F	92	1.12	(0.74, 1.70)
Wu *et al.*, 1985	F	29	1.20	(0.50, 3.30)
Akiba *et al.*, 1986	F	73	1.52	(0.88, 2.64)
	M	3	2.10	(0.51, 8.59)
Lee *et al.*, 1986	F	22	1.03	(0.41, 2.56)
	M	8	1.31	(0.38, 4.54)
Brownson *et al.*, 1987	F	19[a]	1.68	(0.39, 2.97)
Gao *et al.*, 1987	F	189	1.19	(0.82, 1.73)
Humble *et al.*, 1987	F	14	1.78	(0.65, 4.85)
Koo *et al.*, 1987	F	51	1.55	(0.90, 2.68)
Lam *et al.*, 1987	F	115	1.65*	(1.16, 2.35)
Pershagen *et al.*, 1987	F	33	1.20	(0.70, 2.10)
Geng *et al.*, 1988	F	34	2.16*	(1.09, 4.30)
Inoue and Hirayama, 1988	F	18	2.55	(0.74, 8.78)
Katada *et al.*, 1988	F	17	—	[NS; p = 0.23]
Lam and Cheng, 1988	F	37	2.01*	(1.09, 3.72)
Shimizu *et al.*, 1988	F	90[a]	1.10	n/a
Cohort studies				
Garfinkel, 1981	F	88	1.17	(0.93, 1.47)
				(0.20, 4.97)
Gillis *et al.*, 1984	F	6	1.00	(0.59, 17.85)
	M	4	3.25	
Hirayama, 1984b	F	163	1.45*	(1.02, 2.08)
1984a	M	7	2.28*	(1.04, 5.01)

[a]Total number of cases, including unexposed.
*Statistically significant at the 5% level.

parable, each study should be methodologically sound and free from potential biases and confounding factors which could distort the result. As I point out in this paper, those conditions are not met for the studies in question. The small positive associations seen in these studies, to the extent that they are not simply due to chance, may in fact be the result of bias and confounding. If so, a meta-analysis would serve only to provide spurious reinforcement of the invalid results of the individual studies.

Although a formal meta-analysis seems inappropriate, a substantial majority of the 23 studies reported relative risks greater than 1. But even if one assumes that the studies, taken collectively, reflect a statistically significant association between ETS exposure and lung cancer incidence among nonsmokers, it is still necessary to examine the validity of the studies which demonstrate this association before the data can be presumed to support a causal inference. In the remainder of this section I consider various aspects of this question, beginning with a discussion of the five criteria listed in section II.

A. Weight and Validity of Lung Cancer Studies

1. Strength of Association. Even if an association between exposure and outcome is statistically significant, the weaker it is (that is, the smaller the relative risk is) the less confidence we can have in its validity. A weak association is more likely than a strong association to be an artefact produced by bias or confounding factors. Of the 23 studies, four reported relative risks of 1.0 or less for either males or females or for both sexes (that is, no increase or a decrease in risk), 13 reported relative risks between 1.0 and 2.0 for either males or females or for both sexes, and 8 reported relative risks above 2.0 for either males or females or for both sexes.

Although there is no precise definition of a "weak" association, relative risks of less than 2.0 are generally considered to be weak. By this standard, 22 of the 30 sex-specific studies displayed in Table 6–1 represent nonexistent or weak associations. The epidemiologist Jerome Cornfield thought that any relative risk under 3.0 might be considered weak (Wynder 1987). By this standard, all but one of the observed associations between ETS and lung cancer are weak. The one exception was based on only four male lung cancer cases in the exposed group and is not statistically significant; in the same study the relative risk for females was 1.0.

2. Consistency of Results. The studies also lack consistency. Relative risks vary widely between the studies; several reported risks are below 1.0. The differences between inconsistent associations observed in these studies are undoubtedly produced partly by chance variations. But it is also likely that they are partly due to the differential effects of biases and confounding factors.

Some studies display inconsistency with respect to the cell type of lung cancer for which risk elevation with ETS exposure was observed. Lam *et al.* (1987) reported a significant relative risk of 2.12 for adenocarcinoma. But for all other cell types the relative risk was 1.23 and was not significant. On the other hand, Pershagen et al. (1987) reported a significant relative risk of 3.3 for squamous or small cell cancer but for other cancer types (predominantly adenocarcinoma) the relative risk was 0.8.

3. Dose-Response Relationship. A dose-response relationship means that as the extent of exposure and hence the amount of the dose increases, so too does the incidence of the outcome. In assessing the existence of a dose-response relationship, the non-exposed subjects are not considered. None of the 23 studies discussed above demonstrate a statistically significant dose-response relationship. The Japanese cohort study of Hirayama reported an inconsistent dose-response relationship when the subjects were stratified by the wife's age at the time of entry into the study (Hirayama 1984b), as shown in Figure 6–1. Also, in the large American Cancer Society cohort (Garfinkel 1981), women whose husbands smoked 20 or more cigarettes per day had a lower relative risk (1.10) than those whose husbands smoked 1–19 cigarettes per day (1.27). Lack of a dose-response relationship is an internal inconsistency in a study which increases the likelihood that an observed association is due to the effects of bias or confounding, rather than to an effect of exposure.

Some studies have examined more than one exposure measure without finding a dose response. For example, Koo et al. (1987) performed a spousal

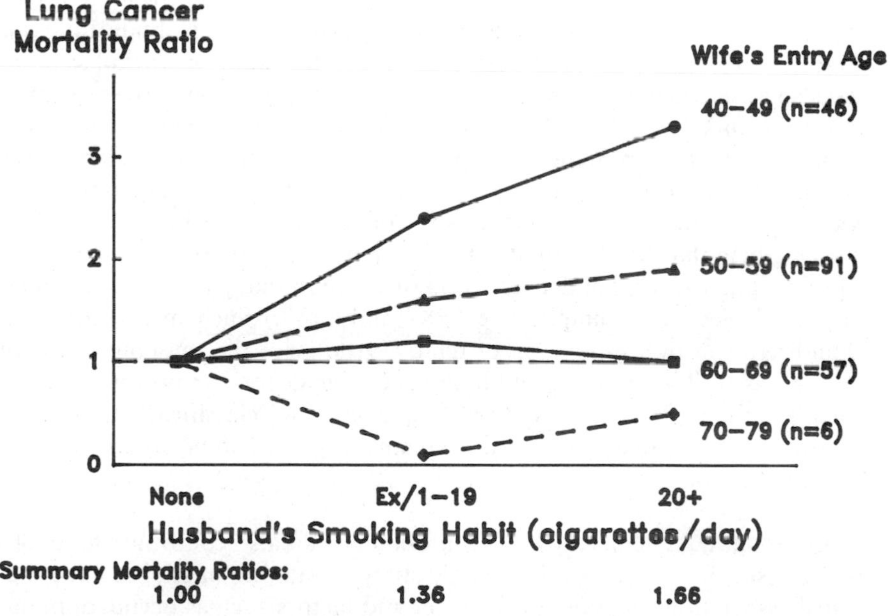

Figure 6–1. Hirayama Japanese Cohort Study: Lung Cancer in Non-Smoking Married Women

smoking analysis by number of cigarettes per day smoked by husband, and calculated relative risks of 2.37, 1.50, and 1.32 for 1–10, 11–20 and 20+ cigarettes per day respectively—a negative dose-response relationship. Several other exposure measures, such as total years exposed, were analyzed, but none of them showed a positive dose-response relationship. Other authors have reported a significant overall increasing trend in risk with a measure of ETS exposure, including non-exposed subjects. As noted above, such an analysis of itself should not be construed as a finding of a dose-response relationship. Lam et al. (1987) reported a significant trend in risk with husband's daily cigarette consumption. But no dose-response relationship was found when attention was restricted to the exposed subjects. (The relative risks reported in this analysis were artificially inflated because smoking-level information was missing for a larger proportion of controls than cases, a point that the authors did not mention.)

4. Biases. The results of epidemiologic studies can be distorted by various types of bias, including interviewer bias, respondent bias, selection bias, and bias arising from misclassification of exposure status and disease diagnosis. Biases can give rise to apparent associations that, on further investigation, turn out to be spurious. Case-control studies are susceptible to selective recall bias, due to the propensity of cases report exposure more completely than the controls. None of the studies of ETS and lung cancer used objective ETS exposure measures such as levels of nicotine or cotinine in body fluids or atmospheric measurements of tobacco smoke in the home or workplace. Bias can also arise when exposure information is obtained from relatives of cases. In the Garfinkel et al. (1985) study, an odds ratio of 1.0 resulted from exposure information from the cases themselves. But when the information was obtained from husbands the odds ratio was 0.92, and when the information was obtained from sons or daughters the odds ratio was 3.19.

One bias that has been consistently cited in connection with studies of ETS and lung cancer is under-reporting of active smoking by professed "nonsmokers." (See, for example, Lee 1987 and 1988.) Such misclassification would result in over-estimation of relative risk, since the smoking habits of spouses, as well as smoking and lung cancer incidence, are positively correlated. On the basis of studies of the frequency of misclassification, Lee concluded that this source of bias could explain most or all of the observed excess lung cancer risk.

5. Confounding Factors. Positive confounding can also contribute to an observed association in an epidemiologic study. A number of studies have suggested associations between lung cancer and factors such as occupation, nutrition and alcohol consumption. To the extent that such factors are correlated with ETS exposure, they could also give rise to a spurious association between ETS and lung cancer. Few of the studies of ETS and lung cancer have been able to control for potential confounding factors.

An example of such potential confounding was seen in a study of dietary beta-carotene intake in a group of nonsmokers for whom ETS exposure information was collected (Sidney et al. 1989). Subjects who reported no ETS exposure in the home were found to have a higher mean carotene intake than those who reported ETS exposure. Since epidemiologic evidence suggests an inverse relationship between dietary intake or blood levels of beta-carotene and lung cancer, beta-carotene status is likely to be a confounding factor in studies of ETS and lung cancer.

Another example of potential confounding is provided by a study by Koo et al. (1988) of Chinese couples in Hong Kong. These investigators found that wives of nonsmoking husbands had "healthier" lifestyles than wives of smoking husbands. They concluded that caution is needed when interpreting data on ETS: "It may not be the hazards of tobacco smoke that are being evaluated, but a whole range of behaviors that result from having a smoking husband, which may in turn increase the risk for certain diseases among their wives and children."

Recent reports by Rylander et al. (1989) and Koo (1989) have suggested that ingested substances, including components of the diet, are risk factors for lung cancer and potential confounders for studies of ETS and lung cancer. Koo stated that data on Chinese women in Hong Kong suggest that consumption of vegetables, meats and fish that are smoked, salted, cured or pickled increased risk of lung cancer relative to fresh versions of these foods, and that the former diet was more frequent among women with smoking husbands relative to women with nonsmoking husbands.

B. *Methodological Issues*

Confidence in the results of an epidemiologic study requires that the study should be methodologically sound. Many if not all of the 23 studies of ETS and lung cancer are open to criticism for flaws in their design and execution. For example, the Greek study of Trichopolous et al. (1983) was subject to a possible selection bias because controls were selected from a different hospital than those from which the cases were obtained. Moreover, the controls were selected by a single physician who was aware of the purpose of the study. The same physician interviewed both cases and controls, so interviewer bias cannot be excluded. Only 65% of the cases were pathologically confirmed, and alveolar carcinoma and adenocarcinoma cases were excluded from the case group, raising the possibility of another selection bias.

Another study that has received considerable critical comment is the Japanese cohort study of Hirayama (1984a,b). Potential problems which have been cited include bias in the selection of the study sample, misclassification of lung cancer diagnosis, misclassification of the non-smoking status of wives and of ETS exposure, failure to control for potential confounders, and inappropriate statistical analysis of the data. Another problem in assessing the quality of the study is the inadequate reporting of the study design, conduct and results. In particular, Hirayama's published reports fail to describe fully the way in which the study cohort was selected, and give no information about the numbers of persons excluded from the cohort on health grounds or the criteria for such exclusions. More seriously, no explicit information has been reported on the number of subjects lost to follow-up. My analysis of the published data indicates that some 10% of the cohort was lost to follow-up, and comparisons with Japanese national mortality statistics strongly suggest that death rates among those lost were at least twice as high as death rates among those successfully traced (Layard and Viren 1989). A mortality differential of this magnitude raises the possibility that selection biases exist in the data which could invalidate an observed relationship between exposure to ETS and cancer mortality.

Comparisons with Japanese national mortality statistics reveal serious internal inconsistencies in the reported cohort mortality experience which cast further doubt on the validity of Hirayama's results. In particular, reported lung cancer mortality among nonsmoking married women in the cohort was 28% less than that projected on the basis of national statistics. For all other women in the cohort, however, reported lung cancer mortality was only 3% less than projected. Also, reported lung cancer mortality among nonsmoking married women aged 60–69 years at entry into the study was 49% less than projected, while for nonsmoking married women aged 40–59 at entry, reported lung cancer mortality was 16% less than projected.

The inconsistent pattern of lung cancer relative risks seen when the Hirayama data are analyzed by wife's entry age (Hirayama 1984b), which is illustrated in Figure 6–1, further detracts from the validity of the study conclusions. These relative risks exhibit a very strong, and highly significant, downward trend with wife's entry age, and there is no elevation of risk at all for women aged 60 years or more at entry. This anomalous pattern is even more surprising because the entry age groups had considerable overlap in terms of attained age during the 16-year course of the study.

In my view, the serious external and internal inconsistencies in the reported results of the Hirayama study require investigation and explanation before this study can properly be used in assessing a possible relationship between ETS and lung cancer.

C. Dosimetric Considerations

The combined lung cancer relative risk of 1.34 derived in the 1986 NRC report from the meta-analysis of 13 epidemiologic studies is much higher than would be expected from comparisons of biological markers of smoke exposure between ETS-exposed persons and active smokers. The NRC report stated that an analysis of urinary levels of cotinine (a metabolite of nicotine) in a group of ETS-exposed persons suggested that ETS exposure was roughly equivalent to smoking 0.1 to 0.2 cigarettes per day. The excess lung cancer risk calculated from the combined epidemiologic studies is about 10 times greater than the excess risk that might be calculated from smoking 0.1 to 0.2 cigarettes per day under a linear dose-response assumption (Lee 1988 and 1989). Arguing that particulate matter is more relevant than nicotine to lung cancer risk, Lee estimated that the inhaled dose of particulates is about one thousand times smaller for ETS-exposed persons than for smokers, and hence that the excess lung cancer risk derived from the epidemiologic studies is about 100 times greater than that suggested by studies of smokers. The effects of ETS exposure and cigarette smoking cannot be precisely compared on the basis of biological markers, since ETS and mainstream smoke are qualitatively different substances (NRC 1986). Nonetheless, this huge discrepancy casts serious doubt on the validity of the observed association between ETS and lung cancer. As noted above, Lee concluded that a more likely explanation for the observed association was misclassification of smokers and ex-smokers as nonsmokers.

IV. Epidemiologic Studies of ETS and Cancer Other than Lung

In contrast to the many studies dealing with ETS and lung cancer, only nine studies have been reported concerning ETS and cancer other than of the lung. Some of the results of these studies are summarized in Table 6–2. As in the case of the lung cancer studies, most of the studies used spousal smoking as the ETS exposure index. These nine studies provide insufficient data to evaluate the effect of ETS on cancer other than of the lung. The reported associations are weak and inconsistent, and are subject to the potential effects of biases and uncontrolled confounding factors noted above in connection with the lung cancer studies. The individual studies are briefly discussed below.

Gillis et al. (1984). In this small Scottish cohort study, there were a total of 43 non-lung cancer deaths among nonsmoking women, and eight among nonsmoking men. This study is flawed by a 20% non-response rate, and by

Table 6–2
Studies of ETS and Cancer in Nonsmokers

Study	*Cancer Site*	*Sex*	*Number of Cases in Exposed Group*	*Relative Risk*
Gillis *et al.*, 1984	All sites except lung	F	33	1.26
		M	2	0.50
Hirayama, 1984a	All sites except lung	F	870	1.11*
	Nasal sinus	F	23	1.99
	Brain	F	31	3.35*
Miller, 1984	All sites	F	34	0.97
Sandler *et al.*, 1985	All sites	Both	118	2.00**
	Endocrine	Both	32[a]	4.40*
	Cervix	F	56[a]	2.10*
	Breast	F	13[a]	2.00
Kabat *et al.*, 1986	Bladder	F	24	1.21
		M	15	0.77
Reynolds *et al.*, 1987	All sites	F	150[b]	1.68*[c]
Burch *et al.*, 1989	Bladder	F	90	0.75 (Home exposed)
			38	0.93 (Work exposed)
		M	37	0.94 (Home exposed)
			25	0.97 (Work exposed)
Sandler *et al.*, 1989	All sites	F	290	1.00
		M	31	1.01
Slattery *et al.*, 1989	Cervix	F	81[+]	1.14 (<1 hr/day)
				1.57 (1–3 hr/day)
				3.43* (3 + hr/day)

[a]All cases, including unexposed.
[b]All cases, including smoking women and unexposed.
[c]Based on a proportional hazards regression analysis which included smoking women.
*Statistically significant at the 5% level.
**Statistically significant at the 1% level.

the exclusion of some eligible subjects from the analysis for apparently unknown reasons.

Hirayama (1984a). The reported relative risk of 1.11 in women for cancer other than lung in the Hirayama cohort study is a very weak association. Confounding and misclassification of smokers as nonsmokers cannot be excluded as explanatory factors. Hirayama's results are not controlled for potentially confounding life-style and socioeconomic risk factors.

Hirayama reported significant associations in women between brain and nasal sinus cancers and spousal smoking. (The result for nasal sinus cancer is not significant when women with ex-smoker husbands are included.) These findings have not been replicated in other studies, so they must be considered inconclusive. The result for brain cancer lacks plausibility, because brain cancer has not been shown to be associated with smoking. Hirayama considered mortality in women for at least 18 different cancer types other than lung, so a question of statistical multiple comparisons arises. When 18 statistical tests are performed, there is a substantial chance that one or more of the 18 will be significant even if there is no association between exposure and disease.

Miller (1984). In this Pennsylvania case-control study of nonsmoking married women, 123 cancer deaths (cases) were compared with 414 non-cancer deaths (controls) with respect to husband's smoking status. The age-adjusted odds ratio was 0.97. Given the substantial number of cases, the power of this study to detect a modest elevation in risk would be reasonably high.

Sandler et al. (1985). In this case-control study, cancer cases aged 15 to 59 years were identified from a hospital based registry in North Carolina. Matched friend controls were obtained for 60% of the cases, and matched population controls for the remaining 40%. For 192 nonsmoking female cases (including at most two lung cancers) the crude odds ratio for cancer of all sites was 2.0. No dose response was found for all-site cancer using as the exposure index either number of years married to a smoker or the number of cigarettes smoked per day by the spouse. Risk was significantly elevated for endocrine cancers (all nonsmokers, odds ratio = 4.4), and for cervical cancer (nonsmoking women, odds ration = 2.1). The odds ratio of 2.0 for breast cancer in nonsmoking women was not quite significant.

The Sandler et al. study has been criticized because it failed to control for known risk factors for specific cancers. A notable example is cervical cancer, with which sexual activity, as indicated by the number of sex partners for example, is strongly related. Since sexual activity is also correlated with smoking habits, it is powerful confounder for cervical cancer. This is demonstrated in the Slattery et al. study discussed below. Other grounds for skepticism about the Sandler et al. results are the unusually high relative risks reported for all-site cancer, and high risks reported for sites which are not generally considered to be smoking related.

Kabat et al. (1986). In this hospital-based case-control study of bladder cancer, analyses of both spousal smoking and self-reported ETS exposure found no significant association between bladder cancer and ETS. The authors stated that their study suggests ETS exposure is not an important factor in bladder cancer in nonsmokers.

Reynolds et al. (1987). In this California cohort study, there were 147 cancer cases diagnosed among 2,385 married women, including an unstated number of lung cancers. A Cox proportional hazards regression analysis, using both smoking and nonsmoking women, gave a cancer relative risk of 1.7 for nonsmoking women with smoking husbands when compared with nonsmoking couples. If only the wife smoked, the relative risk was 2.0, and if both spouses smoked it was 1.5. The implausible implication that cancer risk is lower for couples with two smokers relative to couples with one smoker raises doubts about the validity of the statistical model used. No association was found between cancer incidence and spousal smoking among the husbands, which is a major inconsistency in the study results. Moreover the relative risk of 1.7 reported for women is inconsistent with other studies, particularly with the large Hirayama cohort study.

Burch et al. (1989). This population-based case-control study of bladder cancer was conducted in two Canadian provinces from 1979 to 1982. Of 826 cases, 105 were nonsmoking women and 112 were nonsmoking men. In an age-adjusted logistic regression analysis, no association was found between bladder cancer and self-reported exposure of nonsmokers to ETS at home or at work. This result was not affected by adjustment for several medical and occupational risk factors for bladder cancer.

Sandler et al. (1989). In this cohort study, 28,000 white adult smokers and 19,000 never smokers in Washington County, Maryland, were followed from 1963 to 1975. Mortality from all causes and certain specific causes in nonsmokers was evaluated with reference to smoking habits of others in the household. For death from cancer of all sites, the relative risks of ETS exposure, adjusted for age, housing quality, education and marital status, were 1.01 and 1.00 for men and women respectively. This study had reasonable power to detect an elevation of risk, with 115 cancer deaths among men and 501 among women.

Slattery et al. (1989). This population-based case-control study of cervical cancer was conducted in the Salt Lake City, Utah, area. Of the cases identified, 266 (65%) were included in the study, and of the controls selected, 480 (76%) agreed to be interviewed. This low participation rate is a weakness of the study.

The authors reported a relative risk of 3.4 for cervical cancer in nonsmokers with respect to self-reported ETS exposure of 3 or more hours per day. This relative risk was the same as that reported for current cigarette smokers. In both cases, the relative risks were adjusted for age, church attendance, education and number of sexual partners (but not, surprisingly, for membership in the Mormon religion). In the case of current smokers, the unadjusted relative risk was 10.1, which illustrates the potentially profound effect of confounding variables (the unadjusted relative risk was not reported for nonsmokers). An editorial comment (Layde 1989) pointed out that the most important cause of cervical cancer is thought to be a sexually transmitted infectious agent. Since measures of sexual activity, such as number of sex partners, are unlikely to reflect completely exposure to the causal agent, the editorial noted that the reported relative risk probably overestimates the true risk from ETS exposure. The authors themselves noted that misclassification of sex history could result in inflated risk estimates for ETS exposure.

The association of cervical cancer with ETS exposure reported by Slattery et al. has not been found in other studies, except for Sandler et al. (1985). In particular, Hirayama (1984a) found no association of cervical cancer with spousal smoking among nonsmoking women.

V. Conclusion

The weak and inconsistent associations seen in the epidemiologic studies of ETS and lung cancer, the fact that bias and confounding cannot be ruled out, and questions about the reliability of the reported results, all indicate that these data do not support a judgment of a causal relationship between exposure to ETS and lung cancer. The validity of the observed associations between ETS and lung cancer is also brought into question by considerations of dosimetry.

The data on cancers other than lung cancer suffer from the same deficiencies as those noted in the lung cancer studies, and are sparser, weaker, and less consistent than the lung cancer data. Findings of associations with cancer of sites that are not associated with smoking cast doubt on the validity of all of the ETS-cancer epidemiology, including the lung cancer studies.

VI. Recommendations for Future Research

Resolution of the open questions concerning the possible effects of ETS exposure on cancer incidence will require further epidemiologic studies which avoid as far as possible the pitfalls and problems seen in the currently available data. One important requirement is the measurement of biological markers such as urinary cotinine to validate ETS exposure information. Recognizing the need for such data, the IARC has sponsored an international collaborative study of urinary cotinine levels in nonsmoking married women (Preston-Martin et al. 1987).

There are several reasons for the importance of objective exposure measurements, including measurements of biological markers and direct measurement of environmental concentrations of smoke constituents. Subjective assessments of ETS exposure by the subject or others are inaccurate and unreliable, as are surrogate measures such as spousal smoking. Measurement of biological markers should help reduce bias arising from misclassification of smokers as nonsmokers. Also, biological marker data would help elucidate total exposure to ETS from all sources: home, workplace, transportation, etc. Finally, biological marker data would help establish the presence or absence of a dose-response relationship and, if present, help quantify it.

Apart from collecting information on biological markers, attempts must be made to determine better the present and past smoking status of declared nonsmokers—for example, by cross-validating information from several sources: the subject, relatives and friends, medical records, etc. Also, as much information as possible should be obtained from various sources on the intensity and daily duration of subjects' exposure to ETS at home and elsewhere, as well as on the duration in years of such exposure.

In view of the weak observed associations between ETS exposure and cancer incidence seen in the epidemiologic studies, it is obviously necessary in future studies to collect information on, and take into account, all known risk factors and potential confounders for the cancers under investigation. Koo (1989) and others have suggested that dietary factors are important confounders. Friedman et al. (1983) found that ETS exposure is correlated with marijuana use, alcohol consumption and occupational hazards, all of which are possible risk factors for lung and other cancers.

To shed light on the contradictory results which have been reported concerning ETS and lung cancer of different cell types, future lung cancer studies should ensure that complete histological information is obtained and taken into account in statistical analyses.

Another important need for research is in the area of dosimetric measurements of smoke components for both smokers and ETS-exposed persons. Such data are likely to be valuable in confirming or refuting the results of epidemiologic investigations. A promising avenue of research was described by McAughey et al. (1989), who used a radiotracer to measure tar intake from mainstream smoke in smokers and to estimate, for exposure to sidestream smoke, particulate deposition in the tracheo-bronchial region of nonsmokers' lungs.

References

Alibi, S., H. Kato, and W.J. Blot (1986). Passive smoking and lung cancer among Japanese women. *Cancer Research* 46:4804–4807

Brownson, R.C., J.S. Reif, T.J. Keefe, S.W. Ferguson, and J.A. Pritzl (1987). Risk factors for adenocarcinoma of the lung. *Am. J. Epidemiol.* 125:25–34.

Buffler, P.A., L.W. Pickle, T.J. Mason, and C. Contant (1984). The causes of cancer in Texas. In: *Lung Cancer: Causes and Prevention* (Eds. Mizell and Correa). Verlag-Chemie International, New York.

Burch, J.D., T.E. Rohan, G.R. Howe, H.A. Risch, G.B. Hill, R. Steele, and A.B. Miller (1989). Risk of bladder cancers by source and type of tobacco exposure: a case-control study. *Int. J. Cancer* 44:622–628.

Chan, W.C. and S.C. Fung (1982). Lung cancer in non-smokers in Hong Kong. In: *Cancer Campaign, Vol. 6. Cancer Epidemiology* (Ed. Grundmann). Gustav Fisher Verlag, Stuttgart.

Correa, P., L.W. Pickle, E. Fontham, Y. Lin, and W. Haenszel (1983). Passive smoking and lung cancer. *Lancet* 2:595–597.

Gao, Y.T., W.J. Blot, W. Zheng, A.G. Ershow, C.W. Hsu, L.I. Levin, R. Zhang, and J.F. Fraumeni (1988). Lung cancer among Chinese women. *Int. J. Cancer* 40:604–609.

Garfinkel, L. (1981). Time trends in lung cancer mortality among nonsmokers and a note on passive smoking. *J. Natl. Cancer Inst.* 66:1061–1066.

Garfinkel, L., O. Auerbach, and L. Joubert (1985). Involuntary smoking and lung cancer: A case-control study. *J. Natl. Cancer Inst.* 75:463–469.

Geng, G.Y., Z.H. Liang, A.Y. Zhang, and G.L. Wu (1988). In: *Smoking and Health 1987* (Eds. Aoki *et al.*). Excerpta Medica, Amsterdam.

Gillis, C.R., D.J. Hole, V.M. Hawthorne, and P. Boyle (1984). The effect of environmental tobacco smoke in two urban communities in the west of Scotland. *Eur. J. Respir. Dis.* 65 (Suppl.):121–126.

Hirayama, T. (1984a). Cancer mortality in nonsmoking women with smoking husbands based on a large-scale cohort study in Japan. *Prevent. Med.* 13:680–690.

Hirayama, T. (1984b). Lung cancer in Japan: Effects of nutrition and passive smoking. In: *Lung Cancer: Causes and Prevention* (Eds. Mizell and Correa). Verlag-Chemie International, New York.

Humble, C.G., J.M. Samet, and D.R. Pathak (1987). Marriage to a smoker and lung cancer risk. *Am. J. Publ. Health* 77:598–602.

Inoue, R. and T. Hirayama (1988). Passive smoking and lung cancer in women. In: *Smoking and Health 1987* (Eds. Aoki *et al.*) Excerpta Medica, Amsterdam.

Kabat, G.C., and E.L. Wynder (1984). Lung cancer in nonsmokers. *Cancer* 53:1214–1221.

Kabat, G.C., G.S. Dieck, and E.L. Wynder (1986). Bladder cancer in nonsmokers. *Cancer* 57:362–367.

Katada, H., R. Mikami, M. Konishi, Y. Koyama, and N. Narita (1988). Effect of passive smoking in lung cancer development in women in the Nara region. *Gan No Rinsho* 34:21–27.

Koo, L.C. (1989). Environmental tobacco smoke and lung cancer: Is it the smoke or the diet? In: *Present and Future of Indoor Air Quality* (Eds. Bieva *et al.*) Excerpta Medica, Amsterdam.

Koo, L.C., J.H.-C. Ho, D. Saw, and C. Ho (1987). Measurements of passive smoking and estimates of lung cancer risk among nonsmoking Chinese females. *Int. J. Cancer* 39:162–169.

Koo, L.C., J.H.-C. Ho, and R. Rylander (1988). Life-history correlates of environmental tobacco smoke: A study of nonsmoking Hong Kong Chinese wives with smoking versus nonsmoking husbands. *Soc. Sci. Med.* 26:751–760.

Lam, T.H., I.T.M. Kung, C.M. Wong, *et al.* (1987). Smoking, passive smoking and histological types in lung cancer in Hong Kong Chinese women. *Brit. J. Cancer* 56:763–678.

Lam, T.H., and K.K. Cheng (1988). Passive smoking is a risk factor in never smoking women in Hong Kong. In: *Smoking and Health 1987* (Eds. Aoki *et al.*). Excerpta Medica, Amsterdam.

Layard, M.W., and J.R. Viren (1989). Assessing the validity of a Japanese cohort study. In: *Present and Future of Indoor Air Quality* (Eds. Bieva *et al.*). Excerpta Medica, Amsterdam.

Layde, P.M. (1989). Smoking and cervical cancer: Cause or coincidence? *J. Am. Med. Assoc.* 261:12631–1633.

Lee, P.N. (1987). Lung cancer and passive smoking. *Toxicol. Letters* 35:157–162.

Lee, P.N. (1988). An alternative explanation for the increased risk of lung cancer in nonsmokers married to smokers. In: *Indoor Air and Ambient Air Quality* (Eds. Perry and Kirk). Selper Ltd., London.

Lee, P.N. (1989). Passive smoking and lung cancer; fact or fiction? In: *Present and Future of Indoor Air Quality* (Eds. Bieva *et al.*). Excerpta Medica, Amsterdam.

Lee, P.N., J. Chamberlain, and M.R. Alderson (1986). Relationship of passive smoking to risk of lung cancer and other smoking-associated diseases. *Br. J. Cancer* 54:97–105.

McAughey, J.J., J.N. Pritchard, and A. Black (1989). Relative lung cancer risk from exposure to mainstream and sidestream smoke particulates. In: *Present and Future of Indoor Air Quality* (Eds. Bieva *et al.*). Excerpta Medica, Amsterdam.

Miller, G.H. (1984). Cancer, passive smoking and nonemployed and employed wives. *West. J. Med.* 140:632–635.

National Research Council (1986). *Environmental Tobacco Smoke: Measuring Exposures and Assessing Health Effects.* National Academy Press, Washington, D.C.

Pershagen, G., Z. Hrubec, and C. Svensson (1987). Passive smoking and lung cancer in Swedish women. *Am. J. Epidemiol.* 125:1724.

Preston-Martin, S., B. Dodet, and R. Saracci (1987). Epidemiologic studies of passive smoking. In: *Passive Smoking* (Eds. O'Neill *et al.*). IARC Scientific Publications No. 81, IARC, Lyon.

Reynolds, P., G.A. Kaplan, and R.D. Cohen (1987). Passive smoking and cancer incidence: Prospective evidence from the Alameda County study (Abstract). *Am. J. Epidemiol.* 126:767.

Rylander, R., H.-J. Haussmann, and F.J. Fewes (1989). Lung cancer risk by oral exposure. In: *Present and Future of Indoor Air Quality* (Eds. Bieva *et al.*). Excerpta Medica, Amsterdam.

Sandler, D.P., G.W. Comstock, K.J. Helsing, and D.L. Shore (1989). Deaths from all causes in non-smokers who lived with smokers. *Am. J. Publ. Health* 79:163–167.

Sandler, D.P., R.B. Everson, and A.J. Wilcox (1985). Passive smoking in adulthood and cancer risk. *Am. J. Epidemiol.* 121:37–48.

Shimizu, H., M. Morishita, K. Mizuno, *et al.* (1988). A case control study of lung cancer in nonsmoking women. *Tohoku J. Exp. Med.* 154:389–397.

Sidney, S., B.J. Caan, and G.D. Friedman (1989). Dietary intake of carotene in nonsmokers with and without passive smoking at home. *Am. J. Epidemiol.* 129:1305–1309.

Slattery, M.L., L.M. Robison, K.L. Schuman, T.K. French, T.M. Abbott, J.R. Overall, and J.W. Gardner (1989). Cigarette smoking and exposure to passive smoke are risk factors for cervical cancer. *J. Am. Med. Assoc.* 261:1593–1598.

Trichopolous, D., A. Kalandidi, and L. Sparros (1983). Lung cancer and passive smoking: Conclusion of Greek study. *Lancet* 2:677–678.

Vandenbrouke, J.P. (1988). Passive smoking and lung cancer: a publication bias? *Br. Med. J.* 296:391–392.

Wu, A.H., B.E. Henderson, M.C. Pike, and M.C. Yu (1985). Smoking and other risk factors for lung cancer in women. *J. Natl. Cancer Inst.* 74:747–751.

Wynder, E.L. (1987). Workshop on guidelines to the epidemiology of weak associations. *Prevent. Med.* 16:139–141.

7
Panel Discussion on Lung and Other Cancers

Joseph Wu: Thank you, Dr. Layard. I will now ask the panel of discussants to come to the front and take their seats. First, could we have the comments of Dr. Betton.

G.R. Betton: I would like specifically to address the question of non-lung cancer effects of ETS and in particular those effects that have been purported to exist in children.

The study of parents or spouses and the relationship between their tobacco consumption and the potential carcinogenic effects on children has been reported in a number of papers. Labreque has produced data that nicotine and hence cotinine in breast milk is increased through exposure to ETS as well as through active smoking. So we have a potential, at least, for children to be affected by maternal and paternal smoking, both in utero and by the effects of tobacco metabolites in breast milk and by the normal ETS exposure of the newborn child in a household where the parents smoke.

So there has been, I think quite justifiably, some specific interest in this area. When I refer to childhood cancers, in fact some of the surveys looked at tumors arising in young children all the way through to early adulthood. Of course, the reliability of extrapolating the smoking habits of a parent is highly vulnerable to cloudy judgment since these habits must be remembered back to the time when the parent gave birth. There is also the confounding factor that the time of induction of any postulated tumors is likely to have a certain latency period related to that tumour type. Therefore, whether tumors were related to ETS exposure per se or due to an exposure by the milk of the mother or during intrauterine life has to be taken into account.

Let's look at the series of studies involving brain tumors. The overall results indicate no significant increase in the incidence of brain tumors, although two studies—those of Preston and Martin, and Sandler—have come up with a small increase, at least with both parents smoking.

Looking at leukemias and lymphomas, the effects of radiation and so on have drawn a lot of attention to leukemia clusters and some of the environmental factors that may influence leukemia in children. A summary of studies looking at these tumors in children (again, of mothers and/or fathers who smoke) indicates overall that there are only two studies where significant increases were found.

Again, Sandler's study showed an increase of 1.7-fold when just the fathers smoked. If both spouses smoked, that goes to 4.6-fold with 2.1 in between when the mother smoked. Stjernfeldt published a series in 1986 claiming a 1.8-fold relative risk of childhood leukemia in the children of smokers. However, the much larger series in the U.S. and the U.K. published by McKinney and Stiller and Buckley showed this effect was not reproducible. I think overall these findings indicate that there is no conclusive evidence for a childhood carcinogenic effect of ETS with or without the contributory factors of milk or transplacental exposure.

Nevertheless, I think it merits further monitoring and investigation, particularly as the measurement of transplacental exposure factors, breast milk exposure factors and ETS have not been properly segregated in the epidemiological studies that have been done to date. Clearly, future experience would be important in seeing if any one or a combination of these do in fact have a role in producing childhood neoplasia.

Austin Gardiner: Since I work in clinical medicine in Scotland, I thought it appropriate to comment on the excellent paper from Charles Gillis and his colleagues, which comes from that part of the UK. This paper came from the Scotland Cancer Surveillance Unit, and it's a paper which claims to have some unique features. First, the paper is interesting in that the urban areas of the west of Scotland have the highest national incidence rate of lung cancer recorded and yet, curiously, suburban areas in the city of Glasgow, not many miles from those districts with the highest incidence, have the lowest incidence in the UK. (Gillis, C.R., P. Boyle., D.J. Hole and A. Graham (1982) Cancer incidence in U.K., Scotland, West 1975–77 in Muir C. Shanmugaratriamk, Powell J (eds.) *Cancer Incidence in Five Continents,* Vol. IV, Lyon, IARC Scientific Publications No. 42). Second, it was a prospective cohort study carried out in a geographically defined population whose members are homogeneous by social class and ethnic group. Third, the study examines both sexes rather than simply females exposed to spousal making. And, fourth, no questions concerning exposure to ETS were asked, thus avoiding the bias inherent in self-reported assessment of partnership dosage.

Data were derived from a multi-phasic screening survey for cardiorespiratory disease carried out in two urban areas, Renfrew and Paisley, in which there was an 80% response rate from a randomly sampled group. That group totaled almost 16,000 individuals. The diagnosis of cancer was checked by the West Scotland Cancer Registry; mortality was checked by record linkage.

The results of the study on the effect of ETS related to only about half of the total who attended the multi-phasing screening unit. And although the authors say that this can be accounted for by a discrepancy of those living alone, those living with a partner out of the age range of forty-five to sixty-four years at the time of the survey, and smokers or ex-smokers of five years duration's exclusion, this does not seem to account for the total discrepancy.

Respiratory symptoms were reported by questionnaire and this was standardized for age. In males there was a small but statistically significant increased occurrence of persistent sputum and breathlessness and hypersecretion in ETS-exposed individuals. In females there was a small but statistically significant increased incidence of breathlessness in those exposed to ETS.

But today we are considering lung cancer. The lung cancer incidence was expressed in annual age-standardized mortality rate per ten thousand by smoking categories. For males in the control group who were non-smokers and never-smokers, there were four cases and two deaths. For ETS, thirteen cases and four deaths. And in the smoking group, twenty-two cases and thirty deaths.

In the female group, these figures were: control, four cases and two deaths; ETS, four cases and six deaths. Based on the increasing incidence of lung cancer in the four groups studied—that is, control, ETS, smokers, and smokers plus ETS—the authors imply a dose-response relationship for the males that was not apparent in females for lung cancer deaths. Now, we'll all agree that, as Max Layard has already said, these are very small numbers that we're considering.

Applying Dr. Layard's clear exposition of what constitutes a positive causal relationship to the paper, one can see that Gillis and his coworkers provided some evidence to justify association with disease, that the results seem consistent, and that a demonstration of dose-response relationship in the male group seems as is claimed.

When one turns to freedom from bias and control of confounding factors, however, the data seem less secure. In this paper, the authors make the remarkable statement that lung cancer risk in non-smokers is not importantly related to occupation. The door for criticism on grounds of control of confounding factors is thus opened wide. And confounding factors which have already been mentioned this morning and this afternoon, such as diesel fuel exposure—which has been suggested as an independent risk factor for lung cancer—must confound this study. (Albert, R.E. and C. Chen (1986). Diesel studies on inhalation hazards, in Ishinishi, N., A. Kuizumi, R.O. McLelland, and W. Stobe, *Carcinogenic and Mutagenic Effects of Diesel Exhaust*, pp 411–419). Subjects could have been exposed to diesel at the workplace and as a result of using public transport, both train and passenger bus, or even from their own motorcars. A further confounding factor was indicated by data published in *Nature* in March of this year, in which a statistical analysis by the authors suggests that six percent of lung cancers in the UK may be attributable to radon daughter exposure (Clark, R.H. and T.R.E. Southwood (1989). Risks from ionizing radiation. *Nature* 338: 197–198). It is believed that this exposure is aggravated in effect by methods of modern house construction such as ventilation and insulation in particular. I've already touched on occupation. And more recently still there has been a claim made from Holland for avian contact as an independent risk factor. (Holst, P.A. (1989). Pet birds as an independent risk factor for lung cancer. *Brit. Med. J.* 297: 1319–1321).

Again, one must criticize the Gillis paper and a subsequent 1989 paper by the same group (Hole, D.J., C.R. Gillis, C. Chopra and V.M. Hawthorn (1989). Passive smoking and cardiorespiratory health in a general population in the west of Scotland. *Brit. Med. J.* 299: 423–427) for not mentioning the strong suspicion that air pollution sometime in the lifetime of the respondents in these cohorts may have had an effect. The whole of the urban area of Glasgow in the west of Scotland, until fairly recently, in epidemiological terms, was involved in heavy industry, particularly ship building, and the whole industrial complex in the lifetime of the questionnaire respondents was based on this and on fibre milling.

A fascinating population study reported this summer compares groups of west central Scots who moved to London with peer groups remaining in Glasgow and west central Scotland. (Britton, M. (1989). Mortality-geography. *Population Trends* 56: 16–23). Such factors as smoking, alcohol consumption, diet and lifestyle were compared. The incidence and mortality of coronary artery disease, chronic obstructive pulmonary disease, and lung cancer were significantly lower in the emigrant Scots, attaining the incidence of the native southeast England population the longer the emigrants remained in the London conurbation. The morbidity statistics were similar.

In the same study, it was shown that when the reverse geographical process had taken place—an English population who moved to west central Scotland in the same period—Londoners acquired the smoking, drinking and eating habits of the Scots. The longer they stayed, the more closely the incidence of the above-mentioned diseases approximated that of the native population.

I make this comment merely to emphasize how many important confounding factors obviously exist with respect to disease, and in particular ETS.

Edward Field: Well, I had planned also to address the topic of childhood exposure to ETS, but Dr. Betton has largely anticipated what I had to say. So you'll be relieved to know that my presentation will be that much shorter.

Dr. Layard has reviewed the evidence relating to possible associations between ETS exposure and cancers of nonpulmonary sites and he's advanced a number of cogent reasons why such published evidence can be essentially discounted. Most convincing of these reasons is that misclassification can occur on a substantial scale—a scale probably sufficient to account for any of the associations that have been reported. This misclassification problem has been demonstrated by a variety of objective tests for assessing the accuracy of self-reporting.

Another argument he's advanced concerns the curious observation of apparent associations between ETS exposure and increased risk for cancers that are not related to active smoking, particularly of the hemopoietic system, brain and breast. This effect would seem to be so improbable that such observations only serve to throw additional doubt on the adequacy or validity of epidemiological protocols that had been applied in general to studies of ETS.

Nonetheless, these reports merit closer scrutiny because they introduce some interesting epidemiological principles. For one thing, bias due to misclassification cannot be invoked to explain all of the alleged associations, since the frequency of cancers not related to active smoking will not be increased in the population of putative non-smokers by the erroneous inclusion of some active smokers among them. Further, since the effect of misclassification in cases of smoking-related cancers can be so predominant that it masks any other more subtle sources of bias, studies on non-smoking related cancers provide a better chance to reveal unsuspected confounding factors and to identify them.

Dr. Betton very adequately summarized the current publications that claim to show these associations. Among lymphomas, Sandler's work would suggest that there might be a significant increase in relative risk for children exposed to parental smoking or smoking in the domestic environment. For brain cancers, Hirayama's prospective study claimed to show a significant increase in risk; Preston-Martin in 1982 and Sandler also both have claimed to show significant increases in risk.

In addition, Hirayama and Sandler have reported increased risk for breast cancers. Hirayama's data don't reach significance but Sandler's just about do, although I believe that could be challenged. This effect cannot be attributed to life-style as readily as in the case of cervical cancer. Conceivably, tumor initiation could take place in early childhood or in the developing foetus and later become expressed (promoted) when the adult hormonal activity has been established. But this explanation would require that women from smoking families have a propensity to marry husbands who smoke—a source of concordance that has not yet been explored.

The question is: how much reliance can one place on these observations? The major source of evidence, of course, derives from the series of publications by Sandler, which we've just discussed. Dr. Peter Lee, I believe, in a later session, will be reviewing these studies and will tell us that they suffer from a number of shortcomings that render them highly suspect. Hirayama's studies have been largely discredited on methodological grounds and I have no doubt that serious flaws could also be found in most of the other reports that have been reviewed.

The issue is whether the published evidence linking exposure to ETS in early life with increased risk for certain classes of cancers is so tenuous that it can confidently be dismissed as fortuitous.

I feel that it will be more convincing if, rather than refuting the claims that have been made for these associations, it could be shown that no such association exists by studies that have been properly designed and have controlled for all the foreseeable confounding variables involved in this particular situation. It's quite possible that this information is already available as part of a completed, wider epidemiological study such as the American Cancer Society's Million Person Study or the recent prospective study by Sandler. If so, efforts should be made to retrieve these data and analyze them separately so that this spectre can be finally laid to rest.

Dr. Irving Kessler: The critical question at issue concerns the biological relationship between cancer and ETS, not its statistical significance. This distinction is often ignored, perhaps because epidemiological studies are sometimes improperly regarded as the human analogue of controlled laboratory investigations.

In the typical basic science study, the investigator treats biologically identical clones of animals, exposing cases to the test treatment and observing outcomes in both cases and controls. By way of contrast, epidemiological studies deal with heterogeneous cases and controls, and face ethical and judgmental problems of exposing humans to the test treatment and other largely unavoidable difficulties.

At the completion of the study, the laboratory scientist can usually attribute the outcome to the test treatment without concern for the subjects' genome, prior disease history, method of selection, motivation or degree of cooperation. On the other hand, the epidemiologist is usually left with these problems incompletely resolved and, consequently, faces inferential roadblocks to a full understanding of the biological significance of the study.

Histopathologically distinct neoplasms of a single anatomic site are widely held to be caused by different environmental or hereditary factors. For example, epidermoid tumors of the uterus are regarded as epidemiologically and etiologically distinct from glandular or cervical ones. Yet, in epidemiological studies of lung cancers, squamous and adenocarcinomas are frequently lumped together as if they represented a single disease process.

Imputing disease to a specific factor (like ETS) is reasonable in theory when the study subjects represent the universe of human beings susceptible to the test agent. In the real world, however, the methods adopted for selecting subjects are often designed to satisfy the epidemiologist's convenience rather than to ensure valid inferences of causality. For example, when lung cancer cases are chosen from hospitals accessible to the investigator without regard to their selectiveness with respect to race, social class or ethnic group, the outcome is likely to reflect the particular types of patients studied rather than the universe of individuals subject to lung cancer.

Accumulating cases for study over relatively long periods of time, as a convenience to the investigator, also poses a substantial inference problem because such cases usually reflect a greater diversity in environments, occupations, prior exposures, ethnic distribution, diagnostic fashions, etc. than is true for cases assembled over a relatively short time span in a given geographical area.

Selectivity is also important when cases are derived from tumor registries where the geographically defined reference population is often imprecisely defined. This contrasts with the situation of the laboratory investigator using homogeneous rat or mouse clones for study, a circumstance in which the issue of selection bias is essentially irrelevant.

Issues important in case selection also pertain to controls. Are they similar to the cases in socioeconomic, behavorial, racial and ethnic respects? Were they chosen from the universe of potential study subjects or from less generalizable categories such as "patients without lung cancer or any tobacco-related disease, however defined" or "patients without certain types of cancer?" Were they selected from the same hospitals or communities as the cases?

In recent years, neighborhood controls have become more fashionable among epidemiologists but often without a careful consideration of the advantages and disadvantages. Neighborhood controls may, under the appropriate circumstances, be less pre-selected or more generalizable than hospital controls, but they are not unsusceptible to bias. For example, when potential neighborhood controls decline to participate they are often replaced by second, third, fourth or even fifth choices, a circumstance that may render the statistical analysis questionable or even inappropriate.

In some studies, friends or siblings have been selected as controls, again without due consideration of the potential biases. In the Trichopoulos study, the lung cancer cases were matched with orthopedic controls. While there is no a priori evidence that orthopedic patients react uniquely to ETS, it is unlikely that they are completely representative of the universe of human beings to which the study results are to be generalized.

Quantitative assessment of exposure to the factor under investigation is essential, if only because the demonstration of host responses dependent on dose is an important criterion for causality. Using hospital chart information to quantify exposure to ETS is clearly a weak measure. Since there are hundreds of constituent chemicals in burning tobacco, an effort should also be made to untangle them in studies of etiology; first, because cigarettes vary in their chemical composition and, second, because the lung cancer outcome should be attributed to specific components if possible.

In many epidemiological studies, the operational definitions of "smoker," "non-smoker" and "ex-smoker" are imprecisely stated. For example, is it reasonable to consider a person who smokes one cigarette a day for a year a smoker? What of someone passively exposed to another's smoking of one cigarette a day? Variations among smokers in the number of puffs per cigarette or per time interval also affect a subject's exposure to the suspect agent.

In general, epidemiological studies have not attempted to quantify exposures in the subject's total environment: home, work, leisure, in or out of doors, etc. For convenience, ascertainment has usually been limited to exposures at home and at work. Passive exposures from multiple spouses or from close contacts of unmarried subjects have also been ignored.

Cotinine, the best biological marker for smoking exposure yet available, reflects only recent exposure rather than exposure at the time (ten or twenty years earlier) when the neoplasm was initiated or promoted. Proxies serve as informants on exposure despite general agreement that their information is of lower validity than that from study subjects themselves. Telephone and mailed questionnaires are also less likely to elicit quantitatively valid responses on exposure than head-to-head interviews with subjects or application of biological markers. Neglected, too, are efforts to develop better methods to quantify the changing smoking habits of individuals over their lifetimes.

In the laboratory, the basic scientist does not need to contend with the epidemiological problems of non-response. To epidemiologists, variability in response rates is critically important. While rates higher than 90 percent are considered optimal, the types of individuals who do and do not choose to participate is also decisive. This is much less an issue to laboratory scientists who can safely ignore non-response (due to deaths from other causes, etc.) among identical animals.

For imputing causality, evidence of a quantitative dose/response is widely regarded as essential in epidemiologic studies. Most epidemiologists believe that odds ratios (as a measure of relative risk) less than 3 or 4 to 1 should not be regarded as biologically significant (irrespective of statistical significance) because of the "noise" inherent in human epidemiological studies. It should be noted that most of the studies on ETS and lung cancer risk have yielded odds ratios or relative risks not much greater than 2.0, and usually less.

In human epidemiological studies, it is essential that attention be paid to covariant risk factors (drugs, alcohol, other exposures, other behaviors, hereditary factors, etc.) that may play roles in the etiology of the disease in question. Unfortunately, most of the published studies on lung cancer have failed to provide more than an elementary statistical treatment of such covariants. Adjustment techniques are often misapplied as well, leading to risk estimates of questionable validity.

As undue attention is paid to statistical associations instead of the underlying biological realities, anomalous findings, which are often important, tend to be ignored. For example, the effect of ETS in some studies is greater in young as compared with old subjects, in women as compared with men, and in adenocarcinomas as compared with squamous neoplasms. These findings may simply reflect inadequate control of independent variables relating to age, sex and histopathology. But they may also suggest specific mechanisms for host reactions to ETS.

Another important issue is the practice by some epidemiologists of pooling data from a number of studies in order to increase sample size and reduce confidence intervals. While the statistical procedures for meta-analysis are simple, the underlying assumption that the studies being compared must be similar in methodology is often ignored. Thus, papers reporting on meta-analyses of the lung cancer/ETS issue often do not command the scientific respect that basic science reports, based on a more straightforward application of the classical scientific method, continue to enjoy.

Joseph Wu: The next person to discuss the issue of ETS and cancer is Dr. James Kilpatrick.

James Kilpatrick: Thank you.

I want first to talk about the issue of labeling. Scientists communicate in shorthand; thus, those familiar with the ETS literature know that the phrase "ETS exposure" in fact refers to spousal smoking. The "features of study design are critically important" (Gordis L. (ed.) (1988). *Epidemiology and Health Risk Assessment*, Oxford University Press p. 268) and it is well known that cohort studies are less biased and are more trustworthy than case control studies. However, one of the essential elements of a cohort study is a regular and comprehensive follow-up. Thus, "follow-up over time of the individuals enrolled in a cohort study is the essential feature of the study. The success with which the follow-up is achieved is probably the basic measure of the quality of the study. If a substantial proportion of the cohort is lost to follow-up, the validity of the study's conclusion is seriously called into question." (Breslow, N.E. and N.E. Day (1987). *Statistical Methods in Cancer Research*, Vol. II: The design and analysis of cohort studies. IARC, Lyon, p. 25).

And again, from Last's dictionary of epidemiological terms, "an essential feature of the (cohort) method . . . is observation of the population for a sufficient number of person years to generate reliable incidence or mortality rates in the population subsets." (Last, J.M. (1983). *A Dictionary of Epidemiology*. Oxford University Press, New York). Thus, for example, Elwood (Elwood J.M. (1988) *Causal Relationships in Medicine. A Practical System for Critical Appraisal.* Oxford Univ. Press, Oxford) points out that the British doctors were selected for a cohort study of smoking "because they could be followed through annual registration procedures." (p. 19). In Elwood's critical appraisal of a cohort study, he demands that the "cause-to-effect time sequence be clear" (p. 23) and that "a correct time relationship" be documented." (p. 190). Also, "the interpretation of a cohort study should not depend on a single observed/expected ratio but on the way this ratio evolves with time since exposure." (Gordis L. (ed). (1988) *Epidemiology and Health Risk Assessment.* Oxford Univ. Press, Oxford, p. 188).

I turn now to Dr. Layard's paper. In his paper, Dr. Layard refers to five studies of ETS and cancer as "cohort studies." These are the studies by Hirayama (1984), Garfinkel (1981), Gillis (1984), Reynolds (1987) and Sandler

(1989). Close examination of these papers reveals that they are not cohort studies but "record linkage" studies; that is the term used (in these papers) to describe how the studies ascertain mortality. (See, e.g., Hirayama 1981) In other words, the continuous follow-up of individuals in a true cohort study is absent in these five studies. In terms of follow-up, the best of these appears to be the American Cancer Society study (Garfinkel 1981), which had four follow-up questionnaires over 17 years and in which deaths were reported by ACS volunteers responsible for following subgroups of the cohort. Thus, the ACS study is the closest we have to a true cohort study.

Record linkage studies do not have "time to event" and so omit this important explanatory factor. I have demonstrated in the paper that I presented at the 1988 indoor air conference at the Imperial College in London that the effect of this omission is a likely explanation for the heterogeneity in Hirayama's study. (Kilpatrick, S.J. and J. Viven (1988). Age as a modifying factor in the association between lung cancer in nonsmoking women and their husbands' smoking status. Perry R. and P.W. Kirk (eds.) *Indoor and Ambient Air Quality*, Selper Ltd. London.) Dr. Layard made a point of this in showing his Figure 6–1. Further, I demonstrated at the Brussels conference a couple of months ago (Kilpatrick, S.J. (1989) an example of extra Poisson variation suggesting an under-specified model. Bieva, C.J., Y. Courtois, M. Govaerts (eds.) (*Present and Future of Indoor Air Quality.* Elsevier) that, after introducing a term for over-dispersion to allow for this heterogeneity, the association between "ETS" and lung cancer mortality in non-smoking wives is no longer statistically significant in Hirayama's study.

We need an explanation for why all these statistically significant results have appeared in the literature. One possibility is publication bias, which has been mentioned here. Another that has not been mentioned is "data dredging." It is clear to me that many of these authors take the data and analyze it until they can find a statistically significant result and then publish that. They do not have a prior hypothesis. My friend, Dr. Hirayama, is a good example of this.

Dr. Layard concludes his review with recommendations for further research that would avoid as far as possible the defects of the current literature. In contrast to his suggestion that we should do these studies better, I've come to the belief that such studies are infeasible. The tradition in scientific research that the null hypothesis be retained until it is shown to be untenable has already been violated in the study of ETS and cancer. Under the influence of the past administration, the public have been persuaded that ETS can cause cancer. Those of us who are unconvinced of this have to show that ETS (and here I mean really spousal smoking), is a surrogate for other explanatory variables omitted from the analysis.

As a first step, it is necessary to check the analytical methods used by the authors of these original studies. The statistical analysis of epidemiological data has developed rapidly over the last ten years and yet many of these original studies use archaic methods of analysis and do not validate their statistical models to estimate risks. On the other hand, it has proved well nigh impossible for others to check these analyses because of the paucity of information published in the original reports and the refusal of the authors of the reports to share their basic data. Access to the data would enable us to check the validity of the statistical analyses used to estimate risk.

As a second step, I think we should encourage original research, like that of Friedman (1983) on surrogates for ETS and Koo's 1989 paper, which shows that the introduction of diet as an explanatory variable negates the significance of the association of ETS with lung cancer. (Koo, L.C. (1989). Environmental tobacco smoke and lung cancer: Is it the smoke or the diet? Bieva, C.J., Y. Courtois and M. Govaerts (eds.) *Present and Future of Indoor Air Quality*. Elsevier).

In summary, then, what I have said is that I think we should stop calling these five studies "cohort studies" and call them what they really are—record linkage studies. Further, I think we need to encourage more original studies to discover surrogates for spousal smoking that also are risk factors for lung cancer.

Nathan Mantel: While I am in full agreement with Dr. Layard's position and conclusions, I do consider that he has adopted overly stringent requirements.

Thus, if environmental tobacco smoke has increased the risk of lung cancer, that increase, if any, is unlikely to be in excess of five to ten percent, just undetectable by any reasonable epidemiologic investigation. For similar reasons, it would be difficult to establish dose-response reactions in the ETS-lung cancer association.

The low power of any single investigation is what could make appropriate the use of "meta-analysis," in which the results of individually weak investigations can be reinforcing. Unfortunately, however, the biases in such studies can also be reinforcing, a problem for which "meta-analysis" is not corrective.

One particular problem I see is that any analysis is never on the facts of a situation, but rather on the statements and responses elicited in the investigation conducted. The association found might then relate only to such statements and responses rather than to true situations. Thus, whatever may affect those statements could give rise to the false appearance of associations.

In a report alluded to by Layard, and on which I have elsewhere commented, it was found that when information about smoking at home by the father was elicited from adult offspring, an apparent strong ETS effect arose. But the responses by persons whose mothers developed lung cancer are just not comparable to those from control persons.

One particular situation had made me mindful of this—that of the association between Reye's syndrome and the use of aspirin. Aside from any questions about comparability of the medical situation in Reye's syndrome cases and in control children, it occurred to me that the responses by mothers could have been non-comparable. In one instance, a distraught mother of a Reye's syndrome case is being asked on the spot to identify what medications she may have administered to her child—she could well give a generic reply, "aspirin." The mother of a control child, with favorable outcome, will provide answers in a more relaxed setting and only some time later. I know from my own experience that there are situations in which one just cannot give sensible replies.

Dr. Layard alludes, citing Peter Lee, to the problem of misclassification. But to me, the issue is not simply misclassification, but rather one of not using the right study cohort. A study should properly be conducted, say, among non-smoking wives, differentiating alternatively between those married to smoking or to non-smoking husbands.

Misclassification could occur at this level. But if the apparent cohort of non-smoking wives includes actual smoking wives, that would be "contamination" which, because of the correlation between smoking habits of husband and wife, could give rise to a seeming ETS effect.

In certain situations, respondents may feel it incumbent on themselves to give the "correct" answer in a situation, not the completely truthful answer. That may well have been operative in Hirayama's Japan study, with "non-smoker" perceived as the correct answer for women. But even if Hirayama had elicited truthful answers, the long duration of his study would have militated against the propriety of his analysis. Initially, non-smoking women could have become smokers, and more likely so if the husband was a smoker.

Linda Koo and associates are cited by Dr. Layard as showing that wives of non-smoking husbands had "healthier" lifestyles than wives of smoking husbands. This accords with other studies that have showed smoking rates to be highest in families where the husband was of low socio-economic status, or even unemployed. To the extent that morbidities and even other adverse health effects could be correlates of low income or low socio-economic status, there would be seeming association of these effects with ETS.

Among the studies listed by Dr. Layard is that by Shimizu et al., which showed a relative risk of 1.10 for ETS, presumably non-significant. But, curiously, the ETS effect was most pronounced when the active smoker in the home was either the woman's own mother or even her father-in-law. If this indicated that the family was doubled-up, that too would be suggestive of lower socio-economic status.

It is because of the biases in many individual epidemiologic studies on lung cancer and ETS that collectively, and sometimes even individually, those studies give rise to an apparent association of lung cancer with ETS.

Francis Roe: In his contribution Dr. Layard has analyzed such facts as there are in a way that in my view is both informative and open-minded. Rather than go over the same ground again I propose in this short presentation to do no more than expand on a few of the matters that he raised. My basic proposition, with tongue only partially in cheek, is that "the model has no clothes."

Anyone who is mindful of the welter of really serious health and environmental problems with which mankind is faced must surely be amazed, if not disgusted, by the huge effort and resources that have been and are being devoted to trying to distinguish between "a very low cancer risk" and "no cancer risk" from ETS. Eminent statisticians such as Nathan Mantel (Mantel, N. (1987). Lung cancer and passive smoking. *Brit. Med. J.* 294:440) have repeatedly stated that epidemiology is too blunt a tool to make such a distinction where relative risks are less than 2. Obviously there has to be another attraction in continuing with such research. Can it be that nakedness is attracting the wrong sort of people to the fashion show?

For a subject to merit serious and continuing discussion as distinct from immediate but short-lived interest, it has to be dressed in good quality fabrics that have been expertly tailored. This has not been and cannot be done in the case of the ETS and cancer risk since the fabrics, in terms of accurate exposure data over adequately long periods and in terms of accuracy of diagnosis, are not available. Furthermore, because of the impossibility of controlling for all the important confounding variables and of collecting data about exposure to them in an unbiased way, there is no possibility of expert tailoring by epidemiologists. It is for these reasons that ETS and cancer risk is like a more or less naked model at a fashion show.

Most of the seemingly endless succession of inconclusive papers aimed at seeing if there is a relationship between spouses' smoking habits and lung cancer risk end with the investigators expressing the view that "more research will be needed before firm conclusions can be reached." A more sound conclusion would be that no further research of this kind is warranted because of the impossibility of collecting either accurate exposure data over an adequate time period or accurate diagnostic data based on 100% necropsy rates. Clearly our model is destined never to wear fine clothes. Hopefully, as the attractions of her nakedness diminish with age so will the frequencies of her appearance in the fashion show.

Sooner rather than later not only will preoccupation with things such as the greenhouse effect, gaps in the ozone layer, AIDS, societal hard drug problems, computer-based intrusion into privacy and computer fraud take over from the borderline issues such as ETS and cancer risk. Indeed, those who keep this pot boiling now may well be accused of having got their priorities wrong and having thereby delayed progress towards solving much more serious problems.

Even under conditions of very heavy exposure of humans to potent carcinogens (e.g., as has happened in the past in certain occupations), it is unusual to find examples of cause and effect relationships where the interval between the start of exposure and the diagnosis of cancer is less than ten years. Latent intervals are much more often on the order of 20–50 years. From animal studies it is clear that dose determines not only the incidence of cancer but also the length of the period between first exposure and onset (Druckrey, H. (1967). Quantitative aspects in chemical carcinogenesis. In Rene Truhaut (ed.) *Potential carcinogenic hazards from drugs.* UICC Monograph Series Vol. 7, pp 60–78). Common sense dictates that ETS, if it is carcinogenic at all, cannot be more than very weakly active in this respect. It follows that, for any epidemiological study to have a real chance of throwing useful light on the subject, exposure data will need to be collected for periods of up to 20–50 years prior to the point at which one compares cancer incidence in exposed and unexposed individuals. In this regard, none of the reported studies are adequate and even the prospective studies starting at the age of about 40 may lack information that is highly relevant to exposure earlier in life.

Forty years ago in Britain and in many other industrialized countries, outdoor air pollution was a major problem and a major cause of chronic bronchitis and emphysema. Many studies at that time revealed differences between urban and rural lung cancer death rates ranging upwards from about 1.5 (Curwen, M.P., E.L. Kennaway, and N.M. Kennaway (1954). The incidence of cancer of the lung and larynx in urban and rural districts. *Brit. J. Cancer* 8:181–198. Royal College of Physicians (1970). *Air pollution and health.* pp 1–80). We ourselves quite readily produced skin tumours in mice by applying acetone-soluble extracts of airborne particulates collected over St. Bartholomew's Hospital in London (Roe, F.J.C. and F. Kearns (1967). Comparison of carcinogenicity of tobacco smoke condensate and particulate air pollutants and a demonstration that their effects may be additive. *Alkylierend wirkende Verbindungen*, Second Conference on Tobacco Research, Freiburg, pp 110–111.). Hopefully this problem has receded, although possible lung cancer risk from diesel exhaust fumes is presently a matter for considerable concern (Albert, R.E. and C. Chen (1986). U.S. EPA diesel studies on inhalation hazards. In: N Ishinishi, A. Koizumi, R.O. McClellan and W. Stober (eds.) *Carcinogenic and mutagenic effects of diesel engine exhaust.* pp 411–419).

The point I wish to make is that laboratory studies involving the exposure of animals to carcinogens indicate quite clearly that damage done to the lungs by carcinogenic industrial air pollutants during childhood is likely to have an indelible influence on the risk of developing lung cancer during later life. The same is, of course, true for exposure to other inhalable carcinogens (e.g., radon).

The importance of exposures during the first 10–30 years of life in relation to subsequent lung cancer risk is powerfully illustrated by observations on migrants from Britain to countries that lack substantial industrial air pollution. Such migrants have been found to have a higher risk of developing lung cancer than comparable members of the indigenous population after standardization for personal smoking habits (Roe, F.J.C. and M.A. Walters (1965). Some unsolved problems in lung cancer etiology. *Progr. Exp. Tumor Res* 6:126–227). Obviously, characterization of exposure to ETS based mainly on questionnaire data concerning personal and spouse's smoking habits during adult life falls ridiculously short of what is needed. Further, none of the prospective studies of Hirayama (1981, 1984), Garfinkel (1981) and Gillis et al. (1984) were prospective in respect of potentially important exposures during childhood and early adult life.

It also is apparent that some epidemiologists have little idea of the frailty of medical diagnostic data. Indeed some go so far as to say that inaccuracy of diagnosis only gives rise to false positive associations if bias is involved. As a pathologist I doubt whether this argument really holds good under conditions of extreme variability of diagnostic criteria and of high levels of inaccuracy. Or to put the point in a different way, I doubt whether one could expect to identify all the sources of bias under actual field conditions.

Adenocarcinomas of similar microscopic appearance may arise in many different sites in the body. In women, the breast, ovary, uterus and colon are common sites. All these tumours commonly metastasize to the lungs. The pathologist presented with a biopsy sample of adenocarcinomatous tissue obtained during bronchoscopy is wholly unable to tell the physician/surgeon whether the neoplasm arose primarily in the lung or whether it metastasized from another body site.

None of the epidemiological studies aimed at seeing if exposure to ETS increases lung cancer risk is based 100% on diagnoses made in surgical resection or necropsy specimens. As a consequence, the scope for inaccuracy of diagnosis of lung cancer in many of the studies is enormous. Of particular concern in this regard is the study of Hirayama (1981; 1984). Hirayama relied on death certificate data for the diagnosis of lung cancer while in only 21 of his 200 lung cancer subjects was a necropsy carried out.

A glance at necropsy rates in different countries as reported in the 1988 WHO World Health Statistics Annual shows, first, that necropsy rates are especially low in Japan and secondly that in no country are they high enough for one to be able to base a large epidemiological study on diagnostic data for primary lung cancer established by necropsy.

However, even these rates are misleading insofar as many of the necropsies shown were undertaken merely to establish accidental death or lack of foul play. In other respects such necropsies are often rather superficial in nature so that distinctions between primary and secondary adenocarcinoma of the lung would not necessarily come to light. Generally speaking, persons who are known to have advanced cancer before they die are not subjected to necropsy since the precise site of the primary cancer is considered to be of little more than academic interest in such cases.

In addition to the factors discussed by Dr. Layard, two others need to be considered. First, with the relevant experts agreed that exposure to radon or its daughters in the home is likely to be responsible for thousands of deaths from lung cancer in the USA (National Research Council Committee on the Biological Effects of Ionizing Radiations. *Health risks of radon and other internally deposited alpha emitters. Nat. Acad. Press,* Washington DC, 1988) and Britain (Clarke, R.H. and T.R.E. Southwood (1989). Risks from ionizing radiation. *Nature* 338:197–198), it would be irresponsible to embark on yet further epidemiological studies aimed at assessing lung cancer risk from ETS without attempting to control for exposure to radon. Second, the recent publication by Holst et al. (Holst, P.A. (1988). For debate: Pet birds as an independent risk factor for lung cancer. *Brit. Med. J.* 297:1319–1321) of data suggesting a 6–7-fold increased lung cancer risk associated with the keeping of pet birds in the home after standardizing for smoking habits points to another variable which in future will need to be taken into account. In the case of radon, there is already enough background information to be sure that there really is a lung cancer risk. In the case of the study by Holst et al., the data seem to be sound. However, confirmation in a further larger scale study is needed.

I would offer the following observations, then, in conclusion:

1. Epidemiology is too blunt a tool to distinguish between 'very low risk' and 'no risk' of lung cancer from ETS.
2. One would need to have reliable data for exposure to ETS, mainstream tobacco smoke and numerous other factors (asbestos, radon, urban air pollution, diesel fumes, pet birds, etc.) *from childhood onwards* before one could make epidemiology into a sharper tool.
3. Also one would need to have far more reliable cancer diagnostic data than are presently available.
4. Since there is no prospect of achieving either of these conditions, it is probably morally wrong to devote further resources to research in this area while much more serious threats to human health, society and the environment from other causes are looming larger by the day.
5. Epidemiological studies of the possible association between ETS and lung cancer are like a model for whom there is no prospect of ever being dressed in fine clothes. Her nakedness is bound to pall sooner or later.

Alain Viala: I have five comments to make.

First, studies on smoking have focused on several kinds of cancer. Are they all relevant to ETS?

Second, what compounds should we consider in ETS studies? Studies on ETS have focused on polycyclic aromatic hydrocarbons, terpenes, phenolic compounds, hydroxides and peroxides, nitrosamines, radioactive elements, arsenic, cadmium, cotinine as a metabolite of nicotine, formaldehyde, acrolein, benzene and so on. My question is, must we determine the existence and concentrations of all these compounds in ETS studies? It may depend on the type of cancer being investigated. For example, nitrosamines may be relevant to a study of bladder cancer. Such decisions will be necessary because it will be difficult in practice to determine the concentration of all compounds in ETS.

Third, I think we must try to establish a reliable relationship between nicotine concentration in air and the sum of cotinine plus nicotine, and even all free and conjugated metabolites in urine. This may help to determine true exposure levels of nonsmokers to ETS in future epidemiologic studies.

Fourth, is there a dose-effect relationship for the compounds we consider in ETS studies?

Fifth, many factors must be considered in future epidemiologic studies to enable the classification of the subjects as smokers, non-smokers or never smokers. Questionnaires must be improved; information must be checked. The study must consider occupational exposures other than smoking, outdoor and indoor exposures from air pollutants, heating and cooking at home, radon, formaldehyde, acrolein, asbestos and so on. The importance of diet, social and general health conditions, genetic factors, consumption of alcohol, drugs, narcotics, and so on are also relevant. Reliable histopathological determination of the types of cancer must be made, in order to assure accurate diagnosis of primary lung cancer. The study must also utilize environmental and biological markers to ensure accurate measurement. Finally, a standardized methodology should be applied in epidemiologic studies on ETS.

Joseph Wu: We have concluded the presentation and a discussion on the subject of lung and other cancers. We have some time for questions and answers.

Alan Gross: I'm from the medical university of South Carolina in Charleston, home of Hurricane Hugo. I wanted to make some comments about meta-analysis because I find that methodology to be one of the most troubling. Dr. Layard did an excellent job of pointing out why the NRC/NAS meta-analysis should not have been done. I'm in total agreement with that because of all the confounding issues involved. However, even if one were to accept meta-analysis as being an appropriate tool in this instance, it struck me as rather strange that the estimate that would be used in making the assessments that were made in the NRC report would be the point estimate as opposed to the lower end of the confidence interval. This would result in extremely different conclusions. In fact, using this method, one might even be able to show that ETS exposure is protective. That is a possible conclusion. Another point about the NRC/NAS meta-analysis is it seems strange that the NRC would accept such a meta-analysis when another governmental agency, the Food and Drug Administration, is very rigorous when they're dealing with the drug companies about what kind of meta-analysis they will accept. They have to be done to very stringent specifications. So it seems that a little bit of governmental inconsistency exists here.

James Kilpatrick: May I respond to that? I think we have to face the fact that these meta-analyses exist and are in the literature and there's no use, in my view, saying they shouldn't have been done. I think that what we need to do is to do them better, trying to take into account the possible sources of bias and show that the upper and lower band are so far apart that in fact these meta-analyses have no information in them.

Peter Lee: I would like to offer some additional comments on the Sandler studies, which I think are extremely poor. One of the problems with them is that they use friends and acquaintances of the patients. Now that, in my view, is not an acceptable method of selecting a control population. They also failed to take into account the confounding variables that were mentioned by Dr. Layard.

I just think the results were so much waste paper. I mean they have one study in which they look at colon cancer and claim an association between this and ETS. Now there have been a whole lot of studies in the literature looking at colon cancer in active smoking and they've been fairly universal in showing that colon cancer isn't related to smoking at all. So really, I mean the results just seem to me to have no meaning.

Dr. Layard also mentioned at the beginning of his talk that none of the analyses of lung cancer and ETS showed a significant trend. I produced a similar table to his Table 6–1 for something else I was doing recently. I found six study reports from the literature having a significant trend. I'm not saying this significant trend means a significant causal effect. I just wonder if he meant something different than I do with respect to a "trend."

I have one more point before you answer that. Dr. Layard said at the start of his talk that there are five conditions you must have in order to conclude that an epidemiological study is valid. But even when all of them were satisfied, you still needed to know about biological mechanisms and have biological plausibility. Well, although again this isn't particularly relevant to ETS, I'm not actually sure that is true. I think you need to take into account biological plausibility of marginal cases. But if, for example, you found that workers in four countries in a particular factory all had a vastly increased risk of some cancer that was very rare otherwise, I don't think you'd need to know about biological mechanism in order to infer causal effect.

Maxwell Layard: The question about trend is very simply answered. What I said was that non-exposed persons should not be considered when evaluating those responses and I think the trends that you mentioned did include the non-exposed persons. If, among exposed persons, the effect tends to increase with increasing dose, then this provides some support for the idea of a causal mechanism. But you may see elevated responses at all dose levels without seeing an increasing trend among the exposed only. This could reflect a spurious association due to some confounding or bias. That was my point about no significant dose response. I did not include the non-exposed persons.

On your other point about the criteria, I think I would agree with you when there is such overwhelming evidence. It may in some cases be unnecessary to elucidate a biological mechanism. But I don't think that's the case in every situation. In some infectious disease situations, for example, you may not know the factor involved but it's definitely clear that there's only one mechanism operating. But in a very weak association such as chronic disease like cancer, I think it's necessary to have some corroboration from the biology.

Alan Done: All of the epidemiologic studies of ETS and lung cancer are really quite small as epidemiologic studies go. Has anyone gone to the trouble of doing power calculations to see whether any of them had an eighty or maybe a ninety-five percent chance of showing a difference and failed to do so, so that it could truly be called negative and not just inconclusive?

James Kilpatrick: That is a point that I noted in Dr. Layard's paper that I didn't comment on. He uses the term "negative" rather than "null." Negative to me implies significantly less than one—just as positive would imply significantly greater than one. But I think null would have been a better choice match.

Maxwell Layard: I agree. I just want to say that in answer to the question that I have not myself done many power calculations. I did do one on bladder cancer because of criticism in that particular instance. I did do a couple of calculations and I found that at least in one case, the power of seeing a moderate effect was reasonably high, say sixty percent or something of that order. I think it would be interesting to do more power calculations. But I'm not doing them, at this point.

Since it's relevant, I'd like to say something about Nathan Mantel's comment on power—that he did not think it was surprising to see non-significant effects of these studies because they are so small and have such low power. I agree with that. The fact is, however, that the data we have are these studies, they are small, and even if they have little power, that simply means that there's not much information. So we really do not have much information from these studies on the effect in question.

Nathan Mantel: But that is just why we can't use meta-analysis to let all these weak studies reinforce each other.

David Weeks: I'd like to make a comment directed at this panel from a very personal view point and I want to thank Dr. Roe particularly for kind of keying me to it. We seem to have gone philosophically afield in some of Dr. Roe's comments. I wish to thank both him and Dr. Mantel for bringing me back into focus. I'm a practicing clinician. I am in the business of evaluating risk assessment and then planning risk intervention. I'm also a consultant. I have to evaluate risk assessment and analysis that comes down from the towers. To me, the microcosm of ETS has been brought into focus here in less than a day as a problem of bad science. I think we're discussing a lot of bad science and a lot of bad dissemination of information about it. As a consequence, public policy is getting bad advice. I just personally want to make that comment.

Peter Atteslander: I was especially glad to hear the remarks of Dr. Mantel on the sometimes naive use of questionnaires. Indeed we do not know what distortions there are, especially in the study of Hirayama. But very often, if you are able to see an instrument that was used, it simply does not warrant statistical processing afterwards. We should really be very careful in using survey methods in this field. I can give you an example that is two or three weeks old, in a field that does a lot of research with questionnaires—namely mass media consumption. In France, there is a sample now with an instrument—surveying people behind a screen. The error is not three or four percent but thirty percent. So the interviewed people had a distortion of thirty percent as regarding what has actually been recorded.

Jarnail Singh: I have one comment. ETS adds up to only fifteen percent of total RSP in the air. Thus, eighty-five percent of the RSP in many locations is something other than ETS. So we need to keep that in mind when we are doing all the studies. We are concentrating only on fifteen percent.

Part IV

8

Environmental Tobacco Smoke and Cardiovascular Disease: A Critique of the Epidemiological Literature and Recommendations for Future Research

Lawrence M. Wexler, Ph.D.
New York Medical College

This paper evaluates the current epidemiological literature examining the possible relationship between exposure to environmental tobacco smoke ("ETS") and cardiovascular disease. Based on the available evidence, it is this author's opinion that it has not been demonstrated that exposure to ETS increases the risk of cardiovascular disease. This paper evaluates seven studies that examine this issue (table 8–1). Five of the studies are prospective in nature, one is a case-control design (retrospective), and one is an experimental design examining the biological plausibility of a link between ETS and cardiovascular disease.

Several key points of epidemiology need to be mentioned here, and should be kept in mind when reading the critiques of the seven studies. To prove causality five criteria need to be met. The first relates to the strength of the association. There are three elements to this criterion. First, there must be a statistically significant increase in the incidence of the disease in the exposed population compared with the non-exposed population. Second, for the association to be regarded as meaningful, a relative risk of 2.0 or greater is generally considered necessary. Third, the association should also be dose dependent, i.e., higher doses are associated with higher incidence of disease.

The second point is that consistency of the association must exist among the relevant studies. This means that similar rates of disease must occur at different times and places, under comparable study designs.

A third point deals with the temporal aspect of the association. This means that exposure to ETS should have occurred at a reasonable time before the onset of disease, given what is known about how long it takes for cardiovascular disease to develop.

A fourth point is specificity of the association. With ETS, this means that exposure to ETS must be shown to be associated with cardiovascular disease while controlling for all confounding variables.

Table 8–1
Environmental Tobacco Smoke and Cardiovascular Disease

	Design	*Findings*	*Methodological Problems*
1. Hirayama (1981, 1984)	Sixteen year prospective study of nonsmoking Japanese women classified at start of follow-up by the smoking status of their husbands. 142,857 women 40 and over (91,540 nonsmoking wives).	1. Relative risk of 1.31 for ischemic heart disease for nonsmoking women whose husbands smoked > 19 cigarettes per day compared with nonsmoking women whose husbands did not smoke. 2. Mantel-Haenszel significant at $p < .019$, 1984. 3. "Passive smoking did not seem to increase the risk of developing . . . ischemic heart disease." –Hirayama, 1981.	1. Potential biases. 2. Misclassification o smokers and non-smokers. 3. Misclassification o dose response (number of cigaret smoked per day). 4. Looked at spouse exposure only, not workplace. 5. No control for indoor air pollutio e.g., cooking with kerosene stoves. 6. Not representative Japanese population—only agriculture represented. 7. Non-random sam of prefectures—on a convenience sample.
2. Garland (1985)	Prospective—enrolled 82% of adults ages 50–79 between 1972–1974 in a community in San Diego. Blood pressure and plasma cholesterol measured at entry; interviewed all cohort of 695 current married non-smoking women free of heart disease; ten year follow-up.	1. Elevated cardiac disease deaths in non-smoking women, ages 50–79, whose husbands were former or current smokers. 2. 19 deaths from ischemic heart disease after ten years.	1. Some misgrouping wives of former smoker were grouped with wive of current smoker 2. Small sample sizes value may be inappropriate bas on Mantel-Haensz and may only be a approximation; st p was only $p < .1$ 3. 15 of 19 deaths occurred in nonsmoking wom married to former smokers—puzzlin results.
3. Gillis (1989)	Two urban communities in Scotland. Ten year follow-up report. 8,128 adults ages 45–64.	Non-smokers exposed to cigarette smoke in their homes had a slightly higher rate of myocardial infarction than those unexposed.	1. Small sample size. 2. Few of the results were statistically significant.

ıble 8–1 continued

	Design	Findings	Methodological Problems
Svendsen (1987)	1. Multiple Risk Factor Intervention Trial (MRFIT). 2. Randomized primary prevention trial designed to test the effect of a multifactor intervention program on mortality from coronary heart disease in men with previous cardiac episodes. 3. Men were chosen for participation if they had at least two of three risk factors for heart disease (smoking, high cholesterol levels, high blood pressure).	1. No difference between smoking wives and nonsmoking wives for non-smoking men for blood pressure or cholesterol. 2. Roughly two-fold increase in risk of CHD mortality and morbidity among nonsmoking men exposed to ETS of wives.	1. Sample size small. 2. Results—not statistically significant.
Helsing 1988)	1. Twelve year study executed in Washington County, Maryland. 2. July, 1963 census of 91,909 people. 3. Whites only. 4. Death certificates collected from July, 1963 through July, 1975. 5. Non-smokers, ages 25 and over. 6. 4,162 men and 14,873 women.	1. Death rates from arteriosclerotic heart disease were higher among men (Relative risk = 1.31) and women (relative risk = 1.24) who lived with smokers in 1963, after adjustment for age, marital status, years of schooling, and quality of housing index. 2. For women, relative risk increased significantly ($p < .005$) for dose response (increasing levels of exposure). 3. Men—little evidence of a dose response relationship.	1. Only smoking data collected on every person was in 1963. 2. No measurement of changes in smoking habits. 3. No data on household changes from 1963–1975. 4. Very little other risk factor data for heart disease. 5. No diet, exercise, blood pressure, cholesterol data, or ETS exposure out of home.

Table 8–1 continued

	Design	*Findings*	*Methodological Problems*
6. Lee (1986)	Case-control.	Ischemic heart disease cases and controls did not show a statistically significant difference in their exposure to involuntary smoking, based on smoking habits of spouses or on an index accounting for exposure at home, at work, and during travel and leisure.	Case-control methodological issues
7. Aronow (1978)	Experimental design.	ETS aggravates angina pectoris.	1. Endpoint of angina based on subjective evaluation. 2. Stress not controlled for.

The fifth point is that there must be biological plausibility. This means that under experimental conditions exposure to the pertinent substance (or similar substances) must be shown to cause biological changes that can lead to the disease in question.

All five conditions must be met for causality to be established. We will return to these points at the end of the paper, when we examine recommendations for future research.

I. Summary of Epidemiological Literature

A. Prospective Studies

1. Hirayama. Hirayama (1984) conducted a prospective cohort study in 29 health center districts in six prefectures in Japan between January 1966 and December 1981. In total, 265,118 adults (122,261 men and 142,857 women) aged 40 years and over were followed. Ninety-five percent of the census population was interviewed between October and December 1965. Also, Hirayama established a record linkage system under which he gathered and analyzed death certificates, risk factor records, and a residence list obtained by an annual census. Questions on smoking habits were asked independently of husbands and wives at the beginning of the study. There were 91,540 nonsmoking married women whose husbands' smoking habits were reported by questionnaire.

In 1981, Hirayama (1981) concluded that "husbands' smoking habits seemed to have no effect on their non-smoking wives' risk of developing ischemic heart disease." Hirayama reported age/occupation standardized risk ratios for ischemic heart disease in non-smoking women by smoking habit of husband. When the husband was a non-smoker, the relative risk was 1.0. When the husband was an ex-smoker or smoked 1–19 cigarettes per day, the relative risk was .97. When the husband smoked 20 or more cigarettes/day, the relative risk was 1.03, and the reported p value was not significant at 0.393.

Hirayama (1984), in a 1984 paper, reported an elevated risk of ischemic heart disease morbidity based on further analyses. The relative risk for non-smoking married women for husbands who were non-smokers was 1.0; for husbands who were ex-smokers or smoked 1–19 cigarettes/day the relative risk was 1.10; and for husbands who smoked 20 or more cigarettes per day, the relative risk was 1.31, with a 90% confidence interval of 1.06 to 1.63. The reported p value was significant at .019.

Hirayama's study has several major methodological problems. The first problem is potential misclassification of smokers and non-smokers. Many of the wives who stated they were non-smokers may in fact be ex-smokers or even current smokers, and thus likely to have had or continue to have direct (as opposed to indirect) exposure to cigarette smoke.

The second problem is that Hirayama's study included a disproportionate number of women of lower socioeconomic status. In Japan, these women live in much closer proximity to their cooking quarters and may have more exposure to charcoal or kerosene stoves than women of higher socioeconomic status. This exposure has been associated with lung cancer in women in Hong Kong. Women in Japan of a higher socioeconomic status live farther away from their kitchens and are more likely to use electric burners. The Hirayama study failed to control for these confounding variables, which may be associated with ischemic heart disease.

A third problem is the misclassification of dose response. Ex-smoking husbands were lumped with current cigarette smokers of 1–19 cigarettes/day. Because ex-smokers are very different in their cigarette exposure rates and lifestyles than smokers of 1–19 cigarettes/day, this could skew the data.

A fourth problem is that Hirayama only examined the exposure of the wife in the context of the husband's cigarette smoking behavior. No attempt was made to quantify any exposure to ETS outside of the home, such as in the workplace.

A fifth problem is that the Hirayama study was not representative of Japanese society but only of an agriculturally based population, which is not typical for Japan. In addition, six prefectures were chosen to participate in the study based on the fact that they appear to have had the best conditions for collecting data. Hence, random sampling was not used.

A sixth problem is that the Hirayama study did not control for other risk factors associated with cardiovascular disease, i.e., systolic blood pressure and plasma cholesterol.

Although the Hirayama study offers a large prospective cohort to examine the relationship between presumed exposure to environmental tobacco smoke and ischemic heart disease, one can not draw definitive conclusions because of the aforementioned methodological problems.

2. Garland. Garland (1985) conducted a prospective cohort study commencing in 1972–1974 in Rancho Bernardo, a white middle-class suburb of San Diego, California. The entire adult population was invited to participate, of which 82% agreed. The authors report that the respondents were representative of the total population with regard to age and sex.

All respondents were administered a standardized inventory, including questions about age, cigarette smoking, history of past hospitalizations for heart attack, heart failure or stroke, and number of years married. Cigarette smoking was assessed as current, former or never. Only current smokers were asked the number of cigarettes they smoked per day. No data were obtained for duration of smoking. In addition, blood pressure and plasma cholesterol were obtained.

An annual mailing was utilized to determine vital status for the next ten years. Death certificates were obtained for all decedents. Diagnosis of ischemic heart disease was validated by interviews with family and physicians, and/or examination of hospital records, for 85% of the deceased group.

Six hundred ninety-five (695) currently married nonsmoking women, ages 50–79, with no previous history of heart disease or stroke were followed based on their husband's self-reported smoking status in 1972–1974.

The results, after adjusting for age, systolic blood pressure, total plasma cholesterol, obesity index and years of marriage gave a relative risk of 14.9 of deaths from ischemic heart disease for women married to current or former smokers at entry compared with women married to never smokers. The p value was not significant, $p \leq .10$.

Important methodological problems exist with the Garland study. The first is that Garland later reported a corrected relative risk of 2.7 (not 14.9 as reported in the 1985 publication). The p value is still $< .10$ and not significant.

The second problem is that after ten years of follow-up, only 19 deaths from ischemic heart disease occurred. This small sample size is compounded by the fact that 15 of the 19 deaths occurred in nonsmoking women married to husbands who had stopped smoking at entry. Without more detailed characterization of these women's exposure to ETS, it is difficult to show an association between ETS and ischemic heart disease. As the study did not ascertain number of cigarettes smoked per day in former smokers, it is not possible to measure any sustained effects of ETS in this former smoking group.

Another methodological problem is that wives of former smokers were grouped with wives of current smokers, and it is difficult to determine the exact effect of ETS for this former smoking group.

Although the Garland study does make an attempt in a prospective cohort study to measure the effects of possible exposure to ETS on ischemic heart disease, and does control for important cardiovascular confounders, such as obesity, blood pressure and cholesterol, the small sample size and the lack of adequate measurement of ETS in a former cigarette smoking group make the results only suggestive and certainly not definitive.

3. Gillis. The Gillis study (1989) consists of a prospective cohort comprised of men and women aged 45–64 years who resided in two towns, Renfrew and Paisley, in the west of Scotland, between 1972 and 1976. Residents (15,399) of these two towns who met the age and residency criteria (an 80% response) agreed to participate; 7,997 were subjected to a cardiorespiratory screening examination, a self-administered questionnaire that included questions on smoking behavior. The eventual sample was comprised of 3,960 men and 4,037 women where it was possible to study varying exposures to tobacco smoke by cohabitees. Four groups were established for analysis purposes:

1. Control—neither the case nor anyone living at the same address had ever smoked.
2. Presumed ETS exposure in the home—the case had never smoked but lived at the same address as a subject who had smoked.
3. Single smoking—the case was a smoker or an ex-smoker and lived at the same address as a person who had never smoked.
4. Double smoking: the case was a smoker or an ex-smoker who lived at the same address as a subject who was also a smoker or ex-smoker.

Mortality was used as an endpoint and was obtained from the National Health Service. Cardiovascular signs and symptoms were also noted. Data presented were complete through December 1985, for an average follow-up of 11.5 years.

The authors present relative risks and 95% confidence intervals adjusted for age, sex, social class, diastolic blood pressure, serum cholesterol concentration and body mass index. Total mortality for ischemic heart disease was higher among those reportedly exposed to ETS in the home than controls.

Women with ETS exposure in the home were broken into two dose response categories for further analyses. These included: (1) the high exposure group, where the woman's cohabitee smoked 15 or more cigarettes daily, and (2) the low exposure group where the women's cohabitee smoked less than 15 cigarettes daily. Age-adjusted mortality from ischemic heart disease was higher for those in the high exposure category than in the low exposure group.

Relative risk was adjusted for age, sex, social class and cardiovascular variables including diastolic blood pressure, serum cholesterol concentrations and body mass index. Compared with controls, the relative risk was 2.01 for ischemic heart disease and was not significant.

The Gillis paper has several methodological problems. The first is that it does not have sufficient power to demonstrate an association between ETS and ischemic heart disease. The sample size is too small.

A second problem is that the relative risk of 2.01 for ischemic heart disease for non-smokers compared with controls is too similar to the relative risk of 2.27 for active smokers compared with controls to make sense. An explanation for this is not clear, but may be due to small sample size as well.

Potential biases also exist in the Gillis study. One potential bias is that those exposed to ETS within the home may have had higher exposures to ETS outside of the home compared with controls. A second potential bias is misclassification of women as non-smokers when they may be former smokers or current smokers.

Although the Gillis study suggests an association between ETS and cardiovascular mortality in non-smokers, the data lacks any statistical significance. Also, the study reports some confusing and similar relative risks for active and passive smokers, and is confounded by several important methodological biases. This study should be replicated in a much larger study population, with adequate statistical power.

4. Svendsen. Svendsen (1987) reports the results of the Multiple Risk Factor Intervention Trial (MRFIT), conducted from 1973–1982. The trial consisted of men, aged 35–57, recruited from 18 cities in the United States. Males who fell within the upper 10–15% risk score distribution for heart disease, based on an index comprised of serum cholesterol concentration, cigarette smoking and diastolic blood pressure, and free of overt coronary heart disease were randomized to one of two groups: (1) special intervention or (2) usual care. Participants in both groups were seen annually over six to eight years for risk factor measurement and a medical examination. A detailed smoking history was obtained at baseline and at all subsequent annual visits. Cause of death was evaluated by a committee of three cardiologists after examination of death certificates and other medical records.

Fourteen hundred of 12,866 men reported that they had never smoked at entry into the study. Of these 1400, 1,245 were married. Of the later group, 286 were married to women who smoked and 959 were married to women who did not smoke.

The results compared ETS exposed husbands and non-ETS exposed husbands, where the husbands had *never* smoked. None of the endpoints showed statistical significance between the two groups, before or after adjustment for several variables, including age, baseline blood pressure, cholesterol, weight, alcohol consumption and education.

However, within the exposed group, increasing levels of cigarettes smoked daily by the wife had a statistically significant dose response relationship with husbands' CHD deaths. This is technically significant ($p = 0.04$) but is based on only one death in the 1–19 cigarettes smoked/day category.

A second analysis lumped never smoking husbands with ex-smoking husbands, calling these *non-smoking* husbands. This group was then evaluated on the basis of the smoking status of the wife. Non-smoking husbands of smokers did not show a statistically significant result when compared with husbands of non-smoking wives for mortality from CHD ($p = 0.15$) or from CHD itself as an endpoint ($p = .10$).

Several methodological problems exist in the Svendsen report. One problem is possible misclassification of husband's smoking status either at entry or subsequently. A second problem is that the wife's smoking status was based on interviews with the husband, and not on direct questioning of the wife.

There is also an alcohol-related bias, as MRFIT ETS-exposed husbands' had two drinks per week, on average, more than non-ETS exposed husbands, and this alcohol effect could explain the observed statistical significance in dose response.

Finally, by combining ex-smoking husbands with never smokers, Svendsen confounds any past effects of active smoking by the husband with exposure to ETS.

The MRFIT study serves as an exemplary prospective trial for its design and conduct. However, lack of statistical significance, failure to control for several confounding variables (such as alcohol consumption), misclassification, and misgrouping make it difficult to draw any conclusions from the study.

5. Helsing. The Helsing (1988) paper examines death certificates collected from July 1963 through July 1975 for a population living in July 1963 in Washington County, Maryland. This is based on underlying cause of death of arteriosclerotic heart disease including coronary disease (International Classification of Disease [ICD] −420) and other myocardial degeneration (ICD 422). As of July 15, 1963, 98% of the residents were asked questions that included information on sex, age, race, marital status, years of schooling, housing characteristics, information on cigarette, cigar and pipe smoking habits, as well as frequency of church attendance, for each household member aged 16.5 years or older.

Among 22,973 white men and 25,369 white women 25 years of age and older in the 1963 census, 4,162 men and 14,873 women reported that they had never smoked. The 1971 follow-up population was a subset of these numbers: 3,454 men and 12,345 women.

The results showed that death rates from arteriosclerotic heart disease were higher among men (relative risk = 1.31) and women (relative risk = 1.24) who lived with smokers in 1963, after adjustment for age, marital status, years of schooling and quality of housing index. For women, relative risk increased significantly ($p < .005$) with increasing levels of exposure, but for men, there was little evidence of a dose response relationship.

Several methodological problems exist with the Helsing paper. The first major problem is that the only smoking data that was collected on every person was in 1963. Hence, no changes in smoking habits over the 12-year period were ascertained. In addition, no data were collected on other risk factors for heart disease such as diet, exercise, blood pressure and cholesterol. Finally, no ETS exposure outside the home was measured.

B. *Case-Control Study*

1. Lee. The Lee (1986) study is a case control (retrospective) study to evaluate the possible relationship between cigarette smoking and risk of lung cancer, chronic bronchitis, ischemic heart disease and stroke. The original questionnaire was administered in ten hospital regions in England, between 1977 and 1982. Although not recorded initially, ETS exposure data was subsequently collected in 1979 for married patients in the last four regions.

Two hundred cases and 200 matched controls were collected for each sex (male, female) and age (35–44, 45–54, 55–64, and 65–74) grouping to examine the possible relationship between ETS exposure and diagnosis of ischemic heart disease. Also matched were hospital region and, when possible, hospital ward and time of interview.

Ischemic heart disease cases and controls did not show a statistically significant difference in their exposure to ETS, based either on smoking habits of spouses or on an index accounting for exposure at home, at work, and during travel and leisure.

Although the Lee study is one of the few to attempt to examine non-spousal ETS exposure, it raises the general methodological issues that surround retrospective case control studies. In its finding of non-statistical significance for any trends of association between ETS and cardiovascular illness, the Lee paper confirms the need for execution of better controlled prospective trials.

C. *Experimental Design*

1. Aronow. The Aronow (1978) paper describes an experimental design to examine the possible relationship between exposure to ETS and exercise-induced angina in both a well ventilated and an unventilated room.

The design included ten men (eight non-smokers and two smokers) who exercised upright on a bicycle ergometer with a progressive work load until the onset of angina pectoris. Subjects were randomized to three groups: no smoking, smoking in a well ventilated room, or smoking in an unventilated room.

Aronow has suggested that the results of his study demonstrate that, under the conditions of the experiment, ETS exposure causes anginal pain to develop soon after exercise. In addition, the data from the study indicate that exposure to ETS causes an increase in carboxyhemoglobin, more after ETS exposure in an unventilated room than after ETS exposure in a ventilated room.

Several major criticisms of the Aronow study include: (1) the use of subjective pain as an end point without double blinding, (2) a very small sample size that can lead to a large variance based on just one or two subjects changing their responses, (3) problems associated with the Hawthorne effect [subjects tend to produce symptoms suggested to them], and (4) failure to control for stress.

D. *Conclusions*

The Surgeon General's Report of 1986 (1986) examined the studies of Hirayama, Gillis, Garland and Aronow, and concluded that "further studies on the relationship between involuntary smoking and cardiovascular disease are needed in order to determine whether involuntary smoking increases the risk of cardiovascular disease."

The National Research Council (1986) in 1986 reviewed the prospective studies of Garland, Gillis, Hirayama and Svendsen, as well as several experimental designs examining the biological plausibility of the association of ETS and cardiovascular disease, and concluded that:

> 1. No statistically significant effects of ETS exposure on heart rate or blood pressure were found in healthy men, women, and school-aged children during resting conditions. During exercise there is no difference in the cardiovascular changes for men and women between conditions of exposure to ETS and control conditions.
>
> 2. With respect to chronic cardiovascular morbidity and mortality, although biologically plausible, there is no evidence of statistically significant effects due to ETS exposure, apart from the study by Hirayama in Japan.

It is the opinion of this author that none of the studies critiqued in this paper provides any basis for altering the Surgeon General's and NAS's conclusions concerning ETS and cardiovascular disease.

This conclusion is reinforced by the findings of Schieveblein and Richter (1984). They report that, under real-life conditions, persons exposed to ETS inhale only approximately .02 to .01 of the amount of particulate matter taken up by active smokers. Also, nicotine concentration in serum of ETS-exposed individuals is within a range that is barely distinguishable from the background level, and the increase in carboxyhemoglobin rarely exceeds 1%. The authors conclude that exposure to ETS "is not likely to have an effect on the development and progression of CHD."

II. Recommendations for Future Research

To provide meaningful recommendations for future research, it is necessary to evaluate the existing studies of ETS exposure and cardiovascular disease in light of the five criteria for causality discussed at the beginning of this paper.

The NAS concluded that a relationship between ETS exposure and cardiovascular disease is biologically plausible, and each of the studies reviewed in this paper appears to provide an adequate temporal association between ETS exposure (as measured by spousal smoking) and the onset of cardiovascular disease. However, the studies fail to meet one or more of the remaining criteria for causality.

Of the six studies concerning ETS exposure and cardiovascular morbidity and mortality, only two (Hirayama and Helsing) reported statistically significant relative risks for exposed compared to non-exposed populations, and neither study reported a relative risk greater than 2. Hirayama reported a dose dependent relationship but Helsing did not.

None of the studies demonstrate a specificity of association between ETS exposure and cardiovascular disease. Each of the studies fails to control for one or more important confounding variables, including lifestyle, blood pressure, serum cholesterol, obesity and socioeconomic status. None of the studies provides an accurate measurement of ETS exposure. All of the studies suffer from one or more serious methodological problems, including small sample size and possible misclassification of spousal smoking status. These confounding variables and methodological problems also preclude any demonstration of consistency of association among the existing studies.

In view of the inadequacy of existing studies, it is logical to consider whether the Framingham Heart Study might provide an adequate basis for a definitive evaluation of the relationship between ETS exposure and heart disease.

The Framingham Heart Study, initiated during 1948–1950, is comprised of a study cohort from a random subsample of the adult residents of Framingham, Massachusetts, of which 69% responded. No reports on ETS and heart disease have been published under the Study, but spousal smoking habits could be determined from the Study's data base. Although an effort could be made to measure ETS effects on heart disease in the Framingham Study, this would not be likely to provide an adequate basis for a definitive evaluation of ETS and heart disease.

The critical problem is that the Framingham Study does not provide a basis for an accurate measurement of ETS exposure, especially outside of the home. Use of data on spousal smoking habits as a surrogate for ETS exposure has been shown to present serious methodological and other problems in existing studies.

In any event, the recent paper by Seltzer (1989) suggests that the Framingham Study is not likely to show a significant association between ETS exposure and heart disease. Seltzer's paper compares the Surgeon General's statements regarding the association between active smoking and heart disease with the data in the Framingham Study. Seltzer points out that the Framingham data differ from the Surgeon General's conclusions in several important respects:

1. The Surgeon General asserts a four-fold greater CHD incidence in men who are heavy smokers as compared to non-smokers; Framingham reports relative risk ratios less than two.
2. The Surgeon General asserts that cigarette smoking among women has a predictive association with CHD; Framingham finds no such association.
3. The Surgeon General states there is an increase of CHD with increase of duration of smoking; in the Framingham Study, this increase is absent.
4. The Surgeon General claims that rates of CHD eventually are reduced in ex-smokers to those somewhere between smokers and non-smokers, and sometimes, after many years, falling to the level of non-smokers. The Framingham data are surprising in that reductions in CHD among ex-smokers is below levels for never smokers! This suggests that a selection bias may exist.

Given the relatively small effect of active smoking on heart disease reported in the Framingham Study, it appears unlikely that any effect of ETS exposure on heart disease could be measured under that Study.

In view of the lack of adequate existing data, future studies need to be performed that carefully examine the relationship between exposure to ETS and cardiovascular disease. It is the hope of this author that the critiques presented in this paper, examining many of the methodological problems associated with existing ETS epidemiological studies, will be of use to well-trained scientists. Familiarity with the five key points of causality in epidemiology is critical in designing studies that can clearly show whether any association exists between exposure to ETS and cardiovascular disease.

Based on the analysis in this paper, a meaningful future study should contain at least the following elements:

1. A representative sample large enough to yield adequate statistical power.
2. A design that provides control for important confounding variables, in-

cluding blood pressure, diet, alcohol consumption, plasma cholesterol, body weight, sex, socioeconomic status and exposure to environmental substances other than ETS.

3. A mechanism for accurate measurement of ETS exposure, including exposure outside the home, and adequate follow-up of exposure status.
4. A prospective design specifically developed to satisfy the criteria for causality.

References

Aronow, W.S. (1978). Effects of passive smoking on angina pectoris. *New England Journal of Medicine* 299(1)21–24.

Environmental Tobacco Smoke - Measuring Exposures and Assessing Health Effects, National Research Council, National Academy Press, Washington, D.C., 1986.

Garland, C. et. al. (1985). Effects of passive smoking on ischemic Heart disease mortality of non-smokers. *American Journal of Epidemiology* 121(5).

Helsing, K.J., D.P. Sandler, G.W. Comstock, and E. Chee, (1988). Heart disease mortality in non-smokers living with smokers. *American Journal of Epidemiology* 127(5).

Hirayama, T. (1984). Lung cancer in Japan: Effects of nutrition and passive smoking. *Lung Cancer: Causes and Prevention.* Verlag Chemie International, Inc.

Hirayama, T. (1981). Non-Smoking wives of heavy smokers have a higher risk of lung cancer: a study from Japan. *British Medical Journal* 282:183–185.

Hole, D.J., C.R. Gillis et. al. (1989). Passive smoking and cardiorespiratory health in a general population in the west of Scotland. *British Medical Journal* 299:423–427.

Lee, P.N., J. Chamberlain, and M.R. Alderson, (1986). Relationship of passive smoking to risk of lung cancer and other smoking-associated diseases. *British Journal of Cancer* 54:97–105.

Schievelbein, H. and F. Richter (1984). The influence of passive smoking on the cardiovascular system. *Prevention Medicine,* 13:626–644.

Seltzer, C. (1989). Framingham study data and established wisdom about cigarette smoking and coronary disease. *Journal of Clinical Epidemiology* 42(8):743–750.

Surgeon General's Report (1986). *The Health Consequences of Involuntary Smoking.* U.S. Department of Health and Human Services.

Svendsen, K.H., Lewis H. Kuller et. al. (1987). Effects of passive smoking in the multiple risk factor intervention trial. *American Journal of Epidemiology* 126(5).

9 Panel Discussion on Cardiovascular Disease

Joseph Wu: This paper is now open for discussion. Would the discussants please proceed to the desk.

We'll have the first comment by Dr. Alan Armitage.

Alan Armitage: I would like to congratulate Dr. Wexler on his succinct presentation and to say that I agree with nearly everything that he has said. There's really not too much data and with six discussants all to say their bit, I will be selective in what I say and confine my comments to essentially pharmacological matters. The big question, of course, is whether exposure to ETS represents a health risk for the development of coronary artery disease. We need to remember that CHD is, of course, a common cause of death among nonsmokers. Moreover, although the public health body considers there to be a causal relationship between active cigarette smoking and development of CHD, Seltzer in particular has pointed out much that is not wholly consistent with such a story.

Dr. Wexler referred to five criteria that need to be considered in reviewing the ETS cardiovascular data. It is a good discipline to have this checklist approach and in addition, particularly when a situation is not clear cut, as is the case for ETS and cardiovascular disease, the sensitive, unbiased reviewer needs to have a common-sense "feel for the data."

There are three points I would like to add to the debate about biological plausibility.

First, the question of dosimetry is of particular interest to me because I am a pharmacologist. As we were told this morning, the effective dose of an ETS exposed individual is a function of the dynamic integration of concentration in various environments throughout the day and the time the nonsmoker spends in these environments. Assessing accurate dosage under real life conditions is therefore extremely difficult. Frankly, in many epidemiological studies, the assessment is no more than anecdotal. Merely knowing something about the spouse's or partner's smoking habits is not enough.

Since we are considering possible effects of ETS on the cardiovascular system, we must be concerned with systemic absorption rather than mere deposition. An individual exposed to the diluted smoke which is ETS cannot and does not absorb tobacco constituents such as nicotine and carbon monoxide to any significant degree, or any other putative cardiovascular toxicant like nitrogen dioxide. Thus, cotinine levels in biological fluids, which are generally considered to be a reasonable measurement of nicotine absorption of nonsmokers exposed to ETS, are approximately one percent of those measured in active smokers.

Now, in many studies the association between active smoking and CHD is much weaker, or even nonexistent, in female smokers than in male smokers. If in female active smokers an effect of smoking on the development of CHD cannot be convincingly demonstrated, I find it difficult to believe that such an effect is possible in female nonsmokers exposed to ETS (the favored subjects for epidemiological studies), unless there is something exceptionally noxious in ETS as compared to mainstream smoke.

A second point that to me casts doubt on the possibility of any significant role of ETS in the development of CHD concerns the pipe smoker. Pipe smokers inhale tobacco smoke actively to a limited extent. They also commonly surround themselves in a cloud of tobacco smoke so that they are probably exposed to the highest concentrations of ETS of any group. Yet, they enjoy relative immunity from the three major diseases associated with active smoking.

Finally, Dr. Wexler gave us some ideas on the definitive prospective study that he believes needs to be undertaken to answer the question I posed at the beginning of my commentary. Frankly, I would like to question the need for such a study. It will cost a lot of money that would probably be better spent on other, more important public health issues, as Dr. Roe has suggested. After all, cardiovascular diseases occupied only two pages of the 1986 Surgeon General's Report on the Health Consequences of Involuntary Smoking and did not feature at all in the Fourth Report of the U.K. Independent Committee on Smoking and Health.

So my clear advice to nonsmokers, of which I am one, and to those like me who are fond of good food, is to watch your weight, watch your diet, watch your blood pressure, but don't get too hung up about ETS.

Joseph Wu: Thank you. We will now hear comments from Dr. Joseph Fleiss.

Joseph Fleiss: In general, prospective cohort studies are prone to less serious bias and are subject to fewer sources of bias than are retrospective case-control studies. (Fleiss, J.L. (1981). *Statistical Methods for Rates and Proportions* (2nd ed.) Wiley, New York.) I believe that this general contrast between the two study designs holds for the published studies of the health effects of exposure to environmental tobacco smoke, so that the overall quality of the published studies seeking to associate exposure to ETS with coronary heart disease has been superior to the overall quality of the published studies seeking to link exposure to ETS with lung cancer. This is not to say that the former set of studies, all but one of which have been prospective, are free of bias. My comments, which do not duplicate those made by Dr. Wexler in his excellent review, shall be specific to the biases that may have affected some of the published cohort studies under consideration.

One kind of bias that should have no place in science is prejudgment: deciding beforehand what the final results should be, and then making statistical decisions and expressing the results so that the conclusions turn out the way they were supposed to. Consider, however, the 1985 study by Garland et al., one of the first to have been published. An inappropriate statistical decision the authors made was to perform one-tailed tests. That is, statistical significance would be declared only if the mortality rate of ischemic heart disease among nonsmoking women married to smokers was significantly greater than the mortality rate from ischemic heart disease among nonsmoking women married to nonsmokers. A difference in the other direction was ruled out a priori as either unimportant or unbelievable: "Since we were testing previous findings concerning the risk of passive smoking, statistical significance was assessed at one-sided p levels."

Their reasoning is flawed. The authors were not retesting previous findings. They were testing, for the first time as far as they knew, an association with ischemic heart disease. They were apparently unaware of the chapter by Hirayama that had appeared a year earlier (Hirayama, 1984). Even if theirs was the tenth study of the effect of ETS on ischemic heart disease, and even if each of the preceding nine showed a significant excess incidence in the group exposed to ETS, an attitude of open-mindedness would have led them to a two-tailed test.

I was sorry to see sanction given to one-tailed tests in the 1986 Surgeon General's report on ETS: "Given the strength of the evidence on active smoking and disease risk, one-sided testing in the direction of an adverse effect seems appropriate for most potential consequences of ETS." I have argued publicly that one-tailed tests are almost never appropriate in randomized clinical trials (Fleiss, J.L. (1987). Some thoughts on two-tailed tests. *Control Clin. Trials* 8: 394: Fleiss, J.L. (1989) One-tailed versus two tailed tests: Rebuttal. *Control Clin. Trials* 10: 227–230.), and do not see any valid reasons to excuse epidemiological studies from the requirement for two-tailed tests. More is at stake than the impossibility, with a one-tailed test, of ever finding that nonsmokers exposed to ETS might be at significantly less risk than those not exposed. Biased decisions might be made concerning which potential confounding variables to control for and which not if a difference in the "wrong" direction has been ruled out: a potential confounder that moves the odds ratio or hazard ratio in the hypothesized direction may be more likely to be included in the analysis than one that moves the measure of association in the "impossible" or "unimportant" direction. I am not suggesting that this kind of error actually occurred, only that preconceptions as to the possible direction of association invite biased judgments.

After adjusting for differences between the exposed and unexposed cohorts in risk factors for heart disease, Garland et al. found the relative risk for death from ischemic heart disease to be 2.7, with a one-tailed p-value less than 0.10. (Recall that this corresponds to a traditional two-tailed p-value of $p<0.20$.) The authors concluded that "these data are compatible with the hypothesis that passive cigarette smoking carries an excess risk of fatal ischemic heart disease." Not stated is the fact that the range of uncertainty is so great (the 95% confidence intervals for the relative risk extends from approximately 0.6 to over 12.0) that the data are also compatible with no excess risk and with a markedly reduced risk of fatal ischemic heart disease among those exposed to ETS. Data that are compatible with so many contradictory hypotheses are really compatible with no hypothesis.

The statistical criteria used by Svendsen et al. in their 1987 paper were more appropriate than those used by Garland et al. But the statement of their major conclusion reveals a similar possibility of prejudgment: "Our findings . . . support the hypothesis that passive smoking is associated with an increase in morbidity and mortality among nonsmokers." The only morbidity studied by the authors was coronary heart disease morbidity, and it was analyzed only in conjunction with coronary heart disease mortality. None of the relative risks for the composite endpoint of fatal or nonfatal coronary heart disease was significant at the 0.05 level, even without control for multiple comparison artifacts. Once again, the findings support a number of difference hypotheses, not just the one stated by the authors.

I mentioned a 1984 chapter by Hirayama in which, apparently for the first time, a statistically significant association was reported between a nonsmoking women's exposure to ETS and her risk of dying from ischemic heart disease. There are several problems with Hirayama's analyses. One concerns his erroneously presenting values of critical ratios as values of chi-square. The problem is not a trivial one because the same error was pointed out to him some years earlier in letters written in response to his initial paper linking exposure of ETS with lung cancer (Hirayama, 1981). Another example of possible sloppiness is found in one of his tables (Table 7). When numbers of deaths are first subdivided by the spouse's age group, and are then subdivided by the spouse's age group as well as the spouse's occupation, one expects some reduction in the numbers because of missing data. The last thing one expects are increases in the numbers; that is, more deaths with information on two characteristics than with information on one. Nevertheless, this is exactly what happened.

One must wonder what other statistical mistakes Hirayama has persisted in making. Consider his persistence in controlling for the age of the husband when analyzing data for the wife. This curious and basically indefensible feature of his analytic strategy was also pointed out to him in the correspondence that followed his first paper (Hirayama, 1981) but he never responded adequately. The reason wasn't the unavailability of the wife's age because he finally presented results for lung cancer that controlled for the wife's age in the same chapter in which he presented his results for ischemic heart disease (see his Table 2 on p. 180).

A striking feature of Hirayama's data for ischemic heart disease mortality in nonsmoking wives is that an association with the husband's smoking emerges only after the husband's age is adjusted for:

Smoking Habit of Husband	*Odds Ratio**	
	Before Adjustment	*After Adjustment*
Ex-smoker or 1–19 per day	1.01	1.10 (n.s.)
More than 20 per day	0.99	1.31 ($p<0.05$)

*Versus nonsmoking husbands as the control group.

Until Hirayama analyzes his heart disease data sensibly by adjusting for the effect of the wife's age and not her husband's, and adjusting for the effects of other confounders, I suggest that his findings not be taken seriously.

Peter Lee: Dr. Wexler gave a careful presentation on ETS and cardiovascular disease and I agree completely with his conclusion that the existing epidemiological evidence is inadequate to provide proof of a cause and effect relationship.

I would like to draw attention to a number of points that may assist discussion of this important issue. First, I would like to point out that there is, in fact, a small amount of information in addition to that cited by Dr. Wexler. In his 1988 meta-analysis paper, Wells reports the results of a non-published 1986 study by Martin et al. in Utah purporting to find a statistically significant relative risk of 2.6 despite being based on a total of only twenty-three deaths or cases of CHD. (Wells, A.J. (1988). An estimate of adult mortality in the United States from passive smoking. *Environment Int.* 14: 249–265.)

So we've actually got seven epidemiological studies, six of which report a positive association. Of the six, four of them, Hirayama, Helsing, Martin and Hole report a statistically significant result, either in trend analysis or in simple comparison of ETS-exposed and non-exposed subjects. Garland, Hole, Martin and Svendsen report a relative risk in excess of two (more than a 100% increase in risk) in relation to ETS exposure. In comparison, a mass of literature from large prospective studies shows that active smoking, on average, is associated only with a 60% to 80% increase in risk of heart disease. Given that ETS-exposed nonsmokers are far less exposed to smoke constituents than are active smokers, and also that active smokers have more ETS exposure than ETS-exposed nonsmokers, these results just seem to me to lack plausibility, a priori. They seem far more likely to result from chance or bias than to represent a real effect.

One form of bias that may be particularly important in assessing the relationship between ETS and heart disease is the possibility of publication bias. When you look at the overall literature you see that the total number of reported deaths or cases in ETS studies involving heart disease is similar to those involving lung cancer. When one considers that the incidence of heart disease death in nonsmokers is vastly more common than lung cancer deaths in nonsmokers by a factor of about fifty, it's really rather surprising that so few even moderately sized studies of heart disease and ETS have been published.

Dr. Wexler suggests that the Framingham study might be able to provide data, but really this is only a relatively small study of a few thousand people. Surely the most obvious place to look for more information is the American Cancer Society's Million Person Study. They have published results on ETS and lung cancer involving a hundred and fifty-three deaths. (Garfinkel L. (1981). Time trends in lung cancer mortality among nonsmokers and a note on passive smoking. *J. Natl. Cancer Inst.* 66: 1061–1066.) They certainly have the information to publish results on ETS and heart disease involving, I would imagine, five to ten thousand deaths. The obvious question arises, does failure to publish mean no association was found? Because if that in fact were the case, this would cause an absolutely enormous distortion of the overall evidence.

If you look at the seven published studies on ETS and heart disease, only Helsing's and Hirayama's are based on any sort of substantial numbers of deaths at all. I just want to add a few points regarding these two studies.

First, I note some further weaknesses in the Helsing study. There was no adjustment for number of people in the household. Helsing was comparing people who lived with a smoker and those who did not. So, for instance, people who lived on their own automatically went into the category of people who didn't live with a smoker. There's obvious scope for confounding with factors relating to living alone, overcrowding, etc. The study was also not actually about the probability of dying but about the probability of dying within Washington County, as I understand it. They made no attempt to get death certificates for people who moved outside this relatively small area of the United States. If smoking, ETS exposure or household size related to the probability of leaving the county, bias would result. In contrast, I noticed in the British doctors' study that they took enormous pains to follow up the thirty thousand or so doctors involved. They chased people to the ends of the globe to find out what they died of and I think they only failed to track down fifty or sixty, mainly those doctors who had gone back to India and had gotten lost in the subcontinent somewhere.

The Helsing study also used statistical adjustments by a procedure that wasn't really clear and which had an enormous effect on the relative risk estimates. In women he had an unadjusted 34% reduction in risk which he put through his magical unexplained statistical machine and got a 24% increase. So I'd really like to see rather more before accepting anything from this study.

The only other study with substantially more than 100 deaths is that of Hirayama. Dr. Wexler's paper dealt at length with the weaknesses of this study and he quoted the results on the first two lines in his text. The fact that there was a nonsignificant relationship in 1981 and a significant relationship in 1984 is intriguing. The first result was based on 404 deaths, the next on a further 88, and the analysis was essentially the same apart from the fact that in the first analysis he standardized for age and occupation, in the second analysis, only for age.

Now, if you assume occupational standardization made no difference, you can actually calculate what the relative risks were for the intervening period. You've got this enormously strong relative risk of five. You can also show that there's very highly significant heterogeneity of relative risk between the first period up to 1981 and the period thereafter. But if, in fact, you can't do this because standardization of occupation did have an effect, well why on earth didn't Hirayama standardize for it in 1984? So it seems not to make sense either way.

The question finally is whether a new study is actually worth doing. Dr. Wexler noted that existing data are inadequate for proof of cause and effect and proposed that a large study be carried out. The problem, it seems to me, is that given what we know about the association of active smoking with heart disease and the relative exposure to ETS of nonsmokers, it seems highly implausible that even in the most ETS-exposed nonsmokers you get a relative risk of more than two. I believe Dr. Wexler said in his paper that he feels one actually requires a relative risk of two or more as a precondition to prove causality.

So if that's the case, what's the point of doing the study? Although I believe that a good study can pick up relative risks of less than two, I have my doubts that any study could pick up an effect of the order of magnitude which could plausibly exist in this case.

Joseph Wu: Comments by Dr. Lorimer?

Ross Lorimer: The studies that Dr. Wexler very ably and very extensively reviewed are a testimony to the diligence of medical investigators. More than 100,000 individuals have been assessed from the point of view of cardiovascular disease and ETS and we still have no definite answers, although we do have some impressions.

The question of a meta-analysis of results has been considered. Certainly the Surgeon General's report of 1986 suggested this possibility. Further data have accumulated since then. From the cardiological point of view, there is no doubt that in certain situations meta-analysis has been useful. For example, the use of beta blockade following myocardial infarction has been well substantiated by the use of meta-analysis. The effect of lowering cholesterol levels on the subsequent incidence of coronary heart disease has been shown to be a worthwhile clinical exercise by this method. These studies have employed finite end points, such as survival, and variables, such as cholesterol levels, which can be standardized. Under these circumstances, it is relatively easy for different populations to be compared. However, meta-analysis of the relationship between cardiovascular disease and ETS involves comparing such disparate groups as an agricultural population of Japanese women with a group of Californian women living in a retirement community. The MRFIT/ETS study evaluates American men who are already at increased risk from coronary disease because of raised cholesterol and high blood pressure. This would be compared with a group of men and women with a different range of risk factors living in the environment of the west of Scotland. In these situations, it may be that meta-analysis is not appropriate.

There has been considerable discussion today regarding the Hole study from the west of Scotland. I would like to review their data regarding coronary heart disease deaths. In the control group, there were index case nonsmokers living with nonsmokers. In the ETS exposed group-index case nonsmokers were living with cigarette smokers. The single exposure group were index case smokers living with nonsmokers and in the double exposure group both co-habitants smoked. There were 30 deaths from coronary heart disease in the control group where neither partner smoked. On a pro rata numerical basis one might have anticipated around 48 to 49 deaths in the ETS exposed group. Fifty-four deaths did occur, an excess of only five or six. It is important, however, to recognize that correction of data for age, sex, blood pressure, cholesterol and social class did show a significant increase ($p < 0.008$) for relative risk of coronary heart disease. In the MRFIT study, on a pro rata basis there would appear to be two excess deaths from coronary heart disease and four extra myocardial infarctions. Again, this was a study involving a large number of people followed for around seven and a half years and statistical analysis did suggest an association between ETS and coronary heart disease, although this did not achieve formal statistical significance.

While we can discuss the merits or demerits of the various statistical approaches, it would appear that the actual number of extra deaths is relatively small. From the clinical point of view, I would agree with Dr. Armitage that the important factors with regard to coronary disease are active cigarette smoking, high blood pressure, high cholesterol, life style, and employment or unemployment. There may well be other factors involved. However, it seems unlikely that ETS is contributing significantly to the incidence of coronary heart disease. I would also think it unlikely that it would be possible to confirm or refute this suggestion by mounting a further long-term study. The studies report a small adverse association of ETS and coronary heart disease at most. Any further study would require an extremely large population followed for a very long period of time. This simply may not be possible as a practical matter.

Joseph Wu: We now have comments from Dr. Max Weetman.

Max Weetman: I've had this all my life, beginning with "W" and having most functions in life allocated according to the starting letter of your name. Everything's been said. I've really got very little to add. I'd like to congratulate Dr. Wexler on a really very thorough job of going through the various cases.

I think most of the points have been made here, but I've not come as far as this to actually say nothing, so I want to consider a new "ology". We've talked epidemiology, dosology, and things of this nature. But there's really a rather more fundamental "ology" that we ought to consider, and that's epistemology.

Epistemology is what can we know, what is knowable.

We can't know very much about ETS and cardivascular diseases, I think, because of the problems I will outline here. I would consider all of these problems to be design problems. I'm not going to go through all of them in fine detail, but I have a few points I want to make. Everything I say here applies equally to cancer of the lung as well.

The first weakness really stems from our measurement of exposure to ETS. The best way to control this would be to experiment in a reaction chamber, where you can actually monitor certain surrogates for environmental tobacco smoke and control the number of cigarettes smoked.

Once you go beyond this, to a real world situation, or into a retrospective look at somebody's lifestyle, epidemiology begins to lose all credibility. It's really guessology with respect to exposure at this stage.

Now, how do we actually find out about what possible exposure one might have suffered? We do it by asking people. We ask, "Did you smoke? Did your husband smoke? Did your wife smoke?," etc. Obviously, this approach is prone to an enormous degree of error. We're not likely to get a particularly accurate and true answer there.

Another problem, particularly true for studies of cardiovascular disease, is the use of selected populations. Taking the Multiple Risk Factor Intervention Trial, for example, the patients had high serum cholesterol levels and high blood pressure. In addition, they drank rather more than the control group. Why do we rely on this high risk group for information? Perhaps it's going to tell us something that "normal people"—whatever that might mean—wouldn't.

The second trial where we get some positive information is the notorious—I would say—Hirayama trial. There are even more things wrong with it than have been said here. It's tremendously unrepresentative of the population of Japan because it includes far too few old people, over eighty.

Now, why do we use these peculiar things, the Japanese or high risk or atypical groups, like Hirayama's Japanese cohort or those in the MRFIT? It's because ETS as a problem is quite a recent event. It started with Trichopolous and Hirayama himself in about 1981. Most of the trials considered today did not originate as studies of exposure to ETS, but as studies of other phenomenon, that have been adapted to consider ETS.

The Multiple Risk Factor Intervention Trial had been running for some time. Hirayama's trial was already about twelve or thirteen years old before he started to seek information about ETS exposure.

Epistemologically speaking, the result of this is that you are preselecting the study group, so you have too few subjects to resolve the question. The Garland trial had two deaths in the control group. It's far too brittle a number for a baseline. You can't draw any conclusions about common disease from such small groups.

The use of death certificates is another problem. Not all the trials use death certificates. There are some exemplary attempts where physicians actually review the case to determine the likely cause of death and guard against error. But a lot of the trials, including Hirayama's, use a death certificate only. These are, we know, notoriously inaccurate.

Now, the only thing I would really argue about with our eminent opening speaker involves a little bit of philosophy; I'm talking about biological plausibility. Asking questions about biological plausibility can sometimes be misleading. The worst case arises when you've got a rather weak P-value: you're not quite there but you obviously would like to get there. You then list a number of factors that, had you continued, would have caused you to reach the desired result. You then ask, is it a biologically plausible event that this result will occur? To me, if biological plausibility is used in this sense, it really means "in the absence of evidence, I will now cast one further card, a weak one though it be." The purpose is to fit the results to the preconception brought by the scientist to the experiment. As has already been said, this is the antithesis of scientific investigation. It's wish fulfillment. Maybe our grant bodies are partly responsible for this. We have to publish more and more papers, even though some of them may be nonsense, so that we can obtain the next grant, and do the next run of work.

Similarly, with respect to biological plausibility, Peter Lee has very clearly pointed out that if you have eight factories in quite different places, and people die from some rare disease all having been involved in the same industrial process, you don't say, "Well, I can't see how it's working biologically." If you think about what we know biologically, most things are absurd in the first place, and the rationality in which we place them comes after the initiating discovery.

This is certainly true for most new types of drugs that are discovered. It's interesting to note that carbonic anhydrase had been demonstrated in the stomach many years ago, and was only then discovered in the kidney when they first used sulfonamides and obtained a diuretic response. The only way you could explain this diuretic response was by actually postulating that this enzyme was there and sulfonamides inhibited it. So quite often you get something amazing, biologically implausible and that then promotes discoveries that result in a rational background being discovered.

I think a more economical phrase that we ought to try and use, if we have to be stuck with this notion of biological plausibility, is "freedom from biological implausibility." That's putting the boot on the other foot and asking people to do a little bit of thinking rather than just justifying their orignal thoughts.

Joseph Wu: We'll have the comments from Dr. Philip Witorsch.

Philip Witorsch: Like Max Weetman, I've spent most of my life being at the end of the list. I therefore decided to comment briefly on an aspect that none of the other speakers has addressed, namely the acute effects of ETS exposure on individuals with pre-existing coronary artery disease. Dr. Wexler very eloquently critiqued the Aronow study but there is another, very good study that was published in 1987 by Sheps et al. from the University of North Carolina. The Sheps study raises the issue of the biological implausibility of the acute effects postulated by Aronow.

Aronow and others have suggested that the acute effects of ETS exposure with regard to exacerbation of angina in individuals with pre-existing coronary artery disease relate, at least partially, to elevation of carboxyhaemoglobin from ETS exposure. Superficially, this sounds like it might make sense, until you think about the amount of carbon monoxide actually generated from ETS. Studies have shown only a slight difference in the levels of carboxyhaemoglobin in nonsmokers exposed to ETS as compared to those in nonsmokers not exposed. This result causes the hypothesis to lose its plausibility.

The Sheps study examined thirty individuals with well- documented coronary artery disease and symptomatic angina who had documentation of electrocardiographic changes on exercise typical of angina. They exposed these individuals in an exposure chamber to carbon monoxide, using an endpoint of approximately four percent carboxyhaemoglobin. That compares to levels usually found in nonsmokers and in their controls of about 1.5% carboxyhaemoglobin.

Interestingly, to achieve the 4% carboxyhaemoglobin they had to expose their subjects to one hundred parts per million of carbon monoxide in air for a period of an hour or more. This is probably three to five times the level of carbon monoxide that has been measured in very smoke-polluted areas. They exercised these individuals and measured a variety of cardiovascular parameters, including electrocardiographic evidence of angina, ST-T wave changes, radionuclide imaging of the heart, ejection fraction, and a number of other cardiovascular indices.

They found absolutely no effect on the duration to onset of angina, or any of the objective cardiovascular parameters, despite the subjects' exposure to a hundred parts per million of carbon monoxide and a carboxyhaemoglobin level approaching four percent.

The Sheps study, when added to all the deficiencies cited relative to the Aronow study, should lay this issue to rest. It's very clear that in a real-life situation it is biologically implausible for the degree of carbon monoxide exposure related to ETS to have any effect as far as exacerbation of angina.

I think this might have implications for studies of ETS and reproductive effects as well. Frank Sullivan mentioned earlier that carboxyhaemoglobin is thought possibly to play a role relative to reproductive effects. But it appears implausible that the degree of real-life exposure to ETS results in any significant changes in carboxyhaemoglobin.

Joseph Wu: We have time for a couple of additional comments or questions from the floor. Dr. Roe.

Francis Roe: If I could just address a question to the panel in general. I have the impression that coronary heart disease is not a single disease but at least two. Coronary heart disease in men under the age of fifty seems to be related to different factors than CHD occurring from age sixty onwards. These seem to be two different diseases, but maybe there are many others. I wonder what the implications of this are in relation to studies of ETS.

Secondly, from a causative point of view, one would be concerned with two things. The first is the set of factors that cause arteriosclerosis, and the second is the set of factors that make a fatal coronary occlusion more likely in a person with arteriosclerosis. They seem to be two different things. Aronow obviously was looking at the second of these. The first should not be overlooked.

In examining carcinogenesis, I earlier stressed the point that you need to know what an individual has been exposed to from childhood in order to get any reliable feeling of what happens in lung cancer risk. I suggested that this has not been done so far.

Now, isn't this also true of cardiovascular disease? I mean, the idea of Aronow collecting a lot of old gentlemen and sticking them all on exercise bicycles, to me, is horrific. Would we not be better off if we really started such studies with younger people?

Peter Lee: I would comment on the second of Dr. Roe's points. I suspect lifetime exposure isn't so important in heart disease as it is in respiratory disease. If one takes the analog of active smoking, the evidence seems to suggest that current smoking is important and ex-smoking is not really important because if you give up smoking, your risk reverts fairly quickly. Yet, there may still be something in it even so.

Ross Lorimer: A similar problem arises in studies of women. Coronary artery disease in women expresses itself differently than in men insofar as pre-menopausal women are concerned. From a clinical point of view, the coronary heart disease occurring in women also is usually associated with much smaller diameter of coronary vessels with more diffuse disease than in young men with myocardial infarction, in whom it is not unusual to find single vessel disease, especially involving the left anterior descending and having an acute thrombotic episode. So I'm sure you're absolutely right.

Philip Witorsch: If I can just add a brief comment. I agree that there are different diseases involved. I think lifetime factors are important, but not necessarily lifetime ETS exposure or lifetime cigarette smoking. In many of these studies, people tend to forget that perhaps the most important determinant of coronary artery disease is the choice of parents that one makes. Added to that are diet, lifestyle, exercise and a whole host of other factors, all of which have been very poorly controlled for in the studies to date and are, frankly, very difficult to control for. Assessing cholesterol levels is not an adequate control of many of these factors and that's, perhaps, the most that's been done. It's very analogous to the token control for socio-economic status that has been done in a lot of studies.

Jarnail Singh: I have been doing research on the effect of carbon monoxide levels in animals since 1972. I have a series of papers and a series of experiments where I expose mice from when they are newly born, three, four days old, until they are about eight weeks old. The mice are constantly exposed, except during cleaning and watering, to three levels of CO, 25 PPM, 50 PPM and 100 PPM. At the end of eight weeks, we sacrifice the animals, take all the tissues, lungs, hearts, spleen and kidney, and send them to a pathologist to determine whether there is any dose-dependent effect on these organs. The conclusion is that at these levels, 25, 50 and 100 PPM, there is no dose-dependent effect on the heart or on the lungs.

Part V

10
Effects of ETS Exposure on Pulmonary Function and Respiratory Health in Adults

Philip Witorsch, M.D.
Departments of Medicine and Physiology,
The George Washington University School of Medicine and Health Sciences

I. Introduction

Interest in the effects of environmental tobacco smoke ("ETS") on pulmonary function and respiratory health is a natural outgrowth of the growing concern about possible long term health effects of air pollution in general and indoor air pollution in particular. With respect to possible health effects of ETS, two areas of major research focus have been lung cancer in nonsmokers and respiratory health in children. Compared to studies in children, there are fewer published reports on the effects of ETS on the respiratory system of adults. In 1986, reviews by the U.S. Surgeon General and the National Research Council each found that, specifically with respect to pulmonary function and noncancer respiratory health in adults, the available data were insufficient to determine whether or not ETS exposure had an effect (Surgeon General, 1986; National Research Council, 1986). Several additional studies subsequently have been published. This paper critically summarizes the literature dealing with the noncancer effects of ETS on the respiratory system of nonsmoking adults. In addition, suggestions are made for future studies in this area.

Studies of the respiratory effects of ETS include epidemiologic studies addressing pulmonary function and/or respiratory symptoms or disease in nonsmokers exposed chronically to ETS, as well as experimental studies of the acute effects of ETS on pulmonary function in normal and/or asthmatic individuals. In the epidemiologic studies, ETS-exposed and nonexposed individuals have been compared with respect to pulmonary function, as reflected by spirometry, or prevalence of respiratory symptoms (e.g., cough, phlegm, wheeze) or disease (e.g., chronic obstructive pulmonary disease). In the experimental studies, normal or asthmatic subjects have been exposed to

ETS under controlled conditions and measures of pulmonary function and/or prevalence of symptoms recorded.

II. Epidemiologic Studies

Fifteen epidemiologic studies addressing ETS exposure and pulmonary function and/or respiratory symptoms or disease in nonsmoking adults are listed in Table 10–1. In several instances, reports on the same study population have been published in more than one paper. Since all of the studies, regardless of the endpoint measured, have similarities in design and execution which influence their interpretation, a discussion of these factors is presented before the discussion of the actual findings of the studies.

Table 10–1
Epidemiologic Studies of ETS Exposure in Adults: Pulmonary Function and Respiratory Symptoms

Study	*Source of Subjects*	*Index of ETS Exposure*	*Endpoints Measu[red]*
Schilling et al., 1977	3 U.S. Communities	Spousal smoking	PFT parameters Respiratory sympt[oms]
Simecek, 1980	Czechoslovakia	Spousal smoking	Respiratory sympt[oms]
White and Froeb, 1980	California	Exposure at work >20 yr	PFT parameters
Comstock et al., 1981	Maryland	Household smokers	PFT parameters Respiratory sympt[oms]
Kauffmann et al., 1983	France	Household smokers	PFT parameters
Lebowitz, 1984	Arizona	Household smokers	PFT parameters Respiratory sympt[oms]
Gillis et al., 1984	Scotland	Household smokers	Respiratory sympt[oms]
Kentner et al., 1984 and 1988	Germany	Current ETS exp.	PFT parameters
Brunekreef et al., 1985	Netherlands	>10 cig/d smoked in the home	PFT parameters
Hosein and Corey, 1986	3 U.S. communities	Household smokers	PFT parameters
Kalandidi et al., 1987	Greece	Spousal smoking	Diagnosis of COP[D]
Svendsen et al., 1987	18 U.S. cities	Spousal smoking	PFT parameters
Kauffmann et al., 1989	France[a] 5 U.S. cities	Spousal smoking	PFT parameters Respiratory sympt[oms]
Hole et al., 1989[b]	Scotland	Household smokers	PFT parameters Respiratory sympt[oms]

[a]Same study population reported in Kauffmann et al., 1983.
[b]Same study population reported in Gillis et al., 1984.

A. Methodologic Considerations

In all of the studies, classification of ETS exposure and smoking status, as well as data regarding respiratory symptoms and/or disease where this has been addressed, have been obtained from questionnaires. The questionnaires have been variably standardized, validated and administered. In many of the studies, the index of ETS exposure has been spousal smoking. In others, a more general consideration of household smoke exposure, which usually included spousal smoking, has been used as the index. In a few, exposure to ETS in the workplace was considered.

It is significant to note that in none of these reports has there been verification of ETS exposure using reliable biological or environmental markers. In fact, ETS exposure has generally been assessed through the use of surrogate measures such as spousal smoking or household smoking in general, or ETS exposure in the workplace. Most of the studies rely at least partially on spousal smoking as the index of ETS exposure. This certainly results in misclassification of exposure (Friedman et al. 1983). Some members of the "exposed" population (non-smokers married to smokers) may actually be unexposed if their spouses do not smoke in their presence, and some members of the "unexposed" group (nonsmokers married to nonsmokers) may be exposed through contact with smokers other than their spouses. Since the error introduced is nondifferential, studies that rely on spousal smoking as the index of ETS exposure will tend to underestimate, or perhaps fail to detect, an effect of ETS if it exists (Schwartz and Balter 1988).

However, use of spousal smoking as the surrogate for exposure also introduces a source of differential bias that will tend to overestimate any effect of ETS, or make it seem that one exists when it does not. The error is introduced by the misclassification of smokers or ex-smokers in the study population as non- or never-smokers. Such misclassified smokers bring into the study their own increased risk of pulmonary findings, independent of any effect of spousal smoking. Since there is a tendency for smokers to be married to smokers and nonsmokers to be married to nonsmokers (referred to as marital aggregation or concordance factor), there is a differential effect on the group married to smokers compared to the group married to nonsmokers (National Research Council 1986; Schwartz and Balter 1988).

Another consideration is the possibility that spousal smoking and/or ETS exposure is associated with confounding variables that can, if not adequately controlled for in the design or analysis of the study, affect its outcome. Friedman et al. (1983) noted that the extent of ETS exposure (hours per week) was positively associated with a variety of other health risk factors, such as alcohol consumption, marijuana use and occupational hazards. Koo et al. (1988), in a study of nonsmoking Chinese women in Hong Kong, noted that wives of nonsmokers tended to have healthier lifestyles than wives of smokers.

Socioeconomic status (SES) is another potential confounding variable, known to be associated with smoking status, and potentially associated with other factors that could influence respiratory health (Surgeon General 1986). SES is a complex variable that is inherently difficult to adjust for adequately (Green 1970). The epidemiologic studies of ETS exposure and respiratory function and/or symptoms or disease in adults have treated SES and SES-related factors variably and very few, if any, can be said to have controlled adequately for these potentially important confounding factors. There are complex relationships between cigarette smoking and such SES-related variables as alcohol consumption, income, education, housing, occupation, ethnicity, diet, living space density, transmissible respiratory infections, heating, cooking, transportation, lifestyle, health habits and attitudes. Unless controlled for in the design and/or analysis of the epidemiologic studies of ETS and respiratory health, the possible role of such factors in influencing the outcome of these studies remains uncertain.

III. Studies Using Pulmonary Function Measurements

In studies assessing lung function using objective measures obtained from pulmonary function testing, several commonly used parameters have been employed. These differ with respect to their inter- and intra-individual variability, and the clinical interpretation of findings outside the normal range. The forced expiratory volume in one second (FEV_1) is generally considered to be a reasonably reproducible, although somewhat insensitive, measurement of expiratory airflow. Abnormalities in FEV_1 correlate reliably with certain types of pulmonary dysfunction and disease (Bates 1989). The FEF_{25-75}, i.e., the rate of airflow during the mid-portion of the FVC maneuver, has been suggested as being particularly sensitive to and reflective of disease and dysfunction in the small, peripheral airways (i.e., bronchioles less than 2–3 mm in diameter) but this suggestion remains controversial (Burrows et al. 1983; Miller 1986). Furthermore, FEF_{25-75} and analogous parameters have been found to be much more variable than FEV_1 from test to test in the same individual (Bates 1989).

Since lung function is very much dependent on age, height and sex, determination of normality and abnormality in a given individual requires a comparison between observed values and predicted values derived from prediction formulas that incorporate these variables (Bates 1989; Miller 1986). The results of lung function tests also may be affected by the skill and experience of the technician administering the study, the characteristics of the

ble 10–2
idemiologic Studies of ETS Exposure and Pulmonary Function in Adults

	Reported Change in Parameter					
dy	*FEV*$_1$	*FVC*	*FEF*$_{25-75}$	*PEF*[a]	*MEF*$_{75}$[b]	*Comments*
illing et al., 1977	↔[c]	↔	nd[d]	nd	nd	
ite and Froeb, 1980	↔	↔	↓	nd	nd	↓ FEF$_{75-85}$
nstock et al., 1981	↔[e]	↔[e]	nd	nd	nd	
ffmann et al., 1983	↔	↔	↔	nd	nd	For subpopulation of women ≥40, ↓ FEV$_1$, FVC, FEF$_{25-75}$
m et al., 1984	↔	nr[f]	↔	↔	nd	↓ air velocity index, ↑ total expiratory time
owitz, 1984	nd	nd	nd	↔	nd	
nekreef et al., 1985	↔	↔	nd	↓	↓	
ein and Corey, 1986	↔	nd	nd	nd	nd	↔ MEF$_{25}$, MEF$_{50}$
dsen et al., 1987	↓	nd	nd	nd	nd	↓ greater for spouses smoking 1–19 cig./day than ≥20 cig./day
ffmann et al., 1989[h]	↔	↔	nd	nd	nd	
e et al., 1989	↓	nd	nd	nd	nd	

k expiratory flow rate.
ximum expiratory flow rate at 75% of FVC.
significant change.
t determined.
increased relative risk for FEV$_1$ < 80% of predicted or FEV$_1$/FVC < 70% of predicted.
reported.
nge reported in females only; no change reported in males.
dings for U.S. cohort; findings for French cohort previously reported (Kauffmann et al., 1983).

testing equipment used, and the cooperation, motivation and effort of the subject being tested (Bates 1989).

The findings of epidemiologic studies that used parameters derived from pulmonary function testing as the endpoints for examining the effects of ETS exposure are summarized in Table 10–2. The results of these studies have been variable, with seven reporting differences in one or more parameters of respiratory function associated with ETS exposure, while five found no statistically significant differences between exposed and nonexposed populations.

Many of the studies suggesting effects of ETS (White and Froeb 1980; Brunekreef et al. 1985; Salem et al. 1984) report differences limited to such parameters as FEF$_{25-75}$, without associated significant reductions in FEV$_1$ or related parameters. The physiological significance, clinical relevance and clinical-pathological correlation of reductions limited to such parameters is uncertain, in view of their well-documented wide intra-subject and inter-subject variability (Bates 1989). In addition, as discussed above, the clinical significance of isolated reductions in mid-flow and analogous parameters (e.g., FEF_{25-75}, MEF_{50}) and whether they indicate disease or dysfunction involving the small airways remain unsettled (Burrows et al. 1983; Miller 1986).

There is additional uncertainty regarding the physiological and clinical-pathological significance of the small reductions in pulmonary function parameters that have been reported in these studies (generally in the range of 3–15%). For the most part, none of the reported values represent findings that would be considered abnormal on an individual basis; that is, the values reported for individuals in both the exposed and unexposed groups are within the range of normal values, using generally accepted criteria of pulmonary function parameter normality (i.e., relationship of observed value to predicted value). This makes the clinical relevance of these findings difficult to interpret, since it is uncertain whether or not an individual who experiences a slight decrement in one or more measures of pulmonary function, with all measures still within normal limits, has any clinically significant impairment of function.

Additional concerns regarding these studies also deserve comment. Several of the studies report data that appear internally inconsistent or implausible. For example, Kauffmann et al. (1983 and 1989) report unexplained qualitative and quantitative differences in the effects of ETS in men and women. Further, younger women exposed to ETS (40–45 years of age) exhibited a decrement in pulmonary function (FEF_{25-75}) while older women (55–60 years of age) did not. In the case of age-related effects, one would expect the reverse situation due to a longer period of exposure. Svendsen et al. (1987), in a report of a subgroup of the participants in the Multiple Risk Factor Intervention Trial (MRFIT), a study which was primarily designed to address cardiovascular risk factors, noted a slight but reportedly significant reduction in FEV_1 (approximately 100 ml or 3%) in nonsmoking men whose wives smoked. However, the reported data suggest a dose-response relationship opposite to that which would be expected, i.e., the mean FEV_1 among men said to be nonsmokers married to women said to smoke 1–19 cigarettes per day was less than the value found among such men married to women said to smoke $\geq$ 20 cigarettes per day (a difference of approximately 136 ml or 4%, which was greater than the difference noted between their exposed and nonexposed nonsmokers).

All of the studies, with the exception of White and Froeb (1980), Salem et al. (1984) and Kentner et al. (1984 and 1988), used household or spousal smoking as the index of ETS exposure. As already discussed, this introduces misclassification errors, both nondifferential due to misclassification of exposure and differential due to misclassification of nonsmoking status. Any conclusions derived from the results of these studies must carefully consider the impact of these sources of error. With respect to exposure misclassification, there is a paucity of data that can be used as a basis for appropriately estimating its impact (Schwartz and Balter 1988). Estimation of the impact of smoking status misclassification can theoretically be calculated using the model reported by the National Research Council (1986) for lung cancer. As was the case for lung cancer, however, the data available are inadequate for all of the parameters necessary for calculating the influence of smoking status misclassification (Schwartz and Balter 1988). The impact of smoking status misclassification could be especially important since, unlike the lung cancer studies, most of the subjects comprising the study populations in these studies were classified according to current smoking status. Thus, the nonsmoking groups likely contain a higher proportion of ex-smokers than was seen in the lung cancer studies. While smoking cessation may lead to improvement in pulmonary function, the degree to which this occurs is variable and influenced by a number of factors, including extent and nature of anatomic and physiologic abnormalities present prior to cessation and the specific parameter(s) measured (Bates 1989; Beck et al. 1981; Bosse et al. 1981; Huhti and Ikkala 1980; Speizer et al. 1985; Tashkin et al. 1984; Wright et al. 1983). It has been noted that the effects of cigarette smoking on the airways and lung parenchyma include both reversible and irreversible components, and that ex-smokers often have spirometric values intermediate between those of current smokers and never smokers (Miller, 1986). Thus, the inclusion of ex-smokers in nonsmoker populations in epidemiologic studies could introduce a significant bias.

Little additional information can be derived by looking at the results of the studies that considered other indices of ETS exposure because of deficiencies in those studies. The study by White and Froeb (1980), the first to suggest an effect of ETS, has been questioned on the basis of methodology, statistical techniques, experimental design and instrumentation (National Research Council 1986; Surgeon General 1986). The study of Kentner and associates (1984, 1988) addressed a large number of pulmonary function variables but the paucity of positive findings, even among long-term, active cigarette smokers, raises questions about the sensitivity of their methodology and/or instrumentation.

Most of the epidemiologic studies of ETS and pulmonary function made an attempt to adjust the analysis for some index of SES, although the specific index varied from study to study. However, in view of the difficulty in controlling for this variable and its significance in health-related studies (Green 1970), it is unlikely that SES-related factors can be completely excluded as having potentially confounding effects. Little attempt was made in any of the studies to control for other potentially confounding factors. The finding that the type of cooking fuel used in the home was associated with changes in pulmonary function parameters (Comstock et al. 1981; Hosein and Corey 1986) suggests that this is a factor that should be considered as a potential confounder.

IV. Studies Using Respiratory Symptoms and/or Disease as Endpoints

The eight studies in adults that looked at relationships between ETS exposure and respiratory symptoms and/or disease are listed with their findings in Table 10–3. The studies addressed a variety of respiratory symptoms and/or disease, including cough, sputum production, wheeze, dyspnea and symptoms of bronchitis and chronic obstructive pulmonary disease (COPD). All of the studies used household or spousal smoking as the index of ETS exposure and used a variety of respiratory symptoms as endpoints. The frequency of respiratory symptoms was based on the response to questionnaires, which were variably validated and standardized. For the most part, there was no objective verification of subjective symptomatology. As can be seen from Table 10–3, the reported results are variable. Three reports (Comstock et al.

Table 10–3
Epidemiologic Studies of ETS Exposure and Respiratory Symptoms in Adults

Study	*Findings*
Schilling et al., 1977	No association with cough, phlegm, wheeze
Simecek, 1980	Increased symptoms of bronchitis
Comstock et al., 1981	No association with cough, phlegm, wheeze
Lebowitz, 1984	No association with cough, rhinitis, wheeze, shortness of breath
Gillis et al., 1984	Increased prevalence of expectoration and hypersecretion in males, and dyspnea in males and females
Kalandidi et al., 1987	Increased risk of COPD
Kauffmann et al., 1989	No association with cough or phlegm; in U.S. population, increased prevalence of wheezing; in French population, increased prevalence of dyspnea in women ≥40
Hole et al., 1989	No increased risk of expectoration, dyspnea or hypersecretion

1981; Schilling et al. 1977; Lebowitz 1984)) found no association between ETS exposure and respiratory symptoms. Hole et al. (1989) reported increased symptoms among nonsmokers living with smokers compared to nonsmokers living with nonsmokers but the differences noted were not statistically significant. The four remaining studies (Simecek 1980; Gillis et al. 1984; Kalandidi et al. 1987; Kauffmann et al. 1989) reported an association between household smoking and increased incidence of respiratory symptomatology and/or disease.

Among studies reporting an effect of household or spousal smoking, there was no agreement on the specific symptoms or disease whose incidence was increased. Further, even within a study, apparent inconsistencies in the findings were not explained. For example, Simecek (1980) reports an inadequately explained sexual dimorphism. Symptoms of chronic bronchitis increased in nonsmoking men married to smoking women but not in nonsmoking women married to smoking men. The Kauffmann et al. (1989) report noted a statistically significant increase in wheezing associated with spousal smoking among nonsmoking U.S. women but not among French subjects. No associations of spousal smoking and cough, phlegm or dyspnea were noted in either population group, except for what is described as a "borderline" association of dyspnea with spousal smoking in the subgroup of French women over 40 years of age. The disparate results between French and U.S. women, also seen in the results of pulmonary function testing, are suggestive of confounding by culturally and/or ethnically determined lifestyle factors or, alternatively, the possibility that differences in marital concordance and other parameters differentially affect the quantitative influence of smoking status misclassification bias. While the role of such issues in epidemiologic studies of spousal smoking and pulmonary function remains to be determined, they have been considered to be possibly relevant in analogous studies addressing spousal smoking and lung cancer risk (Schwartz and Balter 1988; Gao et al. 1987; Koo et al. 1988; Koo 1988; National Research Council 1986), and are at least plausibly relevant to this study.

The Kalandidi et al. (1987) study is the only report that examines the incidence of chronic obstructive pulmonary disease (COPD) and ETS exposure. It is a very brief report, published as a letter to the editor, and provides very limited data from a case-control study suggesting an association between spousal smoking and COPD in never-smoking women in Athens. The authors' experience of having obtained a cohort of 103 nonasthmatic, never-smoking women with COPD at a single institution over a two year period is so unique, even for a chest hospital, as to raise significant questions regarding the criteria used to establish this diagnosis. Further, the reported lack of a consistent dose response relationship raises a question about the validity of the authors' conclusions.

V. Experimental Studies

Published reports addressing the acute effects of ETS exposure on pulmonary function generally have utilized spirometric parameters prior to, during and after exposure of subjects to machine-generated tobacco smoke in an exposure chamber. Both normal and asthmatic subjects have been studied. Levels of ETS exposure generated in such studies have been determined by measurement of various environmental markers of ETS, usually carbon monoxide (CO) or respirable suspended particulates (RSP). For the most part, these levels have been equivalent to or greater than levels reported to be found in highly smoke-polluted, real-life environments, such as taverns (Surgeon General 1986; National Research Council 1986).

Bronchoprovocation or bronchial challenge tests also have been performed in some of the studies addressing possible respiratory effects of ETS exposure. These tests involve the inhalation of graded doses of substances known to cause bronchoconstriction, such as methacholine, histamine and cold air, and determination of the dose of the substance at which bronchoconstriction occurs (threshold dose). Individual variation in threshold of bronchial responsiveness has been found to reflect such factors as genetic influences, mucosal damage from environmental agents (irritants, allergens, infectious microorganisms), predisposition to asthma, etc. (Bates 1989). Response to bronchodilator drugs, generally beta-adrenergic agonists, also has been looked at in some studies in children, although not in any systematic fashion in adults. Responsiveness to such agents also varies from individual to individual and is influenced by similar factors as responsiveness to bronchoconstrictors (Bates 1989).

Studies examining the acute effects of ETS exposure on pulmonary function in normal adults have generally reported no effects. Shephard and coworkers, in two studies (Pimm et al. 1978; Shephard et al. 1979a), confined healthy subjects in an unventilated room for two hours in the presence or absence of tobacco smoke, randomly applied on alternate days. The concentration of tobacco smoke was high, as reflected in the reported CO concentration, which was 20–30 ppm. In the second study, the subjects also exercised on a bicycle ergometer for alternating 15-minute intervals. In addition to pulmonary function testing, the subjects noted any symptoms that they experienced during the exposure. The studies revealed that exposed subjects frequently complained of eye irritation, nasal discharge and/or stuffiness and cough, but there was little or no sore throat, shortness of breath, wheezing, chest tightness, dizziness or headache. ETS exposure had little or no effect on most pulmonary function parameters (including FVC and FEV_1) or heart rate compared to ambient air. A lack of effect of such acute ETS exposure on pulmonary function in normal adults also has been observed in the control

able 10–4
xperimental (Exposure Chamber) Studies of Acute ETS Exposure in Asthmatic Adults

udy	*No. of Subjects*	*Findings*
ephard et al., 1977	14	No significant effects on pulmonary function tests
ahms et al., 1981	10	Significant decline in FVC, FEV_1, FEF_{25-75}, symptoms
ight and Breslin, 1985	6	Significant decline in pulmonary function; symptoms; increased sensitivity to histamine challenge
iedemann et al., 1986	9	No significant effects on pulmonary function; decreased sensitivity to methacholine challenge
ankus et al., 1988	21	Significant (>20%) decline in FEV_1 in 7 out of 21 subjects

groups of studies on asthmatics discussed below (Dahms et al. 1981; Wiedemann et al. 1986; Stankus et al. 1988).

In contrast, Salem et al. (1984) reported that a 30-minute exposure to machine-generated tobacco smoke in a room produced a significant decrease in peak expiratory flow rate (PEFR), as well as frequent complaints of eye irritation, tearing, dizziness, headaches and chest tightness. No data were provided regarding levels of environmental markers of exposure, other than the room size and the fact that the smoke was produced by eight cigarettes. Consequently, the relevance of this experimental exposure to real-life ETS exposure cannot be determined.

Five groups of investigators have published reports concerning acute experimental ETS exposure in asthmatics. These are summarized in Table 10–4. In three of the studies, an acute adverse effect on pulmonary function was reported in asthmatic subjects acutely exposed to machine-generated ETS in an exposure chamber (Dahms et al. 1981; Knight and Breslin 1985; Stankus et al. 1988), while in two no such effects were noted (Shephard et al. 1979b; Wiedemann et al. 1986).

Stankus et al. (1988) reported that 7 of 21 asthmatics acutely exposed to ETS exhibited a significant (≥ 20%) and consistent decrease in FEV_1 while 14 did not. They suggested that a subpopulation of asthmatics may be intolerant to ETS. The mechanism for this intolerance did not appear to be allergic, as there was no correlation between intolerance to smoke exposure, as demonstrated by pulmonary function testing, and tobacco leaf immunologic sensitivity, as demonstrated by skin and serologic testing. This finding is consistent with earlier reports, which failed to demonstrate an association between subjectively reported "sensitivity" of asthmatics to tobacco smoke exposure and objective immunologic tests (Lehrer et al. 1984; Lehrer et al. 1985; McDougall and Gleich 1976).

In two of the studies (Knight and Breslin 1985; Weidemann et al. 1986), bronchial reactivity before and after smoke exposure also was assessed, using bronchoprovocation testing. Knight and Breslin (1985) used histamine bronchial challenge and noted increased bronchial reactivity after smoke exposure. Wiedemann et al. (1986) employed methacholine bronchoprovocation and reported the opposite effect, i.e., a decrease in bronchial reactivity after smoke exposure. The reason(s) for these apparently conflicting findings are unclear, although it has been noted that the somewhat different mechanisms of reaction to these two provocative substances may in some cases result in different responses (Bates 1989).

There are several possible explanations for the variable findings that have been reported in the experimental studies of the acute effects of ETS exposure in asthmatics. The differing results may reflect, in part, differences in the intensity of ETS exposure. However, this is unlikely to be an important factor, as the exposures were, for the most part, comparable in intensity. In fact, the levels of ETS exposure reported by Wiedemann et al. (1986), who noted no significant adverse effects on pulmonary function, were much higher than those estimated to be present by Dahms et al. (1981), who reported a significant relationship between ETS exposure and both symptoms and pulmonary function decrements in their asthmatic study population. It is also possible, as suggested by Wiedemann et al. (1986), that the differences may reflect differences in the severity of the underlying asthma and/or the use of bronchodilator medication at the time of the study. Wiedemann's subjects were asymptomatic and off medication, while those studied by Dahms et al. were medicated and exhibited mild impairment of pulmonary function at the time they were studied. It is also quite possible, as suggested by Stankus et al. (1988), that there may be a subgroup of asthmatics who are "sensitive" to some component(s) of ETS, although this sensitivity is unlikely to represent immunologic hypersensitivity.

The possibility that the acute responses noted in some asthmatics (both in experimental chamber exposure studies and in anecdotal reports) result from a psychogenic reaction, as opposed to a physiologic response to ETS, needs to be investigated further. Psychological and emotional influences are known to be of considerable importance in the pathogenesis of asthmatic episodes (Cohen and Lask 1983; Godfrey and Silverman 1973; Knapp and Mathe 1985; Luparello et al. 1968; McFadden et al. 1969; Smith et al. 1970). It has been reported that suggestion may even affect pulmonary function in nonasthmatics (Kotses et al. 1987). Odors also have been reported to worsen asthma by an as yet undetermined mechanism, which could involve psychogenic factors (Shin & Williams 1986).

The study design of Dahms et al. (1981) did not include a control period in the chamber during which there was no exposure to tobacco smoke. Conceivably, the pulmonary function changes they noted could have reflected, at least in part, anxiety and other emotional effects of the testing conditions themselves, as well as a psychogenically mediated reaction to the distinctive odor of tobacco smoke. In the Knight and Breslin (1985) study, in which adverse pulmonary functional effects were reported, the control exposure always occurred on the day preceding smoke exposure, in contrast to the random exposure protocol used in the study of Shephard et al. (1979b), in which no such adverse effects were found. Non-random sequencing of exposure is less likely than random sequencing of exposure to control adequately for potentially biasing psychogenic factors. The use of goggles (to prevent eye irritation) by Wiedemann et al. (1986) may have minimized some of the psychological influences associated with the experimental tobacco smoke exposure situation.

VI. Conclusions and Recommendations for Further Research

The findings of the epidemiologic studies addressing chronic (long-term) ETS exposure and pulmonary function and/or respiratory health in adults have been variable from one report to the next. While seven of twelve studies reviewed reported a relationship between ETS exposure and some decrement in pulmonary function parameters, five did not. Similarly, although four of eight reports noted a significant association between reported ETS exposure and increased frequency of respiratory symptoms and/or disease, an equal number did not report an association. These studies are too variable in results to permit a conclusion concerning an association between long-term ETS exposure and impaired respiratory health or pulmonary function in non-smoking adults.

Further research is needed in this area, and future studies should recognize that if ETS does, in fact, affect the pulmonary health of nonsmokers, its effect is likely to be subtle. Therefore, if future studies are to reliably detect effects, they must be designed to minimize, to the extent possible, the introduction of errors due to misclassification and the presence of confounding factors. Study subjects' ETS exposure must be reliably classified, using questionnaires which have been previously validated. The development of such instruments, validated in conjunction with ETS biomarker studies, is currently under way. Studies should consider all sources of ETS exposure, and not just exposure in the home. This will not only minimize exposure misclassification but will also tend to reduce the impact of some of the confounding factors associated with socioeconomic and lifestyle factors. In addition, if spousal (or household) smoking is not used as the basis for classification of exposure, then smoking status misclassification will no longer introduce differential misclassification error. Nonetheless, it is important that future studies attempt to confine the study population to never-smokers. Finally, future studies should collect data on potential confounding factors, including those related to socioeconomic status, the use of specific types of cooking fuel, occupational exposures and dietary factors in order to identify their contribution to any effects that are seen.

Acute exposure studies in normal individuals generally fail to demonstrate an adverse effect of short-term exposure on pulmonary function, even under artificially extreme conditions. Acute exposure studies in asthmatics have yielded contradictory and inconsistent results. While the majority of asthmatics appear not to respond with impaired pulmonary function upon such exposure, there may be a sensitive subgroup of such individuals in whom ETS exposure does result in increased airflow obstruction. The basis and mechanism of such a change, however, remain to be determined and should be addressed in future studies. While the available data suggest the likelihood of a mechanism other than allergy, this has not been fully explored, and further investigation of possible immunologic mechanisms would still be appropriate.

Another area that needs closer examination is the possible role of psychogenic factors in the reported reactions of some asthmatics to acute ETS exposure. Future studies also should take into consideration such factors as the clinical and physiological severity of asthma and the use of bronchodilator medication by study subjects. Finally, further studies should be done examining the effects of ETS exposure on bronchial reactivity to both nonspecific and specific bronchoconstrictor agents, including methacholine, histamine, cold air, exercise and allergens, as well as to various bronchodilator drugs, such as beta-adrenergic agonists, methylxanthines and anticholinergic agents.

References

Bates, D.V. (1989). *Respiratory Function in Disease,* Third Edition, W.B. Saunders Co., Philadelphia.

Beck, G.J., C.A. Doyle, and E.N. Schacter (1981). Smoking and lung function. *Åm. Rev. Resp. Dis.* 123: 145–155.

Bosse, R., D. Sparrow, and C.L. Rose, (1981). Longitudinal effect of age and smoking cessation on pulmonary function. *Am. Rev. Resp. Dis.* 123: 378–381.

Brunekreef, B., P. Fischer, B. Remijn, R. Van der Lende, J. Schouten, and P. Quanjer, (1985). Indoor air pollution and its effect on pulmonary function of adult nonsmoking women. III. Passive smoking and pulmonary function. *Int. J. Epidemiol.* 14: 227–230.

Burrows, B., R.J. Knudson, S.F. Quan, and L.J. Kettel, (1983). *Respiratory Disorders: A Pathophysiologic Approach,* Second Edition, Yearbook Medical Publishers, Chicago.

Cohen, S.I., B. Lask, (1983). Psychological factors. *Asthma.* Second Edition, Clark, T.J.H., and S. Godfrey, (eds.), Chapman and Hall, London, pp. 184–201.

Comstock, G.W., M.B. Meyer, K.J. Helsing, and M.S. Tockman, (1981). Respiratory effects of household exposures to tobacco smoke and gas cooking. *Am. Rev. Respir. Dis.* 124: 143–148.

Dahms, T.E., J.F. Bolin, and R.G. Slavin, (1981). Passive smoking: Effects on bron chial asthma. *Chest* 80: 530–534.

Friedman, G.D., D.B. Pettiti, and R.D. Bawol, (1983). Prevalence and correlates of passive smoking. *Am. J. Public Health* 73: 267–273.

Gao, Y-T., W.J. Blot, W. Zheng, A.G. Ershow, C.W. Hsu, L.I. Levin, R. Zhang, and J.F. Fraumeni (1987). Lung cancer among Chinese women. *Int. J. Cancer* 40: 604–609.

Gillis, C.R., D.J. Hole, V.M. Hawthorne, and P. Boyle, (1984). The effect of environmental tobacco smoke in two urban communities in the west of Scotland. *Eur. J. Respir. Dis.* 65 (Suppl 133): 121–126.

Godfrey, S., and M. Silverman (1973). Demonstration by placebo response in asthma by means of exercise testing. *J. Psychosom. Res.* 17: 293–297.

Green, L.W. (1970). Manual for scoring socioeconomic status for research on health behavior. *Public Health Reports* 85: 815–827.

Hole, D.J., C.R. Gillis, C. Chopra, and V.M. Hawthorne, (1989). Passive smoking and cardiorespiratory health in a general population in the west of Scotland. *Brit. Med. J.* 299: 423–427.

Hosein, H.R., and P. Corey, (1986). Domestic air pollution and respiratory function in a group of housewives, *Can. J. Public Health* 77: 44–50.

Huhti, E., and J. Ikkala, (1980). A 10-year follow-up study of respiratory symptoms and ventilatory function in a middle-aged rural population. *Eur. J. Respir. Dis.* 61: 33–45.

Kalandidi, A., D. Trichopoulos, A. Hatzakis, S. Tzannes, and R. Saracci (1987). Passive smoking and chronic obstructive lung disease. *Lancet* 2: 1325–1326.

Kauffmann, F., J-F. Tessier, and P. Oriol (1983). Adult passive smoking in the home environment: A risk factor for chronic airflow limitation. *Am. J. Epidemiol.* 117: 269–280.

Kauffmann, F., D.W. Dockery, F.E. Speizer, and B.G. Ferris (1989). Respiratory symptoms and lung function in relation to passive smoking: A comparative study of American and French women. *Int. J. Epidemiol* 18:334–344.

Kentner, M., G. Triebig, and D. Weltle (1984). The influence of passive smoking on pulmonary function: A study of 1,351 office workers. *Prev. Med.* 13: 656–659.

Kentner, M., and D. Weltle (1988). Passive tobacco smoke inhalation and lung function in adults. *Indoor and Ambient Air Quality.* Perry, R., and P.W. Kirk (eds.), Selper Ltd., London, pp. 232–341.

Knapp, P.H., and A. Mathe (1985). Psychophysiologic aspects of bronchial asthma.

Bronchial Asthma, Mechanisms and Therapeutics. Second Edition, Weiss, E.B. et al. (eds.) Little, Brown & Co., Boston, pp. 914–931.

Knight, A. and Breslin, A.B. (1985). Passive cigarette smoking and patients with asthma. *Med. J. Aust.* 4: 194–195.

Koo, L.C., J. H-C. Ho, and R. Rylander (1988). Life-history correlates of environmental tobacco smoke: A study on nonsmoking Hong Kong Chinese wives with moking husbands versus nonsmoking husbands. *Soc. Sci. Med.* 26: 751–760.

Koo, L.C. (1988). Dietary habits and lung cancer risk among Chinese females in Hong Kong who never smoked. *Nutr. Cancer* 11: 155–172.

Kotses, H., J.C. Rawson, J.K. Wigal, and T.L. Creer (1987). Respiratory airway changes in response to suggestion in normal individuals, *Psychosom. Med.* 49· 536–541.

Lebowitz, M.D. (1984). The effects of environmental tobacco smoke exposure and gas stoves on daily peak flow rates in asthmatic and non-asthmatic families. *Eur. J. Respir. Dis.* 133: 190–195.

Lehrer, S.B., F. Barbandi, J.P. Taylor, and J.E. Salvaggio (1984). Tobacco smoke "sensitivity"—is there an immunologic basis? *J. Allergy. Clin. Immunol.* 73: 240–245.

Lehrer, S.B., M. McCants, L. Aukrust, and J.E. Salvaggio (1985). Analysis of tobacco leaf allergens by crossed radioimmunoelectrophoresis. *Clin. Allergy* 15: 355–361.

Luparello, T, H.A. Lyons, E.R. Bleecker, and E.R. McFadden, Jr. (1968). Influences of suggestion on airway reactivity in asthmatic subjects. *Psychosom. Med.* 30: 819–825.

McDougall, J.C., and G.J. Gleich (1976). Tobacco allergy—fact or fancy? *J. Allergy Clin. Immunol.* 57:237.

McFadden, E.R. Jr., T. Luparello, H.A. Lyons, and E. Bleecker, (1969). The mechanism of action of suggestion in the induction of acute asthma attacks. *Psychosom. Med.* 31: 134–143.

Miller, A. (1986). *Pulmonary Function Tests in Clinical and Occupational Lung Disease*. Grune & Stratton, Inc, Orlando.

National Research Council (1986). *Environmental Tobacco Smoke: Measuring Exposure and Assessing Health Effects*, National Academy Press, Washington.

Nemery, B., N.E. Moavero, L. Brasseur, and D.C. Stanescu (1982). Changes in lung function after smoking cessation: an assessment from a cross-sectional survey. *Am. Rev. Respir. Dis.* 125: 122–124.

Pimm, F.E., F. Silverman, and R.J. Shephard (1978). Physiological effects of acute passive exposure to cigarette smoke. *Arch. Environ. Health* 33: 201–213.

Salem, E.S., M. El Zahby, G.A. Senna, and A. Malek (1984). Pulmonary manifestations among "passive smokers." *Bull. Internat. Union Against Tuberculosis* 59: 50–53.

Schilling, R.S.F., A.D. Letai, S.L. Hui, G.J. Beck, J.B. Schoenberg, and A. Bouhuys (1977). Lung function, respiratory disease, and smoking in families. *Am. J. Epidemiol.* 106: 274–283.

Schwartz, S.L., and N.J. Balter (1988). ETS-lung cancer epidemiology: Supportability of misclassification and risk assumptions. *Envir. Technol. Letters* 9: 479–490.

Shephard, R.J., R. Collins, and F. Silverman (1979a). Responses of exercising subjects to acute "passive" cigarette smoke exposure. *Environ. Res.* 19: 279–291.

Shephard, R.J., R. Collins, and F. Silverman (1979b). "Passive" exposure of asthmatic subjects to cigarette smoke. *Environ. Res.* 20: 392–402.

Shim, C., and M.H. Williams (1986). Effect of odors in asthma. *Am. J. Med.* 80: 18–22.

Simecek, C. (1980). Reflection of passive exposure to smoking in the home on the prevalence of chronic bronchitis in non-smokers. *Czechoslovak Med.* 3: 308–310.

Smith, M.M., H.J.H. Colebatch, and P.S. Clarke (1970). Increase and decrease in pulmonary resistance with hypnotic suggestion in asthma. *Am. Rev. Respir. Dis.* 102: 236–242.

Sparrow, D., B. Rosner, and M. Cohen, et al. (1983). Alcohol consumption and pulmonary function: A cross-sectional and longitudinal study. *Am. Rev. Respir. Dis.* 127: 735–738.

Speizer, F.E., D.W. Dockery, and B.F. Ferris, Jr. (1985). A simple model for the loss of pulmonary function associated with cigarette smoking. *Am. Rev. Respir. Dis.* 131: A177.

Stankus R.P., P.K. Menon, R.J. Rando, H. Glindmeyer, J.E. Salvaggio, and S.B. Lehrer (1988). Cigarette smoke-sensitive asthma: Challenge studies. *J. Allergy. Clin. Immunol.* 82: 331–338.

Surgeon General's Report (1986). *The Health Consequences of Involuntary Smoking.* U.S. Department of Health and Human Services, Washington, D.C.

Svendsen, K.H., L.H. Kuller, M.J. Martin, and J.K. Ockene (1987). Effects of passive smoking in the multiple risk factor intervention trial. *Am. J. Epidemiol.* 126: 783–795.

Tashkin, D.P., V.A. Clark, A.H. Coulson, M. Simmons, L.B. Bourque, C. Reems, R. Detels, J.W. Sayre, and S.N. Rokaw (1984). The UCLA population studies of chronic obstructive respiratory disease. VII. Effects of smoking cessation on lung function: A prospective study of a free-living population. *Am. Rev. Respir. Dis.* 130: 707–715.

White, J.R., and H.F. Froeb (1980). Small-airways dysfunction in nonsmokers chronically exposed to tobacco smoke. *New Eng. J. Med.* 302: 720–723.

Wiedemann, H.P., D.A. Mahler, J. Loke, J.A. Virgulto, P. Snyder, and R.A. Matthay (1986). Acute effects of passive smoking on lung function and airway reactivity in asthma subjects. *Chest* 89: 180–195.

Wright, J.L., L.M. Lawson, P.D. Pare, B.J. Wiggs, S. Kennedy, and J.C. Hogg (1983). Morphology of peripheral airways in current smokers and ex-smokers. *Am. Rev. Respir. Dis.* 127: 474–477.

Shettleworth, S. J., R. R. Collins and [illegible] (19[illegible]). [illegible] ... in a [illegible] ... 272–280.

Shettleworth, S. J., R. R. Collins, [illegible] (1979). [illegible] ... 272–278.

Smith, C. and M. H. Williams (19[illegible]). Effect of food [illegible] ... 2[illegible].

Suarez, [illegible] (1980). Effects of [illegible] ... on the [illegible] ... 205–[illegible].

[illegible]

[illegible]

[illegible]

[illegible]

[illegible]

[illegible]

[illegible]

11
Panel Discussion on Adult Respiratory Health

Robert Brown: Dr. Witorsch has summarized the field extremely thoroughly, so I will simply expand on a couple of points and things I think are interesting about this area.

First and foremost, I've been associated over the years with a number of studies of occupational lung disorders. Were data like this presented as part of an attempt to justify compensation for a particular ailment, they would not be accepted. The data are extremely weak. The co-variables are not really controlled for in any of these studies. Surprisingly, in none of the data on the impact of environmental tobacco smoke does there appear to be an equivalent of the healthy smoker effect found in active smokers. Young smokers tend to have better lung function than young nonsmokers because the nonsmoking population includes those with a congenital or some other form of respiratory disease. They choose not to smoke because they are already damaged so their lung function as an average is depressed. You'd think that such people also would choose not to associate themselves with environmental tobacco smoke as well. Thus, you conceivably might find a similar effect in nonsmokers exposed to ETS. Yet, there doesn't seem to be such an effect.

There are several possible explanations for this. The main one is that people who believe themselves to be especially sensitive to environmental tobacco smoke are more likely to classify themselves as being exposed. They're more aware of the exposure. Thus, the difference either disappears or is even exaggerated. People have very different thresholds for describing themselves as being exposed to ETS.

The methods currently available are too insensitive to allow the detection of the effect—if there is one—of ETS exposure. I think there is a need for more study in this area, and I think it's important that all sources of ETS that are of concern be studied. But because exposure occurs in the home, in the work place, during travel and everywhere else, these studies should be associated with personal samplers. Perhaps the data we heard yesterday on hair nicotine might be the best measure. Some measure of individual exposure from all sources could be correlated with lung function disorders.

I must stress, however, that the data presented thus far, including the studies reporting very small difference in lung function, does not justify the conclusion that the individuals studied are ill or severely damaged in any way at all.

Francis Roe: Thank you very much. George.

George Feuer: I congratulate Dr. Witorsch for the excellent presentation. In my comments I should like to emphasize a few points.

The methods used in the various studies were adequate. However, there was no agreement among the fifteen studies of which parameters showed a significant difference. Nine or ten of the papers showed no difference at all in the tests. Even in those studies where some reduction was reported, the degree of the reduction was about three to fifteen percent as compared to the controls. These reductions still fell within the normal range.

The subjects of these ETS studies are quite diverse, covering a wide range of groups regarding lifestyle, occupation and domicile. Reports include nonsmoking housewives who are living in rural areas, white collar workers in highly industrial cities, American women, French women, in relation to different socioeconomical circumstances, office conditions, home environment, influence of affluent society and conditions present in underdeveloped countries. Investigations were carried out on cohorts that live in small towns and in big cities. Some people were taken from moderate climates, and some from sub-tropical and warm, dry climates, some from industrialized, relatively polluted areas, and some from non-industrial regions. The age range was also wide, from thirty to about sixty years. The number of people involved in each study varied considerably.

In the acute studies, the conditions were simulated to resemble the kind of smoky environment that exists in pubs and bars. Still there was no evidence of acute effects of ETS on pulmonary function. Some minor discomforts, such as eye irritation, lacrimation, nasal irritation, discharge, wheezing, sore or dry throat, and coughing were observed in normal subjects and also in some asthmatic patients.

The intensity of some pulmonary responses in asthmatics may also correlate with other psycho-physiological reactions such as elevation of blood pressure, finger pulse amplitude and forehead electromyographic activity.

Despite these observations, there was no physiological or clinical evidence of any adverse reaction apart from the annoying discomfort of mucosa irritation. These adverse reactions were, however, reversible instantaneously after the cessation of the acute ETS exposure.

Finally, we cannot exclude the fact that psychological and other factors influence the response of patients to ETS exposure. Several reports suggest the possibility of psychological interactions. Especially in the acute studies, the level of anxiety associated with the fact that the individual was tested for an effect, and the stressful condition of the experiments themselves may provoke bias and misrepresentation of symptoms.(Shephard, R.J., R. Collins and F. Silverman (1979). Responses of exercising subjects to acute "passive" cigarette smoke exposure. *Environ. Res.* 19: 279–291. Kotses, H., J.C. Rawson, J.K. Wigal and T.L. Creer (1987) Respiratory airway changes in response to suggestion in normal individuals. *Psychosom. Med.* 49: 536–541. Urch, R.B., F. Silverman, P. Corey., R.J. Shephard, P. Cole. and L.J. Goldsmith (1988). McFadden E.R., T. Luparello, H.A. Lyons and E.R. Bleecker (1969). The mechanism of action of suggestion in the induction of acute asthma attacks. *Psychosom. Med.* 31: 134–143.) In fact, some studies found that a mere suggestion of symptoms, without any ETS exposure at all, caused an increased respiratory resistance in normal as well as in asthmatic individuals (Kotses 1987, Urch 1988).

In conclusion, it seems that at present no association has been established between ETS exposure and respiratory effect in normal adults. ETS may cause some annoyance and sensory irritant effects. Reports on its action on various physiological pulmonary parameters are contradictory, and there is no satisfactory evidence of any physical or clinical changes caused by ETS exposure in normal adults, or even in people suffering from chronic lung disease. Considering the wide range of conditions in which ETS was tested, it is unlikely that we ever will find any epidemiological evidence for an association between ETS and impairment of lung function in normal adults.

Does suggestibility modify acute reactions to passive cigarette smoke exposure? *Environ. Res.* 47: 34–47.)

Austin Gardiner: Dr. Witorsch's key analysis was elegant, encyclopedic and, I think on balance, persuasive that ETS exposure has been portrayed as an enormous bogey man.

However, having listened to what he had to say, I'm still left with the feeling that although ETS exposure may not do you much demonstrable harm, it probably doesn't do you any good either.

It has been long known by clinicians that there are certain asthmatics who simply cannot tolerate other people's cigarette smoke and will go to enormous lengths to avoid it. In fact, I remember my chief, Andrew Douglas, in Edinburgh, stating that he had never met a severe asthmatic who could smoke cigarettes and who would try to smoke cigarettes. And I'd remind you that Douglas is one of the co-authors of what is taken to be a standard U.K. text book of respiratory disease. (Crofton and Douglas (1981). *A Textbook of Respiratory Disease.* Blackwell).

I therefore was interested in Dr. Witorsch's comments on the acute exposure studies, especially the Wiedemann paper, in which an integrated pneumotachograph and a rapid xy-recorder were used to obtain data. However, Dahms, Wiedemann and others showed that even large exposures or high concentration exposures had no effect on most subjects, including some asthmatics in remission. But, as Dr. Witorsch pointed out, there were some groups where a significant minority of asthmatics demonstrated unpleasant symptoms and a clear increase in airway obstruction.

One can only speculate on what the mechanism for this might be. Immune reactions to tobacco leaf were tested in some of these patients and did not seem to provide an explanation. I don't think that it's too difficult to explain when one considers the Barnes model of asthma as a bit like dermatitis turned inside out. There's a chronic inflammatory condition and a whole range of "noxious" challenges will evoke acute inflammatory response symptoms and measurable decrease in function secondary to vagally-mediated bronchoconstriction.

I'm sure I can be accused of chauvinism for turning to the work by Hole et al. from the west of Scotland. The data in this study appear worth considering.

These authors identified passive smokers who they categorized as low exposure and high exposure. The high exposure group had a statistically significant reduction in forced expiratory volume in one second. But these changes in parameter are very small indeed and it's difficult to ascribe this to ETS. I think nonetheless that there is virtue in watching the long-term results that come from such a long cohort analysis. I would conclude my remarks by repeating that although ETS does not seem to do very much harm, I'm still persuaded that it doesn't do anybody very much good either.

Leonard Levy: The problem with psychogenic and psychological factors has been raised in Dr. Philip Witorsch's well-balanced and thoughtful review. He cites the work of Kostes et al. (1987) in which healthy individuals showed a change in their respiratory function simply because they thought they were being exposed to something that was going to be harmful to their breathing. Those in occupational health will be aware that there are some analogies here to some of the problems we've had looking at putative cognizant and behavioral changes seen in occupational groups exposed to low levels of organic solvent. Alongside symptomology questionnaires, occupational psychologists have included an assessment of psychological factors which might affect people's test results. This includes commonly used mood scales which assess factors such as stress and anxiety levels. The relationship between these scores and test results can be examined to give an indication of how people's perceptions might be influencing the outcome. Quite clearly, if people believe that something bad is happening to them, and this belief can affect their test results, you need to know about it.

I'm not suggesting that every respiratory study should include a psychologist, but I'm certainly suggesting that there are ways ahead in this particular area. You don't necessarily have to bolt on those scales and tests which are appropriate for other kinds of studies. However, they can be modified fairly easily to include the kind of factors you suspect might affect the outcome measurements in respiratory studies.

A. Poole: The purpose of this symposium, as stated in the brochure, can, for convenience, be divided into two elements. The first is to assess, in the light of current scientific knowledge, the health risk of environmental tobacco smoke exposure and the second is to chart a course for future research. To complement this approach this short review has been divided into two parts, i.e., (1) evaluation of current scientific literature and (2) possible future research.

The literature, unfortunately, is full of contradictions concerning respiratory effects of ETS in adults. Some research has reported that "passive smoking" in occupational, domestic or laboratory/experimental environments can result in adverse pulmonary manifestations, e.g., small airway dysfunction (e.g., see White and Froeb 1980 and Kauffman et al. 1983). Other studies, however, have shown that ETS has essentially no effect on pulmonary function (e.g., Kentner et al. 1984 and Schilling et al. 1977). Consideration has also been given to the effect of ETS on individuals with existing respiratory problems such as bronchial asthma. Once again the results have been inconsistent with some reports describing adverse responses (e.g., Dahms et al. 1980 and Knight and Breslin 1985), while others have found that ETS presents no acute respiratory risks to asthmatics (e.g., Wiedermann et al. 1986).

One possible way to resolve the uncertainty is to scrutinize all of the studies, including the unpublished "raw data," and decide which are the "best" in terms of design, parameters measured, etc. Such an approach can, of course, prove difficult as well as unsatisfactory since, with controversial issues such as ETS, there will always be debate on the methods used, accuracy of assessment, evaluation of data, etc. and conclusions are always open to criticism. This is especially evident when attempting to interpret studies which are subject to a multitude of technical, clinical, sociological, environmental, physiological and behavioral variabilities.

In addition to analytical variables, another problem when examining possible biological effects of ETS is to retain scientific objectivity. There is no doubt that a smoky environment can cause eye irritation, olfactory offensiveness, coughing and irritation. These together with reports of adverse pulmonary effects in active smokers (Chiang et al. 1970) can produce a "persuasive uncertainty" in which, based upon intuitive connections, it would seem logical to take a precautionary stance. However, I am sure that, as scientists, we are all well aware of the uncertainties of extrapolating from one set of circumstances to another. Thus, we must be careful not to use presumptive and inconclusive data to find "logical" causal connections based on what we conceive as reasonable assumptions.

At present there is suggestive evidence that ETS may produce statistically significant changes in certain respiratory parameters. While this evidence cannot be neglected, the negative data should not be ignored. The data are therefore not strong enough to prove that ETS will produce harmful respiratory effects in adults. Neither is it weak enough to assume that it is having no effect. A further confounding factor which must be considered is the possibility that the measured respiratory effects may not be associated solely with ETS but could be due, in part or totally, to other airborne irritants. At this time, it is only possible to reiterate conclusions reached by the National Academy of Sciences that any respiratory effects in normal healthy adults probably reflects the cumulative burden of many pollutants and cannot be blamed solely on ETS.

Given the uncertainties discussed above, how can a better determination of the possible effects of ETS on pulmonary function in adults be achieved? The usual approach is to call for (1) additional testing and (2) better/relevant data. The first of these is easily achieved, requiring only money and volunteers. The second is perhaps more difficult. A problem in attempting to define future work is to decide whether or not further data will be useful in reaching a decision. It is often stated that while it is possible to prove a positive, it is impossible to prove a negative. Thus, those who demand reproducible, sound scientific evidence of a health risk associated with ETS can argue that the burden of proof should rest with obtaining positive proof that ETS is harmful. However, as a general observation, many adverse effects are hidden with the consequence that even well designed studies asking relevant questions have a low probability of discovering effects when they exist. Thus, irrespective of the results obtained there can always be arguments that positive effects could be a result of many other circumstances, e.g., psychological effects, crowded conditions, other indoor pollutants, etc. Conversely, negative data could be interpreted as not examining correct parameters, analytical methods too crude to detect "obvious" physiological effects, etc. The data will therefore always be subject to "cultural/moral" interpretations depending upon whether or not the individual is convinced or unconvinced about the "health effects" of ETS.

This is not to suggest that further work should be discouraged. However, it should be accepted at the onset that it may never be possible to prove categorically that ETS constitutes a health risk or, conversely, that it does not. With this in mind, what can be done to improve our understanding of any risk posed to health by ETS? A possible way to reduce uncertainty is to focus on the key processes which are used in health risk assessments, i.e.—

A. Health endpoint: Risk assessment must be based on a well characterized, relevant health endpoint(s). Risk based on inappropriate endpoint(s) may give poor understanding and misrepresentation of effect.

B. Exposure: Collection of appropriate data to provide better predictive exposure assessment.

C. Delivered dose: Develop methods for monitoring, measuring and interpreting the exposure of the public to ETS.

Risk characterization requires knowledge of the relationship between all three factors. However, in order to evaluate data across many assessments it will be important to have a standardized, consensus approach to estimating health effects and population exposures.

Benito Reverente: I wish to congratulate Dr. Witorsch for such a thorough review and critique on the current literature on the effects of ETS exposure in adults. In light of the controversy on this subject, fueled by the frequent reports in the news media throughout the world, but especially in the West, this paper is not only timely but necessary. In other words, it is time to separate the chaff from the grain, to weed out the reports and papers which cannot be considered reliable and which are not based on generally accepted scientific and research principles, from those that are.

Dr. Witorsch has demonstrated in my view that with one or two possible exceptions, the papers reporting positive effects on ETS had either some flaws in their methodology or reported findings which were not significant. Thus, no research to date provides a sound scientific basis for the conclusion that ETS has an effect on pulmonary function and respiratory health among adults.

Caution dictates, however, that the issue be pursued by better planned, methodologically sound research studies in the immediate future. In the review, for example, of papers which conducted experimental studies on PFT's, by exposing subjects to ETS in exposure chambers, no acute effects were found. But there was no mention of possible chronic effects.

Speaking, however, as an Asian coming from the developing world and schooled in the discipline of occupational health, I would find it inappropriate to be allocating limited research funds in our part of the world for studies on a possible health hazard from ETS. We in Asia in occupational health consider this a lower priority compared to our more pressing health problems such as malnutrition, infectious and endemic tropical diseases, pesticides, and the dumping of toxic chemicals and wastes from industrialized countries to the developing world.

Lastly, I would point out that the papers reporting negative effects have the same methodological flaws as the papers reporting positive effects. The negative findings therefore could not be used as a basis for saying that ETS exposure has no health effects.

The evidence simply is not yet in.

Francis Roe: Thank you very much.

Dr. Witorsch, would you like to respond to the panelists?

Philip Witorsch: I'd like to respond to Dr. Gardiner's comment that while ETS exposure has not been demonstrated to cause harm to respiratory health, there's no evidence that it does you any good. I certainly can't argue with that and it's reminiscent of the line from Fiddler on the Roof, "while it's no great shame to be a poor man, it's no great honor either." That's obviously not the point that we're addressing, but I don't disagree with it.

As far as the response of asthmatics, which Dr. Gardiner alluded to, clearly asthmatics have hyperirritable, twitchy airways and will respond to a whole host of irritants by virtue of mechanisms involving irritant receptors. I have no doubt that some asthmatics may respond to the irritants present in environmental tobacco smoke, with a whole range of thresholds that vary from individual to individual. But it is a nonspecific irritant response in those instances, no different than the response to other kinds of irritants, including smoke from a campfire.

As far as the question about the low exposure and the high exposure subgroup in the Hole study is concerned, there was an observation of reduced FEV_1 in general and in particular in the high exposure subgroup. While that was generally, as epidemiologic studies go, a pretty good study, it still suffers from problems related to smoking status misclassification because of the way the information was obtained and it still has problems with confounding variables. These include the confounders that you've mentioned about the air quality in industrial areas in Scotland where these people work. That certainly may be a factor and we don't know how well that was controlled.

I agree with Dr. Reverente that all the studies, including those with "negative" results, suffer from the same general deficiencies. Based on the data, we cannot conclude either that ETS doesn't cause any respiratory impairment or that it's good for you. I think we need to study it further.

Francis Roe: Thank you very much. Just before I open the discussion I want to ask Phil one question. In studies in which I've been involved in the past, we noticed in Britain seasonal variations in FEV_1 and if you conducted a study looking at the same individuals throughout the year, then you could tell the weather by means of these FEV values. Now, is this an important variable, which perhaps needs to have a little bit more attention?

Philip Witorsch: Not only are seasonal variations important but there are even significant diurnal variations. If you do a forced vital capacity maneuver in the morning versus in the evening, depending on the person's activities, there are going to be significant differences and the differences from one part of the day to another part of the day and one season to another season are in the same range. Sometimes differences of 100m1 have been reported in these studies. So you certainly have to maintain that constant.

Some of these studies did pay attention to at least the seasonal variation and even to the time of day variation. They tried to do the pulmonary function studies on the control subjects and the exposed subjects during the same time of year and at the same time of day. Some of them were successful in doing that, some of them were not successful, and some of them didn't pay attention to that. That varies all over the lot.

Francis Roe: Thank you. Dr. Bacon-Shone.

John Bacon-Shone: John Bacon-Shone, University of Hong Kong.

I'd just like to take up two points, one point made by Dr. Poole and one made by Dr. Gardiner.

Dr. Poole made the point, which I, as a statistician, thoroughly agree with, that we shouldn't simply look at a group of statistically significant levels and become obsessed with them. I think one thing that disturbed me slightly was a reference by Dr. Witorsch to the fact that the pattern of significant levels was not consistent. I think you have to be a little bit careful here because that pattern of significant levels is actually consistent with a number of possibilities.

One of the possibilities, of course, is that there is a misclassification bias that was perhaps even constant across the different studies. Another possibility is that there is an effect that's very small, but it's so small that we're only going to pick up significant effects occasionally. And so I think one thing that is missing is some idea of how big the studies were. I think it's crucial that we keep in mind how big these studies were as well as how well run they were, so we can have some idea whether there was even enough power in any of these studies to show something, if there was something there.

I would be rather suspicious of a selection bias here with the studies of asthmatics. Most asthmatics I know are already well aware of their sensitivity or otherwise to ETS. I would have expected it to be very hard to get people who know or believe they have strong sensitivity to ETS to take part in a study of this sort where in some of these cases they were being exposed to extremely high levels of ETS. Of course, that is in itself a criticism of some of the studies.

Francis Roe: Thank you. There may be various people who want to respond to that, but I'd like to add that I believe that in the Stankus study there were seven individuals who showed some sensitivity. Oddly, they didn't show it in the first hour but instead showed it in the second hour, which I believe is really a rather unusual sort of response in relation to asthma, anyway. Phil, would you like to comment?

Philip Witorsch: The only comment I have on Dr. Bacon-Shone's remarks is that they're well taken. I think clearly in the asthma group there may very well be a selection bias and it may very well be that people are self-excluding themselves from studies like that and that needs to be looked at, certainly.

With regard to delayed response, that's not really that unusual because asthma is now coming to be recognized or asthma attacks are coming to be recognized as a biphasic response. There's been a lot written on the delayed response to various precipitating factors as an immediate response and a four hour or so delayed response. That may be one explanation for some of the delay in those individuals. It's also consistent with any number of mechanisms. It's consistent with an irritant mechanism, an inflammatory process that may take an hour to develop, psychogenic mechanisms and maybe even with an immunologic mechanism. It's not an unusual observation in my experience.

Francis Roe: Thank you. Any more comments?

Frank Sullivan: I think the interesting question is why is it that all the studies of respiratory function don't show anything of any great importance and yet it's common experience that sitting in very smoky atmospheres is unpleasant. I think most of us who are nonsmokers choose to go into nonsmoking carriages in railway trains and nonsmoking parts of airplanes, and so on. So there's obviously some kind of division between what we're measuring and what people are perceiving.

About twenty-five years ago I got involved in some studies on a new cough suppressant drug, and it was just at a time when tape recorders were becoming available. I was doing some work with a consultant at the Brompton Hospital who thought that a good idea would be to develop a very slow moving tape recorder that we could just count people's coughs all night long in this chest hospital.

One of the most important drugs for suppressing cough is morphine and so we used that as our first control. We set up the machine with the microphone under the pillow and we just recorded the number of coughs that patients had when they were getting morphine and when they were not getting morphine. And although the morphine was extremely effective and the patients all felt very much better while they were taking it, there was no difference whatsoever in the number of coughs that they had.

So I think the moral of this story is that in respiratory conditions, what you measure and what people perceive are two quite different things and I think that perhaps the research that we need to do on ETS really should be focused more towards the perception of what ETS is doing to them and how that might be improved in some way. It's no good telling people that lung function tests are not affected. People believe they're affected and we have to do something with that perception.

Hugh Thomas: I'm a consultant psychiatrist and I have done some work in chest medicine long ago. I have an interest in asthmatics and people who are very sensitive to tranquilizer drugs and things of that nature.

Sitting through this conference I've been evolving an idea about what's happening. It seems to me that there's a sort of parallel between what is happening here and a form of psychotherapy. The analogy is this: that we have all this painstaking analytical statistical thinking. On the other hand, there is point by point analysis of the technical problems and the evidence. At the same time, the language which is being used is tremendously the language of anger. We hear about a raging controversy, irritability and so forth. And it's the nature of psychotherapy that the more you analyze the intellectual aspect of the problem, the more you eventually come down to the underlying emotion. And I think the underlying emotion here is very largely anger and there's free-floating anger about and it's not only associated with ETS, it's associated with whatever is very prominent at a particular time for some people, I believe.

Now, I like the idea of asthma as being dermatitis turned inside out. I suppose if we brought back blushing, you know, asthma might decrease. That's another expression of anger, of course, very often.

So that I wonder whether psychological tests could be a helpful aspect of this research, whether it might not be useful to use scales which have to do with the direction and amount of hostility. There already are formalized scales available for just such research.

Francis Roe: Well, thank you for that. I think I must ask Nathan next.

Nathan Mantel: One of the discussants raised and dismissed the possibility of a "healthy smoker" effect. Earlier this year, I raised the possibility of an "unhealthy nonsmoker" effect, that is persons who are already in poor health who just can't smoke. I suggested this as a possible explanation of why Svendsen had found that the nonsmoking husbands of smoking wives had increased rates of mortality and of heart deaths.

Robert Brown: Sorry, I didn't dismiss it, I think it's real. There is the healthy smoker effect in that lung function of young smokers is better than the lung function of young nonsmokers. I think your explanation is quite right.

I've heard a lot here about statistical significance and about what is statistically significant and what is biologically significant and all this sort of thing. I think any and all hypotheses with enough data can and will be rejected eventually. So I think one has to be careful about all this talk about statistical significance and this sort of thing.

Raphael Witorsch: I want to comment on something that Dr. Sullivan introduced. It was followed up with a discussion about the psychological aspects of odor and unpleasantness. But, the issue remains whether or not there is evidence that exposure to ETS has an adverse effect on physical, not psychological health.

I think there is data that a majority of people find cigarette smoking irritating to the nasal passages and unpleasant. But the question is: what is the data base? We're addressing whether or not ETS exposure or what parameters or indices of ETS exposure affect pulmonary health. I think they have to be addressed because of the fact, as a scientist, I like to focus on the use of scientific data to establish a point. The point is to determine whether exposure to ETS enhances your risk of lung cancer, your risk of pulmonary impairment, your risk of cardiovascular disease, and whether your children are at risk. Those are the points that are being raised and those are the issues that we are trying to address scientifically.

The psychological issue is an important issue but I think it's in a slightly different arena. That's the only point. I wanted to bring us back to the focus of this last presentation.

Ross Lorimer: I was very interested, Dr. Roe, in your use of an analog scale to depict where you thought we were in terms of ETS, risk of cancer, risk of heart disease, etc. You'll remember that the analog came somewhere between no effect and very small. I would like to ask members of the panel to use that very helpful analog situation in describing where they think we are in terms of ETS and respiratory problems. Is it zero? Is it very small or is it somewhere towards small? I would be interested in individual views of the panel on that.

Francis Roe: Well, you've had a question. Phil, would you like to kick off?

Philip Witorsch: I think that in terms of plausibility, it is probably somewhat more plausible than the cardiovascular situation. We're talking about ETS effects on adult respiratory health versus cardiovascular health. In terms of chronic effects, I think the data, on the other hand, places it no higher than zero to very slight. And we just don't have enough information to know if it truly is zero or if there is a slight effect that we're just not able to pick up. A slight effect is plausible, but it's not very plausible. Clearly you have a dose-related phenomenon when you're talking about chronic respiratory effects of tobacco smoke. And when you consider the percentage of active smokers who develop chronic respiratory disease and the concentrations of irritants that they're exposed to, I think the plausibility of ETS causing chronic respiratory disease becomes very very slight. But it's theoretically possible. And someone mentioned alpha$_1$-antitrypsin deficiency the other day and, yes, I guess there may be some individuals who might genetically be even more sensitive but that's very hypothetical.

In terms of acute effects, I think that's a different situation. Perhaps in asthmatics the scale would be a little higher but it's still at the low end of Dr. Roe's scale.

Francis Roe: I'll have a panel member. So would you like to comment on this, Len?

Leonard Levy: I'd like to come back to Ray Witorsch's point, please.

I think the psychological aspects shouldn't be dismissed. If they're going to affect the outcome measurement in any way whatsoever, be it a question or a symptom, because of factors you're not certain about, I think you need to know about them. If there's a difference between one group and another because of their perceived risk or because of their general preconceptions about something, they could be quite important. I don't think that you can say that it doesn't have one effect on the other, it might. I think you can allow for this.

Robert Brown: I agree with Dr. Witorsch that it would be surprising if something which many people find irritating didn't have a small effect. He put it very well with somewhere between none and very little. And we could spend a lot of effort trying to actually quantify that very accurately.

On the psychological effect, I wonder if you're looking for an acute effect of tobacco smoke. It wouldn't be advisable to use a self-selected group of those who find tobacco smoke particularly annoying. There are people who are extremely annoyed by ETS and might show very good acute response to tobacco smoke. These people, who are very anti-tobacco smoke, might themselves be a selective sensitive group. It might be a useful approach to try and pick such a sensitive group of people for study.

Austin Gardiner: I must say it seems to me that the effect is slight. I do feel that there are individuals who probably experience very unpleasant symptoms and perhaps temporarily pulmonary dysfunction. And I think that that's likely to be due to the intensity of the tobacco smoke. These long-term cohort analyses come out with numbers of cigarettes smoked by smoking spouses, but we all know perfectly well in a lifetime experience that there are situations where that smoking spouse will smoke an awful lot more of the cigarettes. An individual can, I think, suffer unpleasant symptoms and perhaps certain individuals suffer more than one would imagine. But taking large population groups, it seems to be a very insignificant effect.

George Feuer: We have discussed the scientific evidence on whether ETS has any action on the respiratory health of normal adults and asthmatics.

Considering the wide range of studies, I think the effect of ETS on normal adults is zero or minimal with the exception of an irritation which is transient.

Francis Roe: Dr. Irving Kessler of the University of Maryland School of Medicine could not be with us today. However, he has submitted some trenchant comments for the record.

Irving Kessler: The ultimate objective of studies on ETS/respiratory disease is to draw conclusions about the biological relationship between ETS exposure and pulmonary disease, rather than to derive statistical conclusions about it. In human epidemiological studies, it is sometimes possible to demonstrate (as a result of chance, confounding or bias) statistical significance between diseases and variables that are unrelated. This situation differs from that of the typical laboratory investigation in which the use of homogeneous clones of laboratory animals allow the investigator to ignore most of the hereditary and environmental variables that are likely to affect the outcome of human studies.

Respiratory symptoms (cough, wheeze, etc.) are relatively rare among common laboratory animals and it is difficult to devise methods of studying the effects of environmental tobacco smoke on them. As a consequence, there have been relatively few controlled studies on the relationship between environmental tobacco smoke exposure and respiratory disease in animal models. This has impeded the development of human epidemiological studies as it leaves the epidemiologist with fewer hypotheses and fewer tested variables to investigate. The paucity of animal analogues of human respiratory disease also reduces opportunities for investigators to follow up on human anamnestic studies with randomized experiments in laboratory animals. Thus, the evolution of knowledge on etiology relationships between environmental tobacco smoke and respiratory disease has been impeded by problems in both basic science and epidemiology.

A major focus of epidemiological interest has been on the alterations in pulmonary function and histopathology that result from environmental tobacco smoke exposure. Many of the studies have involved measurements of pulmonary function in human subjects exposed and not exposed to ETS. Unfortunately, the instruments used to measure pulmonary function do not usually permit categorical (black and white) decision-making as to outcome. In part this is due to variations in the subjects' willingness to participate, age, general condition, medications, undiagnosed diseases, other environmental pollutants, variability in the instruments themselves, and skills of the technician, among others.

Case selection is critical in resolving the ETS/respiratory disease dilemma, as it is in many other epidemiological situations. Yet, in most of the studies published, little attention has apparently been paid to selecting the subjects.

It would appear that investigators often utilize subjects that are conveniently accessible to them, rather than those who will best ensure valid causal inferences. Some of the larger studies have utilized previously studied subjects selected for other purposes than the study of respiratory disease and ETS exposure. Other case selection issues I discussed earlier in connection with lung cancer (e.g., accumulating cases over a long period of time, etc.) also apply here.

As for the selection of controls, similar difficulties arise. Since human subjects are extraordinarily heterogeneous with respect to their genetic and environmental characteristics, the epidemiologist finds himself at a major tactical disadvantage vis-a-vis his colleagues in laboratory medicine. He must match the characteristics of the controls to the test subjects in response to variables that may affect the study outcome. However, the very process of matching reduces the possibilities for satisfactory statistical analysis because the relatively few techniques available for matched analysis become less applicable as the number of matching criteria increase. Thus, the epidemiologist who desires to match cases and controls to as many potentially confounding variables as possible finds himself limited for statistical reasons to matching on a limited number of the variables which may affect the study outcome.

Exposure measures for environmental tobacco smoke must be built into the epidemiological studies if its effects are to be validly assessed. However, as I mentioned earlier, measuring such exposures in a valid fashion is extraordinarily difficult.

Response rates and dose/response effects are other critical elements in the evidentiary chain of the epidemiologist. Control of covariant risk factors is another. The investigator must be cautious in attempting to interpret results meta-analytically (when data are pooled from several studies), as well as in pursuing anomalous findings and seeking explanations for unexpected results.

The literature on the relationship between environmental tobacco smoke and non-neoplastic respiratory disease is limited. Perhaps the majority of the published studies are small-scale clinical investigations involving five or ten subject pairs rather than the substantially larger and statistically more adequate numbers that are more commonly found in epidemiological case/control studies. The inferences that can be drawn from such small investigations are usually suggestive or tentative at best, rather than permitting substantive conclusions or resolving major hypotheses.

These clinical studies, as well as the larger investigations, usually suffer from important methodological deficiencies. Exposures are often poorly defined. Data collected previously for other purposes are often utilized, rather than new data designed specifically for the study at hand.

A number of the studies rely on questionnaires to define the exposures and, sometimes, even the clinical outcomes of the subjects. For characterizing such complex symptoms as wheeze, cough, tightness in the chest, bronchial reactivity, changes in respiratory flow, etc., more reliable measures are necessary and yet even those studies in which pulmonary instruments are utilized often suffer from technical deficiencies.

The subjects are often selected in a manner consistent with the convenience of the investigator, so that they are either biased or ungeneralizable to a definable universe of potential patients. Dose/response relationships have also not been observed in the majority of these studies.

With respect to inferences on the ETS/respiratory disease hypothesis, the published studies have not come close to resolution. Asthmatics may or may not be more sensitive than non-asthmatics to cigarette smoke. Cologne may or may not exacerbate the symptoms of asthmatics. Environmental tobacco smoke may or may not adversely affect pulmonary function and/or symptomatology in some asthmatics, though certainly not all. Yet there have been no studies designed to characterize the differences between susceptible and non-susceptible asthmatics in respect to environmental smoke.

Most of the published studies have grossly inadequate sample sizes, as already noted, and in all likelihood are either confounded or biased in one way or another. Furthermore, at the level of pollutants generally found in indoor air in the United States, the anticipated health effects to be evaluated are often of relatively small magnitude. Thus, investigations of the low-level effects of environmental tobacco must be better designed and must include sufficient numbers of suitable subjects to achieve acceptable power levels. Careful consideration must also be given to the problems of misclassifying health outcomes and quantifying individual exposures.

To enhance our knowledge of the effects of environmental tobacco smoke, epidemiological studies must provide better estimates of the low-level effects of environmental pollutants than has been achieved to date. Small effects may be introduced by environmental or host factors not taken into account. Accurate measurements of potentially important covariates must be incorporated into the study design.

Research recommendations on environmental smoke must take into account the extensive data already available on the effects of active smoking. Further research on environmental tobacco smoke is warranted with respect to infants and children, to characterize better the non-malignant effects of ETS on adults, to define the exposures at home and at work as well as to develop precise risk estimates for respiratory disease as an outcome of environmental tobacco smoke exposure.

At the present time, my opinion is that the limited number of studies that have been published have shown that passive exposure to environmental tobacco smoke produces acute, self-limiting symptomatic effects (such as coughing and runny nose) in some children and sensitive adults but that long-term sequelae have not been confirmed.

Francis Roe: I think we've had an excellent basic presentation by Dr. Witorsch. I think the one thing which really stands out in my mind is the comments of Hugh Thomas and I think we would need to have time to consider this. How do you take the capacity for rage into account? People who know me well know that one of the things that I cannot bear is small children eating onion and vinegar chips, both the smell and the noise is quite appalling to me and this would have very profound physiological effects on me, my blood pressure and God knows what! So I think that this aspect, quite seriously, needs somehow to be taken into account. Perhaps we could have more thoughts on this at any future meeting.

12

Parental Smoking and Respiratory Health and Pulmonary Function in Children: A Review of the Literature and Suggestions for Future Research

Raphael J. Witorsch, Ph.D.
Department of Physiology, School of Basic Health Sciences, Medical College of Virginia, Virginia Commonwealth University

I. Introduction

On the basis of the literature available at the time, the reports of the National Research Council of the National Academy of Sciences (NRC/NAS) of the U.S. (1986) and the U.S. Surgeon General (1986) arrived at the following conclusions regarding the relationship between parental smoking and respiratory effects in children:

1. Parental smoking increases the risk of respiratory symptoms and illness in children, especially younger children.
2. Parental smoking may be associated with small decreases in pulmonary function in children and may impair pulmonary growth and development.

In this review I will attempt to analyze the data underlying these conclusions, including studies that have been published since the NRC/NAS and Surgeon General's reports. This review also will include a discussion of possible explanations accounting for the presence or absence of associations between parental smoking and respiratory effects in children. Finally, I will examine directions for future research and suggest ways in which more consistent and objective clinical and physiological information on this issue may be obtained.

II. Basic Design of Studies Relating Parental Smoking and Respiratory Effects in Children

All studies examining the relationship between parental smoking and respiratory effects in offspring have been epidemiologic in nature. These epidemiologic studies have dealt with two fundamental parameters: (1) the incidence of respiratory symptoms and diseases in children; and (2) the level of pulmonary performance in children. All of the relevant studies have employed essentially a similar design. Information about family health and smoking history was obtained from a standardized questionnaire (usually a variant of the ATS-DLD instrument, which was a derivative of the BMRC questionnaire). These questionnaires were usually completed by the parents, sometimes with supervision and sometimes without. In most cases, the questionnaire served as the sole source of relevant health data. In a few studies, however, health data were obtained from medical records or clinical examination. Pulmonary performance was usually obtained by spirometric measurement, normalized for age, sex and height.

The incidence of respiratory symptoms or illness and/or level of pulmonary performance were compared statistically in children classified according to their parents' smoking status (e.g., smoker, ex-smoker or nonsmoker). The underlying assumption of this classification was that parental smoking served as a surrogate for exposure to environmental tobacco smoke ("ETS"). To date, no study of respiratory effects has employed specific biological or environmental markers to verify ETS exposure. In most studies maternal smoking status served as the basis of ETS classification of the child. This is understandable since children generally spend more time with their mothers than with their fathers, and in the case of young children the relationship would be quite intimate. Most of the relevant epidemiologic studies were cross-sectional in design (i.e., providing information about a group of subjects at one point in time) while a few have been longitudinal (where the same objects were examined on more than one occasion over the course of years). Longitudinal studies have focused upon age-dependent effects and issues relating to lung growth and development. Some of the relevant studies have addressed only respiratory symptoms and disease without undertaking or reporting measurements of pulmonary function, others have addressed only pulmonary function data, while yet others have addressed symptoms and diseases as well as pulmonary function parameters.

III. Respiratory Symptoms and Disease in Younger and Older Children

As shown in Table 12–1, at least 25 epidemiologic studies have reported an association between parental, usually maternal, smoking and an increased

Table 12–1
Studies of Parental Smoking and Respiratory Health Effects in Young Children (0–5 Yrs.)

Study	*Symptoms or Illness Increased*
1. Cameron, et al., 1969	respiratory infections
2. Colley, et al., 1974	cough, phlegm, respiratory infections
3. Harlap and Davies, 1974	bronchitis/pneumonia
4. Leeder, et al., 1976	bronchitis/pneumonia
5. Rantakillio, 1978	respiratory illness
6. Speizer, et al., 1980	respiratory illness before 2 yr.
7. Fergusson, et al., 1981	lower respiratory infections and symptoms before 2 yr.
8. Dutau, et al., 1981	respiratory infections
9. Schenker, et al., 1983	chest illness before 2 yr.
10. Ekwo, et al., 1983	respiratory illness before 2 yr.
11. Ware, et al., 1984	respiratory illness before 2 yr.
12. Pedreira, et al., 1985	tracheitis, bronchitis
13. Chen, et al., 1986	respiratory illness
14. Tominaga and Itoh, 1985	respiratory illness, esp. asthmatic bronchitis
15. Fergusson/Horwood, 1985	lower resp. infection and symptoms before 2 yr.
16. McConnochie/Roghmann, 1986	bronchiolitis
17. Strachan/Elton, 1986	wheeze
18. Toyoshima, et al., 1987	wheeze, asthma
19. Malloy, et al., 1988	mortality due to respiratory disease
20. Bisgaard, et al., 1987	wheezing
21. Geller-Bernstein, et al., 1987	wheezy bronchitis in atopic infants
22. Cogswell, et al., 1987	wheezing in atopic and nonatopic children
23. Kershaw, 1987	asthma
24. Taylor/Wadsworth, 1987	bronchitis
25. Chen, et al., 1988	bronchitis/pneumonia

Source: Updated from Witorsch and Witorsch, In Press.

incidence of respiratory symptoms (such as cough, phlegm production and wheezing) and/or illness (such as asthma, bronchitis, tracheitis, pneumonia, chest colds, bronchiolitis and respiratory infections) in infants and children 0–5 years of age. In several of these studies the frequency of respiratory problems in the children varied in a dose-related fashion with the number of cigarettes reportedly smoked by the parents and/or the number of parental (and/or other household) smokers.

Table 12–2
Studies of Parental Smoking and Respiratory Health Effects in Older Children (5 + Years)

Published Study	*Asthma*	*Cough*	*Wheeze*	*Bronchitis*	*Other*
Colley, et al., 1974		+			
Lebowitz/Burrows, 1976		–	–		
Schilling, et al., 1977	–	–	–		–
Bland, et al., 1978		+			
Kasuga, et al., 1979	+		+		
Tager, et al., 1979		–			–
Speizer, et al., 1980				–	+
Weiss, et al., 1980		–	+		
Bonham/Wilson, 1981					+
Fergusson, et al., 1981			–	–	–
Dodge, 1982	–		+	+	
Gortmaker, et al., 1982	+				
Schenker, et al., 1983	–	–	–		+
Ekwo, et al., 1983			+		–
Tashkin, et al., 1984					–
Lebowitz, et al., 1984					–
Charlton, 1984		+			
Ware et al., 1984	+	+	+	+	
Spinaci, et al., 1985		+			+
Fergusson/Horwood, 1985	–		–	–	–
Strachan/Elton, 1986		–	–		–
Burchfiel, et al., 1986	±[1]	–	+	±[2]	±[1]
Willat, 1986					+
Tsimoyianis, et al., 1987	–	+	–	–	
Dijkstra, et al., 1988	–	+		+	
Somerville, et al., 1988	–	+	+	–	
Andrae, et al., 1988	–	+			
Neuspeil, et al., 1989	–		–	+	
Summary: +/– for all studies:	4/9	9/7	7/8	5/5	6/8

Source: Modified and updated from Witorsch and Witorsch, In Press.

Notes: Positive sign indicates that an effect was found. Negative sign indicates than an effect was tested for but not found.

[1]Effect found in boys but not girls.

[2]Effect found in girls but not boys.

In contrast to the consistent association between parental smoking and respiratory effects in young children, studies of the relationship between parental smoking and the incidence of respiratory symptoms and/or illness in children five years of age or older produced less consistent results. Table 12–2 lists the 28 studies that have been published dealing with this issue. Eight of the studies found no relationship between parental smoking and respiratory symptoms or illness. When an association was evident, there was considerable variation from one study to the next as to the particular symptom(s) or illness(es) being reported. As shown at the bottom of Table 12–2, a particular symptom and disease is usually confirmed no more than 50% of the time.

IV. Pulmonary Function

In Table 12–3 are listed 26 epidemiologic studies dealing with parental smoking and pulmonary function in normal children. All involve school-age children or older. This is not surprising since such studies are difficult to administer in pre-school children. Although most of the foregoing studies were cross-sectional in design, five were longitudinal, in which the particular objective was to assess parental smoking on lung growth and development.

Most of the function data were obtained spirometrically using the Forced Vital Capacity (FVC) maneuver. The parameters derived from the FVC maneuver most often examined in these studies were the FEV_1, or its equivalent $FEV_{0.75}$ (forced expiratory volume in one or 0.75 seconds, respectively) and FEF_{25-75} (rate of airflow between the 25% and 75% points of the FVC). These data were usually normalized for age, height and gender.

Table 12–4 summarizes the findings of the 26 functional studies listed in Table 12–3. The results are variable, analogous to the situation above relating parental smoking and respiratory symptoms and illness in older children. For example, twelve of twenty-three reports note a small ($\leq$ 7%) decrement in FEV_1 (or equivalent) associated with parental smoking, while eleven do not. In 4 of these studies, an effect was seen in one sex of offspring and not in the other (three studies show effects in males only and one study shows effects only in females). Variability is also observed among the five longitudinal studies that have evaluated lung growth on the basis of a change in FEV_1 over time (Table 12–4). Two studies report a negative association with parental smoking (studies 4, 7), while three do not (18,22,25). Nine of twelve studies report a reduction in FEF_{25-75} in children of smoking parents compared to children of nonsmoking parents, while three do not. In two of the positive studies, however, the effect was not statistically significant while in three others the effect was seen in females only (Table 12–4). Table 12–4 also reveals variations among studies that measured FVC and/or $Vmax_{50}$, while in four of five studies no apparent effect of parental smoking was evident when PEFR

Table 12–3
Studies of Parental Smoking and Pulmonary Function in Normal Children

Published Study	*Source of Subjects*	*No. Subjects (ages)*
1. Tager, et al., 1976	East Boston, Mass.	140 (5–31y)
2. Tager, et al., 1979	East Boston, Mass.	261 (5–19y)
3. Weiss, et al., 1980	East Boston, Mass.	238 (5–10y)
4. Tager, et al., 1983[L]	East Boston, Mass.	715 (4–28y)
5. O'Connor, et al., 1987	East Boston, Mass.	265 (6–21y)
6. Ware, et al., 1984	Six U.S. cities	7112 (6–9y)
7. Berkey, et al., 1986[L]	Six U.S. cities	7834 (6–10y)
8. Hasselblad, et al., 1981	Seven U.S. areas	16689 (6–13y)
9. Tashkin, et al., 1984	Los Angeles, Cal.	971 (7–17y)
10. Ekwo, et al., 1983	Iowa City, Ia. Western Pa.	183 (6–12y)
11. Vedal, et al., 1984	Turin, Italy	3175 (5–14y)
12. Spinaci, et al., 1985	Turin, Italy	2385 (11y[a])
13. Chen and Li, 1986	Shanghai, China	571 (8–16y)
14. Burchfiel, et al., 1986	Tecumseh, Mich.	591 (10–19y)
15. Yarnell & St. Leger, 1979	Cardiff, Wales	214 (7–11y)
16. Teculesco, et al., 1986	Vandouvre, France	92 (10–16y)
17. Tsimoyianis, et al., 1987	Nassau County, N.Y.	193 (12–17y)
18. Lebowitz et al., 1987[L]	Tucson, Arizona	353 (5.5–25y)
19. Leeder, et al., 1976	London, England	454 (5y)
20. Schilling, et al., 1977	Three U.S. cities	816 (7–18y)
21. Speizer, et al., 1980	Six U.S. cities	5842 (6–10y)
22. Dodge, 1982[L]	Three Arizona towns	472 (8–10y)
23. Lebowitz, et al., 1984	Tucson, Arizona	271 (13.5y[a])
24. Lebowitz, 1984	Tucson, Arizona	24 (4–24y)
25. Dijkstra, et al., 1988[L]	Netherlands	632 (6–12y)
26. Martinez, et al., 1988	Viterbo, Italy	166 (9y)[1]

Source: Updated from Witorsch and Witorsch (1989 and In Press).
[L]Indicates longitudinal study, otherwise cross-sectional.
[a]Average age.
[1]Includes 17 asthmatic children.

Table 12–4
Parental Smoking and Pulmonary Function in Children

Study Number	*FEV_1 or $FEV_{0.75}$*	*FEF_{25-75}*	*FVC*	*Vmax 50%*
1.	decr.[1,2]	NR[3]		
2.	NC[4]	decr.[4]		
3.	NC	decr.[1]		
4.	decr. 7%[1]	NC		
5.	decr. 5–7%[1]	decr. 14–15%[1]	NC	
6.	decr. 0.6–0.9%[1]	NR	incr.	
7.	decr. 0.85%[1]	NR	NC	
8.	decr. 0.5–2.0%[1]	NR		
9.	NC	decr. 2.5%[1,5]	NC	decr.
10.	NC	NC	NC	NC
11.	NC	decr. 4%[1,5]	incr.	
12.	decr.	NC	NC	NC
13.	decr. 3%[8]	decr. 6%[8]		
14.	decr. 4–5%[2]	NR	decr.[2]	decr.[5]
15.	decr. 3%[1,5]	decr. 12%[1,5]	NC	
16.	decr. 5%[2]	NR	NC	decr.[2]
17.	NR	decr.[4,6]	NC	
18.	NC	NR	incr.	NC
19.	NR	NR		
19.	NR	NR		
20.	NC	NR	NC	decr.[5]
21.	NC	NR	incr.	
22.	NC	NR		
23.	NC	NR	NC	NC
24.	NR	NR		
25.	decr. 1.8%[6,7]	decr. 5.3%[6,7]	NC	
26.	NC	NR		
Summary:				
Increase	0	0	4	0
Decrease	12	9	1	4
No change (NC)	11	3	11	4

Source: Modified and updated from Witorsch and Witorsch, In Press.
Numbers in first column correspond to studies listed in Table 12–3.
[1]Associated mainly or exclusively with maternal smoking.
[2]Males only.
[3]Not reported as done.
[4]Effect not statistically significant.
[5]Females only.
[6]Associated with household smoking.
[7]Effect seen only with cross-sectional analysis of the data, not with longitudinal analysis.
[8]Associated with paternal smoking.
Studies 10, 19, 20, and 24 reveal no effect on PEFR, while a 3.3% decrease is seen in this parameter in study 25.

(the maximal airflow achieved during the forced vital capacity maneuver) served as the functional parameter.

When FEV_1 (or equivalent) and FEF_{25-75} were measured in the same study, concurrent decreases in both parameters were observed in four of eleven studies, while two reported a decrease in FEV_1 without a decrease in FEV_{25-75}, four studies reported the converse situation, and in one study no effect was observed on either parameter (Table 12–5). Several of the papers listed in Table 12–4 present results of studies performed on the same population of children at different times (e.g., the East Boston Study, Harvard Six Cities Study, and those conducted in Tucson, Arizona). Table 12–6 summarizes these studies and reveals internal inconsistencies when the same population of subjects were examined at different times.

The most consistent finding in this data base pertains to the possibility of dose-dependency of effect, i.e., the relationship between the magnitude of effects on FEV_1 ($FEV_{0.75}$) and FEF_{25-75} in children and quantitative estimates of parental smoking. In most of the studies, the magnitude of both parameters in children varied inversely with the number of cigarettes smoked by the parent or the number of household smokers (see Table 3, in Witorsch and Witorsch 1989).

The possible relationships between parental smoking and bronchial responsiveness in normal children has been measured using bronchoconstrictors or bronchodilators. Weiss et al. (1985) and O'Connor et al. (1987) using cold air bronchoprovocation and Corbo et al. (1989) using metacholine bronchoprovocation were unable to demonstrate any significant relationship between parental smoking and bronchial construction. On the other hand, Ekwo et al. (1984) noted increased bronchodilation in response to isoproterenol among children whose parents smoked. Martinez et al. (1988) reported increased bronchial responsiveness to carbachol in boys but not girls. They

Table 12–5
Studies of Effects of Parental Smoking on FEV_1 (or $FEV_{0.75}$) and FEF_{25-75} Concurrently

Study Number	*FEV_1 or $FEV_{0.75}$*	*FEF_{25-75}*
2.	NC	decr.
3.	NC	decr.
4.	decr. 7%	NC
5.	decr. 5–7%	decr. 14–15%
9.	NC	decr. 2.5%
10.	NC	NC
11.	NC	decr. 4%
12.	decr.	NC
13.	decr. 3%	decr. 6%
15.	decr. 3%	decr. 12%
25.	decr. 1.8%	decr. 5.3%

Note: Numbers in first column correspond to studies listed in Table 12–3.

Table 12–6
Parental Smoking and Pulmonary Function in Children (Comparisons within the Same Cohorts)

Source and Study Number	*FEV$_1$ or FEV$_{0.75}$*	*FEF$_{25-75}$*	*FVC*	*Vmax 50%*
E. Boston, Mass:				
1.	decr.	NR		
2.	NC	decr.		
3.	NC	decr.		
4.	decr. 7%	NC		
5.	decr. 5–7%	decr. 14–15%	NC	
Six U.S. Cities:				
6.	decr. 0.6–0.9%	NR	incr.	
7.	decr. 0.85%	NR	NC	
21.	NC	NR	incr.	
Tucson, Arizona:				
18.	NC	NR	incr.	NC
23.	NC	NR	NC	NC
24.	NR	NR		

Note: Numbers in first column correspond to studies listed in Table 12–3.

also found in boys a correlation between parental smoking and atopy, as determine by the skin prick test, and suggested that an effect of ETS on bronchial responsiveness and atopy was influenced by the gender of the child. Weiss et al. (1985) also reported an association between maternal smoking and atopy but no sexual dimorphism was noted. Recently, Soto et al. (1987) reported a 14% reduction in specific conductance (a measurement of airway patency) associated with maternal smoking among infants with respiratory syncitial virus bronchiolitis. However, the same study was unable to demonstrate a relationship between family smoking history and the child's responsiveness to the bronchodilator, salbutamol.

The effect of parental or household smoking on pulmonary function in asthmatic children also has been examined, although not extensively. Murray and Morrison (1986) reported 13% and 23% decreases, respectively, for FEV$_1$ and FEF$_{25-75}$ in asthmatic children of smoking mothers relative to those of nonsmoking mothers. Alternatively, Tashkin et al. (1984), Evans et al. (1987), and O'Connor et al. (1987) independently reported no apparent effect of parental or household smoking on pulmonary function parameters, including FEV$_1$, FEF$_{25-75}$, and PEFR in asthmatic children. O'Connor et al (1987) reported hyperresponsiveness to cold air challenge in asthmatic children with smoking mothers compared to such children with nonsmoking mothers but the difference between the two groups was not statistically significant. Martinez et al. (1989) reported that the association between parental smoking and bronchial responsiveness to carbachol for normal children was enhanced in asthmatic children. Murray and Morrison (1986) also reported a fourfold increase in the bronchoconstrictor response to histamine in asthmatic children with smoking mothers compared to children with nonsmoking mothers.

V. Discussion

The fact that parental smoking was consistently associated with increased incidences of respiratory symptoms and disease in young children and that this consistency was diminished as the child approached school age, suggestive of an age-dependent relationship, was noted in both the reports of the NAS/NRC (1986) and the Surgeon General (1986). In agreement with the possibility of such an age-dependency, several studies have shown that as the child ages (e.g., reaches 6 months to 2 years) the association between parental smoking and respiratory effects in the child diminishes or may even disappear (Colley et al. 1974; Fergusson et al. 1981; Ferguson and Horwood 1985; Chen et al. 1988).

Inhalation of ETS by the young child could contribute to increased incidence of respiratory symptoms and illness. To date, however, ETS exposure has been presumed only on the basis of questionnaire data (usually parental smoking status). The relationship between mother and young child is rather intimate and the exposure of the latter to ETS under these circumstances may be unusually intense, especially when maternal smoking occurs in close proximity to the child and in confined or poorly ventilated spaces, as in automobiles. Furthermore, young children may be more susceptible than older children and adults to ETS and this susceptibility may be exacerbated by increased exposure of children to infections of siblings and other children, and adults.

Several factors other than ETS, however, alone or in combination with one another, may account for the association between parental smoking and impaired respiratory health in younger children. Among these are socioeconomic status and related factors, and biologic mechanisms other than ETS associated with the prenatal and early postnatal period.

The effect that socioeconomic status (SES) might have on childhood respiratory health is illustrated by a study conducted by Kerigan et al. on a cohort from Hamilton, Ontario (1986). These workers showed that parental smoking, which is inversely related to family income, is positively correlated with several socioeconomically-related variables that can adversely influence respiratory health such as poorer outdoor air quality, increased parental coughing, higher gas stove usage, frequent change of address, and lower per capita living space. The findings of Harlap and Davies (1974) demonstrate how SES might confound the effect presumed to be caused by parental smoking. These workers reported that while parental smoking was associated with increased respiratory illness in infants, it also was associated with increased hospitalizations of infants due to injury and poisonings. As noted in the 1979 U.S. Surgeon General's Report, this suggests the involvement of parental neglect rather than an effect specifically associated with parental smoking.

SES involves several components and its adjustment in epidemiologic studies is complex. According to Green (1970), the following components of SES are most important: maternal (and to a lesser extent, paternal) education, income, occupation and ethnicity. Accordingly, Green has proposed a weighted formula involving the above components for correction of SES in health-related studies. Most studies pertaining to effects of parental smoking have either used more simplified (and possibly less than adequate) SES corrections or have used none at all. Furthermore, it may be extremely difficult, solely on the basis of even the most rigorously weighted estimates of SES, to adjust for such potentially influential factors as family attitudes and practices concerning stress management, nutrition and exercise.

The apparent age-dependency of the association between ETS and respiratory health effects suggests that biologic mechanisms other than ETS may also play some role, namely *in utero* and lactational mechanisms. The health effects on offspring of maternal smoking during pregnancy and lactation have been reported and reviewed by others (Abel 1980; Kleinman et al. 1987; Malloy et al. 1988; Nyboe-Andersen et al. 1982; Woodward et al. 1986; Witorsch and Witorsch 1989; Witorsch and Witorsch, in press).

The role of *in utero* effects has been examined by Taylor and Wadsworth (1987). These investigators compared the incidence of hospital admissions for lower respiratory tract illness and incidence of bronchitis in young children (aged 0–5 years) according to the following maternal smoking status classifications: (1) continuous smoking (during pregnancy and postnatally); (2) smoking only during pregnancy; (3) smoking only postnatally; (4) never smoking. Rates of hospital admissions in children of mothers who smoked during pregnancy only were found to be as high as mothers who smoked continuously pre- and postnatally. Hospital admission rates of children of mothers who smoked postnatally were not significantly different from children of never smoking mothers. Postnatal smoking may have exerted an effect on the incidence of bronchitis, but the effect was less than that of smoking during pregnancy. While overall incidence of bronchitis was not significantly increased by postnatal smoking, the incidence of bronchitis appeared to be significantly associated with duration of postnatal smoking while no such effect was seen with hospital admission rates. (However, the authors express reservations about postnatal smoking duration data since they were incomplete). According to the authors, these data suggest that maternal smoking effects on respiratory health may be predominantly mediated via an *in utero* effect, and only to a lesser extent through ETS exposure of the child after birth. *In utero* and/or lactational mechanisms, however, do not explain an apparent association between paternal smoking and respiratory health effects in young children from Shanghai households where none of the mothers were reported to be smokers (Chen et al. 1986, 1988).

The diminished consistency of association between parental smoking and respiratory effects in older children may reflect age-dependent phenomona (e.g., transient ETS or *in utero* effect). However, other factors should be considered, such as difficulties associated with using a questionnaire as the major, if not sole, source of acquiring health data in these studies. In the absence of clinical verification, parental memory and characterization of respiratory events regarding their children could involve some inaccuracy. The reliability of such information could be influenced by a variety of factors such as parents' education, family access to professional medical care, and the duration of time between the actual event and completion of the questionnaire. It is conceivable that the lack of consistent confirmation between specific respiratory problems addressed in Table 12–2 could be due in part to the difficulty a parent (lacking medical expertise) might have differentiating between such problems as "wheeze" and "bronchitis."

An association between the reported incidence of respiratory problems in parents and those of their children, which has been documented in several studies (Colley et al. 1974; Ware et al. 1984; U.S. Surgeon General 1979), may reflect either parental recall bias or the transmission of infection from parent to child. Accordingly, a recent report by Vobecky et al. (1988) suggested that maternal recall may be inaccurate. In addition, Enarson et al. (1987) recently raised questions about the usefulness of the ATS-DLS instrument in studies of asthma. Actual medical records and clinical observation no doubt are more accurate and reliable than unverified parental responses. However, such information also may be incomplete, anecdotal or not necessarily acquired in an unbiased scientific fashion.

Since questionnaire data concerning parental smoking status usually served in the studies conducted to date as the sole index of ETS exposure, uncertainty also exists as to the validity of such exposures. Several studies have correlated urinary or salivary levels of cotinine (a metabolite of nicotine) in children with the number of smokers in the family, and particularly with maternal smoking, suggesting that parental smoking status is a reliable indicator of ETS exposure (Greenberg et al. 1984; Jarvis et al. 1985; Strachan et al. 1989). However, use of biologic marker verification of questionnaire data has not been employed to date in respiratory effects studies (or, for that matter, in pulmonary function studies) in children. In addition, recent information regarding the fate of airborne nicotine from ETS, the uncertainties by which nicotine is absorbed by nonsmokers, and problems associated with nicotine pharmacokinetics, indicate that body fluid cotinine is at best only a semiquantitative estimate of ETS exposure (Balter et al. 1988; Lee 1988).

Because parental smoking served as the index of ETS exposure, misclassification of parental smoking status may create biases that distort positively or negatively associations between parental smoking and health effects in children, hence contributing to the inconsistency in the data base in older children. One source of misclassification bias is erroneous reporting of parental smoking status, where respondents in epidemiologic studies claiming to be never smokers are either current or ex-smokers. Estimates of such misclassification vary from 5–10% (NRC/NAS 1986; Lee 1988). Under such circumstances, a child of a misclassified smoker or ex-smoker will be incorrectly classified into the non-smoking or never-smoking parents group.

Change of parental smoking status is another source of misclassification bias. Smoking status has been reported to change at a rate of about 1.25% to 2.5%/year (Berkey et al. 1986), which can be substantial over the course of several years. In studies where subjects are classified according to current as opposed to lifetime parental smoking, such misclassification also would result in a presumed unexposed group containing misclassified exposed children. The foregoing forms of exposure misclassification (i.e., erroneous reporting of and change in parental smoking status) would tend to diminish effects associated with parental smoking.

In studies involving older children, in particular, lack of or inadequate consideration of the fact that children may smoke themselves is another source of error misclassification. Kerigan et al. (1986) reported in their cohort that 24% of the children between 8–13 years of age had smoked previously. As the child aged, a greater percentage of them smoked. For example, 50% of the children smoked at 13 years of age with a significant proportion having smoked in the preceding four weeks. In other studies, estimates of childhood smoking have ranged from 2% or less to 26% (Witorsch and Witorsch 1989).

Furthermore, treatment of childhood smoking among the relevant studies has been variable. Although children were questioned about their smoking habits in the absence of their parents in some studies, it was assumed that children below a certain age did not smoke. The age of this cutoff varied, depending upon the particular study, from 9–15 years of age. In addition, some studies excluded smoking children from the data base while others did not (Witorsch and Witorsch 1989).

It also has been suggested that the likelihood of childhood smoking is greater in families where parents smoke (NAS/NRC 1986; Surgeon General 1986; Lebowitz et al. 1987; O'Connor et al. 1987). Therefore, in a situation analogous to that involving marital concordance in lung cancer (NAS/NRC 1986; Lee 1988), misclassification associated with childhood smoking would tend to overestimate the effect of parental smoking. In view of the variability by which childhood smoking is addressed among the various studies, it is understandable how this source of misclassification error could contribute variability to the data base.

Among the other factors contributing to inconsistency in the association between parental smoking and health effects in older children are confounding variables such as outdoor air quality, home heating, air conditioning, humidity, and occupational exposures, factors which may or may not be related to SES (Witorsch and Witorsch, in press).

Since pulmonary function relies upon quantifiable physiologic parameters, spirometry would seem to provide a more objective indicator of respiratory impairment associated with parental smoking than the foregoing usually unverified health effects. The overall results of spirometric studies conducted in older children are highly variable, verifying those pertaining to health effects. The variability is evident when each of the major pulmonary parameters (FEV_1, $FEV_{0.75}$, FEF_{25-75}, FVC, $Vmax_{50}$) are examined individually (see Table 12–4), concurrently (FEV_1 or $FEV_{0.75}$ and FEF_{25-75}) (see Table 12–5), or when a particular cohort has been re-examined for a particular parameter on separate occasions (see Table 12–6). It is noteworthy, however, that when a particular physiologic decrement associated with parental smoking is demonstrable, the effect is small and within the normal range for FEV_1 and FEF_{25-75} (Bates 1989).

Most of the factors presumed to have contributed to the variability in association between respiratory health and parental smoking could contribute to the inconsistency in pulmonary function data. For example, parental smoking misclassification (erroneous reporting and change of smoking status) would tend to diminish differences in pulmonary function while active smoking in children would tend to exaggerate such differences. Other sources of variability in functional data would be the several confounding variables listed above.

As discussed in a recent review (Witorsch and Witorsch 1989), additional factors are worth noting regarding inconsistencies in the association between parental smoking on pulmonary function in children, namely the possibility of chance variations, genetic factors, and the influence of motivation, learning and SES. Other sources of inconsistency in the data could be the experience and skill of the technician administering the spirometric test, the type of spirometer used, and inherent variability of FEF_{25-75} and $Vmax_{50}$, relative to FEV_1 (Bates 1989).

Based upon the results of selected longitudinal pulmonary function studies that reported decrements in the yearly increment in FEV_1 associated with maternal smoking, both the NRC/NAS (1986) and the Surgeon General (1986) suggested that the latter might be associated with impaired pulmonary growth and development. As discussed above, only two of five studies support this possibility. In this regard, Lebowitz and Holberg (1988) recently examined the discrepant findings between their longitudinal study in Tucson, Arizona (Lebowitz et al. 1987), which failed to show an association between parental smoking and FEV_1 growth, and the longitudinal study of

Tager et al. (1983) in East Boston, Mass., which reported such a relationship. Although differences in study result could not be explained by differences in statistical methodology, they suggest the involvement of differences in ETS and/or other pollutant exposures between the two locales.

Several explanations can account for the apparent quantitative relationship between the decrements in pulmonary function and the amount of parental smoking and/or the number of household smokers (Witorsch and Witorsch 1989). Among these are the amount of ETS exposure, or quantitative aspects indirectly related to misclassification error and/or SES. For example, the incidence and intensity of active smoking in children or confounding variables usually associated with SES (such as outdoor air quality, gas stove usage, etc.) may vary proportionately with the number of cigarettes smoked by the parent or the number of household smokers. The apparent dose-response relationship between pulmonary function decrements in children and the amount of parental smoking and/or the number of household smokers is provocative and requires further examination.

Since only a limited number of studies have examined the association between parental smoking on baseline pulmonary function in asthmatic children and responsiveness to broncho-provocation in normal and asthmatic children, conclusions on these two issues may be preliminary, although the available data are inconsistent. As in the case of children, data relating ETS to asthma in adults are conflicting (Witorsch and Witorsch, in press). Martinez et al. (1989) have suggested that the discrepancies between such studies in children are due to differences in design and the nature of challenges used. Individual variability in the threshhold of bronchial responsiveness, however, is well known and has been found to reflect such factors as genetic influences and exposure to environmental agents such as irritants, allergens and infectious microorganism that might damage respiratory mucosa (Witorsch and Witorsch, in press).

VI. Conclusions

In a recent review, Rubin and Darmus (1988) evaluated 30 studies dealing with ETS exposure and child health. Of these, 28 pertain to respiratory health and/or pulmonary function, all of which are included in the current analysis. These papers were quantitatively rated on the basis of seven individual criteria (such as data collection, estimates of smoke exposure, definition of illness). Although Rubin and Darmus (1988) acknowledged the existence of a few well-designed studies, they noted that most had significant design flaws that prevent reliance on their conclusions.

The current analysis employed a different approach. Rather than attempting to rate the individual studies, the data base was divided into three categories: (1) respiratory health effects in young children; (2) respiratory health effects in older children; and (3) pulmonary function (e.g. spirometry) in older children. The consistency of findings were then discussed for each category and attempts were made to explain the overall findings on a category basis.

The association between parental smoking and increased incidence of respiratory symptoms and diseases in young children is provocative. However, the mechanism for this association remains unexplained. Among the possibilities to be considered are ETS, socioeconomic factors and effects of maternal smoking during pregnancy and/or lactation. The increased inconsistency of this association as the child ages is also unexplained. Among the possibilities to be considered for this apparent age-dependent change are changes in the susceptibility to or intensity of ETS exposure, inaccuracies in the data obtained from questionnaires (e.g., unvalidated clinical data and smoking status misclassification) and confounding variables. The data associating parental smoking with impaired pulmonary function and pulmonary growth, in accord with health effects data in older children, are highly variable and, hence, not compelling. The factors accounting for this variability in functional data are similar to those noted above for health effects.

VII. Directions for Future Research

Future research in the area of parental smoking and respiratory health and pulmonary function in children should be directed toward answering the following questions: (1) What are the mechanism(s) accounting for the association between parental smoking and increased incidence of respiratory symptoms and disease in young children? (2) Can a consistent association between parental smoking and increased respiratory symptoms and disease in older children be demonstrated and, if so, can the mechanism(s) for this association be defined? (3) Can a consistent association between parental smoking and impaired pulmonary function in children be demonstrated and, if so, can the mechanism(s) for this association be defined?

Definition of the mechanism(s) responsible for the increased incidence of respiratory problems in younger children will require epidemiologic studies that pay rigorous attention to socioeconomic factors and attempt to preclude the possibility that such associations are due to nonspecific factors associated with parental neglect. Standardization of socioeconomic correction adjustments would certainly be beneficial in terms of minimizing variability in result. Such studies would also benefit from the implementation of standardized questionnaires administered by trained personnel designed specifically to address respiratory problems in younger children and the implementation of procedures for verification of clinical findings. Insight as to whether ETS exposure contributes to the association in younger children could be obtained by use of body fluid cotinine as a means of verifying exposure in such studies as well as measurement of ETS constituents in the child's environment. More studies similar to the one recently published by Taylor and Wadsworth (1987), discussed above, need to be conducted. The possible contribution of *in utero* effects of maternal smoking on this association could be examined by carefully conducted longitudinal epidemiologic studies that compare health effects of offspring of mothers who smoke during pregnancy (but not postnatally) with nonsmoking pregnant mothers. Possible effects associated with maternal smoking during the early postnatal period (i.e., lactation) could be explored with similarly designed studies of cohorts in which mothers do not smoke during pregnancy but initiate or resume smoking post-partum. Insights concerning the roles of maternal smoking during pregnancy and lactation on the respiratory health of offspring also might be gained from animal toxicologic studies.

Determining whether parental smoking is associated with adverse respiratory health effects and impaired pulmonary function in older children will require implementation of carefully conducted epidemiologic studies specifically designed to minimize sources of variability, such as unreliable, unvalidated clinical data, sources of smoking misclassification (erroneous reporting of and change of parental smoking status, and variability in treatment of childhood smoking status), due consideration to confounding variables, and in the particular case of pulmonary function, standardization of spirometric methodology. This will involve use of professionally administered standardized questionnaires specifically designed to obtain accurate clinical data (that can be verified), as well as the most detailed and quantitative information about childhood exposures to tobacco smoke and other indoor and outdoor exposures. ETS exposure estimates from questionnaire data should be verified with body fluid cotinine measurements and markers for ambient tobacco smoke. Statistical treatment of all studies also should be standardized. In order to determine whether adverse health effects in children predict impaired pulmonary functional impairments, both clinical and functional data should be obtained in the same study.

References

Abel, E.I. (1980). Smoking during pregnancy: A review of effects on growth and development of offspring. *Human Biol.* 52: 593–625.

Andrae, S., O. Axelson, B. Bjorksten, M. Fredriksson, and N-IM Ljellman (1988). Symptoms of bronchial hyperreactivity and asthma in relation to environmental factors. *Arch. Dis. Child.* 63: 473–478.

Balter, N.J., D.J. Eataugh, and S.L. Schwartz (1988). Application of physiological, pharmacokinetic modeling to the design of human exposure studies with environmental tobacco smoke. *Indoor and Ambient Air Quality.* Perry R., Kirk P.W. (eds.), Selper Ltd, London, pp 179–188.

Bates, D.V. (1989). *Respiratory Function in Disease,* Third Edition, W.B. Saunder Co., Philadelphia.

Berkey, C.S., J.H. Ware, D.W. Dockery, B.G. Ferris Jr., and F.E. Speizer (1986). Indoor air pollution and pulmonary function in preadolescent children. *Am. J. Epidemiol.* 123: 250–260.

Bisgaard, H., P. Dalgaard, and J. Nyboe (1987). Risk factors for wheezing during infancy: A study of 5953 infants, *Acta Paediat. Scand.* 76: 719–726.

Bland, M., B.R. Bewley, V. Pollard, and N.M. Banks (1978). Effect of children's and parents' smoking on respiratory symptoms (1978). *Arch. Dis. Child.* 53: 100–105.

Bonham, G.S. and R.W. Wilson (1981). Children's health in families with cigarette smokers. *Am. J. Public Health* 71: 290–293.

Burchfiel, C.M., M.W. Higgins, J.B. Keller, W.F. Howatt, W.J. Butler, and I.T.T. Higgins (1986). Passive smoking in childhood: Respiratory conditions and pulmonary function in Tecumseh, Michigan. *Am. Rev. Respir. Dis.* 133: 966–973.

Cameron, P., J.S. Kostin, J.M. Zaks, J.H. Wolfe, G. Tighe, B. Oselett, R. Stoker, and J. Winton (1969). The Health of smokers' and nonsmokers' children. *J. Allergy* 43: 336–341.

Charlton, A. (1984). Children's coughs related to parental smoking. *Brit. Med. J.* 288: 1647–1649.

Chen, Y., and W. Li, (1986). The effect of passive smoking on children's pulmonary function in Shanghai. *Am. J. Public Health* 76: 515–518.

Chen, Y., W. Li, and S. Yu (1986). Influence of passive smoking on admissions for respiratory illness in early childhood. *Brit. Med. J.* 293: 303–306.

Chen, Y., W. Li, S. Yu, and W. Qian (1988). Chang-Ning epidemiological study of children's health: I: Passive smoking and children's respiratory diseases. *Int. J. Epidemiol.* 17: 348–355.

Cogswell, J.J., E.B. Mitchell, and J. Alexander (1987). Parental smoking, breast feeding, and respiratory infection in development of allergic diseases. *Arch. Dis. Child.*, 62, 336–344.

Colley, Jr. T., W.W. Holland, and R.T. Corkhill (1974). Influence of passive smoking and parental phlegm on pneumonia and bronchitis in early childhood. *Lancet* 2: 1031–1034.

National Research Council (1986). *Environmental Tobacco Smoke: Measuring Exposure and Assessing Health Effects.* National Academy Press, Washington, D.C.

Corbo, G.M., A. Foresi, S. Valente, S. Bustacchini (1988). Maternal smoking and bronchial responsiveness in children. *Am. Rev. Resp. Dis.* 137: 245 (letter).

Dijkstra, I.J., D. Houthuijs, I. Akkerman, and B. Brunekreef (1988). Health effects of indoor exposure to nitrogen dioxide and tobacco smoke. *Indoor and Ambient Air Quality,* Perry, R., and P.W. Kirk (eds.). Selper Ltd., London, pp 277–286.

Dodge, R. (1982). The effects of indoor pollution on Arizona children. *Arch. Environ. Health* 37: 151–155.

Dutau, G., C. Enjaume, M. Petrus, P. Darcos, P. Demeurisse, and P. Rochiccioli (1981). Enquette epidemiologue sur la tabagisme passif des enfants de 0 a 6 ans. *Arch. Fr. Pediat.* 38: 721–725.

Ekwo, E., W.M. Weinberger, P.A. Lachenbruch, and W.H. Huntley (1983). Relationship of parental smoking and gas cooking to respiratory disease in children. *Chest* 84: 662–668.

Enarson, D.A., S. Vedal, M. Schulzer, A. Dybuncio, and M. Chan-Yeung (1987). Asthma, asthma-like symptoms, chronic bronchitis, and the degree of bronchial hyperresponsiveness in epidemiologic surveys. *Am. Rev. Respir. Dis.* 136: 613–617.

Evans, D., M.J. Levison, C.H. Feldman, N.M. Clark, Y. Wasilewski, B. Levin, and R.B. Mellins (1987). The impact of passive smoking on emergency room visits of urban children with asthma. *Am. Rev. Respir. Dis.* 135: 567–572.

Fergusson, D.M., L.J. Horwood, F.T. Shannon, and B. Taylor (1981). Parental smoking and lower respiratory illness in the first three years of life. *J. Epidemiol. Comm. Health.* 35: 180–184.

Fergusson, D.M., and L.J. Horwood (1985). Parental smoking and respiratory illness during early childhood: A six year longitudinal study. *Ped. Pul.* 1(2): 99–106, 1985.

Geller-Bernstein, B., R. Kenett, L. Weisglass, S. Tsur, M. Lahav, and S. Levin (1987). Atopic babies with wheezy bronchitis. *Allergy* 42: 85–91, 1987.

Gortmaker, S.L., D.K. Walker, F.H. Jacobs, and H. Ruch-Ross (1982). Parental smoking and the risk of childhood asthma. *Am. J. Pub. Health* 72: 572–579.

Green, L.W. (1970). Manual for scoring socioeconomic status for research on health behavior. *Public Health Reports* 85: 815–827.

Greenberg, R.A., N.J. Haley, R.A. Etzel, and F.A. Loda (1984). Measuring the exposure of infants to tobacco smoke. *New Eng. J. Med.* 310: 1075–1078.

Harlap, S., and A.M. Davies (1974). Infant admissions to hospital and maternal smoking. *Lancet* 1: 529–532.

Hasselblad, V., C.G. Humble, M.G. Graham, and H. Anderson (1981). Indoor environmental determinants of lung function in children. *Am. Rev. Respir. Dis.* 123: 479–485, 1981.

Jarvis M.J., M.A.H. Russell, C. Feyerabend, J.R. Eiser, M. Morgan, P. Gammage, and E.M. Gray (1985). Passive exposure to tobacco smoke: Saliva cotinine concentrations in a representative population sample of nonsmoking school children. *Brit. Med. J.* 291: 927–929.

Kasuga, H., A. Hasebe, F. Osaka, and H. Matuski (1979). Respiratory symptoms in school children and the role of passive smoking. *Tokai J. Exp. Clin. Med.* 4: 101–114.

Kerigan, A.T., C.H. Goldsmith, and L.D. Pengelly (1986). A three-year cohort study of the role of environmental factors in the respiratory health of children in Hamilton, Ontario. *Am. Rev. Respir. Dis.* 133: 987–993.

Kershaw, C.R. (1987). Passive smoking, potential atopy and asthma in the first five years. *J. Royal Soc. Med.*, 80: 683–688.

Kleinman, J.C., M.B. Pierre, Jr, J.H. Madans, G.H. Land, and W.F. Schramm (1988). The effects of maternal smoking on fetal and infant mortality. *Am. J. Epidemiol.* 127: 274–282.

Lebowitz, M.D., and B. Burrows (1976). Respiratory symptoms related to smoking habits of family adults. *Chest* 69: 49–50.

Lebowitz, M.D., R.J. Knudson, and B. Burrows (1984). Family aggregation of pulmonary function measurements. *Am. Rev. Respir. Dis.* 129: 8–11.

Lebowitz, M.D. (1984). The effects of environmental tobacco smoke exposure and gas stoves on daily peak flow rates in asthmatic and non-asthmatic families. *Eur. J. Respir. Dis.* 133: 190–195.

Lebowitz, M.D., C.J. Holberg, R.J. Knudson, and B. Burrows (1987). Longitudinal study of pulmonary function development in childhood, adolescence, and early adulthood. *Am. Rev. Respir. Dis.* 136: 69–75.

Lebowitz, M.D., and C.H. Holberg (1988). Effects of parental smoking and other risk factors on the development of pulmonary function in children and adolescents. *Am. J. Epidemiol.* 128: 589–597.

Lee, P.N. (1988). An alternative explanation for the increased risk of lung cancer in non-smokers married to smokers. *Indoor and Ambient Air Quality.* Perry, R., and P.W. Kirk (eds.), Selper Ltd, London, pp 149–158.

Leeder, S.R., R.T. Corkhill, M.J. Wysoch, W.W. Holland, and J.R.T. Colley (1976). Influence of personal and family factors on ventilatory function in children. *Brit. J. Prev. Soc. Med.* 30: 219–224.

Malloy, M.H., J.C. Kleinman, G.H. Land, and W.F. Schramm (1988). The association of maternal smoking with age and cause of infant death. *Am. J. Epidemiol.* 128: 46–55.

Martinez, F.D., G. Antognoni, F. Macri, E. Bonci, F. Midulla, G. De Castro, and R. Ronchetti (1988). Parental smoking enhances bronchial responsiveness in nine-year-old children. *Am. Rev. Respir. Dis.* 138: 518–523.

McConnochie, K.M., and K.J. Roghmann (1986). Parental smoking, presence of older sibling, and family history of asthma increase risk of bronchiolitis. *Am. J. Dis. Child.* 140: 806–812.

Murray, A.B., and B.J. Morrison (1986). The effect of cigarette smoke from mothers on bronchial reactivity and severity of symptoms in asthmatic children. *J. Allergy. Clin. Immunol.* 77: 575–581.

Neuspeil, D.R., D. Rush, N. Butler, J. Golding, P.E. Bijur, and M. Kurzon (1989). Parental smoking and post-infancy wheezing in children: A prospective cohort study. *Am. J. Public Health* 79: 168–171.

Nyboe-Andersen, A., C. Lund-Andersen, J. Flack-Larsen, N. Juel-Christensen, J.J. Legros, F. Louis, H. Angelo, and J. Molin (1982). Suppressed prolactin but normal neurophysin levels in cigarette smoking breast-feeding women. *Clin. Endocrin.* 17: 363–368.

O'Connor, G.T., S.T. Weiss, I.B. Tager, and F.E. Speizer (1987). The effect of passive smoking on pulmonary function and nonspecific bronchial responsiveness in a population-based sample of children and young adults. *Am. Rev. Respir. Dis.* 135: 800–804.

Pedreira, F.A., V.L. Guandolo, E.J. Feroli, G.W. Mella, and I.P. Weiss (1985). Involuntary smoking and incidence of respiratory illness during the first year of life. *Pediatrics* 75: 594–597.

Rantakillio, P. (1978). Relationship of maternal smoking to morbidity and mortality of the child up to the age of five. *Acta Paediat. Scand.* 67: 621–631.

Rubin, D.H., and K. Damus (1988). The relationship between passive smoking and child health: Methodologic criteria applied to prior studies. *Yale J. Biol. Med.* 61: 401–411.

Schenker, M.B., J.M. Samet, and F.E. Speizer (1983). Risk factors for childhood respiratory disease. The effect of host factors and home environment exposures. *Am. Respir. Dis.* 128: 1038–1043.

Schilling, R.S.F., A.D. Letai, S.L. Hui, G.J. Beck, J.B. Schoenberg, and A. Bouhuys (1977). Lung function, respiratory disease, and smoking in families. *Am. J. Epidemiol.* 106: 274–283.

Somerville, S.M., R.J. Rona, and S. Chinn (1988). Passive smoking and respiratory conditions in primary school children. *J. Epidem. and Commun. Health* 42: 105–110.

Soto, M.E., P.D. Sly, E. Uren, L.M. Taussig, and L.I. Landau (1985). Bronchodilator response during acute viral bronchiolitis in infancy. *Ped. Pul.* 1: 85–90.

Speizer, F.E., B. Ferris, Jr., Y.M.M. Bishop, J. Spengler (1980). Respiratory disease rates and pulmonary function in children associated with NO_2 exposure. *Am. Rev. Respir. Dis.* 121: 3–10.

Spinaci, S., W. Arossa, M. Bugiani, P. Natale, C. Bucca, and G. de Candussio (1985). The effects of air pollution on the respiratory health of children: A cross-sectional study. *Ped. Pul.* 1: 262–266.

Strachan, D.P., and R.A. Elton (1986). Relationship between respiratory morbidity in children and the home environment. *Family Practice* 3: 137–142.

Strachan, D.P., M.J. Jarvis, and C. Feyerabend (1989). Passive smoking, salivary cotininc concentrations, and middle ear effusion in 7 year old children. *Brit. Med. J.* 298: 1549–1552.

Surgeon General's Report (1979). *Smoking and Health.* U.S. Department of Health, Education, and Welfare, Washington, D.C.

Surgeon General's Report (1986). *The Health Consequences of Involuntary Smoking.* U.S. Department of Health and Human Services, Washington, D.C.

Tager, I.B., B. Rosner, P.V. Tishler, F.E. Speizer, and E.H. Kass (1976). Household aggregation of pulmonary function and chronic bronchitis. *Am. Rev. Respir. Dis.* 114: 485–492.

Tager, I.B., S.T. Weiss, B. Rosner, and F.E. Speizer (1979). Effect of parental cigarette smoking on the pulmonary function of children. *Am. J. Epidemiol.* 110: 15–26.

Tager, I.B., S.T. Weiss, A. Munoz, B. Rosner, and F.E. Speizer (1983). Longitudinal study of the effects of maternal smoking on pulmonary function in children. *New. Eng. J. Med.* 309: 699–703.

Tashkin, D.P., V.A. Clark, M. Simmons, C. Reems, A.H. Coulson, L.B. Bourque, J.W. Sayre, R. Detels, and S. Rokaw (1984). The UCLA population studies of chronic obstructive respiratory disease. VII. Relationship between parental smoking and children's lung function. *Am. Rev. Respir. Dis.* 129: 891–897.

Taylor, B., J. Wadsworth, (1987). Maternal smoking during pregnancy and lower respiratory tract illness in early life. *Arch. Dis. Child.* 62: 786–791.

Teculesco, D.B., Q.T. Pham, W. Varona-Lopez, J.P. Deschamps, M. Marchand, J.C. Henquel, and M. Manciaux (1986). The single breath nitrogen test does not detect functional impairment in children with passive exposure to tobacco smoke. *Bull. Eur. Physiopathol. Respir.* 22: 605–607.

Toyoshima, K., M. Hayashida, J. Yasunami, I. Takamatsu, H. Niwa, and T. Muraoka

(1987). Factors influencing the prognosis of wheezy infants. *J. Asthma* 24: 267–270.

Tominaga, S., and S. Itoh (1985). Relationship between parental smoking and respiratory diseases of three year old children. *Tokai J. Exp. Clin. Med.* 10: 395–399.

Tsimoyianis, G.V., M.S. Jacobson, J.G. Feldman, M.T. Antonio-Santiago, B.C. Clutario, M. Nussbaum, and I.R. Shenker (1987). Reduction in pulmonary function and increased frequency of cough associated with passive smoking in teenage athletes. *Pediatrics* 80: 32–36.

Vedal, R.E., M.B. Schenker, J.M. Samet, and F.E. Speizer (1984). Risk factors for childhood respiratory disease. *Am. Rev. Respir. Dis.* 130: 187–192.

Vobecky, J.S., J. Vobecky, and F. Froda (1988). The reliability of the maternal memory in a retrospective assessment of nutritional status. *J. Clin. Epidemiol.* 41: 261–265.

Ware, J.H., D.W. Dockery, A. Spiro III, F.E. Speizer, and B.G. Ferris, Jr. (1984). Passive smoking, gas cooking, and respiratory health of children living in six cities. *Am. Rev. Respir. Dis.* 129: 366–374, 1984.

Weiss, S.T., I.B. Tager, F.E. Speizer, and B. Rosner (1980). Persistent wheeze: Its relation to respiratory illness, cigarette smoking, and level of pulmonary function in a population sample of children. *Am. Rev. Respir. Dis.* 122: 697–707.

Weiss, S.T., I.B. Tager, A. Munoz, and F.E. Speizer (1985). The relationship of respiratory infections in early childhood to the occurrence of increased levels of bronchial responsiveness and atopy. *Am. Rev. Respir. Dis.* 131: 573–578.

Willat, D.J. (1986). Children's sore throats related to parental smoking. *Clin. Otolaryngol.* 11: 317–321.

Witorsch R., and P. Witorsch (1989). A critical analysis of the relationship between parental smoking and pulmonary performance in children. *Das Öffentliche Gesundheitswesen.* 51: 78–83.

Witorsch, P., and R. Witorsch, Chapter IV. Respiratory effects of ETS other than cancer. *Other People's Tobacco Smoke: Environmental, Social, and Health Issues.* Armitage, A.K. (ed), Ellis Horwood Ltd, London, in press.

Woodward, A., N. Grgurinovich, and P. Ryan (1986). Breast feeding and smoking hygiene: Major influences on cotinine in urine of smokers' infants. *J. Epid. Commun. Health* 40: 309–315.

Yarnell, J.W.G., and A.S. St Leger (1979). Respiratory illness, maternal smoking habit and lung function in children. *Brit. J. Dis. Chest* 73: 230–236.

13
Panel Discussion on Child Respiratory Health

Donald Ecobichon: I'll ask the panel discussants for this topic to come to the front, please.

Robert Brown: There is better evidence that exposure to tobacco smoke has some effect on the respiratory health of children than in other areas. It is perhaps one of the better data bases about the effects of smoking but not necessarily of ETS. Some of the studies probably reflect intrauterine effects of direct smoking by the mother, rather than exposure of the mother to ETS. There is enormous scope for more studies. I personally wasn't aware of the Taylor and Wadsworth paper until fairly recently. I find it extremely interesting that the children of women who smoke during pregnancy showed an effect on respiratory health which tapered off with age. This suggests that the effect was largely a result of in utero exposure, not ETS. It's extremely difficult to understand, however, why exposure through the bloodstream should affect the developing lungs of the embryo and the child later on in life. What would be responsible for effects in these young children not exposed by the respiratory tract? I think there's a need for experimentation and examination along those lines. It would be well worth putting some financial resources into this work, and in particular the very tricky problem which was dealt with so eloquently by Dr. Witorsch about how to examine socioeconomic effects in this area. Examination of other countries with a different socioeconomic distribution of smoking patterns and behavior as well as reproductive behavior would be useful. You could pick the country with the best pattern for the study.

Donald Ecobichon: Dr. Hood?

Ronald Hood: Thank you. There are a few things that I might add.

One point of interest is the fact that almost all of the cited studies relating to childhood ETS exposure have been done on children from white families. It would be of interest to know if similar findings could be obtained from studies of black or Hispanic families. This is particularly true because there's evidence from the literature that there are significant differences among racial groups in pulmonary test results.

Also, such a factor might have influenced the results of Dodge's 1982 study. He had a high percentage of Hispanic children in his study population, but he did not report on the results of the Hispanic and other children separately, so it's difficult to know what effect it might have had on his conclusions.

Four of the reviewed studies on possible effects of ETS in children reported an actual increase in Forced Vital Capacity, FVC. One recorded a decrease, and eleven reported no effect. That was from the data in Dr. Witorsch's Table 12–4. I wonder if this could be indicative of a long-term response to lung function impairment, an adaptive response to respiratory stress. I'm under the impression that such changes do occur under certain conditions, perhaps in asthmatics.

I also want to comment briefly on the suggestion that it might be useful to determine if the effects seen in the reviewed studies were associated with prenatal or postnatal maternal smoking. It was suggested that one might compare the offspring of mothers who smoked during pregnancy but not thereafter with those mothers who had never smoked. Apparently this was done in at least one study. I would think, though, that in general there would be some difficulty in getting groups for such studies. The difficulty would be that mothers, I would think, would be considerably more likely to abstain during pregnancy and then resume, or to begin smoking after term, than to do the opposite. Thus it might be more feasible to compare groups of children from mothers who abstain during pregnancy and thereafter; mothers who abstain during pregnancy and then begin to smoke; and mothers who smoked both during pregnancy and thereafter. Only if the study population is relatively large would it be likely that sufficient numbers of mothers could be included in the fourth category of those who smoke during pregnancy and then cease. Of course, it would be highly desirable to include such a group, especially in trying to determine whether or not there were in utero effects.

Another question deals with how to avoid confounding due to socioeconomic status. I'm not an epidemiologist but I wonder if it would be advantageous to conduct at least some of the studies on ETS with relatively homogeneous populations in order to avoid having to attempt to correct for this factor. That's partly because any correction may be imprecise. We're really not sure what exactly it is that we're adjusting for anyway, because ETS is merely a surrogate. Also, if the study were large enough, it might include different groups that were homogeneous within the larger group, and this might allow comparisons among groups to obtain a ballpark estimate of any effect of socioeconomic status in studies of ETS effects. Thank you.

Jarnail Singh: With respect to the vast literature on health effects of air pollution and ETS, I'd like to make several comments and suggest two conclusions.

First, tobacco smoke forms only up to 15% of the total suspended particulate in the indoor air. However—now this is the key factor—surveys of air quality based on measurements of TSP do not readily identify the excess mass of indoor air from ETS. People exposed to ETS only have about 0.1 to 1.0% of cotinine in plasma, urine or saliva, compared to active smokers. Thus it is unlikely that any effects will be produced in nonsmokers exposed to ETS that are not produced to a greater extent in smokers. Types of effects that are not seen in smokers will probably not be seen in "passive smokers." The effects in nonsmokers are unlikely to be detected unless exposure is substantial and a very large number of people are studied. And in establishing dose-response relationships between parental smoking and respiratory health and pulmonary function in children, maximum effects should be seen in the children of active smokers, followed by the effect in children of pipe and cigar smokers. In many of these studies, we do not have any database from these sub-groups. The children of nonsmoking parents should have the least effect, or they should serve as controls.

Now, in my own research with laboratory animals, I have observed that respiratory health and pulmonary function may be associated with gestational age and birth weight of the young. My research indicates that *in utero* exposure to environmental pollutants such as carbon monoxide, nitrogen dioxide or sulfur dioxide produces dose-dependent, birth-weight deficits. The research further indicates that birth weight may be a key determinant of neonatal development. A 5% birth weight deficit significantly retards neonatal development. The birth weight deficit may mean fewer or smaller cells in the tissues or organs of the body, and smaller or fewer cells in the lung tissues may reduce pulmonary function in children.

The next point I want to make is that these pulmonary functions are influenced by things other than ETS. For example, several studies report that gas cooking stoves have a significant effect on the respiratory health of children. Speizer et al. reported that children living in homes with gas stoves had a greater history of respiratory illness before age two. Nitrogen oxide levels in homes with gas stoves were four to seven times higher than in homes with electric stoves. Lebowitz reported an association of V-max with gas stoves in asthmatics and normal and allergic persons, with outdoor nitrogen dioxide in the same groups, with outdoor CO in asthmatic and allergics, and with outdoor ozone in persons with symptoms of airways obstruction disease. This study further reported that ETS had no effect on V-max or symptoms in children or asthmatic or normal persons.

Other pollutants can have an effect. Spinaci reported that children from urban areas had reduced pulmonary function and higher prevalence of bronchial secretion with common colds than did those from suburban areas. The urban areas had higher levels of sulfur dioxide and total suspended particulates.

The pulmonary functions of children tend to run in families. The functions in children are basically associated with the parents, and there are about seven or eight studies that illustrate this point.

I would also observe that illness during early infancy plays a very big role in the lung function of children. Prolonged hospitalization at birth has been independently associated with lower FVC/FEV_{25-50}. One study reported that older children were better at performing spirometric tests than younger children. That leads me to ask, how efficient were the younger children in these studies in performing spirometric tests.

I have concluded that respiratory health and pulmonary function in children are complex end-points which may be influenced by several confounding factors. The key factors among those, in my view, are gestational age and birth weight. The rest, Dr. Witorsch has discussed.

I also want to emphasize that 85% of the indoor pollution is from non-tobacco sources. In the US, more than half the homes have gas cooking stoves. Infectious and allergic agents and volatile compounds are common in households. Children's respiratory illnesses are extremely common. In addition, the EPA in a recent report estimated that about 20,000 lung cancer deaths in the United States may be caused by radon exposure in homes. Keeping all these things in mind, even a small effect of non-tobacco pollutants could pose a very significant public health problem.

Frank Sullivan: The review by Dr. Witorsch has been excellent and really one can hardly add to it, but there are one or two comments I might make.

The fact that there might be a statistical correlation between ETS and some effect certainly doesn't imply that there's any causal relationship. In terms of reproductive effects, the important fact is that if you choose poor parents, you're very likely to have a poor outcome as far as all aspects of pregnancy is concerned. Abortion rates, stillbirth rates, low birth weight, poor postnatal survival—all fare poorly in low social-class families. There is a very strong social class effect in almost all studies involving pregnancy. I think that in this area, perhaps more clearly than in the ones discussed yesterday, one has to be sure not to confuse a correlation between an effect and ETS, with the conclusion that ETS might be causing that effect.

The second point is that I'm not exactly sure why respiratory disease in children is being discussed in a meeting on environmental tobacco smoke. To my mind, the evidence is much stronger that if there is an effect on respiratory function in children, it's much more likely that it is largely a prenatal effect.

It's important to realize that the majority of the studies looking at respiratory disease in relation to parents smoking do not separate effects of the mother smoking during the pregnancy from the postnatal period. That the effects appear to diminish as the children get older certainly suggests an intrauterine effect. It is comparable, perhaps, to the effect described in the National Child Development Study in the U.K. where all the children who were born in one week in 1958 have been followed up for the rest of their lifetime. One of the results of that study was that, as the children got older, the negative effects attributed to active smoking diminished, and eventually virtually disappeared altogether by the time the children reached puberty (Fogelman, 1980). This effect on respiratory diseases, which could be a prenatally mediated effect, could be related to intrauterine growth retardation in the children and could diminish as the children get older.

Lawrence Wexler: I want to thank Dr. Witorsch for his excellent and very thorough presentation. As an epidemiologist trained in psychosocial variables, I'm interested in the variable of socio-economic status and how it relates to the outcome of these studies. More specifically, I'm interested in the correlations that we saw in children under the age of five. The possibility of *in utero* and lactational mechanisms that may effect children, perhaps up to the age of two, is worth further study. Such a study should look at preschool children between the ages of two to five years to determine whether there is a higher respiratory correlation with ETS in this group as opposed to some sort of *in utero* or pregnancy effect manifesting in children under two.

Another question involves the validity and reliability of the BMRC adaptation questionnaires. With respect to questions adapted and used in different socio-economic groups, and in study populations which haven't been retested, we examine about ten different points to determine internal validity, reproducibility and reliability. I do not feel the data that we are offered in these studies are scrutinized as closely.

One of my co-panelists suggested a long-term prospective trial within one socio-economic group, perhaps one of the socio-economic groups that have been associated with higher risk. Once again, the problem is obtaining significant numbers. The other problem is getting a questionnaire that's been validated for such a group so they understand the questions and that the data that's collected can be meaningfully analyzed.

I'm not sure what the ideal study community would be. We've seen an international list of studies here. I'm a firm believer that 28 different studies are not necessary if we have one or two well-controlled studies in communities where they understand the questions and where we are indeed measuring the effects of ETS, which I think has been a problem in everything we've seen.

Finally, many of the studies are cross-sectional in nature. They're very helpful in evaluating at point prevalence rates and getting a sense of what the problem is, but I would recommend some sort of long prospective trial if we're really going to look at this relationship.

Donald Ecobichon: Ray, would you like to make a comment on any of those points?

Raphael Witorsch: If growth is retarded in general by maternal active smoking during pregnancy, the lungs may be smaller and take a longer time to develop. Unfortunately, there haven't been any good spirometric studies in young children below school age to examine this question. I think it has to be looked at more thoroughly.

Donald Ecobichon: Okay. Some questions, I'm sure, from the floor. I'll start with Peter Lee.

Peter Lee: I've got three points. One thing that hasn't been mentioned is that there's been quite a lot of work done on the relationship between respiratory effects in childhood and respiratory effects in adulthood. There's been quite a lot of work done by Professor Barker's group in Southhampton on this and I'm sure there's quite a lot of other work done. It seems to relate to Francis Roe's point about recording these sorts of things throughout the whole of life.

Secondly, I'd like to ask Dr. Witorsch whether any of the studies of effects in childhood actually measured or adjusted for the birth weight of the child.

Raphael Witorsch: Which studies are you talking about: pulmonary respiratory disease and health studies?

Peter Lee: Yes, any of them.

Raphael Witorsch: I don't believe so.

Peter Lee: I suppose it would be difficult to get hold of the information. It seemed to me this was one possible way of trying to distinguish between maternal smoking effects and possible ETS effects.

The final point is that you listed a vast range of possible confounding factors, but you didn't actually say how many of the studies have recorded these various confounding factors and what the effect of adjusting for these confounding factors were. Are there recorded studies where a significant effect before adjustment has become a nonsignificant or a vastly reduced effect after adjustment?

Raphael Witorsch: To include all the confounding variables and all the studies would require a slide the size of this room. But there is evidence in the literature to indicate that when adjustments are made, associations are greatly minimized. Sometimes they become nonsignificant, sometimes they become less. I can give you examples of various types of socio-economic adjustments. One group used average education of parents as an adjustment for socio-economic status. I thought about this after reading Green's manual.

Imagine that the average father has a Ph.D. and the mother has a high school diploma. The average education level would be fairly high, but Green indicates that maternal education is a very important variable in socio-economic correction. What I'm trying to illustrate is how complicated the issue is. It's really a can of worms.

Joseph Fleiss: With respect to adjustment for confounders and the effects that might have, a name we haven't heard yet today, Hirayama, succeeded in taking unadjusted relative risk in a study of the association between exposure to ETS and coronary heart disease. Without adjustment, absolutely no difference was seen in the study groups—relative risks of one and 0.99 for males and females. After adjustment only did the relative risks become fairly strong and statistically significant. And indeed there were problems with what he chose for adjustments, strange variables, but Hirayama did it again.

Now, with respect to Dr. Hood's questions about measuring socio-economic status and its meaning, I think that in for trying to elucidate the effects of exposure to ETS on respiratory conditions in young children and infants, it's the mother who matters and the mother's education.

Donald Ecobichon: Dr. Roe?

Francis Roe: I would like to point out that, in lower socioeconomic families, the father's indulgences in smoking and drinking and anything else he spends his money on may have quite a serious impact on the family's residual disposable income. This may be a way in which father's smoking could influence health effects of young children.

Secondly, Dr. Sullivan just mentioned the national Birthday Fund Study where they took a cohort of children and followed them for many years. This study gives you an indication of the enormous effect of some socio-economic factors. For children aged eleven, children whose mothers smoked during pregnancy months were four months deficient in their reading age. It's a matter of one's judgment whether one thinks that people can measure reading age with that degree of accuracy. But by comparison, if you looked at children who had three or more elder siblings, there was a 27-month deficiency in reading age. This gives you an example of the kind of background noise against which you may have to judge these effects.

Now, finally, I would like to ask the panel, and perhaps Dr. Hugh Thomas, about the psychogenic influences on children and the way they respond to studies. We're in a television age, and children of the age of four or five are being bombarded with anti-smoking propaganda. As soon as they start going to school, teachers tell them to urge their parents to stop smoking because it's dangerous. Now, can you really conduct the sort of studies which Phil Witorsch has been conducting without taking into account this particular influence?

Hugh Thomas: I think anything concerning the upbringing of children is such an incredibly complicated matter that it's impossible to give a short answer. I'm not primarily a child psychiatrist, although I did work in a dyslexia clinic for quite a time. The most important thing, in my clinical experience, is that one has to accept that every family is different, and it has to have the self-confidence to be different. Every child has to be appreciated as an individual. The one dogma I'm prepared to utter is that dogmatizing is bad.

I would be interested to know whether any of these studies which have made passing reference to differences of lifestyle have done anything to define what a good lifestyle is as opposed to a bad lifestyle. I would have thought one probable ingredient of a bad lifestyle, as far as childhood upbringing is concerned, would be to treat every little cold as a matter of dramatic importance, where the child is kept out of school and not allowed to go out and play because he's got a minor upper respiratory infection. It's a question of the triviality or seriousness of these things that needs to be considered. I think the Renaissance view is correct: we should try to be all-round and allow for individuality and balance.

Donald Ecobichon: Next question?

Frank Lunau: If I understand the presentation correctly, Professor Witorsch, none of these studies relating to school children seem to have taken into account the fact that school children actually go to school. The effect of the school environment upon their respiratory health does not seem to have been considered. Now, the reason why I mention this is that there has been some recent preliminary work by Professor Fanger in Copenhagen which shows that there is a very good correlation between the quality of the indoor air in the school and the prevalence of respiratory symptoms in children. Admittedly, the quality of the indoor air has been judged on a subjective basis, but nevertheless this is probably a very good indication, for instance, of the efficiency of the ventilation in these schools. It seems to me that this is such an important confounding variable that more work should be done on it. If Dr. Fanger's results are confirmed then work that's being carried out on children of school age is probably very suspect if it hasn't taken this variable into account.

Ronald Hood: Those comments made me think of a few things that relate to the real world. It might be possible that the differences seen in younger children versus older children, where the younger ones apparently were more likely to show some differential effect, could be due to the fact that they're at home more. As they get older they begin to go off to school so that a lot of their day is spent away from whatever influences—whether it's ETS or something else at home—that might be causing a differential effect.

Another point is that if smokers are more likely to be lower in socioeconomic status, then perhaps the mother is more likely to be off at work, leaving the children at a day care center or something like that. I'm not absolutely sure about this, but I believe that children in day care centers are more likely to have respiratory illnesses because they get them from other children.

The same thing would happen when the children go to school, but at that point they're all going to school. Earlier, it's mostly the children of working mothers who are going to the day care centers and are exposed to additional diseases.

Myron Weinberg: As we listen to this discussion, I notice that a lot of people search for a physical or a biological answer to some observation, and I'd like to add a psychosociological observation, Dr. Witorsch, which perhaps you'll comment on.

The literature from 1987 to the current time contains over 50 studies which indicate that smokers are defined psychologically as risk-takers. There are two things that are well defined as affecting both the incidence of childhood disease and things such as birth weight. Those two things are the level of maternal care and the level of household care. The psychological literature is replete with the fact that risk-taking is associated with minimal maternal care and therefore risk-taking is associated with reduced birth weight. And clearly risk-taking in parents is associated in the psychological literature with an increased incidence of respiratory disease in the household.

One may look, as epidemiologists frequently do, for things associated with the same thing or associated with each other. If you have cigarette smoking parents, you tend to have increased risk-taking. If you have increased risk-taking, there's data on birth weights, and there's data on increased infection. That might be a psychological effect.

The second point I'd like to make is that the literature is replete with the fact that marijuana consumption is directly associated with the incidence of cigarette smoking. In the 1989 literature we have a disease now known as "fetal marijuana effect," which concerns *in utero* defects produced by marijuana consumption. I don't know anything about what happens if you smoke marijuana in the household, and children aged zero to five smell it, inhale it or do anything with it. But those are two pieces of information which are in the psychosocial literature, risk-taking and drug use, which parallel cigarette smoking and which might affect both in utero development and post-natal development.

Raphael Witorsch: That's a point well taken. The risk phenomenon is associated in the literature usually with Koo's study and Friedman's study, where smoking is associated with other lifestyles. A good study might look at respiratory effects in children of parents who invest in the stock market after October 1989. That might be a good form of risk-taking.

There was a question about school environment and what effect it has. If my memory serves me correctly, in the 75 or so studies that have dealt with these effects, a number of studies have mentioned the possibility that exposure to other children and being in a school environment could be a source of increased disease, but it's never been addressed as a parameter for correction. It's a point well taken. In many cities, at least in the United States, some schools have deteriorated to the point where asbestos is falling from the walls, there's bad heating, cracks in the windows, etc. It's something that really should be considered.

Jarnail Singh: What we call the "ETS effect" in the literature really may be what I call the effect of poverty. As most of our international colleagues know, the District of Columbia has the highest infant mortality rate in the U.S. Next is a county in the State of Alabama called Green County. The University of Alabama has done studies there on why infants in this county are dying. They came up with three conclusions. The first one is late or inadequate prenatal care, the second is inadequate prenatal nutrition, and the third is inadequate early childhood medical care. It is poverty, not ETS, that did these things.

Robert Brown: On a much lighter note, the Action on Smoking and Health group in Britain, a pressure group against all forms of tobacco use, issued a press statement recently pointing out that if you smoked you were more likely to have a motorcycle accident, and they seemed to attribute a causal relationship to this. They seemed to feel that people actually smoked while driving their motorcycles.

They also went on to say that if your parents were smokers, you were more likely to have a motorcycle accident as well. It's a health effect which we haven't touched on but which could be related, at least as much as some of the others which do get publicity.

Donald Ecobichon: Any other comments?

Frank Sullivan: I was interested in this last comment about psychological makeup. Those of us who've been interested in the effects of smoking for a good number of years will remember the big argument that used to rage about constitutional factors in smoking. The early Yerushalmy studies that were carried out were interpreted to show that women who smoked tended to have small babies, and that it didn't matter whether they took up smoking after or before they had their babies. They had small babies, and this was regarded as a constitutional factor in the women.

What's happened now is that all of the studies that were used to support the constitutional hypothesis of smoking have now been transferred over to environmental tobacco smoke. All these things that we used to say were due to the psychological or the physiological makeup of the women or the men are now ascribed to ETS. This is really quite important. ETS is very in vogue to talk about, but I think it's very important for us to try and separate out what is an ETS factor from what is a psychological-constitutional factor.

Part VI

14

An Assessment of Potential Effects of Environmental Tobacco Smoke on Prenatal Development and Reproductive Capacity

Ronald D. Hood, Ph.D., Biology Department
University of Alabama

This review addresses the potential effects of exposure to environmental tobacco smoke ("ETS") on the developing embryo and fetus. Most of the available studies are concerned with the possible relationship between maternal exposure to paternal smoking and lower birth weight, and the review accordingly focuses on this issue. The review concludes that the available data on ETS and birth weight are limited in scope and inconclusive. This review also addresses data on ETS and reproductive potential and related endpoints, and concludes that the data in this area are even more limited.

Because the unborn individual cannot smoke, the terms "passive" and "involuntary" smoking have at times been used to refer to prenatal exposure due to maternal active smoking. The current review addresses only the issue of exposure of nonsmoking mothers to ETS. The review does not consider transplacental responses to maternal active smoking products, as these are not directly relevant to assessment of ETS and are beyond the scope of this inquiry.

This review examines the literature from the perspective of a reproductive and developmental toxicologist, and covers the literature regarding ETS and fetal weight, mortality and malformation, as well as reproductive endpoints in adults, including spontaneous abortion and fecundity. The review also offers a critique of available data and highlights major research needs in this important area.

I. Review of Current Literature on Potential ETS Effects

A. Animal Studies

A literature search for studies directly relevant to possible effects of ETS exposure on the developing fetus did not reveal any appropriate laboratory animal studies. The limited animal data on developmental effects following maternal exposure to tobacco smoke were derived from investigations attempting to mimic active smoking (e.g., Haworth and Ford 1972; Abel 1980; Reznik and Marquard 1980; Peterson et al. 1981; Bertolini et al. 1982; Tachi and Aoyama 1983, 1986, 1989; Bassi et al. 1984). They used simulated mainstream smoke and employed exposure levels equal to or greater than those expected from active smoking. Thus, their results are not appropriate for assessment of the likelihood or nature of ETS effects.

B. Epidemiologic Studies

Most of the data pertinent to an assessment of ETS effects are from epidemiological reports. Virtually all of these studies relied on unverified questionnaire data and used paternal smoking as a surrogate for maternal ETS exposure. Most of the studies dealt with possible effects on birth weight, although a few studies addressed other endpoints.

1. Birth Weight and Body Measurements

Early Studies. The initial published studies attempting to investigate effects of prenatal ETS exposure were conducted in the 1960s and early 1970s. They include reports by Yerushalmy (1962, 1971), MacMahon et al. (1966), Comstock and Lundin (1967), Ravenholt and Levinski (1965), Underwood et al. (1967), Terris and Gold (1969) and Mau and Netter (1974). These investigators generally used reports of paternal smoking as their only measures of ETS exposure. Mean birth weight or incidence of low birth weight or prematurity, defined as birth weight below 2500 g, were their major endpoints. Their results were almost uniformly negative. Only two reports by the same author (Yerushalmy 1962, 1971) claimed to find a statistically significant association between decrements in infant birth weight and maternal exposure to paternal smoking.

In 1962, Yerushalmy published the results of a study of the relative effects of maternal and paternal smoking on the outcome of 982 pregnancies, comparing the incidences of low birth weight babies. Compared with data for offspring of two nonsmoking parents (incidence = 5.7%), there was no effect on the incidence of low birth weight offspring when the father smoked and the mother did not (incidence = 6.2%, relative risk = 1.1, NS). Yerushalmy reported, however, that the effect of the father's smoking (incidence = 6.2%) appeared to be greater than that seen when the mother alone smoked (4.6%) (Table 14–1), a finding that lacks biological plausibility. Moreover, Yerushalmy stated that when both parents smoked, the likelihood of delivering a low birth weight baby (incidence = 9.4%) was significantly greater than was the case for pregnancies where only one or neither parent smoked.

Since spousal smoking habits tend to be correlated ("concordance"), the wives of smokers in Yerushalmy's study may have smoked more heavily then did the wives of nonsmokers. Such potential sources of bias were not corrected for. Also, the difference in incidences of low birth weight babies born to smoking vs. nonsmoking fathers, independent of maternal smoking habits, was nonsignificant, and Yerushalmy's data do not support a dose-response relationship between paternal smoking and lowered birth weight. These considerations led Goldstein and coworkers (1964) to state that "[Yerushalmy's] data failed to establish any association between birth weight and the father's smoking habits independent of the mother's smoking habits."

In a larger study, Yerushalmy (1971) examined the outcome of over 13,000 pregnancies. Again the incidence of low birth weight live born infants was found to have been unaffected by paternal smoking if the mother was a nonsmoker (Table 14–2). Data from white and black parents were analyzed separately. For whites, if the father was a smoker, the incidence of low birth weight offspring was significantly increased, but only if the mother was also a smoker. The data on birth weights of black parents were apparently similar in trend and relative magnitude (percentage increase) but the difference was nonsignificant.

The data of Yerushalmy (1962, 1971) were not adjusted to compensate

Table 14–1
Percentage of Low Birth Weight Infants by Paternal and Maternal Smoking Habits

Mother	*Father*	
	Smoker	Nonsmoker
Smoker	9.4%*	4.6%
Nonsmoker	6.2%	5.7%

Source: From Yerushalmy, 1962.
Note: ≤ 2500 g.
*$p \leq 0.05$ (different from all other groups).

Table 14–2
Percentage of Liveborn Low Birth Weight Infants by Paternal and Maternal Smoking Habits and Race

Paternal Smoking Status	*Maternal Smoking Status and Race*			
	White		*Black*	
	Nonsmoker	*Smoker*	*Nonsmoker*	*Smoker*
Nonsmoker	3.43	4.83	5.80	9.50
Smoker	3.10	6.74*	6.11	13.41

Source: From Yerushalmy, 1971.
Note: ≤ 2500 g.
*$p \leq 0.05$ for difference associated with husband's smoking status.

for potential confounding factors. Yerushalmy himself suggested that the observed relationship between paternal smoking and incidence of low birth weight was probably not causal, and indeed, such a conclusion appears reasonable.

The remaining early studies fail to support Yerulshalmy's finding of an association between paternal smoking and an increased incidence of low birth weight infants. For example, MacMahon et al. (1966), in an examination of more than 12,000 pregnancies, concluded that the mean weight of newborns from nonsmoking mothers was only slightly decreased (20 g for male and 23 g for female infants) if the father smoked. When the authors corrected the data for the mother's smoking level, they concluded that there was "no association between infant birth weight and paternal smoking habits." No dose-response was found for the level of paternal smoking.

More Recent Studies. Several additional studies are available dating from the late 1970s. These studies can be divided into two groups: (1) those using only reported paternal smoking as a surrogate for exposure to ETS and (2) those using other ETS measures, including exposure indicators such as thiocyanate or cotinine assays. The data from the more recent studies are mixed. Five of the studies found no positive association between birth weight decrement and maternal ETS exposure (Hauth et al. 1984; Magnus et al. 1984; Little and Sing 1987; MacArthur and Knox 1987; Chen et al. 1989). Six others, however, reported finding significant or marginally significant associations between maternal ETS exposure and decreased birth weight (Borlee et al. 1978; Rubin et al. 1986; Schwartz-Bickenbach et al. 1987; Haddow et al. 1988b) or incidence of low birth weight infants (Martin and Bracken 1986; Nakamura et al. 1988).

Studies Using Paternal Smoking as the Only Measure of ETS Exposure. The first of the more recent studies to report positive results was that of Borlee and coworkers (1978). This study was incidental to a larger retrospective case-control investigation of birth defects and environmental factors conducted at eight hospitals in southern Belgium. According to the authors, children of nonsmoking mothers and smoking fathers weighed 228 g less at birth than children whose parents did not smoke, and this difference was significant (Table 14–3). This reported effect seems implausibly large, however, since it is equivalent to differences that have been attributed to maternal active smoking of some 20 cigarettes per day (Kramer 1987). Further, height and head circumferences of the newborns were unaffected by the father's smoking status.

The authors also found that birth weights of offspring whose parents were both smokers were 175 g *higher* than was the case when only the mother smoked. This finding is at odds with the data from nonsmoking mothers and decreases the likelihood that the reported association with paternal smoking was meaningful. Conversely, when only smoking fathers were considered, both the height and head circumference of the newborns were significantly decreased, but only if the mother was also a smoker. Infant's body weight was not significantly altered by maternal smoking status when the father was a smoker.

Unfortunately, the inconsistent data reported by Borlee and coworkers (1978) were not adjusted for possible confounders, even though several variables, such as maternal age and weight gain, had been shown by the authors

ble 14–3
ssociation of Mean Birth Weight, Height, and Head Circumference with ternal and Maternal Smoking Habits

	Maternal Smoking Status					
	Birth Wt.[1]		*Height*[2]		*Head Circumference*[2]	
ternal oking tus	*Nonsmoker*	*Smoker*	*Nonsmoker*	*Smoker*	*Nonsmoker*	*Smoker*
nsmoker	3399 ± 875	2838 ± 675	50.45 ± 2.94	50.00 ± 1.73	34.84 ± 1.27	34.00 ± 0.00
oker	3171* ± 692	3013 ± 538	50.27 ± 2.57	48.03** ± 3.35	35.19 ± 2.56	33.94** ± 1.91

urce: From Borlee et al., 1978.
grams.
centimeters.
ifferent from offspring of nonsmoking fathers ($p \leq 0.05$).
Different from offspring of smoking fathers and nonsmoking mothers ($p \leq 0.05$).

themselves to affect significantly the parameters of interest (infant's body weight, height and head circumference). These data are thus difficult to interpret.

Rubin and coworkers (1986) reported a study of maternal exposure to rnal smoking on birth weight of offspring of 500 Danish women, of which 202 acknowledged having smoked during pregnancy. Among the fathers, 230 were said to have smoked during their partner's pregnancy. When the father's smoking was treated as a continuous variable in a multiple regression analysis, and a number of other variables (including maternal smoking) were controlled for, a decrement of 6 grams in birth weight was seen for each additional cigarette, cigar or pipe bowl smoked by the father. This effect was declared to be significant, as was also the apparent effect when the amount of smoking by each parent was analyzed as a discrete variable. According to the authors, paternal smoking had an effect 66% as great as did maternal smoking.

An ETS effect of this relative magnitude seems improbable, however, when the relative degrees of exposure are considered. Moreover, in their regression analysis of paternal smoking effects, the authors failed to include interaction terms. This is true even though they reported finding a significant interaction between social class and paternal smoking effects, and earlier studies had reported interactions between effects associated with maternal and paternal smoking status. Rubin and coworkers failed to control for a number of other potential confounders as well.

In 1987, Schwartz-Bickenbach and coworkers in West Germany published preliminary data from a prospective, longitudinal study of 54 matched pairs of smoking and nonsmoking mothers who intended to breast feed. Birth weights of the infants from 28 mothers who reported being nonsmokers with smoking husbands averaged 205 g less than weights of the 26 offspring of nonsmoking families (Table 14–4). This was a difference of −5.74 %, equivalent to half the weight decrement the authors reported to be associated with having a smoking mother, and the effect thus seems implausibly large. Moreover, no mention was made of any statistical analysis, and the significance of these differences was not stated. When the newborn's head circumference and body length were compared, no differences were observed among groups.

Interestingly, when cotinine levels were measured in the mother's milk over a six-month period following delivery, amounts of that metabolite were generally quite low and did not differ between individuals with smoking versus nonsmoking husbands (Schwartz-Bickenbach et al. 1987). Comparable values from smoking mothers were consistently much greater. This finding casts suspicion on the author's contention of a causal relationship between exposure to paternal smoking and a considerable decrease in birth weight, especially when the relative magnitude of the reported weight decrements is considered. It seems unlikely that the relative smoke exposure of nonsmoking

Table 14–4
Association of Mean Birth Weight, Height, and Head Circumference with Paternal and Maternal Smoking Habits

Parental Smoking Status	*Birth Wt.*[1]	*Body Length*[2]	*Head Circumference*[2]
Mother smokes	3165 ± 518	50.0 ± 2.5	35 ± 1.5
Father smokes	3365 ± 360	50.7 ± 1.7	35 ± 1.2
Neither smokes	3570 ± 495	51.8 ± 2.5	35 ± 1.5

Source: From Schwartz-Bickenbach et al., 1987.
[1]In grams.
[2]In centimeters.

mothers could have been high enough to produce an effect on their offspring half as great as that reported for offspring of smoking mothers when the difference in relative maternal exposure was much greater. Also, the effects reported for exposure to paternal smoking in this study are as great as those claimed for active maternal smoking in other studies (Abel 1980) and seem biologically implausible. Moreover, the effect reported by Schwartz-Bickenbach (1987) is much greater than those associated with paternal smoking in studies with considerably larger numbers of subjects (e.g., Underwood et al. 1967; Magnus et al. 1984; Martin and Bracken 1986).

Nakamura and colleagues (1988) conducted a study of 2483 Japanese women who had single live deliveries in Osaka prefecture between July 1984, and June 1986. Data on smoke exposure and twenty-four potential confounders were obtained by questionnaire and related to incidence of low birth weight in all deliveries and in term births alone, and to incidence of preterm births (<37 weeks). Comparisons were made among pregnancy outcomes of nonsmoking women with nonsmoking or smoking husbands, ex-smokers with smoking husbands, and smokers with smoking husbands.

When the crude data were analyzed, the overall risk of having a low birth weight infant for nonsmoking mothers with smoking partners appeared to be increased but the association was only marginally significant (RR = 1.5, CI = 1.0–2.2). Unadjusted relative risks for preterm births or low birth weight at term were nonsignificant. In an attempt to remove any confounding influence from possible additional ETS exposure at work, a separate analysis was done on data from only nonworking women. The risk of having a low birth weight child for nonsmoking women married to smokers was apparently increased but again the increase was only marginally significant (RR = 1.6, CI = 1.0–2.5) and the risks of preterm delivery and low birth weight at term were nonsignificant.

When the data were adjusted for 22 confounders by use of multiple logistic regression analysis (two possible confounders were omitted due to low numbers of affected subjects), the overall risk of delivering a low birth weight infant was nonsignificant (RR = 1.4, CI = 0.9–2.2). Results of a similar analysis on only nonworking women were marginally significant (RR = 1.7, CI = 1.0–2.9).

Studies Using Other Measures of ETS Exposure. As part of the Yale Pregnancy Outcome Study that examined the relation of pregnancy outcome to a variety of maternal exposures, women who intended to deliver at the Yale-New Haven Hospital were interviewed shortly after their first prenatal visit (Martin and Bracken 1986). Records obtained on over 3800 birth outcomes were used to examine the relationship of ETS exposure to incidence of low birth weight (<2500 g) or premature delivery (<37 weeks from the last menstrual period). Effects on mean birth weight and mean gestational age were also considered. ETS exposure was defined as being subjected to someone else's cigarette smoke for at least two hours per day during gestation, either at home or at work.

The data were based on responses to questionnaires. Exposures were divided into four categories: (1) no exposure, (2) ETS exposure only, (3) active smoking only and (4) ETS exposure plus active smoking. Association of ETS and altered mean birth weight was examined by use of multiple linear regression analysis, and potential confounders were eliminated if they were not significant at the 0.10 level. Incidence of low birth weight infants was subjected to a stepwise multiple logistic regression analysis, and variables that were significant at the 0.10 level were added to the model containing the ETS variable.

According to Martin and Bracken (1986), their initial crude analysis indicated a significant effect of maternal ETS exposure on mean birth weight for nonsmokers (−61 g) but not for smokers (Table 14–5). When all deliveries were considered (preterm and full term), no significant effect of ETS on incidence of low birth weight infants was seen for either nonsmokers or smokers. There were also no significant effects of ETS exposure on mean gestational age at birth or on rates of preterm deliveries in either nonsmokers or smokers.

When effects of ETS exposure on mean birth weight were examined according to whether the delivery was preterm or term, the only significant association was for nonsmokers with term deliveries (Table 14–6). The final logistic regression model, employing gestational and maternal ages, parity and race (white vs. nonwhite) as significant confounders, yielded an estimate of 2.17 (CI = 1.05 to 4.50, $p = 0.037$) for the adjusted relative risk of having a low birth weight infant following ETS exposure. As to mean birth weight,

Table 14–5
Association of Parental Smoking Habits with Mean Birth Weight and Low Birth Weight for All Deliveries

Maternal Smoking	*Paternal Smoking*	*Additive Effect on Mean Weight (g) (unadjusted)*	*Low Birth Weight[1] (%)*	*Relative Risk of Low Birth Weight[1] (unadjusted)*
No	No	—	3.00	1.00
	Yes	−61	3.91	1.30 (CI = 0.85–1.98)
Yes	No	—	6.06	1.00
	Yes	−34	6.10	1.00

Source: From Martin and Bracken, 1986
[1]<2500 g.
*$p \leq 0.005$ for difference associated with husband's smoking status.

the final model for linear regression analysis included three confounders (gestational age, parity and race) and resulted in a nonsignificant value of −23.5 g (CI = −59.9 to 12.8, $p = 0.21$).

Martin and Bracken (1986) also calculated an overall adjusted relative risk associated with ETS (smoking and nonsmoking mothers combined) for having a low birth weight infant and obtained a nonsignificant value of 1.52. A similar calculation for mean birth weight yielded a significant decrement of −30 g. These overall values were thus opposite in terms of statistical significance from those for nonsmoking mothers alone. Also, no effects of ETS exposure on mean gestational age or premature delivery were found by regression analysis.

The analyses reported by Martin and Bracken (1986) are inconsistent and difficult to interpret. This may be due, at least in part, to the authors' use of a relatively crude estimate of ETS exposure. Their findings would have been more meaningful if further information had been available regarding exposure intensity and duration. Further, since questionnaire data were solicited early in gestation, intensity and duration of ETS exposure may have changed considerably for a number of subjects over the remainder of pregnancy.

It is puzzling that the authors used statistical significance as the criterion for inclusion of potential confounders in their multiple regression analyses when, according to various experts (e.g., Breslow and Day 1980; Kleinberg et al. 1982), this may eliminate important confounders (e.g., because of low statistical power or multicollinearity). This is particularly likely to have been a problem in the analysis of the incidence of low birth weight infants as the

Table 14–6
Association of Parental Smoking Habits with Mean Birth Weight and Low Birth Weight for Term Deliveries Only

Maternal Smoking	*Paternal Smoking*	*Mean Birth Weight (g)*	*Additive Effect on Mean Weight (g) (Crude)*	*Additive Effect on Mean Weight (g) (Adjusted)*	*Low Birth Weight (%)*	*Relative Risk of Low Birth Weight[1] (Crude)*	*Relative Risk of Low Birth Weight[1] (Adjuste[d])*
No	No	3507			0.86	1.00	
	Yes	3422**	−75	−23.5	2.34	2.72*	2.17*
Yes	No	3336			2.99	1.00	
	Yes	3295	−41		3.27	1.09	

Source: From Martin and Bracken, 1986.
[1]< 2500 g.
*$p \leq 0.005$ for difference associated with husband's smoking status.
**$p \leq 0.0002$ for difference associated with husband's smoking status.

sample size was small (34) and thus the statistical power in the multivariate analysis was low. Potentially important confounders, such as maternal weight and the child's sex, were apparently not determined during the data collection, and thus were unavailable for the analysis, although such variables may significantly influence birth weight. Also, fairly crude measures of socioeconomic status were employed.

Another puzzling aspect of Martin and Bracken's (1986) study is the great discrepancy between the percentage of low birth weight infants reported in that study and the study reported by Yerushalmy (1971). For example, for nonsmoking families, Yerushalmy reported a value of 3.43% for low birth weight infants born to nonsmoking white parents and 5.80% for low birth weight infants born to black parents. These percentages are considerably higher than the values of 0.86% for infants of nonexposed mothers and 2.34% for infants of ETS exposed mothers reported by Martin and Bracken for a mostly white (78%) population.

This discrepancy may have been due to major differences in socioeconomic status or other factors, but it is clear that the population studied by Martin and Bracken differs considerably from those examined in a large number of other studies. For example, studies reviewed by Abel (1980) reported incidences of low birth weight infants in populations of nonsmokers (presumably including both ETS exposed and non-exposed) ranging from 2.6% to 11.8% (the values over 8% were all from studies of black families). These data raise the possibility that Martin and Bracken's results cannot be extrapolated to more typical U.S. populations and make their data difficult to compare with those of other studies.

In another recent report, MacArthur and Knox (1987) provided data on birth weights of the offspring of women who said they were former smokers who had stopped smoking by the second month of pregnancy. The raw data indicated that the birth weights of children whose fathers smoked were 14 g lighter than those of the offspring of nonsmoking fathers, but the data did not show a dose response when evaluated by level of father's smoking. When birth weights were standardized for maternal height and parity, the infant's sex, and gestation length, the infants in the group with smoking fathers were found to be significantly *heavier* than those with nonsmoking fathers, with a calculated difference of 123 g. Although the study population was not large, totalling only 180 women, these findings are of considerable interest because they show how much adjusting for possible confounders may influence study outcome.

Recently, Haddow et al. (1988b) reported an analysis of effects of ETS on birth weights of infants of women who claimed to be nonsmokers during pregnancy and had been included in an alpha-fetoprotein screening program in the state of Maine. The authors used second trimester maternal serum cotinine measurements as an index of ETS exposure and assumed that women whose serum cotinine levels were ≥ 10 ng/mL had not been truthful in stating that they were not smokers. These women were omitted from the group, leaving 1231 apparent nonsmokers. They then compared birth weights of infants from 386 women with serum cotinine levels greater than 1.0 but less than 10 ng/mL (said to be equivalent to urinary cotinine levels of 10 and 30 ng/mL, respectively), who were classified as "ETS exposed," with birth weights of babies from 376 women whose cotinine levels were less than 0.5 ng/mL. The latter group was assumed to have been relatively unexposed.

According to Haddow and coworkers (1988b), the mean birth weight in the ETS exposed group was 107 g less than that of infants from the unexposed group (Table 14–7). A similar difference (−108 g) remained after a multivariate analysis that took into account some of the relevant potential confounders (maternal weight, height, age, gravidity, and years of education, as well as the infant's sex). When the birth weights of infants from women in the 0.5 to 1.0 ng/mL serum cotinine range were compared with those of the unexposed group, there was no difference.

When Haddow and coworkers (1988b) modified their regression analysis to consider cotinine as a continuous variable, the linear coefficient for birth weight decrement associated with ETS exposure was −28 g/ng/mL (p = 0.04). The authors also stated that the proportion of low birth weight babies (≤ 2,500 g) was increased by 29% in the group with maternal serum cotinine values above 1.0 ng/mL in comparison with those in the below 1.0 ng/mL maternal cotinine group, but did not state whether this difference was significant.

Haddow and co-workers (1988b) concluded from their data that the apparent relationship between serum cotinine levels and birth weight was not

Table 14–7
Mean Birth Weight According to Second Trimester Serum Cotinine Level in Nonsmoking Women

Serum Cotinine (ng/mL)		*Mean Birth Weight (g)*			
Range	*Mean*	*Crude*	*Difference*	*Adjusted*[a]	*Difference*
<0.5	0.28	3588		3535	
0.5–1.0	0.71	3591	+3[b]	3531	+4[b]
1.1–9.9	2.14	3481	−107[c]*	3427	−108[c]*

Source: From Haddow et al., 1988b.
[a]Adjusted for maternal weight, height, age, gravidity, and education, and for infant's sex.
[b]Difference between low and middle serum cotinine group.
[c]Difference between low and high serum cotinine group.
*$p < 0.001$.

linear because it predicted that the birth weight decrement for the highest ETS exposed group should have been 60 g, rather than 108 g as found by their nonlinear model. They stated in a previous study (Haddow et al. 1987) that they had found a decrease of approximately 140 g for birth weight of infants born to mothers with "light active exposure to cigarette smoke." These women consumed 10 cigarettes per day, resulting in serum cotinine levels of 25 to 137 ng/mL. This suggests that the data from the studies of Haddow and coworkers were indeed exceedingly nonlinear and that unaccounted variables may have determined the results.

Hauth and coworkers (1984) assayed umbilical cord and maternal serum thiocyanate levels at term as indicators of relative smoke exposure of healthy American women with normal deliveries. Three groups were evaluated: (1) women who smoked 10 or more cigarettes per day, (2) nonsmoking women who were unexposed to ETS and (3) nonsmoking women who lived or worked with a smoker. Thiocyanate levels were higher in smokers than in nonsmokers, while the two nonsmoking groups did not differ in this regard. Umbilical cord thiocyanate levels were similar to maternal levels and showed this same relationship among the three study groups. For infants of smoking mothers, thiocyanate levels were negatively correlated with decreased birth weight. This was not the case for offspring of either the ETS exposed or unexposed mothers, nor did these two groups differ in mean birth weight. The number of subjects in each category was small, however, with only 51 ETS exposed, 29 actively exposed and 83 unexposed.

The most recent study relating maternal ETS exposure to birth weight was conducted by Chen et al. (1989). This group reported data collected on 1058 infants born to nonsmoking women in Shanghai. The results were grouped according to daily cigarette consumption by all family members and by the father alone. According to the results presented, maternal ETS exposure was unrelated to either mean birth weight or incidence of low birth weight.

2. Perinatal Mortality. Relatively few studies have addressed the issue of possible effects of maternal ETS exposure on pre- or perinatal mortality. Comstock and Lundin (1967) evaluated 238 nonsmokers randomly chosen from the population of Washington County, Maryland. They adjusted the data for two confounders, sex of the offspring and paternal educational level. An apparent increase in neonatal death rate for infants of nonsmoking mothers and smoking fathers was observed. But it was not clear from the information present whether the increase was significant, and the association of stillbirths with paternal smoking was not found to be significant. The numbers of total births, stillbirths and neonatal deaths were so low, however, that the results are not very meaningful.

Tokuhata (1968) obtained data on 1322 deceased women from Memphis and Shelby Counties in Tennessee, and categorized them as smokers or nonsmokers married to smokers or nonsmokers. Information on smoking status and other data, such as cause of death, race, age at death, education, occupation, and husband's occupation, education, and race were obtained from surviving family members. Data were obtained on 4577 pregnancies, and miscarriages and stillbirths were considered together as "fetal losses." Fetal losses of 11% were seen for both nonsmokers with nonsmoking husbands and for nonsmokers with smoking husbands (Table 14–8).

Smoking women married to nonsmoking men were reported to have 20% fetal loss, compared with 16% for smoking women with smoking husbands. This difference is suspect, however, because there were only 52 cou-

Table 14–8
Association of Parental Smoking Habits with Prenatal Mortality

Maternal Smoking	*Paternal Smoking*	*Percent Prenatal Mortality*	*Relative Risk*	*P*[1]
No	No	10.52	1.00	NA[2]
	Yes	11.35	1.08	NS[3]
Yes	No	20.00	1.90	0.001
	Yes	16.19	1.54	0.03

Source: From Tokuhata, 1968.

[1]Probability of differing from pregnancy outcome for nonsmoking wives with nonsmoking husbands.

[2]Not applicable.

[3]Nonsignificant.

ples in the category of smoking wives with nonsmoking husbands. The reliability of obtaining information merely from birth and death certificates and relatives' responses to questionnaires is doubtful, and it was not definitely known if smoking occurred during any specific pregnancy. Also, half of the women included in this study were chosen because they died of certain types of cancer, and the remainder were matched controls. Thus, the study population may not be representative of the general population.

In his previously discussed 1971 paper, Yerushalmy also addressed the issue of neonatal mortality in low birth weight infants. In this case, his finding was that offspring of nonsmoking mothers had a *higher* survival rate if the father was a smoker, whereas for smoking mothers, the opposite was true. The trend was similar for both whites and blacks. Although these data are puzzling, possible explanations include the fact that the numbers of affected individuals in some of the categories were "too small," according to the author, and as previously mentioned, the data were not adjusted for potential confounders.

According to Mau and Netter (1974), who reported the results of almost 3700 pregnancies of nonsmoking mothers evaluated at 20 different clinics in Germany, paternal cigarette smoking was associated with a significant (by Chi-squared) but not dose-related increase in perinatal mortality. The mortality rate was 3.1% for infants with nonsmoking parents, 2.2% for those whose fathers smoked from 1 to 10 cigarettes per day, and 4.8% for infants whose fathers smoked over 10 cigarettes daily (Table 14–9). It is of interest to note that when maternal smokers and nonsmokers were analyzed together, with an N of nearly 5200, a similar pattern emerged. The perinatal mortality rate was 3.0% when the father was a nonsmoker, 2.5% if the father smoked less than 10 cigarettes per day, and 4.5% if the paternal smoking rate was higher, an association that was also declared significant.

Table 14–9
Association of Paternal Smoking Habits with Perinatal Mortality in Infants of Nonsmoking Mothers

Paternal Daily Cigarette Consumption	*Perinatal Mortality (%)*	
	Nonsmoking Mothers[1]	*All Mothers*[2]
none	3.1	3.0
1–10	2.2	2.5
>10	4.8	4.5

Source: From Mau and Netter, 1974.
[1] $X^2 = 9.4, p \leq 0.01$.
[2] $X^2 = 10.4, p \leq 0.01$.

When these latter data were corrected for the influence of prematurity, however, the difference was no longer significant. Such an analysis was not done for children of nonsmoking mothers only. The data from pregnancy outcomes of nonsmoking mothers were construed to mean that heavy paternal smoking was related to increased perinatal mortality. Since there were only two categories of paternal smokers (light and heavy), however, Mau and Netter's data also could be taken to mean that newborns whose fathers were light smokers were more likely to survive than if the father did not smoke.

When Mau and Netter (1974) evaluated the possible influence of various confounders on the data, the effects were said to have remained significant, but each confounder was evaluated separately, one at a time. The authors also questioned whether there was a causal relationship between paternal smoking and perinatal mortality, as their results were reversed for both reduced birth weight and mortality when the data were from smoking versus nonsmoking mothers. According to the authors, this suggested that the cause of increased perinatal mortality among children of heavily smoking fathers must be related to other characteristics of the father.

3. Incidence of Congenital Defects. Very few studies appear to have addressed the issue of whether ETS exposure is associated with birth defects. Mau and Netter (1974), whose study was considered above, analyzed data on congenital defects across all mothers, regardless of smoking status. They reported a significant increase in the incidence of infants born with "severe malformations" as paternal cigarette smoking increased, yet they found no effect due to maternal smoking (Table 14–10). The relationship of paternal smoking and malformation rate was unaffected by parental age, social status on the particular clinics from which the data were obtained. A variety of different defects were seen in the population, and when specific defects were examined, the association with paternal smoking was significant only for

Table 14–10
Association of Paternal Smoking Habits with Malformations in Infants of Both Smoking and Nonsmoking Mothers

Paternal Daily Cigarette Consumption	*Percent Malformed*	*Number Malformed/ Total Examined*
none	0.8	21/2563
1–10	1.4	15/1089
>10	2.1	32/1509

Source: From Mau and Netter, 1974.

Note: When results for children of smoking and nonsmoking mothers were analyzed separately, there was no difference related to maternal smoking status.

$X^2 = 12.4, p \leq 0.01$.

facial clefts. The absence of an effect of maternal active smoking suggests that the observed correlation between congenital defects and presumed ETS exposure was not a causal relationship. Mau and Netter (1974) suggested that either there was an effect of paternal smoking on the male gametes or the correlation was a spurious one.

The most recent published report concerning ETS and congenital defects appears to be the finding of Swedish workers (Holmberg and Nurminen 1980) that fathers of infants born with central nervous system defects were not more likely to be smokers than were fathers of normal case controls. Parents of 120 affected infants and a like number of controls were included in the study population, and the father's smoking habits were assessed only for the time prior to conception.

No other studies that mentioned birth defects and ETS were found in a search of the literature. A consideration of interest is that teratogenic agents rarely are capable of causing a significant increase in the malformation rate when present only at very low doses. Thus, since studies of maternal active smoking have not generally found an increase in the rate of congenital defects (Nash and Persaud 1988), this suggests that ETS is also unlikely to be found teratogenic in man.

4. Effects on Other Reproductive Parameters. There is relatively little mention in the literature of any effects of ETS exposure on fertility-related endpoints. Spira and Lazar (1979) failed to discern any relationship between exposure to paternal smoking and history of spontaneous abortions in a group of 751 French women who had given birth to defective children. The same observation was made by Mau and Netter (1974) in their study of German women. Tokuhata (1968), in his case-control study of deceased cancer patients, reported that more nonsmoking women who had nonsmoking husbands had never been pregnant, although other aspects of their gynecological health were unremarkable. When neither spouse smoked, 18% of the women were "infertile" by Tokuhata's definition, in that there was no record of their having had a child (Table 14–11). If the wife did not smoke, but the husband did, only 13% had never given birth, whereas 23% of smoking women married to non-smokers and 19% of those with smoking husbands were childless. Tokuhata's study had several deficiencies as previously mentioned, however, and it is questionable whether these results are meaningful.

Recently, Koo and coworkers (1988) described a study of a large number (97) of lifestyle variables of 136 nonsmoking women with either smoking (N = 66) or nonsmoking (70) husbands. The smoking husbands were classified as light (< 20 cigarettes/day) or heavy smokers. Wives of smoking husbands appeared to be more likely to have had a miscarriage but the trend was not significant. The proportion of wives having a dilatation and curettage (D & C) was significantly greater if their husbands smoked. The authors

Table 14–11
Association of Parental Smoking Habits with Infertility as Defined by Never Having Given Birth

Maternal Smoking	*Paternal Smoking*	*Percent Infertile*	*Relative Risk*	*P*[1]
No	No	17.55	1.40	0.03
	Yes	12.51	1.00	na[2]
Yes	No	22.76	1.82	0.002
	Yes	19.38	1.55	0.003

Source: From Tokuhata, 1968.
[1]Probability of differing from nonsmoking wives with smoking husbands.
[2]Not applicable.

stated that D&Cs were generally not used as a means of birth control in the age group making up the study population. Nevertheless, they also commented that "only a few mentioned induced abortions as a method of birth control." Since the study groups were small, even a few D & Cs used for birth control could have greatly skewed the data.

The number of pregnancies was also significantly greater in the group with smoking husbands, and the number of live births appeared greater but not significantly so. There were no effects of ETS exposure on menstrual cycle cessation and onset of menopause. The authors also found significant associations between having a smoking husband, especially if he was a heavy smoker, and a variety of lifestyle variables, such as lower socioeconomic status, improper diets and diminished health, as reflected by chronic cough and greater need for chest X-rays. They suggested that such correlates, if not corrected for, would confound data using paternal smoking as a measure of ETS exposure.

Wilcox and coworkers (1989) conducted a retrospective investigation of 631 Minnesota women. The authors reported that those who had been exposed to ETS as children under ten years of age had higher fecundability (the per-cycle probability of conception) than those who were not exposed (Table 14–12). Furthermore, the authors reported an apparent dose-response according to the number of smokers in the home and that the relationship persisted after adjustment for five possible confounders.

Additionally, a comparison was made between women who had been ETS exposed only after birth (because their mother was the only smoker in the home and she had not started until after she had given birth) and those who were never exposed to ETS in the home. In that case, the fecundability ratio was 2.0, again indicating an apparent beneficial effect associated with childhood ETS exposure. The group size (N = 17) for women exposed only

Table 14–12
Relationship of Fecundability to Childhood ETS Exposure

Number of Smokers in the Home	*Fecundability Ratio*[1]	
	Minnesota Study[2]	*North Carolina Study*[3]
one	1.3 (1.1–1.6)	1.3 (0.9–1.8)
two	1.4 (1.1–1.8)	1.6 (1.0–2.4)
three or more	1.6 (1.1–2.2)	NR[4]

[1]Ratio and 95% CI.
[2]From Wilcox, et al. (1989).
[3]From Weinberg et al. (1989).
[4]Not reported in the study.

in childhood was quite small, however and no effects on other reproductive parameters were found to be associated with ETS exposure.

In another recent investigation, the same research group prospectively assessed the relationship of childhood ETS exposure to the fecundability of 217 women in their late twenties to early thirties who lived in North Carolina (Weinberg et al, 1989). The authors again reported that women who had been exposed during childhood to smoke from other family members appeared to exhibit increased fecundability in comparison with women who had not been exposed to ETS during that time (Table 12).

According to the authors of the two previously discussed studies (Weinberg et al. 1989; Wilcox et al. 1989), the apparent association between childhood ETS exposure and increased fecundability is puzzling in terms of a biologic mechanism for such results. Nevertheless, the relationship was relatively consistent across two studies, one prospective and the other retrospective. At present, it is unclear how these data should be interpreted.

II. Research Needs

Much remains to be done in order to determine whether ETS has any effect on human reproduction or development. Improvements in design of epidemiologic studies of ETS effects, particularly in the areas of exposure assessment and validation and elimination of confounders, are especially important. In addition, appropriate animal studies would be helpful in allowing definitive conclusions to be drawn.

Even a small number of well designed epidemiologic studies might provide far more useful information than those currently found in the literature. In particular, exposure assessment must be refined before reliable experiments can be performed. This should include obtaining information on total hours of ETS exposure, both at home and elsewhere. Independent confirmation by appropriate means must also be done because subjective estimates alone are not sufficiently precise or reliable (Jarvis and Russell 1984; Matsukura et al. 1984; Haddow et al. 1988a) and misclassification, especially of smokers as nonsmokers, is likely to occur (Lee 1987).

Both types of data should be obtained at several time points. For example, in a study of prenatal exposure, information on maternal ETS exposure status and marker levels should be obtained as soon as pregnancy is confirmed, at several points during gestation, and at term. Data on fetal marker levels can be acquired at parturition by sampling cord blood (Sorsa and Husgafvel-Pursiainen 1988). Further, data must be obtained on as many potential confounders as possible, such as those suggested by Friedman et al. (1983), Kramer (1987) and Koo and coworkers (1988), and these should be employed in appropriate multivariate analyses in order to correct for their possible influence on the study outcome.

The control of confounding variables is especially important in ETS studies examining birth weight and similar endpoints. Kramer (1987) reviewed 895 reports in the literature on determinants of low births weight and identified 43 factors that could be involved. Among those with "well established direct causal impacts on intrauterine growth" were a number that may have influenced the studies on ETS effects covered in this review. The design of future studies must include appropriate controls to prevent confounding by these factors, which include infant's sex and racial/ethnic origin, maternal prepregnancy weight, parity, history of low birth weight infants, gestational weight gain and caloric intake, and general morbidity and episodic illness, and paternal weight and height, among other factors.

According to Kramer (1987), many studies of effects on birth weight are difficult to compare because they fail to distinguish associated factors from actual causal determinants. This is certainly true of ETS studies conducted to date, and as Kramer states, many potential determinants are highly correlated, and their effects thus mutually confounded. Such effects must be controlled for in order to avoid spurious associations between ETS and decreased birth weight.

Indeed, the problem is especially acute in ETS studies on pregnancy outcome because ETS exposure has been shown to correlate positively with a number of known determinants of decreased birth weight, including lower socioeconomic studies, ill health and poor nutrition (Friedman et al. 1983; Koo et al. 1988). The tendency of some individuals to make false or inaccurate statements regarding their smoking status or that of others, coupled with the greater likelihood of smokers to marry other smokers (Lee 1987), further complicates the interpretation of ETS studies. Another factor that makes such studies problematic is the difficulty of assessing the degree of ETS exposure merely by use of questionnaires or interviews without an objective measure of actual exposure (Jarvis and Russell 1984; Haddow et al. 1988). All of these shortcomings of past studies must be taken into account in designing future research.

In order to assess prenatal effects, randomized control trials might be conducted with prospective parents. In these, a portion of the husbands of non-smoke exposed women might be asked to cease smoking, at least prior to conception and throughout gestation. Compliance of both parents would be monitored by appropriate marker analyses. This type of study has been done with smoking mothers (Sexton and Hebel 1984) and would decrease the possibility of confounding due to factors associated with having a smoking husband. Of course, it would still be important to stratify the two groups according to known possible confounders such as socioeconomic status (Guyatt and Newhouse 1985).

Epidemiologic studies generally do not provide conclusive proof of causation. Interpretation of such data is often aided by studies on laboratory animals. Although such studies apparently have not been published to date, they should be considered for the future and should include assessment of both toxicity end points and determination of actual exposures of the embryo/fetus.

Appropriate exposure methodology must be a major consideration for animal studies pertinent to assessment of ETS effects. This is a particularly difficult problem, however, because ETS is not a single, well defined entity. It is a complex mixture that varies in composition with both source and receiving environment and over time (Reasor 1987). Also, it is important that exposure levels be analogous to human experience. Careful attention must be given to ensure that observed effects are not simply the result of maternal toxicity and systemic stress resulting from excessive doses.

III. Summary and Conclusions

A. Incidence of Low Birth Weight Infants

Nine published studies include data on the incidence of low birth weight infants, generally defined as newborns weighing less than 2,500 grams. These studies provide conflicting and inconsistent data. Four of the studies, including the largest of those reviewed (Underwood et al. 1967) reported no effects. The remaining five studies report mixed results. (Appendix). Two reports (Yerushalmy 1962 1971), the second of which apparently was an enlargement of the first study, found a positive association between low birth weight and maternal ETS exposure for smoking mothers but not for nonsmoking mothers. One study (Martin and Bracken 1986) reported a positive association only for nonsmoking mothers but not for smoking mothers, and another (Nakamura et al. 1988b) described a "marginally significant" association for nonworking mothers only. The remaining report (Haddow 1988) implied that there was a modest positive association with ETS (RR = 1.29) but did not state whether the relationship was statistically significant.

The findings of Yerushalmy are inconsistent and appear biologically implausible for the reasons previously discussed. The findings of Haddow (1988b) consist of a marginal increase based on small numbers of low birth weight infants, and the data of Martin and Bracken (1986) suffer from a variety of deficiencies previously identified. Thus, it appears that the evidence for an association between ETS and low birth weight is, at best, equivocal.

B. Mean Birth Weight

Fourteen studies addressed the issue of ETS exposure and decreased mean birth weight. Four studies were positive (Borlee et al. 1978; Martin and Bracken 1986; Rubin et al. 1986; Haddow et al. 1988b), one did not state if the observed weight decrement was significant (Schwartz-Bickenbach et al. 1987), and nine were negative (Ravenholt and Levinski 1965; MacMahon et al. 1966; Comstock and Lundin 1967; Underwood et al. 1967; Hauth et al. 1984; Magnus et al. 1984; Little and Sing 1987; MacArthur and Knox 1987; Chen et al. 1989) (Appendix).

Of the negative studies, one (MacArthur and Knox 1987) actually reported an increased adjusted birth weight for offspring of ETS-exposed mothers. One of the positive studies (Borlee et al. 1978) was inconsistent in finding that while infants of ETS exposed nonsmoking mothers had a birth weight decrement of 228 g, those of ETS exposed smoking mothers had a weight excess of 175 g.

Most of the reported weight decrements were relatively small but some (Borlee et al. 1978; Haddow et al. 1988b; Schwartz-Bickenbach et al. 1987) were as large as or larger than those that have been reported for effects of maternal active smoking. Considering the deficiencies of both positive and negative studies, particularly in areas such as exposure assessment and accounting for possible confounders, the mixed findings seen in the available literature do not permit a conclusion with respect to the effects of ETS exposure on mean birth weight.

C. Perinatal Mortality

Only four reports (Comstock and Lundin 1967; Tokuhata 1968; Yerushalmy 1971; Mau and Netter 1974) considered the possible relationship between maternal ETS exposure and perinatal mortality, and study size was often small (Appendix). Again, the results were inconsistent across studies, measures of ETS exposure were questionable, and results were not appropriately corrected for possible confounders.

D. Congenital Defects

There is relatively little information on ETS exposure and birth defects in the available literature. One German study (Mau and Netter 1974) reported positive effects. The most recent report (Holmberg and Nurminen 1980) reported no such effect (Appendix). In view of the scarcity of data, reliable conclusions cannot be drawn.

E. Other Reproductive Effects

With regard to effects on other reproductive parameters, such as fertility, there are three negative studies (Tokuhata 1968; Spira and Lazar 1979; Mau and Netter 1974) (Appendix). Koo and coworkers (1988) reported an association between ETS and the proportion of women who had had D & Cs, but their study groups were small, and the relevance of this finding is not at all clear. Two recent studies (Wilcox 1989; Weinberg 1989) suggest an association between ETS exposure and increased fecundability but the significance of these observations is also not clear. Thus, the available data on reproductive effects are largely negative.

IV. Overall Summary

In general, the literature dealing with ETS exposure and effects on prenatal development and reproduction is inconsistent and inconclusive. Only epidemiologic studies have addressed this issue. Although some researchers have shown positive associations, primarily between paternal smoking (as a surrogate for presumptive maternal ETS exposure) and decreased birth weight, others have failed to find an effect. In several cases, the purported effects on infant's weight were far greater than would seem biologically plausible and are inconsistent with the results of the remaining studies. Most of the available studies adjusted the data for none or only a few of the numerous potential confounders that plague reports of pregnancy outcome in general and birth weight in particular. The general lack of objective measures of actual ETS exposure during gestation, and reliance on unverified paternal smoking as the sole measure of maternal passive smoking, are additional flaws in the existing studies.

References

Abel, E.L. (1980). Smoking during pregnancy: A review of effects on growth and development of offspring. *Human Biology* 52(4):593–625.

Bassi, J.A., P. Rosso, A.C. Moessinger et al. (1984). Fetal growth retardation due to maternal tobacco smoke exposure in the rat. *Pediatric Research* 18(2):127–130.

Bertolini, A., A. Bernardi, and S. Genedani (1982). Effects of prenatal exposure to cigarette smoke and nicotine on pregnancy, offspring development and avoidance behavior in rats. *Neurobehav. Toxicol. Teratol.* 4:545–548.

Borlee, I., A. Boukaert, M.F. Lechat et al. (1978). Smoking patterns during and before pregnancy. *Europ. J. Obstet. Gynec. Reprod. Biol.* 8(4):171–177.

Breslow, N.E., and N.E. Day (1980). *The Analysis of Case-Control Studies.* IARC, Lyon, France.

Chen, Y., L. Pederson, and N.M. Lefcoe (1989). Passive smoking and low birth weight. *Lancet* 2:54–55.

Comstock, G.W., and F.E. Lundin (1967). Parental smoking and perinatal mortality. *Am. J. Obstet. Gynecol.* 98:708–718.

Friedman, G.D., D.B. Petitti and R.D. Bawol (1983). Prevalence and correlates of passive smoking. *Am. J. Public Health* 73(4):401–405.

Goldstein, H., I.D. Goldberg, T.M. Frazier et al. (1964). Cigarette smoking and prematurity. *Public Health Reports* 79:553.

Guyatt, G.H., and M.T. Newhouse (1985). Are active and passive smoking harmful? Determining causation. *Chest* 88(3):445–51.

Haddow, J.E., G.J. Knight, G.E. Palomaki et al. (1987). Cigarette consumption and serum cotinine in relation to birth weight. *Br. J. Obstet. Gynaecol.* 94:678.

Haddow, J.E., G.J. Knight, G.E. Palomaki et al. (1988a). Estimating fetal morbidity and mortality resulting from cigarette smoke exposure by measuring cotinine levels in maternal serum. *Progress in Clinical & Biological Research Ser.* 281:289–300.

Haddow, J.E., G.J. Knight, G.E. Palomaki et al. (1988b). Second-trimester serum cotinine levels in nonsmokers in relation to birth weight. *Am. J. Obstet. Gynecol.* 159:481–484.

Hauth, J.C., J. Hauth, R.B. Drawbaugh et al. (1984). Passive smoking and thiocyanate concentrations in pregnant women and newborns. *Obstet. Gynecol.* 63(4):519–522.

Haworth, J.C., and J.D. Ford (1972). Comparison of the effects of maternal undernutrition and exposure to cigarette smoke on the cellular growth of the rat fetus. *Am. J. Obstet. Gyencol.* 112:653–656.

Holmberg, P.C., and M. Nurminen (1980). Congenital defects of the central nervous system and occupational factors during pregnancy. *Am. J. Indust. Med.* 1:167–176.

Hughes, J.R., L.H. Epstein, F. Andrasik et al. (1982). Smoking and carbon monoxide levels during pregnancy. *Addictive Behaviors* 7:271–6.

Jarvis, M.J., and M.A.H. Russell (1984). Measurement and estimation of smoke dosage to non-smokers from environmental tobacco smoke. *Eur. J. Respir. Dis.* (suppl. 133):68–75.

Kleinberg, D.G., L.L. Kupper and H. Morgenstern (1982). *Epidemiologic Research*. Van Nostrand Reinhold, New York.

Koo, L.C., J.J-C. Ho and R. Rylander (1988). Life-history correlates of environmental tobacco smoke: A study on nonsmoking Hong Kong Chinese wives with smoking versus nonsmoking husbands. *Soc. Sci. Med.* 26(7):751–760.

Kramer, M.S. (1987). Determinants of low birth weight: Methodological assessment and meta-analysis. *WHO Bull.* 65:663–737.

Lee, P.N. (1987). Passive smoking and lung cancer association: A result of bias? *Human Toxicol.* 6:517–524.

Little, R.E., and C.F. Sing (1987). Father's drinking and infant birth weight: Report of an association. *Teratology* 36:59–65.

MacArthur, C., and E.G. Knox (1987). Passive smoking and birth weight. *Lancet* 1:37–38.

MacMahon, B., M. Alpert and E.J. Salber (1966). Infant weight and parental smoking habits. *Am. J. Epidemiol.* 82:247–261.

Magnus, P., K. Berg, T. Bjerkedal et al. (1984). Parental determinants of birth weight. *Clinical Genetics* 26(5):397–405.

Martin, T.R., and M.B. Bracken (1986). Association of low birth weight with passive smoke exposure in pregnancy. *Am. J. Epidemiol.* 124:633–642.

Matsukura, S., T. Taminato, N. Kitano et al. (1984). Effects of environmental tobacco smoke on urinary cotinine excretion in non-smokers. *N. Engl. J. Med.* 311:828–832.

Mau, G., and P. Netter (1974). The effects of paternal cigarette smoking on perinatal mortality and the incidence of malformations. *Deutsche Medizinische Wochenschrift* 99(21):1–16.

Mulcahy, R., and J.F. Knaggs (1968). Effect of age, parity, and cigarette smoking on outcome of pregnancy. *Amer. J. Obstet. Gynecol.* 101:844.

Nakamura, M., A. Oshima, T. Hirayama, N. Kutota, K. Wada, and K. Yana (1988). Effects of passive smoking during pregnancy on birth weight and gestation: A population-based prospective study in Japan. In: Aoki M., S. Hisamichi, S. Tominaga, eds., *Smoking and Health 1987; Proceedings of the Sixth World Conference on Smoking and Health*. Elsevier, New York:267–9.

Nash, J., and T.V. Persaud (1988). Embryopathic risks of cigarette smoking. *Exp. Pathol.* 33:65–73.

Peterson, K.L., R.W. Heninger and R.E. Seegmiller (1981). Fetotoxicity following chronic prenatal treatment of ice with tobacco smoke and ethanol. *Bull. Environ. Contam. Toxicol.* 26:813–819.

Peterson, W.F., K.N. Morese and D.F. Kaltreider (1965). Smoking and prematurity. *Obstet. Gynecol.* 26:775.

Ravenholt, R.T., and M.J. Levinski (1965). Smoking during pregnancy. *Lancet* 1:961.

Reasor, M.J. (1987). The composition and dynamics of environmental tobacco smoke. *J. Environ. Health.* 50(1):20–24.

Reznik, G., and G. Marquard (1980). Effect of cigarette smoke inhalation during pregnancy in Sprague-Dawley rats. *J. Environ. Pathol. Toxicol.* 4:141–152.

Rubin, D.H., J.M. Leventhal, P.A. Krasilnikoff et al. (1986). Fathers' drinking (and smoking) and infants' birth weight. *N. Engl. J. Med.* 2:415–417.

Sexton, M., and J.R. Hebel (1984). A clinical trial of change in maternal smoking and its effect on birth weight. *JAMA* 251:911–915.

Schwartz-Bickenbach, D., B. Schulte-Bobein, S. Abt et al. (1987). Smoking and passive smoking during pregnancy and early infancy: Effects on birth weight, lactation period, and cotinine concentrations in mother's milk and infants' urine. *Toxicology Letters* 35:73–81.

Sorsa, M., and K. Husgafvel-Pursiainen (1988). Assessment of passive and transplacental exposure to tobacco smoke. *IARC Sci. Publ.* 89:129–32.

Spira, A., and P. Lazar (1979). Spontaneous abortions in sibship of children with congenital malformations or malignant disease. *Eur. J. Obstet. Gynecol. Reprod. Biol.* 9(2):89–95.

Tachi, N., and M. Aoyama (1983). Effect of cigarette smoke and carbon monoxide inhalation on gravid rats on the conceptus weight. *Bull. Environ. Contam. Toxicol.* 31:85–92.

Tachi, N., and M. Aoyama (1986). Effect of restricted food supply to pregnant rats inhaling carbon monoxide on fetal weight compared with cigarette smoke exposure. *Bull. Environ. Contam. Toxicol.* 37:877–882.

Tachi, N., and M. Aoyama (1989). Effects of cigarette-smoke exposure on early stage embryos in the rat. *Bull. Env. Contam. Tox.* 43(3):467–472.

Terris, M., and E.M. Gold (1969). An epidemiologic study of prematurity. *Am. J. Obstet. Gynecol.* 103:358–379.

Tokuhata, G.K. (1968). Smoking in relation to infertility and fetal loss. *Arch. Environ. Health* 17:353–359.

Trichopoulos, D. (1986). Passive smoking, birth weight, and oestrogens. *Lancet* 2:743.

Underwood, P.B., K.F. Kesler, J.M. O'Lane et al. (1967). Parental smoking empirically related to pregnancy outcome. *J. Obstet. Gynecol.* 29:1–8.

Weinberg, C.R., Wilcox, A.J., and Baird, D.D. Reduced Fecundability in women with prenatal exposure to cigarette smoking. *Am. J. Epidem.* 1989; 129, 5:1072–1078.

Wilcox, A.J., Baird, D.D., and Weinberg, C.R. Do women with childhood exposure to cigarette smoking have increased fecundability? *Am. J. Epidem.* 1989; 129,5:1079–1083.

Yerushalmy, J. (1962). Statistical considerations and evaluation of epidemiological evidence. In: James, G.J., and T. Rosenthal, eds., *Tobacco and Health*. Charles C. Thomas, Springfield, Ill.:208–222.

Yerushalmy, J. (1971). The relationship of parents' cigarette smoking to the outcome of pregnancy-implications as the problem of inferring causation from observed associations. *Am. J. Epidemiol.* 93(6):433–456.

ppendix 14–A
ımmary of Data from Studies of ETS Exposure and Human Reproduction or evelopment

·ference	*End Point*	*Study Size*	*Magnitude of Effect*	*Significance*[a]
		Low Birth Weight		
·en et al. (1989)				
?aternal smoking low		754	RR = 1.79	—
?aternal smoking high		612	RR = 1.24	—
·amily smoking low		584	RR = 1.45	—
·amily smoking high		764	RR = 1.23	—
·ddow et al. (1988)		1231	RR = 1.29	?
·rtin and Bracken, 1986				
·onsmoking mothers		2473	RR = 2.17	+
moking mothers		1137	RR = 1.09	—[b]
·moking and nonsmoking mothers		3610	RR = 1.52	—
·u and Netter (1974)		3696	RR = 1.36	—
·kamura et al. (1988)				
ll mothers		2483	RR = 1.4	—
·onworking mothers		<2483	RR = 1.7	±
·ris and Gold (1969) (black)		197	RR not given	–
·lerwood et al. (1967)				
·aternal smoking low		13,040	RR = 0.9	–
·aternal smoking medium		19,950	RR = 0.9	–
·aternal smoking high		10,877	RR = 1.0	—
·ushalmy (1962)				
·onsmoking mothers		606	RR = 1.1	–
·moking mothers		376	RR = 2.0	+
·ushalmy (1971)				
·onsmoking mothers (white)		6067	RR = 0.9	–
·moking mothers (white		3726	RR = 1.4	+
·onsmoking mothers (black)		2219	RR = 1.1	–
moking mothers (black)		1071	RR = 1.4	–
		Decreased Mean Birth Weight		
lee et al. (1978)				
·onsmoking mothers		238	dif. = −228	+
·noking mothers		92	dif. = +175	–
·n et al. (1989)				
·aternal smoking low		754	dif. = −9	–
·aternal smoking high		612	dif. = −11	–
·amily smoking low		584	dif. = −4	–
·amily smoking high		764	dif. = −15	–
·nstock and Lundin (1967)		238	dif. = −42	–
·dow et al. (1988)		762	dif. = −108	+
·th et al. (1984)		134	dif. not given	–
·e and Sing (1987)				
·noking and nonsmoking mothers		377	dif. not given	–
·Arthur and Knox (1987)		180	dif. = +123	+

Appendix 14–A continued

Reference	*End Point*	*Study Size*	*Magnitude of Effect*	*Significan*
	Decreased Mean Birth Weight			
MacMahon et al. (1966)				
(male infants)		3041	dif. = −20	−
(female infants)		2894	dif. = −23	−
Magnus et al. (1984)				
smoking and nonsmoking mothers		3130	dif. = −4.9	−
Martin and Bracken, 1986				
nonsmoking mothers		2473	dif. = −24	−
smoking mothers		1137	dif. = −41	−[b]
smoking and nonsmoking mothers		3610	dif. = −30	+
Ravenholt & Levinski, (1965)				
smoking and nonsmoking mothers		1096	dif. not given	−
Rubin et al. (1986)				
smoking and nonsmoking mothers		500	dif. = −6 g[c]	+
Schwartz-Bickenbach et al. (1987)		108	dif. = −205	?
Underwood et al. (1967)				
Paternal smoking low		13,040	dif. = −7	−
Paternal smoking medium		19,950	dif. = −5	−
Paternal smoking high		10,877	dif. = −3	−
	Perinatal Mortality			
Comstock and Lundin (1967)				
(stillbirths)		238	RR = not given	−
(neonatal mortality)		238	RR = 1.4	?
Mau and Netter (1974)				
smoking and nonsmoking mothers		4098	RR = 1.2	+[d]
nonsmoking mothers		2958	RR = 1.5	+[d]
Tokuhata (1968)				
nonsmoking mothers		982	RR = 1.08	−
smoking mothers		340	RR = 0.81	−
Yerushalmy (1971)				
mothers of low birth weight infants				
nonsmoking mothers				
(white)		197	RR = 1.4[a]	?
(black)		129	RR = 1.6[a]	?
smoking mothers				
(white)		237	RR = 2.5[a]	?
(black)		132	RR = 2.4[a]	?
	Congenital Defects			
Holmberg and Nurminen			RR =	+
		240		−
Mau and Netter (1974)				
smoking and nonsmoking mothers		4072	RR = 2.6	+[d]

ppendix 14–A continued

ference	End Point	Study Size	Magnitude of Effect	Significance[a]
	Other Reproduction Endpoints			
o et al. (1988)				
spontaneous abortions)		136	RR = 1.4	—
D & C)		136	RR = 2.0	+
number of pregnancies/woman)		136	dif. = +1.15	+
u and Netter (1974)				
spontaneous abortions, smoking nd nonsmoking women)		5183	RR = 1.1	—
ra and Lazar (1979)				
spontaneous abortions)		751	RR not given	–
uhata (1968)				
women with one or more children)				
nonsmoking women		1165	RR = 0.71	+
smoking women		443	RR = 0.85	[c]
inberg et al. (1989)				
ncreased fecundability)				
cox et al. (1989)				
ncreased fecundability)				

= Significantly different from control, – = not different from control, ? = significance not stated, ± arginally different" from control.

adjusted.

cigarette, cigar, or pipe bowl per day.

aviest smokers only (over 10 cigarettes per day).

imated from graph of data.

15
Panel Discussion on Reproductive Effects

Joseph Wu: Thank you, Dr. Hood. I would now like to ask the discussants to proceed to the desk, please. We'll first have a comment from Dr. Butler.

William Butler: Dr. Hood had done an excellent job of reviewing the large body of inconsistent literature in this area. To avoid duplication, I will restrict my comments to only one of the potential health effects addressed by him: ETS and birth weight. I will further restrict my comments to two recent studies which attempted to measure ETS exposure by means other than spousal smoking habits, since, as pointed out by Dr. Hood, this surrogate measure has substantial limitations.

My perspective for this review is that of a biostatistician and epidemiologist. My view is somewhat different from that of Dr. Hood, in that I will focus on the statistical and methodological strengths and weaknesses of these studies which affect the interpretation of their results.

The first of the studies I'll consider was conducted by Martin and Bracken (1986). Their exposure assessment is based on the subjects' responses to a single ETS question contained in a 45-page interview form. The question asks: "Since you became pregnant, have you been exposed to someone else's cigarette smoke most days for at least two hours per day, either at home or at work?"

This data collection instrument has the advantage of specifically soliciting information on non-household (and thus non-spousal) sources of ETS exposure. As Dr. Hood pointed out, however, it does not collect information on the source, intensity or duration of the subjects' exposure. Neither does the questionnaire collect information to distinguish between household, workplace or other sites of ETS exposure. Thus, it is not possible to examine the patterns of association so as to evaluate better whether ETS exposure is a risk factor for low birth weight. (Elwood, J. (1988). *Causal Relationships in Medicine: A Practical System for Critical Appraisal,* Oxford University Press, Chapter 8). In addition, these responses were not confirmed either by questioning the women at a later point in time or through the use of an appropriate biological marker. Thus, the potential for differential misclassification has not been addressed in their study design.

The majority of the statistical analyses of the papers focus on pregnancies that went to term; that is, gestational age was estimated to be at least 37 weeks. However, sufficient information is contained in the article to include pre-term infants in the statistical analysis. Substantially different patterns are observed in these two groups of infants. When one looks at the crude data presented by Martin and Bracken, it is clear that ETS exposure is not associated with the frequency of pre-term infants either among non-smoking or smoking mothers. Also, the relative risk of low birth weight for non-smoking mothers with ETS exposure was 1.3 (= 3.91/3.00; 95% confidence interval = 0.86, 1.98). Thus, considering all the non-smoking mothers, there is only a weak, non-significant association between ETS exposure and low birth weight.

However, the authors chose to restrict their univariate and multivariate analysis to term births. Among these pregnancies there was a much larger and statistically significant association (crude RR = 2.71; 95% confidence interval = 1.38, 5.34). Importantly, this positive association in term infants was accompanied by a non-significant, protective effect among pre-term infants (crude RR – 9.77; 95% confidence interval = 0.48, 1.22). The same pattern of reversal was also observed among smoking mothers but the magnitudes were much smaller and a distortion was not introduced in this group.

Martin and Bracken state that they restricted attention to term infants in order to examine intrauterine growth retardation. This restriction is unnecessary and, in this particular study, could be misleading. The association between intrauterine growth retardation can and should be examined in both term and pre-term infants. In fact, intrauterine growth retardation is defined with respect to the attained gestational age of the infant. For example, Kallen (1988) writes: "A growth-retarded infant is said to be small for gestational age (SGA) or small for date. Any factor which shortens gestational length will reduce mean birth weight, but does not necessarily cause an intrauterine growth retardation . . . In principle, the two phenomena should be kept apart: low birth weight due to short gestational length and low birth weight due to intrauterine growth retardation." (Kallen, B. (1988). *Epidemiology of Human Reproduction*. CRC Press, Boca Raton, p. 38).

Next I turn to a statistical analysis of the crude data for all infants of non-smoking mothers. The relative risks for ETS exposure in the two gestational age categories are significantly different from each other ($p < 0.003$). This observation motivates the search for either biological or methodological explanations for an interaction.

A possible biological explanation is that the magnitude of the association is less for pre-term infants due to the shorter length of time of gestation during which the agent could act on the fetus. Or perhaps the potential decrease in birth weight associated with ETS might be substantially reduced (or completely absent) among pre-term infants due to their already low birth weight. Alternatively, a methodological explanation is that the pattern may be an artifact of the creation of an arbitrary dichotomy of infants with gestational ages either greater or less than 37 weeks.

Both explanations could be examined by carrying out the statistical analysis using infants from all gestational ages. Specifically, one could analyze the data using three or more gestational age categories, for example, gestational age less than 36 weeks, between 36 and 38 weeks, and greater than 38 weeks. In addition, one could include indicator or continuous predictor variables for gestational age in a multivariate logistic regression model.

If the first (biological interaction) explanation were true, then one would expect to see increasing magnitudes of the relative risk for ETS exposure equal to unity for infants of low gestational age with increasing magnitudes of this relative risk with increasing gestational age. However, it is somewhat difficult to accept this as the entire explanation since the observed increase in the relative risk is quite steep and the resulting difference quite large. There is even the suggestion that ETS exposure is negatively associated with low birth weight among pre-term infants, a relationship for which a biological explanation is not immediately apparent.

If the second (methodological artifact) explanation were correct, then one would not expect to see a pattern in the relative risks among the gestational age categories. In addition, one would expect a summary measure comparable to that observed by combining the data for the term and pre-term infants. When all the crude data (term and pre-term infants) on the association between ETS exposure and low birth weight are examined using standard methods of statistical analysis (Kleinbaum, D.G., L.L. Kupper and H. Morgentern (1982). *Epidemiologic Research: Principles and Quantitative Methods*, Lifetime Learning Publications, Belmont, Cal., Chapter 17), the observed association is more modest than the RR = 2.72 reported by Martin and Bracken. In fact, the association is relatively small (either 1.30 or 1.15) and not statistically significant. Even this small association would be removed if the adjustment from the confounders is of at least the same magnitude for the entire data set as it was for the term infants.

An additional comment on the Martin and Bracken paper concerns the method utilized to select potential confounding factors for their multivariate regression model. As was pointed out by Dr. Hood, the method they utilized is specifically warned against in standard epidemiologic textbooks. In spite of this, the variables that were selected by their procedure are known to be potential confounders for reproductive outcomes and the reported associations for these variables are not unreasonable in either direction or magnitude. However, Martin and Bracken's statistical approach does not allow for the consideration of interactions among these potential cofounders.

An interaction between mother's age and parity is particularly relevant to Martin and Bracken's data since they report that non-smoking mothers without ETS exposure differ from those with ETS exposure in both age and parity. The ETS-exposed non-smoking mothers are younger and more likely to be primiparious than are the non-ETS-exposed non-smoking mothers. The younger, primiparious mothers are more likely to deliver low birth weight infants. Failure to include this interaction in the multivariate model could distort the comparison between these two groups.

Another curious feature of the multivariate adjustment of their data is the different magnitudes of effects due to confounding that were observed for mean birth weight and the frequency of low birth weight. The mean difference in birth weights between ETS exposed and unexposed non-smoking women was substantially reduced by the consideration of confounders. Specifically, the difference was reduced from 75 gms (p-value < 0.0002) in the crude analysis to 23.5 gms (p-value = 0.2050) in the adjusted analysis. On the other hand, the relative risk for low birth weight was reduced from 2.72 (p-value < 0.05) in the crude analysis to only 2.17 (p-value – 9.0370) in the adjusted analysis.

To demonstrate why this is unexpected from a statistical analysis perspective, consider the distribution of birth weights for smokers and non-smoking women as reported by MacMahon et al (1966). The difference in mean birth weights between these two groups is accompanied by a difference in the frequency of low birth weights (that is, below 2500 gms). Thus, the difference in means is associated with a relative risk of low birth weight which is greater than unity.

The adjustment for confounders typically results in a reduction in the difference in means which would be represented by the two distributions shifting towards each other. This shift would result in a greater overlap between the two curves and, thus, be accompanied by a reduction in the difference in the frequency of low birth weights. Thus, a substantial reduction in the difference in the means is expected to be accompanied by a similar reduction in relative risk. The fact that this concordance was not observed in the Martin and Bracken data set raises questions as to the shape of the distribution of the birth weights of the infants born to these two groups of women. It also raises the question as to whether a few aberrant data points with low birth weight (possibly influenced by uncontrolled confounders such as alcohol consumption) might be distorting the analysis. Thus, further analysis to explain the disconcordant effects of controlling for confounders in this data set are needed.

Moving on to the second study, Haddow et al. (1988) used a single serum cotinine level taken during the second trimester of pregnancy. As with the Martin and Bracken (1986) report, Haddow et al. (1988) has left substantial gaps in their analysis which raises substantial uncertainty as to the interpretation of their results. Recall that in this study, serum samples of 1508 pregnant white women who enrolled consecutively for maternal alpha-fetoprotein screening and who declared themselves to be non-smokers were analyzed for cotinine. The average elimination half-life of cotinine is about 20 hours. Statistical analyses were carried out on 1202 (80%) women who had viable, singleton births and for whom "complete demographic and biophysical data were available." Twenty-nine women with serum cotinine levels of 10 ng/ml or more were dropped from the analysis since it was assumed they were smokers.

In the adjusted analysis controlling for maternal weight, infant's sex, maternal height, maternal age, gravidity and maternal education the highest cotinine level is associated with a mean birth weight decrease, relative to the lowest cotinine level, of about 108 grams, essentially the same as the decrease of 107 grams in the unadjusted analysis. An effect of this magnitude seems to be implausibly large when compared to the effects reported in other studies of ETS exposure and in studies of maternal smoking. In the Martin and Bracken (1986) study, for example, the adjusted mean birth weight difference for self-reported ETS exposure is 24 grams. Kramer (1987) reviewed 30 reports on maternal smoking and birth weight, and calculated a sample-size weighted birth weight deficit among smoking mothers of 11.1 grams per cigarette per day. The deficit of 108 grams reported by Haddow *et al* is thus the same as the deficit reported as being associated with maternal smoking of about 10 cigarettes per day. It is biologically implausible to suppose that such a large effect could be produced by ETS.

No data were presented on mean birth weight for sublevels of serum cotinine concentration in the 1.1–9.9 ng/ml category, and the authors do not mention the presence of a dose-response. Of course, the documentation of a dose-response relationship is critical in the examination of epidemiologic data (Elwood, J. (1988). *Causal Relationships in Medicine: A Practical System for Critical Appraisal*, Oxford University Press, Chapter 8). If the authors had found such a dose-response relationship, it is reasonable to expect they would have reported it. Since there was no such report, it is likely then that either the authors did not carry out such an analysis or, if they did, no dose-response relationship was found.

The authors imply that the source of the measured cotinine is exposure to ETS. However, the above comparison strongly suggests that part of the cotinine they measured in the high level (1.1–9.9 ng/ml) group resulted from smoking by a number of the women. This conclusion is reinforced by the fact that the authors dropped 29 declared non-smokers. It should be noted that only one blood sample per woman was assayed in this study. Since cotinine has a short half-life, a single sample can give only limited information about smoking during the entire pregnancy period. It is quite possible that some women refrained from smoking for a few days immediately before their clinic visit. (It is noteworthy that because of cotinine's short elimination half-life, a woman whose measured cotinine level was between 9 and 9.9 ng/ml would have had a measured level of over 10 ng/ml if she had been tested two or three hours earlier, and would have been dropped from the study as an assumed smoker.)

The results of this study indicate that perhaps cotinine levels alone may not be sufficient to distinguish between direct smokers of low intensity and non-smokers exposed to ETS. To overcome this problem, it would be necessary to add at least one additional dimension to the instrument to distinguish between these two sources of nicotine exposure. Candidate measures might include carbon monoxide and thiocyanate, though the NRC lists a number of chemical constituents which vary widely in concentration between sidestream and mainstream smoke. It would be of interest to develop one or more of these which could be used in conjunction with cotinine to distinguish better between those with ETS versus direct smoking exposures.

Edward Husting: I agree entirely with Dr. Hood's conclusion about the literature in this area, and I also agree with Dr. Butler's remarks, particularly with regard to Martin and Bracken. I would like to say just a few words about confounding.

The problem of bias recurs throughout the ETS literature. Confounding is one of three commonly recognized types of bias. The three are selection bias, information bias and confounding. Each detracts from the validity of epidemiological or other research. The categories of bias are not always clearly separate. However, for practical purposes, confounding is distinguished by the fact that it can be controlled in data analysis. This discussion focuses on confounding.

Most studies of pregnancy outcome have adjusted for none or only a few potential confounders. For example, Nakamura et al. (1988) adjusted for 22 confounders using multiple logistic regression but omitted at least two. They also examined data from nonworking women separately. MacArthur and Knox (1987) adjusted for confounders and found that the birthweight of infants with smoking fathers were actually greater than those with nonsmoking fathers. Haddow et al. (1988) found only a one gram difference in birth weight of ETS exposed infants when the data were reanalyzed using a multivariate analysis that considered maternal weight, height, age and other factors. However, the non-linearity of data in their 1987 paper suggests the effect of uncontrolled confounders. The results of Mau and Netter (1974) remained significant after evaluating confounders, although the confounders were evaluated separately and not simultaneously. Koo et al. (1988) listed a number of potential confounders. From these examples, it is clear that confounding is a serious problem in this literature.

Confounding is a mixing of effects, or a distortion of the effect of the exposure of interest. In the present context, confounding could cause under-

or over-estimation of the effect (if any) of ETS on perinatal development or reproductive capacity. Confounding could even change the apparent direction of an effect from positive to negative, or vice versa.

To be a confounder, a risk factor must satisfy certain conditions:

- the confounding factor must be associated with both the exposure and the disease of interest;
- it must have an effect, that is, be predictive of disease, but the effect need not be causal;
- the effect must become mixed with the effect under study;
- the confounder should be related to risk of disease among individuals not exposed to the primary factor, i.e., ETS;
- the confounder should be associated with exposure in the source population, and not merely among cases; and
- the mechanism of action should be different from the one under study.

The Dictionary of Epidemiology defines confounding as follows: "A situation in which the effects of two processes are not separated. The distortion of the apparent effect of an exposure on risk brought about by the association with other factors that can influence the outcome." A confounding variable "must be controlled in order to obtain an undistorted estimate of the effect of the study factor on risk."

According to Rothman a confounding factor must be a risk factor for disease among unexposed subjects, be associated with the exposure variable in the base population, and not be an intermediate causal link between the exposure of interest and disease. (Rothman, K.J. (1986). *Modern Epidemiology*. Little, Brown, & Co., Boston, p. 358). Age is a common confounding factor. Confounding can be limited in study design by restricting subjects, by matching, and by randomization. Confounding is controlled for in the analysis phase of a study by statistical techniques such as stratification or regression.

The Surgeon General (1986) listed some confounding factors for ETS and lung cancer and noted that these are "of particular concern when the effects of the exposure of interest are expected to be small." Possible confounders for ETS include occupational exposures, diet, other combustion products, other indoor air pollutants and socioeconomic status. Presumably, these same confounders can affect studies of reproduction.

The review of ETS by the National Research Council (1986) lists 30 or more potential confounding factors, including marijuana use, and fourteen separate factors related to the indoor air environment.

Adjustment of confounding, or confounding, may result in low or insignificant associations, and could affect publication bias. Uncontrolled confounding in individual studies can seriously affect the outcome of a meta-analysis, especially when the anaylsis combines data or results from studies which controlled for different confounders.

Sandler et al. found that exposure to ETS was associated with age, personal smoking status, marital status, education and location of residence. They mentioned, but did not examine, possible differences in diet and exercise between unexposed and exposed nonsmokers. (Sandler, D.P., K.J. Helsing, G.W. Comstock and D.L. Shore (1989). Factors associated with past household exposure to tobacco smoke. *Am. J. Epidem.* 129: 380–387.)

Koo et al. (1988) compared never-smoker wives whose husbands never smoked with never-smoker wives with ever-smoker husbands in Hong Kong. Wives with never-smoker husbands had healthier lifestyles, including better socioeconomic status, diet, housekeeping practices and family cohesiveness. They had lower frequency of miscarriages, abortions, breathing through the mouth, chronic cough and chest x-rays.

A recent study by Sidney et al. clearly illustrates a dietary confounder related to ETS, although in the context of lung cancer rather than reproductive effects. A cross sectional study of more than 2000 nonsmokers showed that the mean dietary intake of carotene was lower in nonsmokers exposed to ETS at home than in unexposed nonsmokers. The difference was statistically significant after controlling for age, sex, race, educational status, body weight and alcohol intake by multiple linear regression. The authors conclude that dietary beta-carotene intake is a potential confounder. (Sidney, S., B.J. Caan and G.D. Friedman (1989). Dietary intake of carotene in nonsmokers with and without passive smoking at home. *Am. J. Epidem.* 129: 1305–1309.)

Alberman has noted that low birthweight is associated with parity, social class, maternal height, pre-eclampsia and smoking. Sex and ethnic specific birthweight, as well as fetal growth and gestation, are influenced by maternal occupation, alcohol use, abnormalities of the cervix and uterus, infection, diet, genetic effects, hypoxia and other factors. (Alberman, E. (1984). Low birthweight. *Perinatal Epidemiology*, Bracken, M.B. (ed). Oxford University Press, pp. 86–98.)

Kallen (1988) noted that the choice of regression model can influence conclusions regarding the epidemiology of reproduction. In a linear model, maternal age seems to play no role for low birthweight risk but it actually does, as is evident when a curvilinear model is applied. He lists various confounders, including maternal age, previous reproductive outcomes, parity, changes in population reproductive patterns, socioeconomic conditions, use of antibiotics or other medications, occupation, alcohol or drug abuse, and racial and ethnic differences. (Kallen, B. (1988). *Epidemiology of Human Reproduction.* CRC Press, Inc., Boca Raton, p. 197.)

Joffe has discussed the spurious association which can arise between employment status and birthweight because of such confounders as age, parity, family size and spacing, social class, work experience, educational level, country of origin, use of health services, height, pre-pregnancy weight and pregnancy weight gain. (Joffe, M. (1985). Biases in research on reproduction and women's work. *Int. J. Epidem.* 14: 118–123.)

Some authors have controlled for a number of potential confounders. For example, Chen et al. (1989) controlled for infant's sex, parity, father's education, maternal age at birth and average income using multiple linear and logistic regression. They did not control, however, for other variables such as maternal height and weight. They found an absence of relation between exposure of mothers to ETS from paternal smoking and either mean birthweight or low birthweight.

Other authors have not adequately addressed the issue of confounding in their analyses. For example, the apparently paradoxical results of Yerushalmy (1962) may be the result of uncontrolled confounding. The percentage of low birth weight infants was higher when both parents were nonsmokers than when only the mother smoked. Borlcc ct al. (1978) found that birth weights were higher when both parents smoked than when only the mother smoked.

Martin and Bracken (1986) controlled for a number of potential confounders, including age, marital status, ethnicity, education, current employment, gestational age, parity and race. They admit the possibility of uncontrolled confounding, as well as misclassification bias. They concede that their results could have been due to some "unknown factor which was not controlled for in the analysis," such as socioeconomic status or an occupational factor. They conclude that "Whether the association found is due to passive smoking or some other related factor is unclear."

The associations reported for ETS and various reproductive and developmental effects are weak, and frequently not statistically significant. Issues of mis-classification bias are rampant. However, the failure to control for confounding casts a shadow of doubt over this entire literature. The issue of an effect of ETS on reproduction or development will remain unresolved until studies are available which deal with confounding.

George Leslie: I agree fully with the summary of the evidence presented by Dr. Hood. The published data are few, often flawed and inconclusive. They do not support the hypothesis that ETS exposure of a pregnant woman represents a risk to her fetus.

The evidence upon which we must base any judgment is at present confined to epidemiological studies. Out of about 20 papers published in the last few decades, only a minority report adverse effects—mostly in terms of reduced birth weight of infants. I cannot be sanguine about the prospect that conducting better quality, larger studies which adequately control for confounding factors and accurately quantify ETS exposure will give us any satisfactory resolution to this issue.

If we had a dozen such studies with entirely negative results, they would not convince those who wish to believe that ETS exposure is harmful. They would still point to the few studies purporting to show adverse effects, as did for example the fourth report of the UK Independent Scientific Committee on Smoking and Health. If several more studies report such effects and others do not, we will be left with the present inconclusive situation.

In view of the many published studies showing no effect, it would be surprising if well-conducted studies suddenly started to show conclusive effects. Dosimetry considerations also make such an outcome unlikely.

In summary, I do not think that epidemiology is going to help us.

As a toxicologist I find that the experimental animal approach offers opportunities to provide some hard evidence in many situations where epidemiological studies are inconclusive. We have at present (so far as I have found) no published studies of the effects of ETS exposure on pregnant animals. Such studies have many technical problems in experimental animals since rodents are a poor model for humans in terms of their respiratory anatomy. The larger respirable particles which could reach the human lung would not reach the lungs in rodents. ETS studies in dogs or primates would probably not be feasible in terms of ethics or costs.

I think it may be feasible to conduct studies in rodents, bearing in mind their limitations, but it seems unlikely that such studies will resolve the issue. It would be very difficult to establish suitable conditions for exposure, dose levels, ETS generation, etc. It would also be difficult to control for the effects of stress on reproductive parameters.

C.E. Steele: As an experimental scientist I found the epidemiological papers on the subject of the effects of ETS on human reproduction difficult and frustrating. There is, therefore, little I can add to the detailed and comprehensive review given by Dr. Hood concerning these studies. I did note in particular one publication which stated that "the degree of inaccuracy which might exist in the data obtained cannot be determined." In light of this kind of observation it seemed a good idea to look at the animal data (albeit relating to mainstream smoke) that are available. Dr. Hood touched very briefly on some of this work.

These data are no more helpful than the epidemiological studies on the question of the reproductive toxicity of ETS. Several bioassays have been conducted in pregnant mice and rats held in smoke exposure chambers through most or all of gestation to assess the reproductive effects of exposure to tobacco smoke. All of these studies were explicitly designed to be active smoking studies. The animals were exposed to mainstream tobacco smoke at high concentration levels. The COHb blood concentration levels reported in these studies ranged from 5–10% (roughly comparable to active smoking levels) to 50–55% (eleven times active smoking levels).

I should also note that even these active smoking studies are at best preliminary. Although some of them have attempted to analyze the effects of carbon monoxide exposure alone (Tachi, N., and M. Aoyama (1983). Effect of cigarette smoke and carbon monoxide inhalation by gravid rats on the conceptus weight (1983). *Bull. Environ. Contam. Toxicol.* 31: 85–92) or of undernutrition by using pair-fed controls (Bassic, J.A., P. Rosso, A.C. Moessinger, W.A. Blanc and L. Stanley James (1984). Fetal growth retardation due to maternal tobacco smoke exposure in the rat. *Pediatric Research* 18: 127–130), the animal data, which tend to be uncritically cited in clinical/epidemiological publications, do not provide full answers to these questions.

In general, there are inadequate numbers of animals used in these active smoking studies. In one study there was a control group with only two mice (Peterson, K.L., R.W. Herringer, and R.E. Seegmiller, (1981). Fetotoxicity following chronic prenatal treatment of mice with tobacco smoke and ethanol. *Bull. Environ. Contam. Toxicol.* 26: 813–819). This should be compared with the group of 25 rats used for reproductive studies on substances being developed for pharmaceutical use.

Another problem with the active smoking studies is that there were no attempts to establish dose-response relationships. Again, for pharmaceutical development, there are typically four groups: a control, a low dose group (to determine a no-effect level), a high dose group (to determine the target organs and general toxic effects) and an intermediate dose group. There was none of this in the animal studies I reviewed. In fact, in one study (Peterson, K.L., et al.) the mice in the single exposed group were comatose for four hours a day!

But at bottom, for the subject of this conference, the problem is that none of these studies are really designed to evaluate the possible reproductive effects of ETS exposure. What is needed are studies designed to explore precisely this question. The problem of concentration must be dealt with, as must the problem of the substance to which the animals are exposed. It must be ETS, not mainstream smoke. These problems are not insignificant. I listened with interest to the comments of the first two panels on ETS characterization and exposure, and I appreciate the difficulties of what I am proposing. But if we really want to resolve questions about the reproductive effects of ETS through animal tests, these difficult issues must be addressed.

I also must urge that any studies on ETS avoid the problems that are apparent in the active smoking studies on reproductive effects that are described above. Studies should follow the guidelines provided by the United States Food and Drug Administration for reproductive toxicity studies. These include male and female fertility, teratology, and peri- and post-natal studies. In addition, these studies should include detailed assessment of maternal, fetal and neonatal exposure with assays involving blood, urine, amniotic fluid and milk as well as whole body autoradiography. The choice of marker compounds has been described in detail by Dr. Reasor, though the timing of the measurements is open to question.

Frank Sullivan: I also was very impressed with Dr. Hood's review of the studies. My approach to examining the effect of ETS is slightly different. I like to look first at the effect of direct smoking in pregnancy and then in comparison with that to see what plausibility there would be in the effects ascribed to ETS.

Direct smoking during pregnancy is reported to lead to reduced birth weight, increased perinatal mortality, and perhaps to have some effect on postnatal development. However a review of the literature on the effect of direct smoking on birth weight shows that the studies are even poorer than the ETS studies, in part because they were mostly done rather longer ago and also used poor methods. In a good review by Sidle (1982) of the effects of smoking on birth weight, published by the Spastics Society, he came to the conclusion, after reviewing all the studies, that if you do very small and carefully controlled studies, you couldn't detect any effect from smoking on birth weight, but if you do very large studies which are less well controlled, then you can show an effect of smoking on birth weight. The implication is that if you do a study which is small enough to be able to control adequately for the various important confounding factors that we know about, then the effect is too small to measure. So it's a kind of philosophical problem of how to do a big study that is at the same time well controlled for confounders.

We have already discussed at some length the effect of socio-economic factors as confounders and one cannot overestimate the importance of these in pregnancy. I would like to talk, however, about two other confounders that have not been discussed so far and which are relevant both to the direct smoking studies and to the ETS smoking studies.

There are numerous studies which show that there is a correlation between smoking and drinking alcohol. It correlates both qualitatively in that the people who smoke tend to drink and quantitatively in that people who smoke heavily tend to drink heavily. There's also a correlation between smoking and caffeine consumption, and again, the heavier smokers tend to drink more cups of coffee or consume other sources of caffeine.

Both of these substances are also reported to cause reduced birth weight. Alcohol certainly has a clear effect on birth weight and perinatal mortality, and very clear effects on postnatal development. One of my interests has been to try to assess the relative contributions of smoking and alcohol to reduced birth weight and other adverse effects on pregnancy. The problem is that almost all the studies, except the Mau and Netter study, failed to control for alcohol or had quite inadequate controls for alcohol intake. The adverse effect of alcohol in pregnancy is probably much bigger than the effect of smoking, but people seem to be willing to admit that they smoke but less willing to admit that they drink at all.

Since we have had some discussion of Scottish studies, there was one rather remarkable study in the north-east of Scotland on smoking and drinking habits of pregnant women. They found that none of the women would admit to ever having had a drop of alcohol pass their lips. I think that anybody who has ever lived in the north of Scotland would know that that's not very likely to be the case.

So I think that we really have to look at the evidence underlying the claim that direct smoking actually does cause reduction in birth weight. Other studies have shown that the effects of smoking on birth weight seem to be very sensitive to the nutritional status of the mother, so that if you actually do improve the nutritional status of the mother, then the effects are very much reduced. Dr. Hood contrasted the results of Martin and Bracken on the incidence of low birth weight with the Yerushalmy study. The former had 1–2% of low birth weight babies while the latter had 3–6% of low birth weight babies. The effect in the Yerushalmy studies between the white and the black populations was also very marked, with a much higher rate in the black population. My impression is that the more you study a deprived population, the bigger the effect of smoking and other confounding factors is.

So I think that what we have to do is to look very closely at the studies that were reviewed by Dr. Hood and see to what extent they controlled, not just for socio-economic status, but also for alcohol intake, which I think is probably a more powerful factor.

Now, I think that the Martin and Bracken study probably is the most criticized because it is to date the best study that has been done. They have done quite complex modelling, in an attempt to take account of confounding factors.

In the Martin and Bracken paper, it's interesting that the effect that they got from ETS was just marginally significant, but they identified twelve other factors which were highly significantly different between the wives of smokers and the wives of non-smokers. Things like age, educational status, race and marital status—more of them were unmarried—employment and gravidity, almost all of which are known to have quite important effects on birth weight. So I think that it's very important, when one is talking about wives of smokers versus wives of non-smokers, to realize that these are really two quite different types of populations of people. I think one of the strengths of the Martin and Bracken study, and one or two of the other studies, is that they do actually highlight the differences between the two groups of women, irrespective of the effect of ETS. So that it's quite clear in the pregnancy area that confounding factors are extremely important. Of these, alcohol and nutrition are especially important to take into account.

Joseph Wu: We have one other discussant who's been added to the panel, Pamela Allen.

Pamela Allen: First, as did the other discussants, I would like to compliment Dr. Hood on a very detailed account of the available literature.

My comments mostly have been covered by the other panel discussants, but I would just like to state that in all the other papers we have heard, both today and yesterday, there has been discussion of the need to be able to quantify the exposure and dose of ETS. That is very much the case with studies on the effects of ETS on pregnancy outcome.

The majority of the studies categorize the women as either exposed or non-exposed simply on reported spousal smoking habits, and that not in relation to the time when the couple are together. This totally imprecise measurement is then related to differences in mean body weight at birth of the order of tens of grams.

I reiterate Dr. Hood's comments that future research requires well-designed epidemiologic studies in which exposure assessment is refined. Exposure both at work and at home must be taken into account, and there should be independent confirmation of the exposure, using biological markers such as cotinine. Assessment of exposure should also be obtained at several time-points during gestation, and particularly during the final trimester.

Second, as many potential confounders as possible should be taken into account.

Thirdly, the sample size of the study should be large enough to be able to accommodate all the confounding variables and still have results that are meaningful.

One point on which I differ from the views expressed by Dr. Hood, and also by Dr. Steele, is the need for animal experiments. I think people underestimate the difficulties presented in designing animal experiments that would really be meaningful for extrapolation to the human situation.

For one thing, the actual dose inhaled into the lungs by, for example, a rat, would be considerably less than that inhaled by man for equivalent ETS exposure, because of the very different anatomical structure of the nasal turbinates in the rat, and the fact that the rat is a nose-only breather and man is not.

Raphael Witorsch: I agree with Dr. Hood that the available epidemiologic data associating ETS exposure in pregnancy with a reproductive toxic effect lack consistency. To my knowledge, 15 studies have examined whether ETS exposure is associated with a decrease in average (mean or median) birth weight of offspring. Ten of these have not demonstrated a statistically significant decrement in birth weight, while 5 studies have reported such a decrease ranging in magnitude from 100–250 g. In two of these latter studies, however, the statistical significance of this effect is uncertain. Schwartz-Bickenbach et al. (1987) did not provide statistical analyses of their data that paternal smoking is associated with a decrement in mean birth weight The mean decrement in birth weight was about 200 g., the error terms were quite large, and the sample size was small (or about 50). Borlee et al. (1978) found the effect of paternal smoking to be statistically significant only if analyzed by t test (in a data set involving more than 2 means). Analysis of the data by analysis of variance, however, found no statistically significant effect of paternal smoking on mean birth weight of offspring. In view of this, the authors suggest that the paternal smoking effect may be mediated through its association with another factor.

While Martin and Bracken (1986) have been unable to show a statistically significant decrement in mean birth weight of offspring, they have reported that exposure of nonsmoking pregnant women to ETS for 2 or more hours is associated with about a two-fold increase in the incidence of delivering low birth weight (e.g., less than 2500 grams) term infants. More recently, both Nakamura et al. (1987) examining a cohort in Osaka, and Chen et al. (1989) examining a cohort in Shanghai, reported no statistically significant association between paternal smoking and the incidence of low birth weight term offspring. Nakamura et al. also reported that the association between paternal smoking and incidence of low birth weight offspring (both preterm and term) was of borderline statistical significance. However, a series of reports published in the 1960's and 1970's find no statistically significant association between paternal smoking and the increased incidence of low birth weight (pre-term and/or term) offspring of nonsmoking mothers.

Birth weight was chosen in most of these studies because it is considered to be the most sensitive indicator of fetotoxicity (intrauterine growth retardation, IUGR) and a reliable predictor of perinatal mortality (Abel, 1980). It is noteworthy, however, that there is little or no evidence associating paternal smoking and infant mortality.

The issue of fetotoxic effects of ETS is very difficult to resolve because: (1) birth weight is influenced by a wide variety of factors and (2) misclassification of both smoking status and ETS exposure are, at present, difficult to control in epidemiologic studies.

As noted in the reviews of Thomson (1983) and Kramer (1987), and emphasized by Dr. Hood, numerous factors have been identified that influence birth weight. To adjust for all of these adequately in an epidemiologic study would be a substantial undertaking. Furthermore, the physiologic bases of these factors are poorly understood. Since adjustment for these variables has not been standardized in the epidemiologic studies in question, it is reasonable to assume that this could contribute, in part, to the lack of agreement in results from one study to the next.

All but one of the epidemiologic studies dealing with the potential fetotoxicity of ETS lacked verification of such exposure with a specific tobacco marker (such as body fluid cotinine). In most of the studies, paternal smoking served as the surrogate for ETS exposure. As pointed out repeatedly during this symposium, spousal smoking per se is an imprecise surrogate for ETS exposure.

In the future, epidemiologic studies should, at the very least, attempt to validate ETS exposure with some specific and reliable biological marker. Environmental monitoring would also be beneficial. Every attempt should be made to control for all of the confounders that influence birth weight, socioeconomic status, and potential sources of error in smoking status and ETS exposure classification. Furthermore, consideration and treatment of confounding variables should be standardized.

The problem of birth weight as an index of fetotoxicity is made more complex by the fact that relatively little is known about the mechanisms determining fetal growth and the pathophysiologic mechanisms responsible for fetal growth retardation. The field of fetotoxicity in general would benefit from studies relating specifically to placental function (i.e., transport of nutrients, placental hormones and growth factors) and its relationship to fetal growth and development. Such studies should be performed both in animals and in humans.

Since a limitation of epidemiologic studies is the appropriate adjustment for a wide variety of variables, there is value in conducting studies of the potential fetotoxicity of ETS in animals. Numerous toxicologic studies have been published on the effects of tobacco smoke and birth outcome using animal models, most often the rodent. However, these studies have little relevance to the issue of ETS since they involved exposures to mainstream smoke at levels that were equivalent to, or in far excess of, that seen with active smoking. There is a real need for studies involving the exposure of pregnant animals to aged mixtures of sidestream and mainstream smoke that attempt to simulate ETS. Assuming that these experiments will employ a smoking machine, the levels of nicotine and CO in the smoke chamber should be monitored and be maintained to approximate those seen in real life situations, while body fluid cotinine levels in these exposed animals should be comparable to that seen in nonsmoking ETS individuals. In addition to size, birth weight, and length of offspring, these studies should also monitor postnatal development and placental function during pregnancy.

Joseph Wu: We'll take questions from the floor now.

Roger Jenkins: I'm Roger Jenkins from Oak Ridge National Lab. I wanted to address some of Dr. Leslie's comments concerning the utility of animal studies—perhaps not the utility of the studies, but rather their feasibility.

Based on the available literature we've got concerning particle size of environmental tobacco smoke, it appears that most of the particles are fairly small—on the order of a tenth of a micron mass median diameter. So it shouldn't be a question of the large particles not getting into the animal's lungs, because there are probably not a lot of large particles present in true ETS. And to reiterate what Dr. Witorsch said about the utility of animal studies, I think it would be very easy to use diluted sidestream smoke and dilute it down to something on the order of five hundred or seven hundred micrograms per cubic metre particulates and expose the animals for a long term period. In other words, that kind of smoke could be generated fairly easily. If you're concerned about the addition of exhaled mainstream smoke, to make this atmosphere more relevant, it certainly could be accomplished by bubbling mainstream cigarette smoke through some sort of washing apparatus which strips some of the more volatile components of the smoke. Using this method, you could end up with something that represents the 10–15% of exhaled mainstream smoke that comprises ETS.

I'm not going to comment on the relevance of using a Fischer or a Sprague-Dowley rat for an animal model. That's up to my more learned colleagues in the area of toxicology. But from the standpoint of accomplishing animal studies by generating a "relevant atmosphere," I think that's possible.

Joseph Fleiss: The discussion concerning confounding reminded me of the turmoil that exists in biostatistics and epidemiology about what confounding is and how we adjust for it. It's not as simple as we once thought. A confounder, in simple terms, is a variable or a factor that's associated both with the risk factor and with the response variable. In the old days, I think—1984, 1985 and before then—we would have identified confounders on the basis of significance tests, correlated with both the input factor and the output factor. But that's verboten nowadays. Nowadays, we see in some standard epidemiology texts the statement that "a confounding variable is one that exerts a meaningful change in the relative risk." "Meaningful change." That appears in a text by Kleinbaum and Cooper and others. How soft and subjective and prone to bias that is.

So I agree with everything that was said about the need to control for confounders but, again, it's not as easy as it once was.

Jarnail Singh: Two points were alluded to by the panelists.

The first one was that maybe more studies should be done, perhaps using ETS surrogates, CO or nicotine. And the second was that nutrition may play a big role in fetal weight or neonatal weight. And I've been looking at these subjects.

First of all, my work on the effect of CO on fetotoxicity is published and I want to make two points on that. One is that fetal mortality is dose-dependent. The second point is that fetal weight is inversely related to the dose.

On the nutrition point, I just finished analyzing this data, and three points come out very clearly. The first is that fetal weight is dependent on the level of proteins in the mother's diet. The higher the protein level, the higher the fetal weight; the lower the protein level, the lower the fetal weight. The second point is that a low protein diet enhances the carboxyhaemoglobin concentration in the fetal blood but not as much as in the maternal blood.

And the third point that comes out very clearly is that the incidence of low birth weight was enhanced in the low protein diets in each concentration of CO.

Joseph Wu: We'll take the last question from Dr. Roe.

Francis Roe: I'd just really like to ask the panel, is there any more mileage to be got by looking at the placenta? Ray Witorsch discussed placental function, and that presumably can be done before parturition. But what about looking at the placenta? Is that likely to be helpful? What happens in the case of active smoking?

Raphael Witorsch: The placenta of the rodent and the placenta of the human are quite different, structually. Endocrinologically, it's turning out in certain areas that there are some parallels. So if one goes into an area using an animal model, you have to go in with your eyes open.

Francis Roe: I wasn't really asking about the animal. I was asking about using human material, for a human study.

Raphael Witorsch: Well, it would be very good. There are studies which have shown, for example, that an association exists between maternal smoking and levels of placental actogen. It's an inverse relationship, at least in one study that I know of. The interpretation there was that it would be a good marker for placental function. When I looked at that, my ears perked up. I said, "Well, maybe that's not only a marker for placental function." If the secretion of that particular hormone is impaired during late pregnancy (which is the period at which birth weight is most affected) and this particular hormone is believed to have a role in nutrient shift (mobilizing nutrients to the mother transplacentally to the fetus), maybe that or something like that is a final common denominator of this intrauterine growth retardation effect.

Again, the reason one should also do animal studies is that at least in an animal environment you don't have the problem of confounding variables because—if you're working with a homogeneous strain of animals—you can just focus in on the phenomenon that you're looking at, be it tobacco smoke, alcohol, etc.

So, really, to get new knowledge, I think both approaches have validity.

Joseph Wu: Dr. Sullivan?

Frank Sullivan: There have been a number of studies of the placenta in human smokers, and one of the problems with placentas is that, as a famous placental pathologist once said, "It's physiological for the placenta to be pathological." So the placenta gets more and more infarcted as pregnancy goes on, until eventually the baby is holding on by a thread, really, and is born not a moment too soon, normally. That's why, you know, increased gestation becomes really very dangerous.

There have been studies on placental pathology and smokers. There is an increase in pathology, but I don't think that the evidence is clear enough to say that that's a significant factor. I mean, that's with direct smoking. There's nothing on indirect smoking that I'm aware of, but for direct smoking it's not clear. It's too difficult to quantify, really, because placentas can be very infarcted and yet the baby can do very well.

The other thing, I think, that's very important is that, as far as we know, the effects of smoking in pregnancy are not seen if the mother stops by the fourth month of gestation, so that it's the late effect in pregnancy that's important.

Part VII

16
Risk Assessments Relating to Environmental Tobacco Smoke

Alan J. Gross, Ph.D.
Department of Biometry
Medical University of South Carolina

This paper describes the technique of environmental risk assessment and then considers representative examples of the application of the technique to environmental tobacco smoke ("ETS"). As will be seen, the risk assessments that have been conducted in this area thus far are fraught with serious problems that call their validity into question. Much more scientific work is still necessary before one could conclude with any confidence that exposure to ETS involves a quantifiable risk of any particular health hazard.

First, I describe the risk assessment technique in general terms. Then I consider representative risk assessments of exposure to ETS, noting their various methodological problems. I conclude with some brief observations on features common to those risk assessments and indicate what remains to be done in this area.

I. Risk Assessment

A. Procedure

Risk assessment, as defined in the report of the National Research Council ("NRC") (1983), is a technique that is used to estimate the effects on the health of individuals or populations exposed to certain materials or situations that are regarded as hazardous. It is generally accepted that risk assessment consists of the following four seemingly simple steps:

1. Hazard identification: Determining whether a particular agent is causally linked to certain health effects.
2. Dose-response assessment: Determining the relationship between the amount of exposure to the agent and the probability of occurrence of the health effects in question.

3. Exposure assessment: Determining the extent to which humans are actually exposed to the agent.
4. Characterization of risk: Describing the nature and often the magnitude of the risk to humans, including the uncertainty involved.

If a risk has been quantified, it can form the basis for a public policy decision on whether and how the risk should be managed.

As Park and Snee (1983) point out, carcinogenic risk assessment, which is the centerpiece of the efforts considered by this paper, typically is a quite complicated process that can be based on a number of different types of studies: mutagenicity, acute studies in animals, subchronic animal studies, metabolism, chronic animal studies, epidemiology, and route and amount of exposure. As far as the possible basis for a risk assessment for ETS is concerned, however, the primary focus thus far has been on only the latter two types of studies, namely, epidemiological studies and studies concerned with route and amount of exposure.

B. The Data Base for ETS Risk Assessments

To date 23 epidemiologic studies (20 retrospective case-control and three prospective cohort studies) have been carried out to assess a possible association between ETS and the incidence of lung cancer in humans. In nearly all of these studies, spousal smoking has been used as the means to assess the exposure of nonsmokers to ETS. This in itself produces a bias, as ETS from co-workers and others is not considered in these studies. Thirteen of these studies form the basis for the relative risk factor presented in the NRC (1986) report on ETS.

In addition to these epidemiologic studies, studies of the amount of exposure to ETS have been employed by Repace and Lowrey (1985a), Repace (1987) and Robins et al. (1989). Also, Wells (1988) discusses a number of additional epidemiologic studies dealing with a possible association between ETS and cardiovascular disease, as well as cancer at sites other than the lung. Finally, Robins (1986) and Robins et al. (1989) obtain epidemiologic and dosimetric estimates of the number of cigarette equivalents allegedly inhaled daily by a nonsmoker through exposure to ETS. From this estimate and the aforementioned epidemiologic studies, an attempt has been made to assess the risk of lung cancer deaths in nonsmokers due to ETS.

The manner in which these sets of data have been employed in specific ETS risk assessments is described below.

C. The NRC (1986) Report

As noted, 13 of the 23 lung cancer epidemiology studies that have been conducted thus far form the basis for the summary relative risk ratio of 1.34

presented in the NRC (1986) report. As Dr. Layard demonstrated earlier in this symposium, both these 13 studies and the 10 additional studies manifest numerous fundamental problems that call their validity into question. For example, all data were subject to misclassification of disease. That is, the possibilities of false-positive and false-negative findings in the diagnosis, or missed diagnosis of lung cancer, are among the items for which a proper accounting was not given. Furthermore, the studies failed to deal with the possibility of misclassification of smoking status. That is, many individuals who were classified as nonsmokers with regard to ETS actually may have been smokers. When Letzel et al. (1988) adjusted for the impact of these misclassifications, their conclusion was "there are presently two alternatives—accepting the null hypothesis or creating new empirical evidence and performing a really good study."

In addition, these epidemiologic studies do not control for numerous important confounding variables, such as diet, alcohol consumption, occupation, socioeconomic status, and so on. This was pointed out by Koo et al. (1988) in the Hong Kong study. In summary, the present epidemiologic studies are not sufficiently well done to justify an inference of an association between exposure to ETS and an increased risk of death due to lung cancer for nonsmokers. Accordingly, the NRC (1986) risk assessment fails at step one of the technique; because it is based on data that do not support an inference that ETS is a health hazard to begin with, it possesses no reliable basis from which to calculate a risk of the alleged hazard.

I note that the 13 epidemiologic studies employed in the NRC report (1986) formed the basis for a "meta-analysis" in which the studies were combined to obtain an overall risk ratio of 1.34 for nonsmokers "exposed" to ETS versus those deemed "unexposed." The use of this procedure is problematic. Aside from the obvious point that each individual study contained in a meta-analysis must be valid for the population studied—a condition that has not been met for the studies in question—it is also crucial that the studies be sufficiently comparable to justify adding their results together to obtain a risk factor that is valid for a wider population. Such comparability is not present in the studies in question because they evidence a wide disparity in major factors such as the social and demographic characteristics of the populations examined. Indeed, how can studies in Europe, Asia and North America be combined into a meta-analysis when the cross-cultural differences in the populations studied are so obvious? Simply put, one cannot add apples and oranges in this fashion—and indeed, to persist with the metaphor, no number of bad apples will add up to any quantity of good apples.

D. Repace and Lowrey

Like the NRC report (1986), Repace and Lowrey (1985a) simply assumed, on the basis of the epidemiologic studies mentioned above, that there is a causal link between ETS and lung cancer. They then attempted to quantify this perceived risk.

Repace and Lowrey (1985a) conducted field surveys to determine levels of respirable particles (RP) both indoors and outdoors in both smoke-free and smoky environments. They used what they termed "controlled experiments" to develop a model to estimate exposures to these particles. The model predicts that exposure of U.S. nonsmokers is in the range of zero to 14 mg of cigarette "tar" per day, depending on the nonsmokers' "lifestyle." For non-smoking adults of working age, the model predicts an average total exposure of 1.43 mg/day at home and at work "with an 86% exposure probability." This means that 14% of adults are estimated to be completely non-exposed, which is taken into account in the average exposure caculation.

It appears that this 1.43 mg/day estimate is not really representative since it does not distinguish exposure by sex or by environment (i.e., whether exposure is at home or the workplace.) Futhermore, the estimate is based on cross-sectional data but patterns of exposure, especially for women, have changed greatly since the end of World War II due to changing work patterns and the role of women in society in general. Finally, the workplace exposures modeled by Repace and Lowrey (1985b) are likely to be too high. The same observations hold true for their assumption of an average cigarette consumption by smokers of two cigarettes per hour. The use of a mere arithmetic average in this instance may also be incorrect.

Repace and Lowrey base their estimate of an excess lung cancer death rate due to ETS on a comparison by Phillips et al. (1980a, 1980b) of a group of 25,264 Seventh Day Adventists (SDA's) with a comparable group of 50,216 non-SDA's; both groups consisted of self-reported never-smokers whose ages ranged from 35 to 85. They calculated an age-adjusted SDA-to-non-SDA lung cancer rate ratio of 0.41 averaged over both sexes. This is their basis for the claim that the non-SDA group had an average lung cancer mortality rate 2.4 times that of the SDA group. Based on this rate ratio, Repace and Lowrey calculated that ETS caused 4,700 lung cancer deaths (LCD's) among the 62.4 million U.S. non-smokers aged 35 or over in 1980. This is an excess rate of 7.4 LCD's per 100,000 person-years due to ETS.

Repace and Lowrey's use of this SDA analysis is open to criticism for several reasons. Some of the more important of these reasons are:

1. Contrary to Repace and Lowrey's assertion, the difference in lung cancer deaths between the groups may well be due to any number of causes other than ETS. SDA's and non-SDA's tend to differ in major lifestyle variables such as alcohol consumption, occupation and dietary habits, not to mention racial and ethnic differences.
2. Selection bias is possible since SDA participants were selected from active

church members whereas the other non-smoking participants were part of an American Cancer Society study cohort which was selected from among friends, relatives and acquaintances of American Cancer Society volunteers. Neither sample was random.

3. Among SDA members, the causes of about 10% of the deaths out-of-state (the study took place in California) were not ascertained. There is also an 8–10% under-ascertainment of causes of death among older subjects.

Based on the assumption of a linear dose-response, Repace and Lowrey calculated an ETS dose-response relation of roughly 5 LCD's/100,000 per 1 mg of tar per day, by dividing 7.4 LCDs/100,000 by 1.43 mg./day of average tar exposure. Since Repace and Lowrey estimated a tar exposure range of 0–14 mg/day, this dose-response function yields roughly 70 lung cancer deaths/100,000 for the most "exposed" lifestyle, e.g., a nonsmoking musician who performs regularly in a smoky night club and lives in a small apartment with a chain-smoker. The problem with this exercise is that there is no direct evidence of a linear dose-response relationship (or indeed of any dose-response relationship).

Repace and Lowrey also derived an ETS dose-response relationship by extrapolating from estimates of lung cancer risks based on mainstream smoke. Under a one-hit linear model (essentially a linear dose-response extrapolation in the low dose region), this corresponds to a dose-response of roughly 0.6 lung cancer deaths/100,000 per 1 mg/day, which is an order of magnitude lower than the dose-response estimate based on the SDA data. Repace and Lowrey claimed that the larger estimate accords better with the results of the epidemiologic studies than the model extrapolated from mainstream smoke. However, as pointed out above, the risks suggested both by the epidemiologic data and the SDA-based dose-response model may well be statistical artifacts produced by biases and confounding factors, so the mere fact that they are similar proves nothing.

Given these problems with the work by Repace and Lowrey, it must be concluded—even assuming that it had been demonstrated that ETS could be regarded as a health hazard in the first place—that they have failed to provide convincing dose-response and exposure models on which to base a risk assessment.

E. Wells

Wells (1988) obtained a mortality projection for nonsmokers exposed to ETS based on epidemiologic data for lung cancers, other cancers and cardiovascular disease. He acknowledged that in the Surgeon General's (1986) report and the NRC (1986) report, data on other cancers and cardiovascular disease were not considered adequate to support a causal judgment or to "calculate reliable overall risks." However, he asserted that considerable new epidemiological information has become available since 1985. That claim is dubious in view of the problems that have been detected in these later studies, as shown by Drs. Wexler and Layard earlier in this symposium.

Wells used two risk assessment models in his paper. His primary model combined the relative risks from disease and sex-specific studies under the assumption that the relative risk is constant with respect to age. In his secondary model, the combined relative risk was allowed to vary with age. Wells estimated that a total of 61% of male nonsmokers and 76% of female nonsmokers were exposed to ETS. These overall exposure fractions were adjusted to give higher fractions at younger ages and lower fractions at older ages.

Wells estimated never-smoker death rates using data primarily from the American Cancer Society 25-state cohort study (Hammond, 1966; Garfinkel, 1981). From these estimates of relative risks, population fractions exposed and death rates, he then calculated annual numbers of deaths due to ETS exposure. The calculations yield an estimated U.S. annual total of 3,000 lung cancer deaths, 11,000 deaths from other cancers, and 32,000 deaths from heart disease, giving a combined total of 46,000 deaths.

Wells's estimates of both the exposed fractions and never-smoker death rates can be criticized on a number of grounds, including, especially, the sources of the data that form the basis of the estimates and the assumptions and methods used to calculate them. For example, the American Cancer Society 25-state cohort was a selected group whose death rates differed from those of the general U.S. population. Furthermore, the meta-analytic assumptions and methods used to derive summary relative risks from disparate epidemiologic studies are of doubtful validity, as other speakers at this symposium have noted. However, the critical element in Wells's death projections is the assumption that the combined relative risks derived from the epidemiologic studies of ETS and disease represent causal relationships. Since that assumption has not been justified, any attempt to estimate the number of disease-specific deaths from ETS is an ill-founded exercise.

Detailed reviews of the epidemiologic evidence in each of the three disease areas considered by Wells have been presented by other speakers at this symposium and need not be repeated here. Therefore, based on their conclusions that consideration of the usual criteria for evaluating epidemiologic evidence, such as strength and consistency of association and freedom from bias and confounding, indicate that the currently available epidemiologic data do not support a causal inference for lung cancer, other cancers, or heart disease, Wells's estimates of the number of deaths from these diseases due to ETS must be regarded as nothing more than groundless speculation.

F. Robins et al.

J. Robins presented a lung cancer risk assessment in an appendix to the NRC (1986) report. (The appendix was prepared too late to be considered critically by the NRC committee in assembling its report.) A journal article containing essentially the same analysis has just been published (Robins et al. 1989). The various assumptions underlying the analysis, and the computational details, are too complex and lengthy to review exhaustively in this paper. Nevertheless, it is possible to outline the main results of the analysis and comment on the major problems and uncertainties inherent in Robins' estimates.

The main results of the Robins risk assessment were estimates of the annual number of deaths among nonsmokers due to ETS exposure and of the lifetime risk of death from lung cancer due to ETS:

1. Estimates of lung cancer deaths due to ETS exposure: Of an estimated 7,000 U.S. deaths among lifelong nonsmoking women in 1985 due to this disease, Robins estimated that between 1,770 and 3,220 could be attributable to ETS. Of an estimated 5,200 U.S. lung cancer deaths among nonsmoking males, he estimated that between 720 and 1,940 could be attributable to ETS.
2. Estimate of lifetime risk of lung cancer death due to ETS: The estimated lifetime risk of death from lung cancer attributable to ETS for a nonsmoker with moderate ETS exposure was between 390 and 990 per 100,000 persons at risk.

The estimates of the number of lung cancer deaths among women in 1985 were obtained from National Health Interview Survey data on the number of nonsmoking women at risk and from death rates in the American Cancer Society 25-state cohort study (Garfinkel 1981). The number of lung cancer deaths attributable to ETS was then estimated by using estimates of the age-specific average relative risk among nonsmoking women. These estimates were in turn obtained from age-specific estimates of the probability of being married to a smoker (derived from the Garfinkel et al. (1985) case-control study) and from estimates of the "true" relative risk in "exposed" and "unexposed" subjects. In this analysis, an "unexposed" subject is defined as a nonsmoker married to a nonsmoker, and an "exposed" subject as a nonsmoker married to a smoker. The average "unexposed" subject is assumed to receive ETS exposure from sources other than spousal smoking amounting to one third of the total ETS exposure received by the average "exposed" subject. The calculation with regard to lung cancer deaths in males in 1985 was similar.

"True" relative risks are defined by Robins to be those relative to a person receiving zero ETS exposure. Robins estimates these true relative risks for the "exposed" and "unexposed" in a very convoluted manner. The computation requires estimates of age-specific ETS exposure of "exposed" and "unexposed" subjects relative to the current ETS exposure of an average adult "unexposed" subject. Since no data exist on which to base such estimates, Robins performs a sensitivity analysis with 30 different hypothetical exposure histories. The analysis assumes that smoking and ETS exposure affect the same first and fourth stages of a 5-stage carcinogenesis model, and requires an estimate of β_4/β_1, where β_1 and β_4 are, respectively, the magnitudes of the smoking effects for the first and fourth stages. Robins obtains two estimates of this ratio, one from the British doctor study (Doll and Peto 1978) and one from a European case-control study (Lubin et al. 1984). Finally, Robins assumes that the ratio of the true relative risks for the "exposed" to the "unexposed" at age 70 is 1.3. (The number 1.3 is the summary relative risk from the NRC (1986) meta-analysis of 13 lung cancer studies, which Robins assumes reflects a causal association.) The resulting estimated range of the true relative risks, when the calculations are performed for each of the 30 exposure histories and both estimates of β_4/β_1, is 1.41 to 1.87 for the "exposed" and 1.09 to 1.45 for the "unexposed."

As in the case of Wells's risk assessment, the critical assumption in the Robins analysis is that the summary relative risk derived by the NRC meta-analysis is causal. As noted above, because that assumption cannot be justified on the basis of the epidemiologic studies carried out thus far, an estimation of the number of deaths due to ETS is mere speculation. Other problems with Robins' estimates are:

1. Many further assumptions are made in the course of the analysis for which there is no empirical basis.
2. Although sensitivity analyses were done for some parameters, the width of the interval estimates for numbers of deaths would have been considerably greater if other sources of uncertainty, such as statistical variability, had been taken into account.
3. Use of an alternate carcinogenesis model could have a considerable impact on the estimates.
4. As Robins concedes, an attempt to compare ETS dose in cigarette equivalents calculated from (a) epidemiologic data on smoking and on ETS exposure and (b) dosimetric measurements failed to provide support for the observed ETS-lung cancer association. The first calculation gave a cigarette equivalent dose for an "unexposed" subject in the range 0.12 to 0.93. Based on dosimetric data on respirable suspended particulates ("tar"), the cigarette equivalent dose was estimated as 0.0001 to 0.005. To resolve this issue, Robins et al. (1989) recommend that careful dosimetric measurements be made of the exposure of smokers and nonsmok-

ers to suspected carcinogenic components of mainstream smoke and ETS. This work remains to be done.

In summary, while the Robins analysis is more complicated and sophisticated than the other assessments discussed in this paper, and he is more candid about his assumptions of causality, his work does not justify the conclusion that ETS exposure increases the risk of nonsmoker lung cancer.

II. Conclusions

The most striking aspect of the ETS risk assessments that have been carried out thus far is that the authors have seen fit to undertake them at all. As we have seen, these assessments have feet of clay: Because they are based on epidemiologic studies that themselves are not reliable, they lack the necessary foundation of an inference that exposure to ETS causes disease of any sort in humans. Thus, employing the data in those studies to perform the remaining steps in a risk assessment has been a futile exercise. The first order of business, therefore, is for proper studies to be carried out with respect to a possible causal link between ETS and particular diseases. If studies justifying a causal inference were to become available, we could then employ the remaining steps in the risk assessment technique.

Still, considerable work also remains to be done in devising a proper methodology in the areas of dose-response and exposure assessment. Further efforts in these areas would have to take into account the serious, perhaps debilitating difficulties in deriving ETS dosimetry measurements by low-dose ETS extrapolation from animal bioassay data or epidemiologic data relating to mainstream smoke. In this regard, we clearly need to develop a much better understanding of the constituents and behavior (e.g., "aging") of ETS before these areas of inquiry can proceed beyond their current speculative stage.

Only if these conditions were to be met could we begin to take seriously any assertion that ETS exposure elevates the risk that one will contract certain diseases. It is most unfortunate that, in the meantime, projections of large numbers of deaths due to ETS have sown considerable fear and confusion among the public.

References

Doll, R.D., and R. Peto (1978). Cigarette smoking and bronchial carcinoma: Dose and time relationships among regular smokers and lifelong non-smokers. *J. Epidemiol. Comm. Health* 32:303–313.

Garfinkel, L. (1981). Time Trends in Lung Cancer Mortality among nonsmokers and a note on passive smoking. *J. Nat'l Cancer Inst.* 66:1061–1066.

Garfinkel, L., O. Auerbach, and L. Joubert (1985). Involuntary smoking and lung cancer: A case-control study. *J. Natl'l Cancer Inst.* 75:463–469.

Hammond, E.C. (1966). Smoking in relation to the death rates of one million men and women. *Nat. Cancer Inst. Monogr.* 19:127–204.

Koo, L.C., J.H-C. Ho, and R. Rylander, (1988). Life-history correlates of environmental tobacco smoke: A study on nonsmoking Hong Kong Chinese wives with smoking versus nonsmoking husbands. *Soc. Sci. Med.* 26: 751–760.

Letzl, H., E. Blumner and K. Überla (1988). Meta-analysis on passive smoking and lung cancer effects of study selection and misclassification of exposure. *Environmental Technology Letters* 9:491–500.

Lubin, J.H., W.J. Blot, F. Berrino et al. (1984). Patterns of lung cancer risk among filter and nonfilter cigarette smokers. *Int. J. Cancer* 33:569–576.

National Research Council: Committee on Passive Smoking (1986). *Environmental Tobacco Smoke: Measuring and Assessing Health Effects.* National Academy Press, Washington, D.C. xiii + 337 pp.

National Research Council: Committee on the Institutional Means for Assessment of Risks to Public Health (1983). *Risk Assessment in the Federal Government: Managing the Process.* National Academy Press, Washington, D.C. xii + 191 pp.

Park, C.N. and R.D. Snee (1983). Quantitative risk assessment: state of the art for carcinogenesis. *The American Statistician* 37(4): 427–441.

Phillips, R.L., L. Garfinkel, J.W. Kuzma et al. (1980a). Mortality among Californian Seventh-Day Adventists for selected cancer sites. *J. Nat'l Cancer Inst.* 65:1097–1107.

Phillips, R.L., J.W. Kuzma, W.L. Beeson et al. (1980b). Influence of selection versus lifestyle on risk of fatal cancer and cardiovascular disease among Seventh-Day Adventists. *Amer. J. Epidemiol.* 112:296–314.

Repace, J.L. 1987). Indoor concentrations of environmental tobacco smoke: Models dealing with effects of ventilation and room size. *IRAC Scientific Publication 81. Environmental Carcinogens: Selected Methods of Analysis:* 25–41.

Repace, J.L. and A.H. Lowrey (1985a). A quantitative estimate of nonsmokers' lung cancer risk from passive smoking. *Environment International* 2:3–22.

Repace, J.L. and A.H. Lowrey (1985b). An indoor air quality standard for ambient tobacco smoke based on carcinogenic risk. *New York State Journal of Medicine* July:381–383.

Robbins, J.L., D. Blevins, and M. Schneiderman (1989). The effective number of cigarettes inhaled daily by passive smoking. Are epidemiologic and dosimetric estimates consistent? *J. Haz. Mat.* 21:215–238.

Robbins, J. (1986). Risk assessment—exposure to environmental tobacco smoke and lung cancer. *Appendix D. NRC Report on Environmental Tobacco Smoke,* National Academy Press, Washington, D.C.: 294–337.

Surgeon General's Report (1986). *The Health Consequences of Involuntary Smoking.* U.S. Department of Health and Human Services. xix + 359 pp.

Wells, A.J. (1988). An estimate of adult mortality in the United States from Passive Smoking. *Environment International* 14:249–265.

17
Panel Discussion on Risk Assessment

Donald Ecobichon: We'll start off in alphabetical order with the exception of the last three people, when I'll ask Dr. Starr to go ahead out of order because Dr. Schwartz and Dr. Voytek tell me they're doing something in tandem. Dr. Atteslander, please.

Peter Atteslander: I would like to thank Dr. Gross for his paper. I'm especially glad that he really put his finger on what for me, at least, are the most important aspects of risk assessment: validity and quantification. These are the two points that I would like to address now.

Risk assessment depends on the definition of risk. There is no generally accepted definition of risk known to me that both meets the requirements of the stringent natural sciences' logic and takes into account the human and societal implications that are the logic of the social sciences.

Empirical tests on risk depend not only on the more or less discernible definition of risk that researchers use but even more on the quality of "operationalization." In other words, reports on risks must answer the questions:

- what has been measured?
- how has it been measured?
- when and how many cases have been measured?

We usually are confronted with highly aggregated sets of data referring to health risks, without the possibility for the reader to trace the genealogy of the data-gathering. Before one can decide how valid data are, one has to know how they emerged and with what degree of exactitude they were isolated from and within the existing complex network of interrelating factors of physical and social life.

Dr. Gross and, before him, Dr. Wexler, have clearly shown that most if not all epidemiological studies on health risk regarding ETS do not meet these requirements (Lebowitz, M. D. (1986). The potential association of lung cancer with passive smoking. *Environment International* 12: 3–9). Notwithstanding their questionable validity, epidemiological data have served as the alibi for numerous administrative rules, legal prescriptions and political interventions.

Before one should talk of "risk acceptance" or "risk refusal" it might be helpful to accept the necessity of an interdisciplinary approach, which is at least being attempted in the field of acceptance of new technologies. "There are a number of analysts who point out that the term 'risk acceptance' is an improper persepective: society, or an individual within a society, does not accept or reject risks in isolation; rather, one accepts or rejects technological developments that have a multiplicity of risk attributes as well as inherent benefits and costs of other kinds. These include a wide range of beneficial and adverse effects on the natural and human environments that are direct and indirect, intended and unintended, quantifiable and intangible, short and long term, and rather certain or probabilistic of realization." (Spangler, M.B. (1982). The role of interdisciplinary analyses in bridging the gap between the technical and human sides of risk assessment. *Risk Analysis* 2(2):101–114.).

As an example of careless use of health data for official campaigns, I may quote a recent example from Switzerland, where an official brochure was published in early 1985 that took the position that smoking should be banned altogether (Bundesamt für Gesundheitswesen (1989). *Schw. Sanitätsdirektorenkonferenz und Arbeitsgemeinschaft Tabakmißbrauch; Rauchen und Sterblichkeit in der Schweiz* (Bern)). Thirty-three member states, including Switzerland, decided in 1984 on a common strategy for promoting "health for all by the year 2000." Ilona Kickbusch, an employee of the European Regional Office of the World Health Organization in Copenhagen, pointed out entirely correctly that this programme must, in view of the failure in the case of "civilization illnesses," be regarded as entirely utopian and its goal thus unreachable. Equally remarkably, she stated: "What health can not be is a fixed normative state which permits interventions, medically or by the police, on the basis of deviations from the norm." (Kickbusch, I. Vom Umgang Mit der Utopie: Anmerkungen zum Gesundheitsbegriff der Weltgesundheitsorganisation, in: Abholz, op. cit. pp. 267–276.)

If government departments—as in the present case—propagate the necessity of preventive measures, it must be clarified whether they have fulfilled the requisite duty of care in handling official statistics. Lamentably, this is not the case. In various places, the brochure of the Swiss Health Office just mentioned creates the impression that the figures presented were scientifically significant and could unreservedly be used as grounds for political-administrative measures.

Even allowing for the good intentions of those concerned, it is necessary to ask whether this is not a misuse of official statistical data. Although various passages in the text speak of estimates, an impression of scientific accuracy is nevertheless unhesitatingly created in the very first introductory sentence, which reads: "Smoking is the single most important avoidable cause of disease and premature death in Europe."

It has been known for many years in professional circles that such a statement is unsupportable scientifically. As Abholz states: "As is known, epidemiological findings are only feature associations, and it is impossible to determine causal relationships" (Abholz, H.H. (1982). Konzeptionelle und ethische probleme des risikofaktoren-konzepts in seiner therapeutischen anwendung In: Abholz, H.H.; D. Boigers; W. Karmaus, und J. Korporal (Eds.): *Risikofaktorenmedizin—Konzept und Kontroverse* (Berlin-New York). Rutsch has indicated: "Lack of clarity regarding the parameter to be calculated and the dearth of health-statistical data can have the result that, as the measure of excess mortality, a figure is calculated which does not meet the factual and logical requirement and the expectations which it has raised." (Rutsch, M. (1979). Mortalität, Rauchen und Statistik. *Statistische Hefte* 20: 160–171). As early as ten years ago, Rutsch examined the mortality comparisons available at that time and critically evaluated the generally accepted calculation of the excess mortality of smokers. Unfortunately what he then found also applies fully to the mentioned brochure: "Confusion of definitions, some eccentric calculation methods and an obscure origin of the starting figures; all these are reasons for the enormous latitude in the allegations regarding the mortality excess in (cigarette) smokers."

I would like to make three statements at this point:

1. The so-called civilization illnesses are increasing in developed societies.
2. The number of diseases that represent a combination of different causes (polyaetiology) are also increasing proportionately.
3. This makes the epidemiological determination of the number of cases more difficult and, with few exceptions, prohibits the establishment of causal relationships between disease symptoms and the causing factor.

In conclusion: We should not so much discuss individual figures in the reports, but rather their research artifacts. That means complete research designs have to be reviewed. Dr. Gross has shown how such artifacts have been established in the studies he mentioned. As a result, research artifacts, if not identified, may become a political reality.

We should discuss maybe in another meeting why there is a strong urge to quantify even in areas where quantification is not the proper procedure. Quantification is not what determines whether something is more or less scientific; this depends, rather, on theory and on research design. What is my "medicine" for tomorrow? Fewer and better epidemiological questionnaires, and more participant observations. The latter is difficult, more expensive, but probably more valid, at least if human behavior is involved.

Gary Flamm: I've had occasion to look at quite a lot of the literature in the ETS area over the last couple of months and I'm compelled to agree with both Max Layard and Alan Gross. Professor Gross in his review criticized the allegedly positive epidemiologic studies as flawed. I think it's fair to say that all epidemiological studies are flawed. It's a matter of degree—but the degree to which these ETS studies are flawed is pretty severe.

Professor Gross essentially put meta-analysis in its place by showing that erroneous apples-and-oranges comparisons have been conducted. Nathan Mantel put it differently. He essentially said that you can amplify biases in a meta-analysis and it's quite conceivable that that happened in the instance of ETS. But I think the meta-analysis with the claimed 1.34 relative risk looms extremely large and I don't think that it can be dismissed entirely by what I have heard over the last couple of days. I don't really know what the answer is. It may be that additional work in the area of sensitivity or meta-analysis might be fruitful. I don't know; but from what I've seen in the literature, the assumption, erroneous though it may be, that there is an increase in relative risk is getting stronger, not weaker. This, despite the fact the studies that have been most recently conducted are not as strong as the studies that were done in the early eighties.

As I look at this whole area, I see features and characteristics that I've never experienced before in science. We've been holding back here on the political and the sociological aspects of ETS and I think it quite proper that we do so, but as you review the whole literature, you cannot help but be impressed that standards are being applied in this area that are certainly not common. And yet it seems to me that the question we are here to discuss is an important public policy question. It does have to be addressed rigorously. I think there is a need for open discussion and deliberation so that we might actually develop a consensus that is suggested by data in the literature. The record in the open literature is going to be very confusing to anyone who isn't prepared to sit down and really go through it thoroughly.

I think we probably have to go back and do more critical review and analysis and look at meta-analysis more thoughtfully. I also think we need to consider to what extent the meta-analysis was affected and biased by the multiple comparisons and whether in the meta-analysis a good enough job has been done at balancing what is on the negative side.

Clearly the weakness of the epidemiologic studies that have been addressed by nearly everyone today has caused people to look for alternative ways of answering the critical question. The alternative in the minds of many is through exposure assessment. What I heard over the last couple of days is that we can't even agree on the principles by which we should try to do that, and I think Peter Lee brought that out quite nicely the other day.

So I would say we do have a lot of work to do. And to those who say that this is not an important public health problem, they may be quite right, but it is perceived as such. While we're not here to talk about the perception, if we're reflecting on importance, if we're reflecting upon which way things are going to go, we can't ignore public perception because it will certainly influence outcome. I think additional work, additional study and analysis and certainly open deliberation will be necessary in order to get better resolution and move closer to what is an acceptable, credible consensus.

James Kilpatrick: I'm going to amplify what Dr. Flamm has said, and I'm going to be more direct. I'm first going to make some general comments concerning risk analysis, then some specific comments on Judson Wells's paper and then on Repace and Lowrey, and I'm going to conclude with some recommendations.

Members of this panel are not alone in their concern for the misapplication of risk assessment techniques. Thus, quoting from a recent editorial in the Journal of Risk Analysis, "regulatory science, the science that forms the basis for regulatory decisions, is marked by unusually high levels of uncertainty and expert disagreement." (Janasoff, S. (1989). Norms for evaluating regulatory science. *Risk Analysis* 9(3): 271–274.) It is therefore not surprising that, according to Gordis (Gordis, L. (ed.) (1988). *Epidemiology and Health Risk Assessment.* Oxford Univ. Press (Oxford)), "there is concern that preliminary or tentative epidemiological findings may be over-interpreted, and this may lead to inappropriate anxiety or regulatory pressure."

Indeed, in my view, even if we disregard the whole question of causality, the epidemiologic studies of ETS currently in the literature lack the specificity required for risk assessment. Thus Gordis says that "risk assessors have found that many epidemiologic studies are missing important information, such as the measure of dose in relation to the risk of disease." (Gordis 1988). As we've heard repeatedly throughout this conference, one of the most frequent criticisms of studies of the health effects of ETS is that ETS exposure is indeterminate, the authors relying instead on surrogates such as spousal smoking classification.

Again, the majority of epidemiologic studies use the case control design, and yet case control studies, again quoting from the same source, "case control studies are unable to evaluate dose or the related measure of latency, both of which are needed for dose risk assessment." (Gordis. 1988)

Early in this conference I have made what might appear to you to be a quibble, but to me it is meaningful: I've made the point that the association of ETS with lung cancer has not been confirmed by cohort studies. The design used is prospective, but rather than being true cohort studies, these are, in my view, record linkage studies in which the time to event is omitted.

My conclusion, therefore, is that risk assessment of ETS cannot be based on the results from epidemiology. Nevertheless, Judson Wells (Wells, A.J.

(1988) An estimate of adult mortality in the United States from passive smoking. *Environment Int.* 14: 249–265.) does just that. Some of my specific comments on his article are as follows:

Wells assumes that marriage to a smoker is synonymous with ETS exposure, and yet we well know that Friedman et al. (Friedman, G.B., D.B. Petit and R.D. Bawol (1983). Prevalence and correlates of passive smoking. *Am. J. Pub. Health* 73: 401–405.) have found that 47% of nonsmoking wives had no ETS exposure from their husband's smoking.

Again, Wells combines mortality and morbidity and appears to believe that a statistically significant association is the same as a demonstration of cause and effect. Wells also combines adjusted and unadjusted risk estimates and does not describe the factors that are used in the adjusted estimates. Wells includes cancer, other than lung cancer in females, but omits other cancer in males. It's difficult to understand how ETS could cause other cancer in one sex but not in the other unless by other cancer—and this is not clear—he means cancer of the breast. And I refer to a recent study which has shown no association between active smoking and breast cancer.

In any event, Wells uses the wrong weighting system to combine his estimates. Current statistical analysis uses log linear or logistic regression. Under these models the canonical weighting system is to use the logarithm of the reciprocal of the variance of the odds ratio to combine the log odds ratios from different studies. Wells also uses the wrong estimate for Hirayama's large and heavily weighted record linkage study. If my estimates are used for lung cancer on the basis of my reanalysis of Hirayama's data (Kilpatrick, S.J. (1989). An example of extra-Poisson variation suggesting an under-specified model. In: *Present and Future of Indoor Air Quality* (Bieva, C.J., Courtois, Y., Govaerts, M. (eds.). Elsevier.)then his combined relative risk estimates from his so-called "cohort" study which he gives as ranging from 1.0 to 1.64, become 0.92 to 1.57.

Wells's calculations of the numbers at risk can also be shown to be incorrect. Enough for Wells. I turn now to Repace and Lowrey (Repace, J.L. & Lowrey, A.H. (1985). A quantitative estimate of nonsmokers' lung cancer risk from passive smoking. *Environment Int.* 11: 3–22.)

In my 1986 rebuttal of Repace and Lowrey's paper (Kilpatrick, S.J. (1986). Letter to the Editor. *Environment Int.* 12: 29–31.) I criticized their model on the following grounds. The one-hit model used by Repace and Lowrey has a zero intercept term. This is equivalent to assuming that the mortality rate of lung cancer is zero in the absence of ETS; thus Repace and Lowrey assume ETS to be the sole cause of lung cancer in the nonsmoker!

Also I made the point that nowhere in their argument do the authors consider the aggregation of smokers with smokers and nonsmokers with nonsmokers. Instead, they assume perfect mixing of smokers and nonsmokers in deriving their estimates. If, on the other hand, all smokers work with smokers and nonsmokers with nonsmokers, the global statistics that they used would still apply, but there would be zero exposure to ETS!

My objections to Repace and Lowrey, then, are best summarized as follows. The relationship of ETS with lung cancer has not been shown to be one of cause and effect so that modelling is, at best, premature. "The assumption of a no-threshold effect from carcinogens is also unproved." (Abelson, P.H. (1984). Environmental risk management (Editorial). *Science* 226 (4678): 1023.) The ambient measurements may have little or no bearing on the amounts that actually reach the target tissue." (Doll, R. (1985). Occupational Cancer: A hazard for epidemiologists. *Int. J. Epidemiology* 14(1): 22–31.)

In conclusion, in my letter to the editor in 1986 I stated, "the null hypothesis that passive smoking and lung cancer mortality are causally unrelated still stands. Until it is rejected, I consider it irresponsible to apply risk management to ETS, even if it had been applied correctly." (Kilpatrick 1986)

That was 1986. What has happened since then? Neither Repace and Lowrey nor I have changed our opinion concerning the interpretation of the published data associating ETS with disease or the relevance or irrelevance of risk assessment of ETS. The period since Repace and Lowrey's alarmist publication has seen no crucial evidence published to confirm or deny their assertions. We have a few additional studies using the same methods and now a considerable body of papers, mostly criticizing the methodologies and analyses of the original study.

And now I come to my recommendations. By their very nature, risk assessment predictions cannot and will not ever be validated. What shall we do then in these circumstances? Here I disagree with some of the previous speakers.

In my view, no matter how pertinent, our criticisms are insufficient. We need basic research studies that show, on the basis of published information or known relationships, that risk assessment studies of ETS are not trustworthy. Robins used a sensitivity analysis in his recent paper. We should use sensitivity analysis, but much more broadly, to show how robust are the conclusions of a risk assessment, and we can also use bootstrapping to get more reliable confidence intervals.

In fact, since coming to this conference I've seen a similarity between meta-analysis and risk assessment and my point is that it's simply not enough to criticize. These criticisms will not really be heard by the scientific public, let alone the general public. We must repeat both meta-analyses and risk assessments of ETS, allowing for the biases inherent in both approaches.

Maxwell Layard: I have a few remarks on low-dose extrapolation.

Figure 17–1 illustrates a fit of the Moolgavkar carcinogenesis model to the British doctor cohort data (Moolgavkar et al. 1989). Very briefly, the

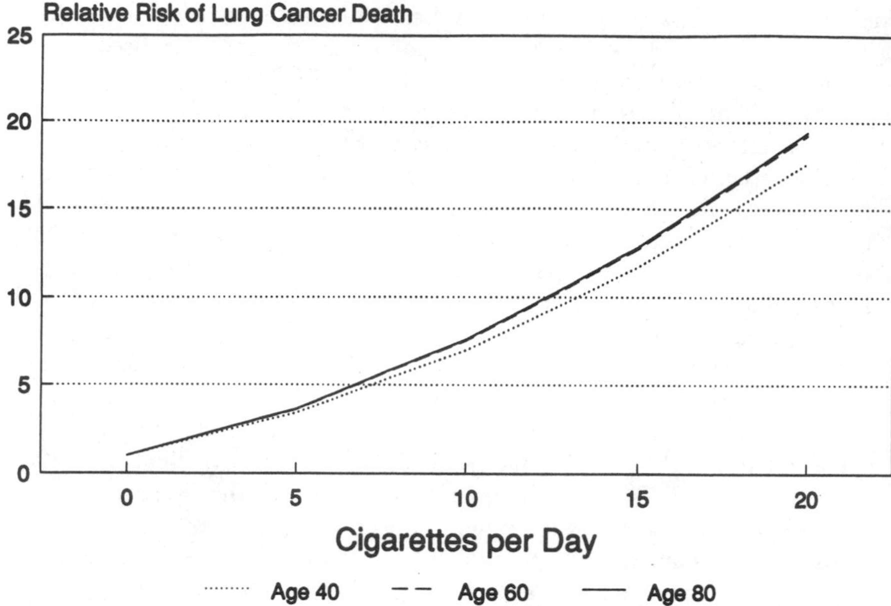

Figure 17–1. Lung Cancer Relative Risk: Moolgavkar Model Fit, Brit. Doctor Data

Moolgavkar model is a two-stage model that allows for cell growth kinetics of first-stage cells. This is a dose response function relating the relative risk of lung cancer death to number of cigarettes consumed per day.

In figure 17–2, we see the very low-dose end of this model fit, from zero to one cigarette per day, and as you see it's essentially a straight line. The function is that relative risk is equal to 1.0 + 0.3d, where d is the number of cigarettes per day. This is based on exposure from age 22.5 and present age of 60. Calculation of a similar function for exposure since birth gives relative risk equal to 1.0 + 0.47d.

In figure 17–3, there is a similar low-dose extrapolation, except that this is based on a multi-stage model fit. This fit was done by Darby & Pike (1989): they fit a five-stage model to the British doctor data. Again, in the low-dose region, the relative risk function is essentially linear but now, instead of 1.0 + 0.3d, it is 1.0 + 0.46d, based on exposure from ago 20 to present age 65.

Now, we've heard some reference to comparisons of dosimetry measurements with low-dose extrapolation, and I just want to mention briefly two or three of these.

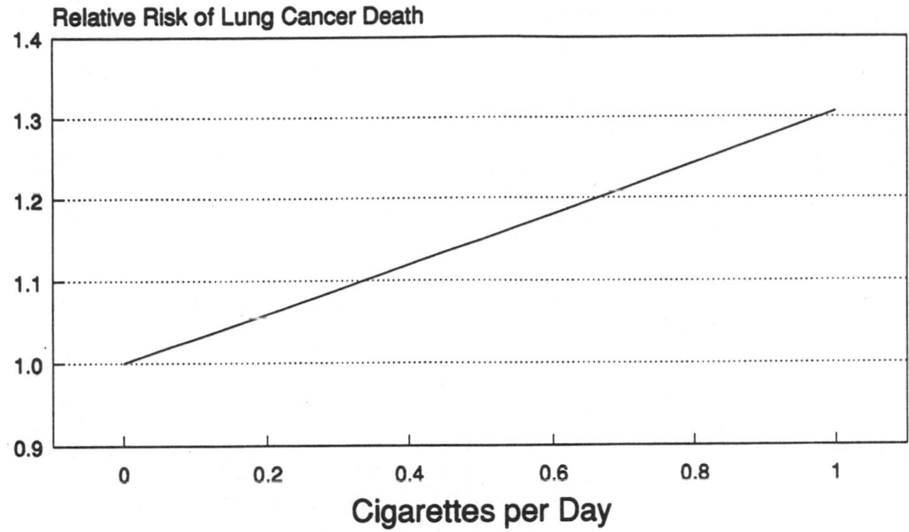

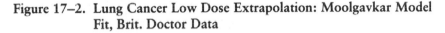

Exposure period: Age 22.5 to 60 years
[Moolgavkar et al. 1989, JNCI 81:415-20]

Figure 17–2. Lung Cancer Low Dose Extrapolation: Moolgavkar Model Fit, Brit. Doctor Data

First, in a recent paper by McAughey et al. (1989) the authors used a radiotracer, and for smokers they had volunteers smoking thirty cigarettes a day, and for sidestream smoke they used nonsmokers exposed to two cigarettes burning continously. For tracheobronchial particle deposition, the cigarette equivalent of sidestream smoke they found was .006 cigarettes per day. From the low-dose extrapolation from the Moolgavkar model with exposure beginning at age 22.5, this gives a relative risk of 1.002.

Second, in the Robins risk assessment (NRC 1986), an RSP-based cigarette equivalent was calculated from dosimetry measurements reported in the NRC publication, of .0001 to .005 cigarettes per day, and the relative risk equivalent here from the Moolgavkar fit (exposure beginning at 22.5) ranges from 1.00003 to 1.0015.

And lastly, in a recent paper Peter Lee (Lee 1988) has calculated a retained dose ratio for males of .02%. This is for respirable suspended partic ulates. Lee adjusted this ratio up by a factor of 3 to .06%, based on the difference between exposed and non-exposed nonsmokers. And multiplying this ratio by thirty cigarettes a day—and I'm not sure whether that's appro-

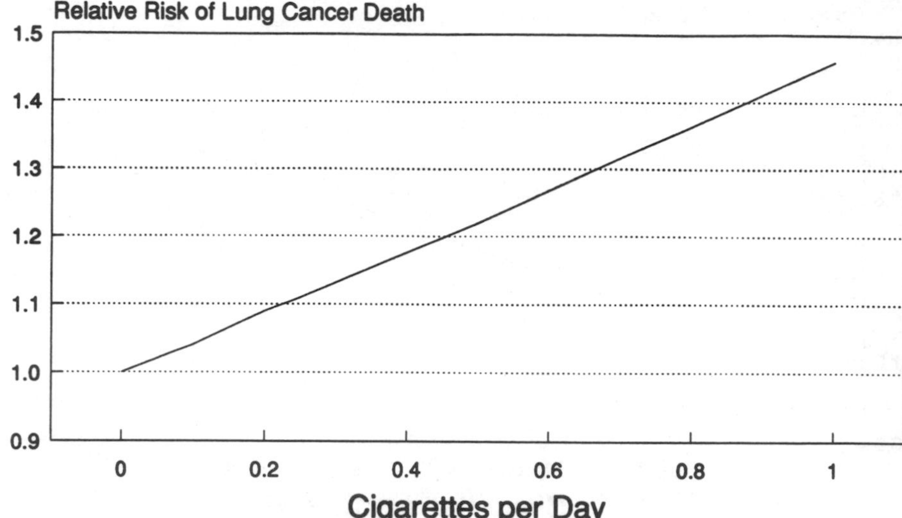

Figure 17–3. Lung Cancer Low Dose Extrapolation: Multi-stage Model Fit, Brit. Doctor Data

priate; maybe it should be twenty—gives a cigarette equivalent of .018 per day. The relative risk from the Moolgavkar fit is 1.0054 (exposure beginning at age 22.5). Using the multi-stage fit, these relative risks would be slightly higher.

Darby and Pike also calculated the relative risk for exposure from birth, and instead a relative risk of 1.46 for one cigarette per day, they calculated 1.77. So, extrapolation based on exposure from birth would increase these relative risks slightly.

But the point, of course, is this: all of these relative risks I've quoted, based on dosimetry measurements and comparisons with low-dose extrapolation from smoking data are far lower than the epidemiology studies would have us believe.

Peter Lee: I think I'm next. Yes.

I'm glad I was invited to speak today. There's a special reason for this. I consider I'm actually uniquely qualified to be considered an expert on risk assessment because 21 years ago I married a risk. My wife's maiden name was Risk. I won't give you the outcome of the assessment yet. It's an on-going experiment.

I'd just like to make one or two points on Professor Gross's interesting presentation.

First, with respect to criticisms of the epidemiologic evidence, Professor Gross seemed to be saying that because there is misclassification of disease, misclassification of ETS exposure, and confounding in the epidemiologic studies of ETS, you can't rely on them. I'm not sure this approach is right in principle, because in fact all epidemiology suffers from all these things. What you've actually got to do is look at how large all these effects are and what direction these biases work in.

There is also another source of bias, misclassification of smoking status which I believe is by far the most relevant source of bias. Misclassification of disease and ETS exposure generally tend to reduce the relative risk if a true effect of ETS exists, but random misclassification of active smoking tends to produce an artificially raised relative risk if no true effect exists, and I can demonstrate that it's probably of a similar order of magnitude to the effect to 1.3 or 1.4 that you get from the meta-analysis.

I'll also comment about meta-analysis. Meta-analysis has its place in some situations. It has both weaknesses and strengths. But I don't think it is valid to say, as I believe Professor Gross was saying, that you can't combine the evidence just because the populations you are meta-analyzing come from studies with different social and demographic characteristics. If you study the relationship of an agent to a disease, and you find evidence that the agent increases incidence in exposed populations of whites, blacks, yellows, reds, greens and blues, I think this is stronger evidence of an effect than if we find evidence in only one population. There are a lot of problems with using meta-analysis in the ETS situation, but I think that isn't one of them. It's a mistake to argue that in principle one can't combine inferences from studies in different populations.

Finally, I'd like to turn to the central theme of Professor Gross's paper. He confines his attention to studies in the United States. There's actually a considerably larger literature than this. Wigle (Wigle, D.T., N.E. Collishaw, J. Kirkbride and Y. Mao (1987). Deaths in Canada from lung cancer due to involuntary smoking. *Can. Med. Assoc. J.* 136: 945–951.) has produced estimates for Canada; Kawachi (Kawachi, I., N.E. Pearce and R.T. Jackson (1989). Deaths from lung cancer and ischemic heart disease due to passive smoking in New Zealand. *New Zealand Med. J.* 102: 337–340.) recently for New Zealand; Russell (Russell, M.A.H., M.I. Jarvis and R.I. West (1986). Use of urinary nicotine concentrations to estimate exposure and mortality from passive smoking in non-smokers. *Brit. J. of Addict.* 81: 275–281.) and the Independent Scientific Committee (Froggatt, P. (1988). *Fourth Report of the Independent Scientific Committee on Smoking & Health*. Her Majesty's Stationery Office, London.) in the UK; and Arundel and Sterling (Arundel, A., T. Sterling and J. Weinkam (1987). Never smoker lung cancer risks from exposure to particulate tobacco smoke. *Environ. Inter.* 13: 409–426.) in Vancouver produced estimates for a wide range of countries including the United States. And there are probably others I've forgotten about.

There certainly are differences in detail in all these papers—and in the ones that Professor Gross referred to—but there's a striking point about them which I felt didn't come out clearly enough in the paper, although it came out to some extent in what Dr. Layard was saying just now. There are two completely different basic methods of carrying out the estimation at risk, and the two methods come up with completely different answers. Both methods start by using information on relative risk of lung cancer according to smoking habits and the frequency of smoking in the population, to come out with an estimate of the number of lung cancer deaths due to ETS among never smokers (or in some cases never plus ex-smokers).

Before I go on to describe how the two methods differ, I'd like to make a point no one ever seems to make in any of these risk assessment papers: if there is misclassification of smoking status, the actual total number of deaths among never-smokers will be substantially overestimated, so your answers by either method will be too high.

Let me now describe the two methods. The first is based solely on the observed epidemiologic data on ETS and lung cancer, with all its known deficiencies. This produces very high estimates. In fact, if one divides by two those estimates applicable to never and ex-smokers combined to make them approximately applicable to never smokers, one ends up with the following figures:

(i) Repace and Lowrey—U.S.—2500,
(ii) Wells—U.S.—1500,
(iii) Arundel—U.S.—1850,
(iv) Robins—U.S.—2010,
(v) Kawachi—New Zealand—30, for a country with about a 75 times smaller population than the U.S.,
(vi) Wigle—Canada—480, for a country with about a 10 times smaller population than the U.S., and
(viii) Independent Scientific Committee—U.K.—"several hundred," for a country with about a three times smaller population than the U.S.

Obviously there are differences in detail, and in national frequencies of smoking and ETS exposure, but it is abundantly clear that using this first approach in the U.S. gives an answer of a few thousand deaths a year, with 2000 probably the most appropriate round estimate.

The second approach completely ignores the epidemiologic data on ETS, and combines epidemiologic data on active smoking with dosimetric information on relative exposure of smokers and nonsmokers to "appropriate" smoke constituents to come up with an estimate of lung cancer deaths due to ETS. This approach assumes a linear, non-threshold model, which is questionable but a fairly standard procedure in risk assessment. The answers achieved depend strongly on which constituent one uses to estimate relative exposure. While it is clear that gas phase components give higher answers than particulate phase components, it is generally held that the relationship of active smoking to lung cancer risk results primarily from the particulate phase, so I will concentrate on the latter here.

Russell, based on the observation that nonsmokers (i.e., never and ex-smokers) had, on average, urinary cotinine levels of 0.7% of that of smokers, calculated that 1050 deaths from all causes would occur among U.K. nonsmokers from ETS exposure. He suggessted that urinary cotinine, if anything, underestimated relative particulate matter exposure, though this is highly questionable. Converting his estimate to deaths from lung cancer only among U.S. never smokers, I calculated a figure of about 440 per year.

Repace and Lowrey estimated that on average U.S. nonsmokers inhaled 0.28% of the particulate matter of U.S. smokers and estimated a number of lung cancer deaths a year, which would convert to about 280 deaths a year among never smokers.

Robins carried out estimates for the U.S. based on the assumption that nonsmokers married to nonsmokers had a particulate matter exposure of 0.01 cigarettes a day. Roughly speaking, this is equivalent to stating that nonsmokers as a whole have an exposure about 0.1% of that of smokers. His estimates for female never smokers ranged from 31 to 259 a year and his estimates for males ranged from 14 to 137 a year.

Finally, Arundel estimates that the relative retained particulate matter exposure of nonsmokers was in males about 0.02% and in females about 0.01% of that in smokers. This resulted in an estimate of 8 for the total number of lung cancer deaths among nonsmokers. McAughey (McAughey, J.J., J.N. Pritchard and A. Black (1989). Relative lung cancer risk from exposure to mainstream and sidestream smoke particulates. Bieva et al. (eds) *Present and Future of Indoor Air Quality*, Excerpta Medica, Amsterdam.) has reported similar estimates of 0.02% for relative particulate deposition in the tracheo-bronchial region for ETS exposure to active smoking, and it is arguable that this is the most appropriate method available to estimate risk.

Overall it seems that, while epidemiologically based estimates give around 2000 deaths a year, estimates based on cotinine, nicotine or inhaled particular matter give an order of magnitude less while those based on retained particulate matter give 20 orders of magnitude less. The striking difference between the epidemiology and the dosimetry is further illustrated when one compares relatives risks for ETS with relative risks for active smoking elsewhere (Lee, P.N. (1988). An alternative explanation for the ıncrease risk of lung cancer in nonsmokers married to smokers. Bieva et al (eds.), *Indoor Air and Ambient Air Quality*, Excerpta Medica, Amsterdam.) that a number of the epidemiologic studies seem to suggest passive smoking has 10–20% or more of the effect of active smoking, a percentage which is totally inconsistent with the dosimetric evidence, and which casts further doubt on the validity of the epidemiologic evidence.

Maurice Le Vois: I would like to comment briefly on a point that has already been made by Dr. Gross, as well as by earlier speakers, but it is so central to the debate about the validity of ETS risk assessment that it cannot be overstated. The point is that all so-called "phenomenological" risk assessment calculations turn on the assumption that the true risk of lung cancer among ETS exposed nonsmokers is about 30% higher than among nonsmokers who are not exposed to ETS, yet we can be confident that this is not the true measure of risk. The figure 1.3 cannot presently be accepted as the true relative risk because: (1) the meta-analysis that produced this estimate is based upon a series of studies of inconsistent quality, (2) all of the ETS studies are highly vulnerable to a host of potential biases and (3) misclassification bias is a serious problem in all of the studies, and this bias alone can explain the observed increased risk.

There are now numerous epidemiologic studies of the ETS/lung cancer association. While many of these studies have reported relative risks of around 1.3, some studies have failed to find any association, and most show inconsistent levels of association across subgroups, with some groups even demonstrating a protective effect of ETS exposure. An uncritical pooling of the results of all of these studies adds nothing to our understanding of the true relative risk because it ignores the effects of variable study quality, especially differences in vulnerability to systematic biases common to all of these observational studies.

The 1986 NRC report is most often cited as the basis for accepting 1.3 as the true relative risk for ETS exposure. In the discussion of their meta-analysis, the NRC Committee states: "Otherwise our analysis used data from all the studies, thereby reducing the possibility of bias arising out of selecting only some of the studies that met minimal standards." "Otherwise" refers to the fact that the authors first chose to exclude 5 studies that failed to meet minimal standards before selecting the 13 studies they included in their meta-analysis. The authors of this section of the NRC report must know that it is essential to select for meta-analysis only studies that meet minimal standards of quality and comparability. Unfortunately, such a critical review of each of the studies comprising the epidemiological literature on ETS was not undertaken by the authors. The resulting meta-analysis, using Dr. Gross's metaphor, ignores the difference between "good and bad apples," and the resulting pooled relative risk cannot be accepted as a valid (or even improved) estimate of the true risk. (Letzel, H., E. Blumner, K. Überla (1988). Meta-analysis on passive smoking and lung cancer: effects of study selection and misclassification of exposure. *Environmental Technology Letters* 9: 491–500.) have demonstrated that the 1.3 relative risk of the NRC report depends disproportionately on the contribution of three studies judged to be of lowest quality. Remove those three studies, and the confidence interval for the pooled relative risk includes zero for all other combinations of ETS studies.

The limitations of observational study designs employed in epidemiologic research in general, and the methodological problems in the ETS literature in particular, have been discussed in detail by other speakers at this conference. It is important to bear in mind that when conditions exist that create systematic bias, bias will be present in each and every study that fails to address the problem. No matter how many studies are conducted, or how large the studies are, if a basic study design problem permits a confounded or otherwise biased observation to be confused with a true effect, all of the studies of the same basic design will produce the same confused result.

Such a problem is known to exist in the ETS literature. Many current and former smokers are likely to be misclassified as nonsmokers. This error, in conjunction with a strong aggregational tendency for smokers to select smoking spouses (Lehnert, G.L., L. Garfinkel, T. Hirayama et al. (1984). Roundtable discussion. *Preventive Medicine* 13: 730–746. Lee, P.N. (1987). Lung cancer and passive smoking: association an artefact due to misclassification of smoking habits. *Toxicology Letters* 35: 157–162. Wald, N.J., K. Nanchahal, S.G. Thompson, H.S. Cuckle (1986). Does breathing other people's tobacco smoke cause lung cancer? *British Medical Journal* 293: 1217–1222. National Research Council (1986). Committee on Passive Smoking. *Environmental tobacco smoke: measuring exposures and assessing health effects*. National Academy Press, Washington, D.C.), causes this error to be systematic and forces the observed association to overestimate the true relative risk of ETS exposure. While there is disagreement as to the probability that this error accounts for all of the ETS/lung cancer association, as Peter Lee believes, even the NRC's conservative calculations demonstrate that this is a very real possibility. The NRC report states: "We can say, therefore, that while the epidemiologic studies show a consistent and, in total, a highly significant association between lung cancer and ETS exposure of nonsmokers, the excess might, in principle, possibly be explained by bias." The NRC report goes on to speculate that another design problem common to all of the ETS studies could cause the observed 1.3 relative risk to be an underestimation of the true ETS affect. (This is because in every study some of the so-called "unexposed" controls have probably received some degree of ETS exposure.) However, that calculation depends once again on the assumption that there is a non-zero true ETS effect.

Detecting a 1.3 relative risk is pushing the very limits of the methods of epidemiology. The problem is not a matter of achieving statistical significance. Large epidemiologic studies are able to demonstrate the statistical significance of observed differences even smaller than rr = 1.3. Unfortunately, at that low level of effect even subtle biases due to study design and measurement limitations may result in observed associations that are due entirely to artifact and not to a true effect. Before such a small effect can be accepted as real, very high standards of proof are required. This cannot be achieved by repeating the same basic flawed studies over and over again.

Sir Austin Bradford Hill, in his President's Address to the Section of Occupational Medicine, Royal Society of Medicine (1965), has summarized nine elements of evidence required to permit a reasonable inference of causation from studies that purport to show association. This list is representative of many such lists that have been discussed in the literature. I will just mention each element, in order of priority:

1. An association should be strong.
2. It should be consistent across a variety of subjects, settings and circumstances.
3. It should be specific.
4. Exposure must precede the observed outcome.
5. A biological gradient (dose-response) should be evident.
6. The association should be biologically plausible.
7. Evidence from all relevant scientific disciplines should be coherent.
8. Experimental, or quasiexperimental, evidence should be sought whenever possible.
9. Analogy to similar cause and effect relationships may be informative. (Hill, A.B. (1965). The environment and disease: association or causation? President's address - Section of occupational medicine. *Proceedings of the Royal Society of Medicine* 58: 295–300.)

Other lists, and other ways of prioritizing the evidence, can be easily cited. The point I wish to make is that few, if any, of the widely accepted criteria of causation have been met by the current collection of ETS studies. To proceed to make general population risk calculations based on these data is premature. First we must satisfy the most basic requirements of establishing causation.

Torbjorn Malmfors: Ladies and gentlemen, I am certainly going to divert considerably from the paper by Dr. Gross and the comments of this panel. I hope you can bear with me.

My first question is: what is risk? I want to point out what I think is very important: risk relates to the future. What we have been discussing most of the time is the past, the statistics. That is what we know or what might be concealed. The risk is foreseeable or unknown. I can define risk as our imagination about what harm might happen in the future, or say that risk is a harmful happening according to the rule of probability. In other words, risk doesn't exist outside our body.

But in order to study risk, we must at least have some models and I propose that we talk about the risk situation where we can identify a hazard, a vulnerable object, and an initiating event.

How do we then assess risk? I'm using a slightly different terminology. This terminology is used in Europe in a different way.

I think the first step, the risk estimation, can be done in several ways. There is the statistical method, which I can call the temporal extrapolation, which is used in epidemiology and so on and has been talked about a great deal. Then there is the experimental method, including species extrapolation, where mathematical models also come into consideration. We have the theoretical methods, e.g., fault free analysis, and so on. We also have the "expert method," that is, how the experts do it.

We then have risk evaluation, and I certainly can't avoid talking about risk evaluation because I think that it influences the risk estimation. And there are many ways of doing this: risk benefit analysis, risk comparisons, expert opinion; regulatory decisions and referenda.

I should also mention the terms risk communication, risk management, and risk perception in this context, not to forget that these are also involved in the concept of risk assessment.

How do we then assess the risk of ETS? That's a difficult problem. The obstacles are: what is the toxicity; how to determine exposure; which health effects, if any, are induced. We must decide whether we are dealing with a stochastic or a deterministic event, which risk estimation methods to use, and what the risks are, as well as variations in the risk perception. And risk communication is certainly in jeopardy.

What to do then? It's important that we identify the uncertainty. We have to estimate the minimum risk that can be detected. In this way we can at least get some idea of how large the ETS risk could be. We should also study risk perception in detail; I think that's most important and also improves risk communication.

Dennis Paustenbach: The question was raised a moment ago whether a regulatory health risk assessment for ETS would be the first one to be based on human epidemiologic data. In fact, ETS would not be the first one. The benzene, arsenic and hexavalent chromium regulations are based on human rather than animal data, and there may be others.

I want to begin by saying that I agree with most of what Dr. Flamm said in his remarks. I doubt very much that regulatory agencies will be restrained from evaluating ETS for regulation due to the scientific inadequacies that have been identified during this symposium.

For the benefit of those of you who are not entirely familiar with risk assessment, I thought it might be interesting for me to describe how a regulatory agency might conduct a risk assessment based on what has been said over the last two days of discussions. I would, however, like to make it clear that this hypothetical scenario is based on my observations of the regulatory community's tendencies, and is not an endorsement of that process or of the postulated conclusions that the process might yield regarding ETS.

For the hazard identification step, an agency might conclude that the data regarding ETS and lung and other cancers are suggestive, weak or inconclusive. I believe that they would say that the data on cardiovascular effects are suggestive or unlikely—with a heavier emphasis on unlikely. The evidence that ETS can produce respiratory effects in adults would probably be considered adequate for the hypersusceptible individuals. The evidence that ETS can produce respiratory effects in small children would probably be considered adequate but the clinical importance is unclear. The evidence for developmental and/or reproductive effects of ETS would probably be classified as inconclusive or unlikely.

To properly conduct a risk assessment on ETS, you would essentially have to conduct five risk assessments; one for each potential adverse health effect. You would have not only five different hazard identifications but several low-dose extrapolations to perform. Some low-dose responses might be based on non-threshold models and some would have a threshold. The knowledge of the toxicology of ETS, unfortunately, is severely lacking. Anyone would have a difficult time doing a low-dose extrapolation because of the uncertainty regarding the dose to use. Although it has numerous shortcomings, an interim measure of dose might be one based on the number of cigarettes smoked per hour; with corrections for the ventilation rate, room size, wall adsorptivity and humidity. A better dose term would be based on a biologic marker. Some of the parameters that were suggested during this meeting sound promising.

A number of the speakers mentioned that finding a biologic marker would be difficult due to confounding exposures. Although this is an important consideration, it may not preclude identification of a marker. I think that we might, with further effort, find a good biologic marker or a characteristic set of markers. There is nothing wrong with tracking a group of two, three or four chemicals as a marker. We have used this approach to monitor other chemicals and mixtures. When conducting a proper low-dose assessment for cancer risk, a likely mechanism of action needs to be proposed. This would allow us to select the most appropriate model, as we have done with other potential carcinogens.

When conducting the low-dose extrapolations, I would pay particular attention to the postulated late stage nature of lung tumors invoked by mainstream smoking. A model similar to the Moolgavkar model would probably be most appropriate for such events. It is likely that any carcinogenic hazard that might be associated with ETS might be best described by a biologically based model like Moolgavkar's rather than by one of the older quantal models.

The third segment of this hypothetical regulatory risk assessment would be exposure assessment. Here again, we are left with very little to work with. Based on what I have heard from this group of experts, I would be hard pressed to conduct a high-quality exposure assessment that I would want to publish and discuss with my peers. We simply do not have a good dose or dose surrogate for ETS. There appears to be no stable conservative marker for integrating exposure to ETS. An assumed dose surrogate could be selected, such as cigarettes smoked per day per 1000 cubic feet of room, but more needs to be known before it could be considered appropriate or relevant.

In the exposure assessment, we need to quantitatively incorporate a number of important considerations in our calculation. Again, more than one agent should be monitored in order to help understand the puzzle. I am not surprised, or disappointed or alarmed by yesterday's discussion regarding the difficulties in estimating exposure. I have worked in the area of ventilation for a number of years. Numerous models had been developed and validated to describe contamination over time to account for dilution. I feel confident that a number of them could acccurately predict the air contaminant levels over time.

Along these lines, I do not believe that the apparent conversion between vapor and particulates for the various ETS contaminants necessarily makes the exposure assessment process unmanageable. As mentioned earlier, the particles are generally quite small (less than 1–2 μ). These particles are going to behave, to a large extent, like vapors with respect to their uptake. If a biologically active chemical were a systemic agent, no difference in biological response would be expected if it entered the respiratory tract as a vapor or a particle.

One technique that would make a more valid risk assessment than those that have been conducted thus far is to use statistical bounding techniques when estimataing dose. In this approach, each exposure parameter would have a range placed on the bounds and a probability assigned to each value. This is one of the arguments that has been received well within the regulatory agencies.

The fourth component of a risk assessment is the one that seems to be the most difficult: risk characterization. The goal is to quantitatively estimate the likelihood of occurrence (for a specific dose) of each alleged effect (hazard). One would want to isolate each of the five or six possible adverse effects of ETS and put each into perspective. From a societal standpoint, this is very important because society now views the ETS mixture and its potential adverse effects as a "chemical soup." We have had this problem with other chemicals in the past. Dioxin may be the best example. The zealots kept the scientists at bay by saying: "No one knows if there is a safe level of exposure. It produces effects on every organ. It works through many, many mechanisms and therefore we'll never determine its true hazard. Consequently, it should be regulated to very low levels." This attitude prevented some useful research from being conducted on Dioxin. I hope the same does not occur with ETS.

However, this meeting reminds me of one held about seven years ago on Dioxin in which I participated. Everyone concluded that the toxicology data were not very useful for risk assessment and the epidemiology data were very poor. Too little was known about the mechanism of action to know which low-dose model was best. Nevertheless, the government went on to regulate Dioxin to levels that were among the most stringent ever imposed. To many persons' credit, this did not discourage the industry. They asked themselves, "what do we need to do to bring about more fair regulations before it is too late; before the resources of the various nations are wasted? We need to know if Dioxin contamination is a nonproblem or a small problem compared to some of the larger ones that we face." As a result of the meeting, long-term agressive research programs were undertaken.

The same could occur with ETS. Consequently, I would like to suggest that some groups do what the Dioxin experts did some seven years ago. That is, establish a research program to address the weaknesses of the poor data base on which the public's and agencies' fears have been based. For Dioxin, it required seven years of research programs and the publishing of over thirty papers in respected journals to change public and agency opinions. The United States and most other countries no longer place Dioxin on center stage, and it appears that future regulatory measures will be more objective. If appropriate, less of these various nations' resources will be directed to controlling insignificant levels of Dioxin in soil, air, water and food. I believe that this is the sort of research effort that is needed to restore rationality in the case of ETS.

The "weight of the evidence" scheme is a term that I would suggest this group become more comfortable with. It is one that is currently used in risk assessment circles. Weight of evidence is the basis on which IARC classifies carcinogens for hazard identification, and the concept is being applied to exposure assessment and low-dose response modeling. It simply means that data of equal quality will be considered equally influential, and that poor data will be given little weight in the decision-making process. This approach should also be incorporated into any risk characterization of a high-quality ETS risk assessment.

The importance of quantitatively evaluating uncertainties in risk assessment has already been discussed. I suggest that any subjective views about the wisdom of spending large sums of money to resolve whether or not ETS poses a potentially significant or insignificant hazard need not be discussed in this section. Based on my first-hand experience with Dioxin and some other controversial chemicals, we might all do better to limit our views to those based on objective data and analyses.

If I were asked to do a risk assessment on ETS in 1989, I would be at a loss. I would have to conclude that the current data appear to be insufficient for conducting a convincing quantifiable risk assessment. I remain optimistic, however, that those data could be developed in a reasonable period of time. I do not know if you think seven years is reasonable or not, but that is what it took us to better understand and to properly characterize the risks of low-level exposure to Dioxin.

I have some closing suggestions. Better data need to be collected to do future work. Of equal importance is the need to conduct careful analysis of better data sets in an open forum. I was pleased to see that the two or three key papers in this field have received comments in the journals. Such open discussion does make a difference. I would suggest that interested scientists continue to critique the less-than-high quality studies that have appeared in the literature on ETS. In the United States, criticisms of these less-than-high-quality studies do not have to be considered by the regulatory agency if they do not appear in a peer-reviewed journal. The importance of peer-reviewed papers is something that needs to be kept in mind by scientists studying ETS. Like Dr. Flamm, I believe that regulations for ETS may be written in a number of other contries and in the United States in the not-so-distant future. Only a more persuasive data set and more rigorous analysis will prevent unjustified regulatory action.

Thomas Starr: There are only a few additional points that need to be made or just reinforced. In my view, if quantitative estimates of lung cancer risk from exposure to environmental tobacco smoke are to have any validity at all, then the apparent risks observed in epidemiologic studies of ETS-exposed individuals must be real. However, these studies have numerous shortcomings, as many speakers have noted in the past two days. In fact, we are probably all quite tired of the epidemiology bashing that's gone on here.

However, Peter Lee demonstrated clearly that the excess lung cancer risk observed among reportedly never smoking spouses of active smokers may be due entirely to contamination of that group with smokers or ex-smokers. Thus, the excess risks observed in these studies seem to be artifactual, arising from bias, and not causal in origin.

Furthermore, as Nathan Mantel noted in his remarks yesterday, a combination of any number of weak and biased studies with meta-analysis serves only to strengthen or reinforce the bias of the individual studies.

So I'm in essential agreement with Professor Gross that the data base on ETS presently available for quantitative risk estimation of lung cancer, at least, is very poor in quality. Consequently, it is likely to yield only results whose nature is appropriately characterized as worst case, if such an exercise is carried out.

One could also inquire whether the apparent relative risk of 1.3 or so for ETS, when combined with epidemiologic information regarding active smoking, produces an exposure estimate in equivalent cigarettes per day that is at all consistent with the dosimetric measurements of ETS. Such consistency, as Robins and his colleagues pointed out, would strengthen the credibility of the epidemiologically derived estimates.

In the 1986 NRC report and the subsequent 1989 paper by Robins and his colleagues a very elaborate attempt was made to address this question. As the authors of these studies themselves noted, a number of critical assumptions had to be made in order to effect their analyses and, in particular, a dose response model had to be selected and further assumed to be equally representative of both smokers and nonsmokers exposed to ETS. Robins et al. chose a five-stage version of the Armitage-Doll multi-stage model with only the first and fourth stages affected by exposure.

At present I'm unaware of any direct evidence that the process of carcinogenesis is comprised of five stages for any carcinogen. The number five is, rather, inferred indirectly from the steep rate at which lung cancer deaths increase with age among smokers and, as well, from the steep rate at which they decline following the cessation of smoking. There are, as Dr. Layard pointed out, other mechanisms that may well be responsible for these features. In particular, the cytotoxicity of tobacco smoke in respiratory tissues and the sustained compensatory elevation in cell-proliferation rates at the high exposures that smokers receive would equally well, and more parsimoniously, account for the steep rates that are seen in the epidemiologic studies of active smokers.

However, the low dose risks predicted by models that include these factors could differ radically, as Dr. Layard pointed out, from those derived from the five-stage model. Indeed, Robins et al. are refreshingly honest with respect to this dilemma. In their own paper they state, and I quote, "Although this version of the multi-stage model reproduces the qualitative shape of the dose response curve in active smokers fairly well, there is no compelling reason to believe that the model can accurately predict the lung cancer rate of groups such as passive smokers exposed to low levels of carcinogen. It follows that our estimates of d_0 could be badly biased if the above multi-stage model fails to actually describe the dose response curve at the low levels of exposure."

They conclude additionally, and I quote again,"Unfortunately, it is impossible to develop a model-free estimate of the background level of exposure from epidemiologic data alone."

Finally, the dosimetric measures of environmental tobacco smoke that Robins and colleagues present vary over a range that spans orders of magnitude. As the authors themselves note, the dosimetric data are far too uncertain to provide any consistency check on the estimates derived from epidemiologic studies of active smokers.

So in summary, I would concur with Drs. Gross and Layard that there is little, if any, scientific justification for the quantification of lung cancer risk from ETS exposure at the present time, except possibly in a worse case scenario sense. Thank you.

Sorell Schwartz: We've discussed cause and risk, and I wish to reinforce the individual nature of causal inference and risk assessment. Estimating injury by environmental chemicals is generally in response to one or both of two pertinent questions. One, given an effect following an exposure, is the exposure the cause of the effect? Second, given that the exposure is the cause of the effect, what is the probability that a particular dose of the agent involved in the exposure will result in some level of the effect? The first question concerns causal inference, and the second question pertains to risk; both involve the logic of uncertainty.

Causal inference is just that: inference. It is not causation. Causation involves far too much of an implication of certainty to be applied in cases of environmental injury to anything other than situations involving uniquely singular exposure circumstances where dose and dose-response relationships are unequivocally defined.

In an attempt to fulfil the presumed necessity for rigid objectivity, statistical methods are often applied to causal inference. It is usually, but not always, recognized that statistical approaches at best facilitate identification of associations. It is also usually, but not always, recognized that association and causal inference are distinguishable and that the latter is a step beyond association.

The well-known Hill criteria used to assess the degree to which the available epidemiologic evidence support a causal inference have been often cited and utilized, but they present the paradox of being at once too conservative and too permissive, depending upon the application of the particular criteria. The point being made here is that, irrespective of the outward appeal of the notion that scientific objectivity is our gold standard, enforced objectivity can be illusory. Approaches recognizing the subjective nature of causal analysis can be made realistic and—paradoxically—are thereby more legitimate scientifically.

Now, logically, risk assessment must follow causal inference. However, this is not always the case. It is quite common to calculate what the risk would be "if" the suspected agent caused the health disturbance in question. This is appropriate under some circumstances, provided that the major qualification is recognized.

It is, however, inappropriate to use the risk assessment as a basis for confirming or even supporting a causal inference, much less causation per se. Despite the illogic of such an application, the results of risk assessment have at times been cited in both the lay and scientific literature as implicitly or explicitly establishing causation.

Estimating carcinogenic risk is probably the source of more controversy because, for the most part, the risk is at too low a level to be determined observationally by epidemiologic studies. Carcinogenicity of chemicals in animals is generally low enough so that experimental studies involve effective doses that are very difficult to extrapolate to the low levels of exposures of most environmental and occupational settings.

Most extrapolation procedures used by quantitative carcinogenesis models involve some articulation of the linear extrapolation methods. All are probabilistic. Outside of long-held radiobiological concepts of carcinogenesis, few mechanistic considerations enter into current modeling approaches.

Attempts to mold the ETS data into one view or another using available risk assessment techniques present a striking illustration of a reality. That reality is that the non-threshold, linearized, regression-derived staging paradigm is a risk assessment approach that is perilously close to being exhausted. If there is to be any true progress, then a quantum leap in conceptual models must precede any attempt to improve mathematical models.

In attempting to identify a new archetype, some effort should be directed at allowing the emergence of procedures that have a greater deterministic element than we now use. Part of the strategy for increasing the deterministic component of risk assessment will depend on identifying useful mechanistic information, and I think that Dr. Paustenbach very wisely pointed this out in his discussion.

Admittedly, at this time, any risk assessment procedure based solely on mechanistic understanding is doomed to failure. Such complete understanding is not within our grasp and there is virtually no likelihood that this fact will ever change. However, this does not preclude the possibility of significant improvement in risk assessment techniques. For example, we have heard some mention of the two-stage model, which is conceptually based not on mathematical extrapolation but on biological mechanism.

Peter Voytek: Since I've already been aligned with Dr. Schwartz, I have no alternative but to agree with everything that he said.

However, I thought I might start out by reminiscing for just a moment. I spent well over ten years at the U.S. Environmental Protection Agency, and before coming to the EPA I worked at the National Cancer Institute, where I was very much a bench scientist, and a basic researcher. I remember during my first year there one of the tasks that I had was to evaluate information on a particular chemical. It was a pesticide, as I recall. It was being produced in fairly large quantities, and we felt that there was going to be a sizeable population that was going to be potentially exposed to this particular pesticide. When I saw the data it didn't take me long to see that they were very insignificant. And certainly I didn't see any way that I could use the information to come up with a qualitative risk assessment, let alone a quantitative risk assessment.

Essentially, what I had was an Ames test, and a rat study in which the chemical was given IP, one dose. The animals were sacrificed after a year, and some had liver tumors. Well, with only this information available to me, I talked to the regulatory people, and said there was nothing I could do with it. They answered, "You have to do something, even if we have inadequate types of data."

I then went back and used the data, and was able to come up with a number. I put in all the necessary caveats that you could imagine, saying that it was more or less a first approach, it was really a back of the envelope type of calculation, and from a scientific standpoint it really couldn't be justified. The one thing that was remembered about that risk assessment was not my caveats, but the number that I came up with, and that's what primarily was the driving force.

One has to be a bit sympathetic with the regulator, because you have to balance not just the science with the law that you have to administer, but you have to deal with the public. This balancing act is quite difficult, and I certainly found this out in my ten or so years within the agency, where I was intimately involved in risk assessment, in mutagenicity studies, and reproductive and cancer risk assessments.

Well, given this, I think the point I want to make is that it would probably be difficult to refute the use of epidemiology data, for example epidemiology data on ETS that is controversial, and expect the regulatory agencies not to use it.

Another alternative, I think, that may be more acceptable would be to look at the different types of models that have been used in the last decade or so, namely the linear, one-hit model, or the linearized multi-stage model, and determine how they can be improved on.

Like other people here, I have a certain preference for the two-stage model with clonal expansion, which was established by Moolgavkar and Knudson, and from a biological standpoint it makes sense to me to use this particular model. It can be used to model much of what we know about chemical processes. You can account for initiation (chemicals that cause a transition from a normal cell to a preneoplastic cell) and chemicals that are not mutagenic, that are not initiators, which can influence the growth of the preneoplastic cell. And finally you can account for completors or, as we prefer to call them, "second initiators," which results in a mutational event from a preneoplastic clone into a neoplasm that eventually develops into a tumor.

The Moolgavkar model can account for other things, such as chemicals that affect the growth of normal cells. (The stem cell growth rate or death rate may be affected, possibly by excess toxicity.) So, from a biological standpoint it makes a lot of sense to consider seriously this particular type model and apply it to the cancer risk assessment process.

The advantage, I suppose, is that the exposure term in there is of the second power as compared to the existing models where they are linear. As one goes down in the dose, one might expect to get a lower cancer risk.

We found that the two-stage model seems to be quite universal. We've looked at cancer data in male and female rats, in male and female mice, for a particular liver carcinogen, and found that there are some parameters of the two stage model that seem to be independent of the species, whereas others are species-dependent.

When one gets this particular result where the model seems to be fitting different types of data sets, it strengthens one's confidence in its use.

There are some studies by Grimmer in Germany in which ETS was divided into different fractions. And he did a cancer assay—a lung implantation bioassay—and, interestingly, the soluble fraction did not produce lung tumors whereas the non-volatile fraction which had PAHS of three ring structures or less was relatively weak. However, the fraction with PAHS with ring structures of four or more represented most of the carcinogenic activity in ETS.

One could use this information and compare the potencies of the various fractions with benzo(a)pyrene. The complex mixture (ETS) could be put into cancer potency units comparable or matched to benzo(a)pyrene. An inhalation bioassay with benzo(a)pyrene is available, so the equivalent units of ETS can be correlated to the inhalation bioassay for benzo(a)pyrene, and extrapolation using the two-stage model could be used to estimate the risk of ETS to humans.

The model derived from the animal studies could be used to predict at least the range of types of cancers that are being reported in the epidemiology studies. Then, if the model is not over or underestimating the human risk, a certain level of credence would be established and there would be more confidence in extrapolating downward to lower doses.

From a regulatory and scientific standpoint, this model would have a certain amount of appeal. I know the U.S. EPA is certainly looking at the two-stage model very seriously, and the National Academy of Sciences and other government agencies in the U.S. are also looking at it.

The last thing I want to mention is the consideration of sensitive individuals in the population. There may be certain types of individuals representing small amounts of the total population whose chances of getting cancer through exposure to cigarette smoke or whatever, could be very, very high, 80–90%, whereas the greater part of the population has a very, very low risk. Therefore, the epidemiologic data may be skewed, not taking into consideration sensitive types of populations.

Part VIII

18

Indoor Pollution: Sources, Effects and Mitigation Strategies

Gray Robertson
Healthy Buildings International, Inc.
Fairfax, Virginia

I. Introduction

It is somewhat ironic that I should be asked to give a presentation at an international conference focusing on environmental tobacco smoke ("ETS"). Based on my own research and experience, the focus of this conference is far too narrow, particularly if the goal is significantly improved indoor air. While indoor air contamination and associated health effects rightly have become objects of concern, ETS is rarely the cause of the problem. In fact, the U.S. National Institute for Occupational Health and Safety (NIOSH) has reported that of the buildings it has investigated in response to occupant complaints, only two percent were attributable to ETS. My own company, Healthy Buildings International (HBI), has investigated hundreds of public and private buildings. Of these, tobacco smoke has been a major contributing factor to air quality problems in only about three percent.

The consistency of these findings makes clear that ETS is blamed for poor indoor air quality and its associated effects primarily because it is one of the few indoor pollutants that we can see and smell. Office workers plagued with sore eyes, dry throats, nose irritation, fatigue, coughing, itching skin, nausea, headaches and respiratory problems often assume that ETS is the cause of their problem because they can see people smoking. The coincidence of smoking employees and an outbreak of symptoms is simply assumed to be causally related.

In reality, ETS is merely a symptom of an invisible problem, not a cause. Without question, the leading cause of sick buildings is inadequate ventilation. If visible pollutants like smoke accumulate inside a building, so too do pollutants that are invisible. The symptoms often wrongly attributed to ETS can be caused by a veritable garden of contaminants. Scores of nontobacco pollutants such as formaldehyde, carbon monoxide, oxides of nitrogen, ozone, fungal and bacterial spores, cotton fibers and fiberglass fragments—coupled with poor ventilation—are generally found on investigation to be the real cause of the problems reported by building occupants.

The Surgeon General's 1986 report on "involuntary smoking" questioned the effectiveness of ventilation as a mitigation strategy for ETS. We have found, however, that proper ventilation quickly dissipates ETS. Indeed, ventilation experts frequently gauge the operational efficiency of ventilation systems by using smoke tests. If smoke persists, it is a clue that a serious ventilation problem exists. Once the underlying problem of poor air circulation is corrected, so too is the high level of ETS.

II. Sources of Indoor Pollutants

Virtually everything we use in buildings sheds particulate matter and/or produce gases. When a building is new, some compounds are given off quickly and then disappear. Others continue "off-gassing" at a slow pace for years. Common office supplies and equipment have been found to release dangerous chemicals—especially duplicators and copiers. We even have found formaldehyde being released from bulk paper stores.

People themselves also are a major contributor to indoor air pollution since each person sheds literally millions of particles, primarily skin scales, per minute. In addition, people contribute significant amounts of carbon dioxide to the spaces they occupy.

Clothing, furnishings, draperies, carpets, etc. contribute fibers and other fragments. Cleaning processes such as sweeping, vacuuming and dusting normally remove the larger particles but often increase the airborne concentrations of the smaller particles. Cooking, broiling, grilling, gas and oil burning, smoking, coal and wood fires also generate airborne particulates, vapors and gases. If the ventilation is inadequate, all of these will accumulate in an internal environment.

A simple classification of indoor pollutants is shown in Table 18–1. The Table shows gases and vapors—both organic and inorganic; fibers and dusts that can be subdivided into Total Suspended Particulates (TSP) and Respirable Suspended Particulates (RSP)—the latter being the more important since these are the particulates that can pass through the natural filters of the upper respiratory tract and enter the lungs; and, finally, microbiological organisms, which can be viable or nonviable.

A. Organic Chemicals

Organic chemicals are arguably the widest variety of indoor pollutants. Thousands of specific types occur in very dilute concentrations, usually expressed as parts per million or billion. Most of these are presumed to be safe at the very low levels encountered, although synergism between different organics can occur. In addition, over time people can develop a sensitivity to a

Table 18–1
Indoor Pollutants

Gases — Vapors (Organic/Inorganic)		
Examples:		
Radon	Methylene Chloride	SO_2
Formaldehyde	NO(X)	CO/CO_2
NH_3		
Fibers		
Asbestos		
Fiberglass: mineral wools		
Textiles/cotton		
Dusts		
Allergens		
Household dust (mites)		
Pollens: Feathers, danders, spores		
Smoke/Fume: Coal, wood, environmental tobacco smoke		
Microbes		
Bacteria		
Fungi		
Viruses		

particular chemical that elicits no reaction in others. Usually the organics are more a problem in the home than the office since concentrations in the home are usually higher, mainly due to lower air exchange rates. Recent research, however, shows new office buildings have higher levels of these gases than older buildings.

B. Radon Gas

Radon, a decay product of uranium, is present in variable quantities in bedrock and soil. Some building aggregates like cinder blocks also contain radon. Radon can move from the soil by diffusion into air pockets or water. It then can migrate indoors through unvented crawl spaces, building foundation cracks and the like. In other cases, radon enters a building via the water supply. Some radon is released when there is turbulence such as a running tap. It has been estimated by some researchers that anywhere from 10 to 15% of the radon we are exposed to comes from water used indoors.

C. Inorganic Oxides

Carbon dioxide is produced by respiration and combustion. Oxides of nitrogen and sulphur are associated with gas stoves, wood, coal fires and kerosene heaters. Carbon monoxide is emitted from unvented kerosene heaters and wood stoves and frequently diffuses into buildings from automobile exhausts generated in adjacent garages. Small to trace quantities of each of these gases and other organics also are present in cigarette smoke.

Ozone is another gas that is generated, usually in very small quantities, by copying machines and electrostatic precipitators. In one specific case that we studied, the maintenance staff of a building had a policy of switching off the main air supply fan over the weekend but not switching off the electrostatic precipitators. As a consequence, ozone accumulated inside the air handlers and was delivered to the staff first thing each Monday morning—resulting in severe, though temporary, discomfort to the people working in the areas involved.

D. Fibers

1. Asbestos. Prior to 1973, asbestos was the material of choice for fireproofing and thermal and sound insulation. It was used as a spray-on insulation material for ceilings and steel girders; as thermal insulation for boilers, pipes, ducts, air conditioning units, etc.; as an abrasion resistant filler in floor tiles, vinyl floor coverings, roofing and siding shingles; as a flexible, though resistant, joining compound and filler for textured paints and gaskets; as a bulking material for automobile brake shoes; and in countless domestic appliances such as toasters, broilers, dishwashers, refrigerators, ovens, clothes dryers, electric blankets, hair dryers and similar products. In fact, the U.S. Environmental Protection Agency has estimated that approximately 733,000 or 20% of all government, residential and private non-residential buildings in the U.S. contain some type of friable asbestos-containing material.

Many asbestos bearing materials or products pose no health risk when used as intended or continue undisturbed in their original state. Wear, abrasion, friability or water damage, however, can cause asbestos fibers to be released into the air and inhaled. Any quantity of airborne asbestos should be considered potentially dangerous.

2. Glass and Other Man-Made Fibers. The glass fiber or "fiberglass" industry is in its infancy compared with asbestos. Glass fibers are not shed in such large quantities as asbestos and most of the resins bonding the fibers appear to be extremely effective and long lasting. However, some fragmentation does occur and this is especially noticeable when loose fiberglass insulation, often used in attics and ceiling voids, is disturbed. Most of us have experienced itching on contact with fiberglass. Other man-made fibers can cause similar reactions.

3. Microbes. The area of indoor pollution that has received the least study has been microbial contamination. Eight percent of the major buildings studied by HBI have exhibited high levels of potentially pathogenic or allergy causing bacteria, including the actinomyces and flavobacterium species. In addition, legionella pneumophila, the cause of Legionnaires' disease, frequently has been isolated inside air conditioning systems.

Perhaps more significantly, we have found over twenty-eight different species of fungi contaminating air handling systems (see Table 18–2). Of the buildings studied by HBI since 1981, 31% have been found to contain high levels of potentially pathogenic or allergy causing fungi, including alternaria, aspergillus, cladosporium, fusarium and penicillium species. In many buildings with excessive staff complaints, aspergillus and/or cladosporium fungi were found growing to excess in the building's ductwork system. A number of studies have confirmed severe allergic reactions to the spores of these fungi. Subsequent cleaning and removal of fungal contaminants have resulted in a complete abatement of complaints.

III. Causes of Building-Related Illnesses

The study of indoor air quality is relatively new. Until recently, no one had heard of concepts such as "sick buildings" or "indoor air pollution." In part, this is a function of central air conditioning, which began to be widely used in the U.S. and elsewhere during the 1950s and 1960s. This enabled buildings to create for the first time their own sealed "mini climates." The true beginning of the "sick building," however, corresponds to the "energy crisis" of the early 1970s. Rising fuel costs led building professionals, business proprietors and property owners to seek ways of conserving energy. Of these con-

Table 18–2
Fungi Isolated from Air Conditioning Systems by HBI Inc.

A ternaria sp.	Aspergillus sp.
Aureobasidium sp.	Candida sp.
Cephalosporium sp.	Chaetomium sp.
Chrysosporium sp.	Cladosporium sp.
Curvularia sp.	Diplosporium sp.
Fusarium sp.	Helminthosporium sp.
Monilia sitophila	Monosporium sp.
Mucor sp.	Mycelia sterila
Oospora sp.	Paecilomyces sp.
Penicillium sp.	Phoma sp.
Rhizopus sp.	Rhodotorula sp.
Saccharomyces sp.	Scopulariopsis sp.
Streptomyces sp.	Tricothecium sp.
Verticillium sp.	Yeasts

servation measures, one of the most critical was the 1973 decision by the American Society of Heating, Refrigeration and Air Conditioning Engineers (ASHRAE) to reduce its standard for the proper ventilation of offices from a minimum of 15 cubic feet of fresh air per minute (cfm) per person to 5 cfm.

The result of the lower standard and other associated energy conservation measures was a dramatic reduction in the natural infiltration of fresh air. To save energy, building managers and designers tightened buildings and sealed windows. Building engineers, often poorly trained, sometimes simply sealed fresh air intakes and, on top of this, often shut down air conditioning systems during off-hours, allowing condensation to build up inside ductwork.

HVAC systems also are often badly designed and carelessly maintained. Inadequate and cheap filtration allows large quantities of dirt to enter with the supply and return air. The dirt often is not alone. Both HBI and NIOSH have discovered dead insects, birds, rodents, snakes, rotting food and dangerous levels of bacteria and fungi in air supply ducts, even in supposedly sanitary environments like hospitals. The dirty ductwork and condensate build up and function as a breeding ground for germs and fungi. Poor ventilation systems that recirculate indoor air instead of bringing in fresh outdoor air then redistribute infectious microbes, allergenic dusts and spores from office to office and floor to floor.

To put these problems into perspective, we have reviewed our data base on over 400 buildings. Our data (see Table 18–3), as well as data published by NIOSH (see Table 18–4), confirm three factors as the major causes of sick building syndrome.

A. Poor Ventilation

Poor ventilation often stems from acts of commission and omission. As already noted, the concern with energy conservation in the 1970s led many building owners and operators to reduce the quantity of fresh air entering their buildings. They accomplished this by reducing the speed of fans pushing air through the air handling system, sealing up the cracks around windows and doors and closing air-intake dampers—thus eliminating all "fresh" outdoor air and forcing occupants to breathe only recycled air. In addition, building renovations too often have been undertaken without regard to air distribution considerations. New walls sometimes are constructed or moved in ways that leave pockets of dead air, wholly separated from the building ventilation system; diffusion fans to particular spaces are shut down or fail; or other changes are made in the air handling system, typically in response to specific problems or needs, in ways that interfere with the system's overall operation or efficiency.

Table 18–3
Sick Building Syndrome Causes: HBI Experience, 1980–1988

Total Building Studies	412
Number of Square Feet	63,000,000
Poor Ventilation	62%
Including No Ventilation	33%
Inefficient Filters	61%
Including Careless Installation	18%
Dirty Air Handlers	58%
Including Contaminated Ductwork	22%

Summary of Most Significant Pollutants Found

Major Pollutants in Air	*% of Buildings*
Allergenic Fungi	31
Dust Particles	29
Low Humidity	26
Allergenic or Pathogenic Bacteria	8
Formaldehyde	7
Vehicle Exhaust gases	6
Tobacco smoke	3
VOCs	3
Fibrous Particles	2
Ozone	1

Table 18–4
Completed NIOSH Indoor Air Quality Investigations By Type of Problem, Through December 1983

Problem	*Number*	*Total*
Contamination (inside)	36	17.7
Contamination (outside)	21	10.3
Contamination (building fabric)	7	3.4
Inadequate ventilation	98	48.3
Hypersensitivity pneumonilis	6	3.0
Cigarette smoking	4	2.0
Humidity	9	4.4
Noise/illumination	2	1.0
Scabies	1	0.5
Unknown	19	9.4
Total	203	

B. Inadequate Filtration

Filters catch only larger dirt particles, and often become loose, torn or clogged, rendering them ineffective. Unfortunately, many building owners persist in buying cheap, low efficiency filters that are woefully inadequate. On many other occasions, the filters are installed improperly, rendering them, in the worst cases, virtually useless (see Figures 18–1 and 18–2).

C. Contamination

Air conditioning systems—often consisting of miles of dirty ductwork—are prime breeding grounds for bacteria, molds and fungi, many of which can cause illness and even death. Remarkably, ductwork tends to be installed without provision for subsequent access or cleaning. This out-of-sight, out-of-mind mentality often leads to a massive build-up of ductwork contamination that is spread to building occupants as air passes through the ductwork (see Figures 18–3 and 18–4).

In one hospital, for example, HBI discovered an air supply system completely compromised by dirty ductwork. Smoke detectors and fire dampers were blocked by dirt; reheat coils, turning vanes and exhaust grilles were completely sealed; and large quantities of bacteria and fungi were found throughout the system (see Figures 18–5, 18–6, and 18–7). Predictably, cross infections were high and doctors and patients alike complained of poor indoor air quality. Similarly, a NIOSH microbiologist found fungi in a government office building in Washington with levels of up to 83,700 fungi per cubic meter, characterizing the building's environment as "sort of like a chicken coop." The irony is that these problems easily could have been prevented by the simple expedient of responsible maintenance of the HVAC system and good ventilation.

It has taken many years and many buildings to discover the true causes of indoor air contamination and the hidden costs of inadequate ventilation. For a while, the only immediately obvious effect of lowered ventilation rates appeared to be an increase in smoke-filled rooms. Many people jumped to the easy but erroneous conclusion that "tobacco smoke" and "indoor pollution" were synonymous. In response to rising concern, ASHRAE published in 1981 a new, dual ventilation standard of 5 cfm of fresh air per person in a smoke-free environment and 25 cfm in a smoking environment. Rather than incur the additional costs of ventilating to the higher standard, some cost-conscious managers decided simply to ban smoking in their buildings.

Because tobacco smoke has been found to be the real cause of reported discomfort in only two to three percent of the cases, however, smoking bans failed to solve the problem. The realization that smoking bans are no cure for the sick building has led ASHRAE within the past few months to publish

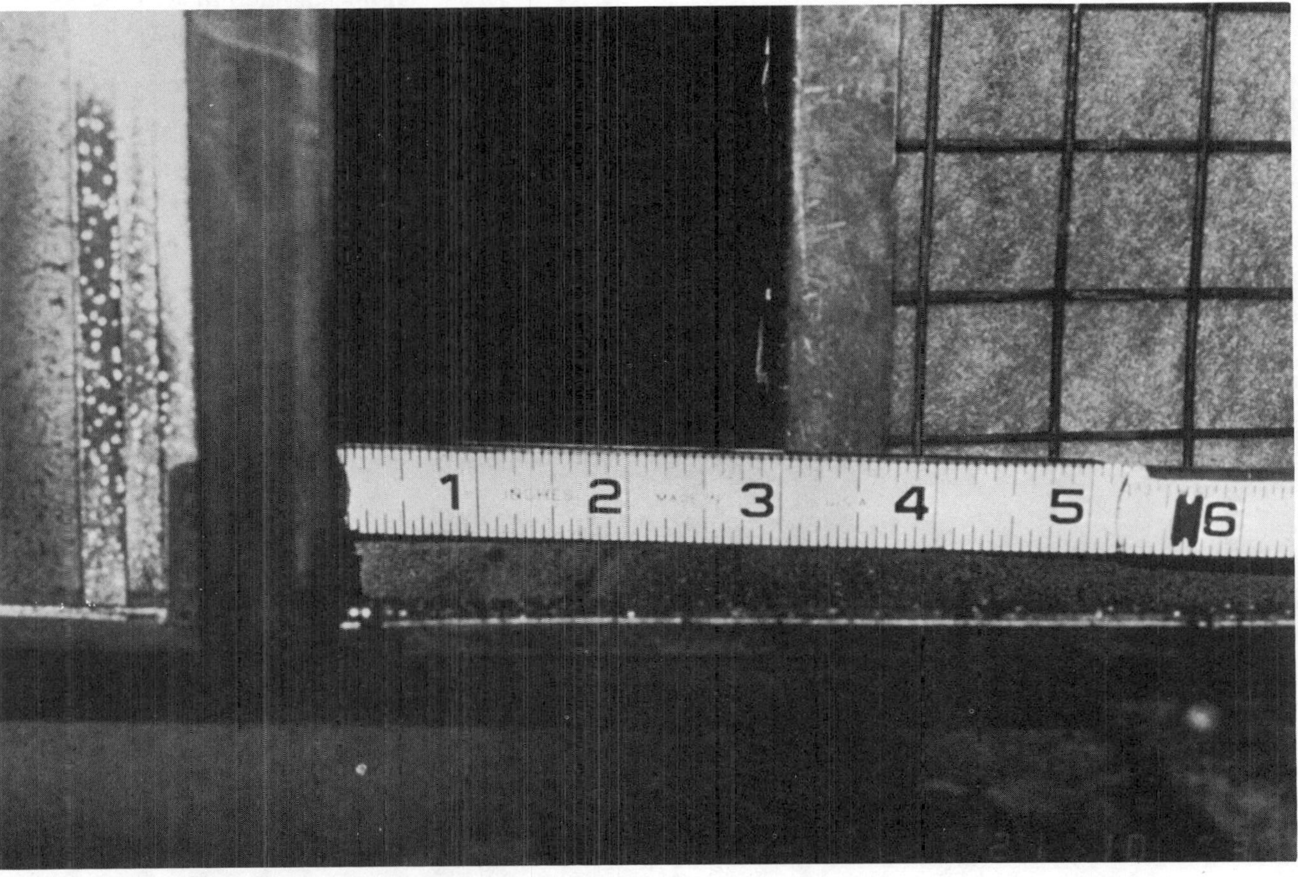

Figure 18–1. Air Bypass around Filter, Typical of Many Air Handling Systems.

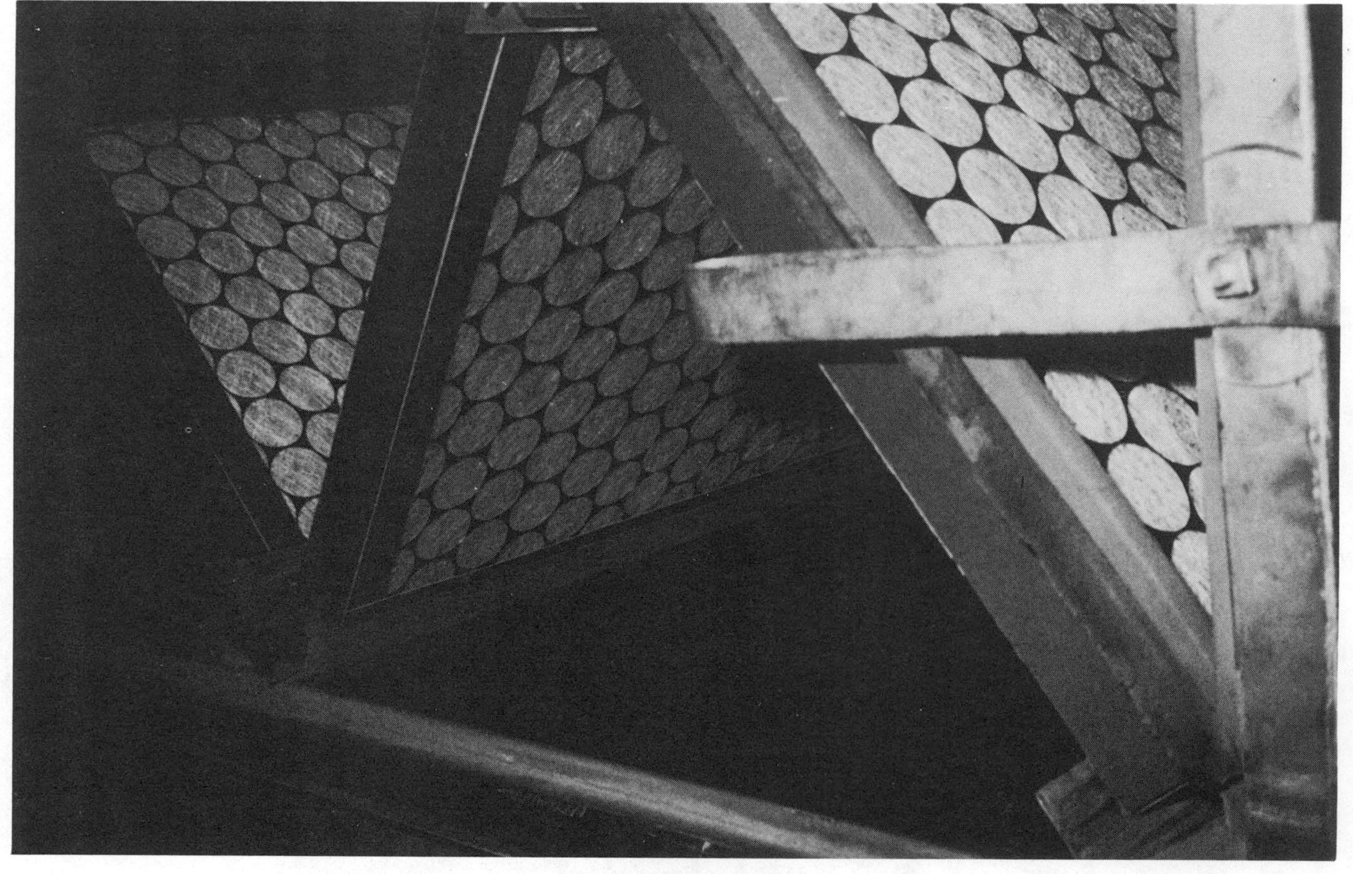

Figure 18–2. Typical Cheap and Very Inefficient Filter. These stop less than 15% of respirable dusts.

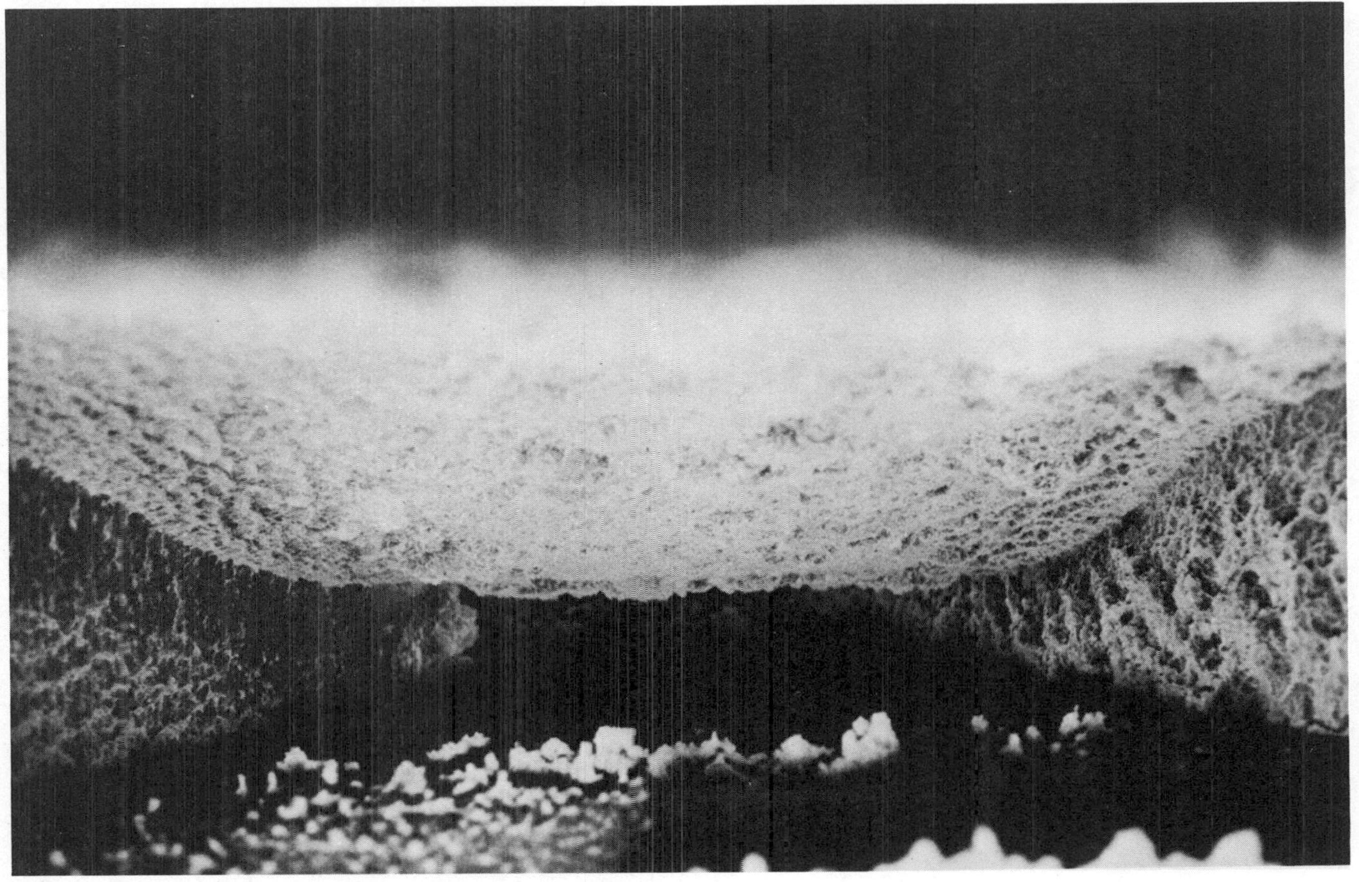

Figure 18–3. Air Duct before Cleaning.

Figure 18–4. Fungal Isolates.

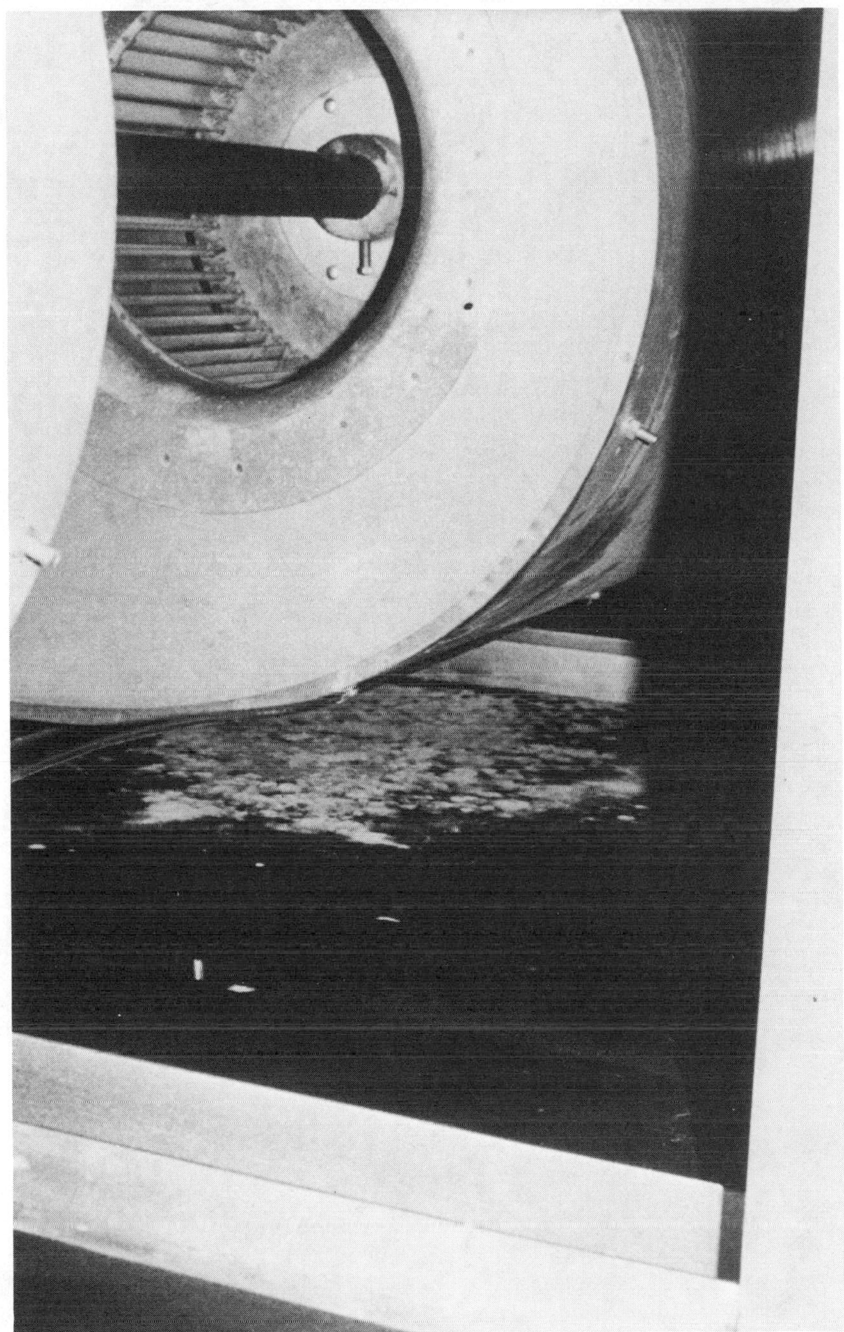

Figure 18–5. Fungus Inside Fan Chamber Serving Operating Room.

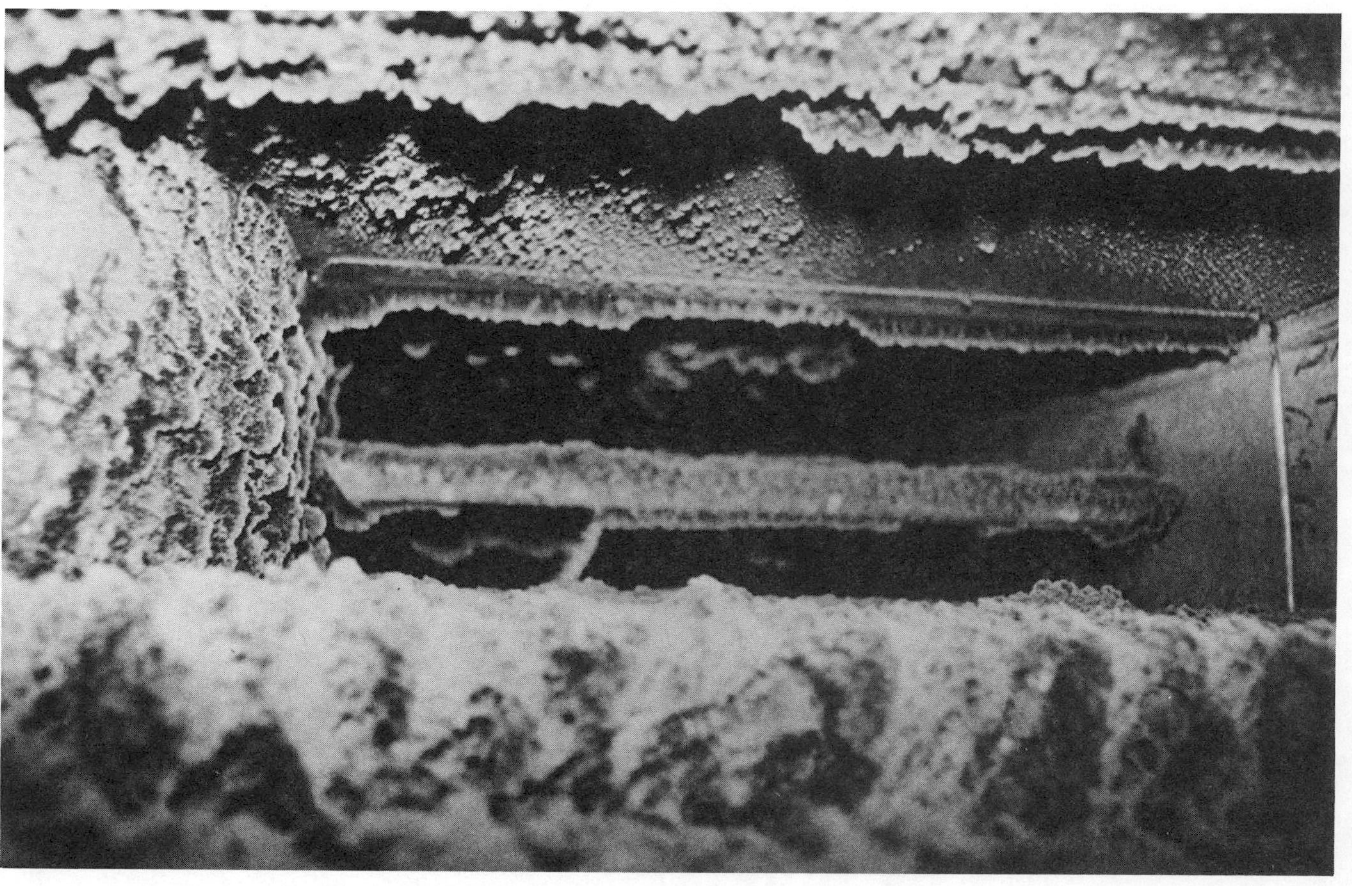

Figure 18–6. Hospital Air Duct Showing Damper before Cleaning.

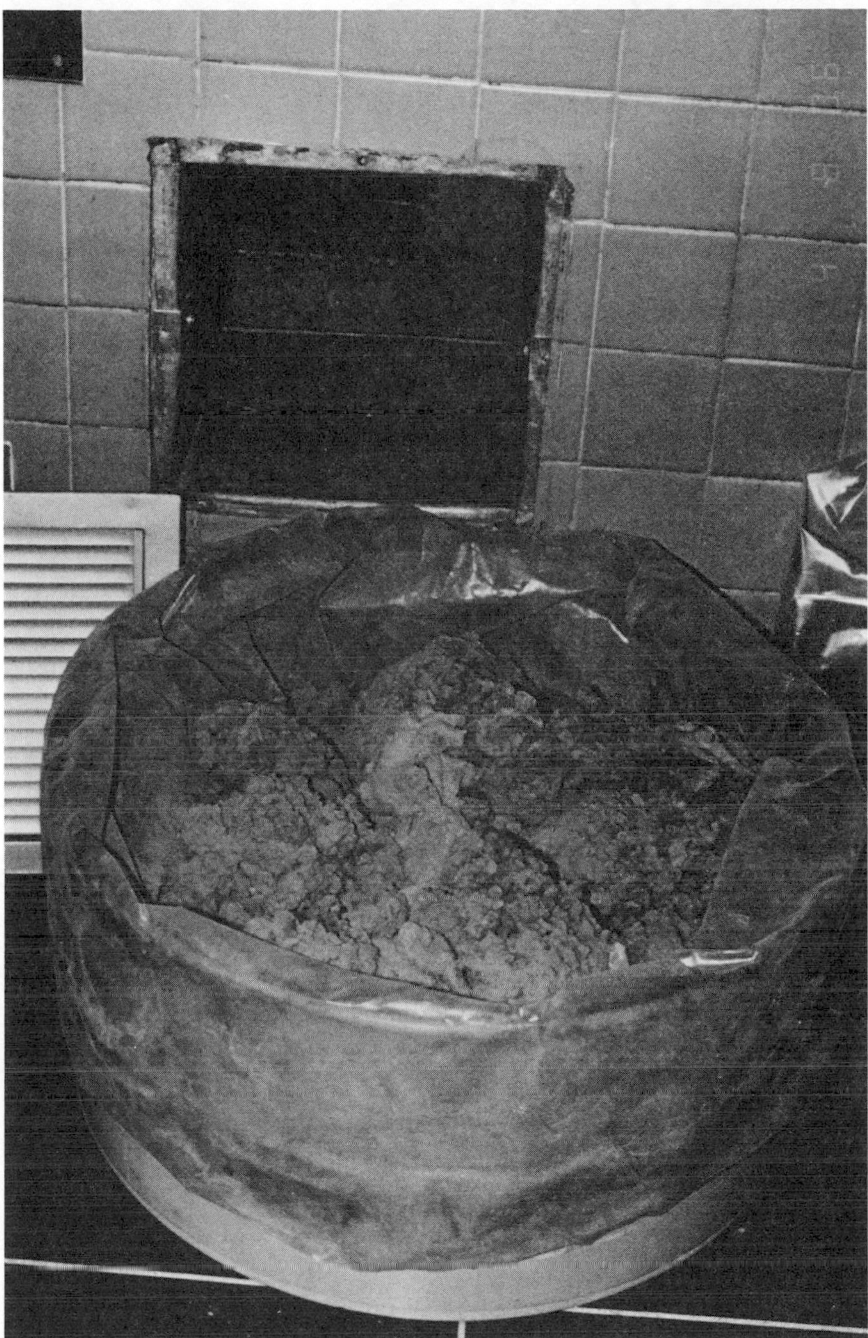

Figure 18–7. Inside Operating Room of a Naval Hospital: Dirt Removed from Ductwork.

a revised ventilation standard for new buildings. Rather than recommend different ventilation rates for general office space depending upon whether smoking is permitted, ASHRAE Standard 62–1989 ("Ventilation for Acceptable Indoor Air Quality") recommends a unitary ventilation rate of 20 cfm per person in offices, with 15 cfm as an absolute minimum. The standard recognizes that the rate previously recommended for nonsmoking areas was inadequate to ensure a reasonable degree of occupant comfort and that a single higher ventilation rate will result in measurable and immediate air quality improvements in all occupied spaces. A ventilation rate of 20 cfm of fresh air per person deals adequately with typical smoking activities as well as other contaminants in buildings. The new ASHRAE ventilation standard therefore should ameliorate the sick building syndrome in ways that a smoking ban could never do.

IV. The Special Case of Air Quality in Commercial Aircraft

Recently, the battle over ETS and indoor air quality has expanded to commercial airlines. Passenger discomfort with the cabin environment has prompted government regulators and others to focus, yet again, on tobacco smoke as a possible culprit.

As with sick buildings, the cause of poor cabin air quality can be traced directly to poor ventilation and misguided efforts to conserve energy. Between 1973 and 1980, aviation fuel prices soared by 800 percent. In response, McDonnell Douglas advised its cost-conscious DC-10 customers in 1980 that reducing fresh air intake by 50% would result in an 0.8% fuel savings on each trip. On a 1,050 mile trip, McDonnell Douglas calculated that a 50% reduction in fresh air would save 42 gallons of fuel. If the aircraft were used to maximum potential, that equaled a fuel savings of 62,000 gallons per year, per plane. McDonnell Douglas also recommended retrofitting the DC-10 to install recycled air systems. Air quality has deteriorated steadily ever since.

In 1986, the U.S. National Academy of Sciences (NAS) undertook a study of cabin air quality. The study was precipitated by escalating complaints from passengers and flight attendants. Reported symptoms paralleled those associated with sick buildings: sore eyes, scratchy throats, nasal irritation, headaches, coughing, shortness of breath, fatigue and dizziness. Among other findings, the study reported that the ventilation rate in the economy class of a 747 is less than 7 cfm of fresh air.

Contaminants found in the atmosphere of the average airliner include carbon dioxide, carbon monoxide, ozone, particulate matter, nicotine, nitrogen oxides, volatile organic compounds, microbes and cosmic radiation. Such compounds originate from humans, dry ice, exhausts, atmospheric and electrical discharges, fabrics, smoke, cleaning materials and processes, fuel, food and toilets.

The studies surveyed by NAS measuring the concentrations of these contaminants did not find carbon monoxide, nicotine or airborne particulates to present any significant threat to air quality. Carbon dioxide and ozone, however, have been found in unacceptably high concentrations in many airplanes. In addition, low relative humidity exacerbates irritation from other pollutants.

As with buildings, microbes are a major cause of cabin air quality problems. Continuous recirculation of stale cabin air is an extremely effective way to spread contagious diseases. Enclosed air cabins always have functioned to some extent as germ incubators, and bad ventilation has worsened the problem. One study examining the impact of one passenger with influenza on a Boeing 737 flight to Alaska, for example, found that 38 out of 54 passengers had influenza within three days of the flight. Similarly, in a 1976 Canadian experiment on a Boeing 707, bacillus subtiles spores were released in the cabin to simulate three sneezes. Prior to pressurization, with the aircraft still on the ground, 100% of the cabin was found to be contaminated by the spores.

Alarmed by its findings, the NAS made the following recommendations to reduce the risk of infections and other air quality problems on airplanes:

- When the ventilation system is inoperative, passengers should leave the plane within 30 minutes. Opening doors will not suffice.
- The amount of outside air during flight should be maximized.
- Full ventilation should be maintained with heavy passenger loads both on the ground and in the air.
- All recycled air should be filtered to two micron size.
- The U.S. Federal Aviation Administration (FAA) should introduce a program to ensure that ozone concentrations comply with regulations.
- FAA should establish a monitoring problem for air contamination in airliner cabins.
- FAA should review its carbon dioxide standard.
- Ban smoking on all flights.

Of these recommendations, only one was not justified on the basis of the data reviewed by NAS: the ban on smoking. The available data indicate that flight attendants, the most heavily exposed group, receive minimal doses of ETS constituents. One study published in the New England Journal of Medicine, for example, studied flight attendants on a transoceanic flight (Foliart et al. 1983). The study found that the attendants' blood nicotine levels increased from a mean of 1.6 ng/ml to 3.2 ng/ml. In comparison to the levels found in typical smokers (15–45 ng/ml), the study concluded that physiologic effects were unlikely.

Other studies by Muramatsu et al., Oldaker and Conrad, and Drake and Johnson using nicotine as a marker for ETS found that smokers as well as nonsmokers are exposed to minimal amounts of ETS on commercial aircraft with reasonably well operated ventilation systems. Similarly, a 1977 French study found that even on long flights carrying a high number of smokers, carbon monoxide concentrations did not exceed 5 ppm, far below the standard set by the U.S. Environmental Protection Agency and Occupational Safety and Health Administration.

The most recent and comprehensive study of air quality in passenger cabins has confirmed these findings. (Malmfors, et al. 1989). The study analyzed air samples from forty-eight DC-9 and MD-80 Scandinavian Airline System (SAS) flights under various conditions. The study concluded that nicotine concentrations were approximately one-tenth of the standard for the working environment. Carbon monoxide concentrations were about one-tenth of the standard for general indoor air. The study also found relatively high levels of carbon dioxide. As with sick buildings, high carbon dioxide levels are an indication of inadequate ventilation.

Paradoxically, not one of the NAS's recommendations has been implemented in the U.S. other than a partial smoking ban. The reasons for this are similar to the reasons why smoking bans have been a popular reaction to sick buildings. Smoking is the only visible pollutant, and it has been thought to be cheaper for airlines to turn on "no smoking" signs than to improve ventilation.

HBI has calculated that improving ventilation to acceptable levels would cost an airline between 30 and 60 cents per passenger per trip, depending on the size of the aircraft and the length of the trip. This seems to be something of a bargain compared to the benefits conferred: decreased carbon dioxide, carbon monoxide, ETS, odors and microbes, and better air mixing and movement. This in turn means healthier, more comfortable passengers.

V. Mitigation Strategies

A major step toward better indoor air quality has been taken with the recent publication of ASHRAE's new ventilation standard. In addition to higher ventilation standards, however, there remain many constructive strategies that building owners and occupants can use to improve indoor air quality in all respects.

A. Education

The single most important factor in preventing indoor pollution problems is education.

1. Building owners, managers and maintenance staff need to understand the vital necessity of adequate ventilation. In line with current ASHRAE standards and recommendations from the Building Officials and Code Administrators International (BOCA), we recommend that occupied buildings have a minimum intake of 20 cfm/person of outside air, even under extremes of outdoor temperatures.
2. Designers, building engineers and maintenance staff must ensure that filters in their buildings' air handling systems are correctly installed to preclude air bypass, are routinely inspected and when necessary changed, and meet at least the 30% to 60% efficiency standard defined in ASHRAE Standard 52–76 (Atmospheric Dust Spot Test) or its equivalent.
3. Engineers and maintenance staff must maintain a high standard of cleanliness throughout their ventilating systems. Rotting leaves, dead insects, windblown soil and other debris should be cleaned routinely from the various chambers of the air handling system and ductwork. Equally important, all places where water can collect (cooling towers, humidifiers, condensate trays, etc.) should be examined and cleaned frequently. Drains should be installed in condensate traps to remove all standing water.
4. HVAC maintenance and operating costs should be integrated into overall staff budgets so that priority is given to the most important and expensive costs—staff costs—as distinct from incremental savings in service costs that can adversely effect the overall profitability of the organization.
5. Recognize the important role of those in charge of building system maintenance and environmental services. Educate them, motivate them and reward them financially for actions they take affecting positively the health and productivity of all other staff.

B. Air Cleaning Equipment

Under normal conditions of occupancy, any building operating to the new ASHRAE standard should cope adequately with varied activity levels and a moderate amount of smoking. However, if local regulations demand or management opts for designated smoking areas, the judicious use of supplementary air cleaners may be justified. Today many area filtration systems are available that dramatically reduce airborne respirable particulates, including those from tobacco smoke. Electrostatic precipitators and high efficiency filters such as HEPA grade filters are ideal for these applications provided that they are serviced correctly. By placing activated charcoal filters in series with particle filters, most of the odorous pollutants and higher molecular weight vapors will be removed.

C. *Local Exhausts*

ASHRAE Standard 62–1989 already identifies areas where ventilation rates above 20 cfm/person are necessary. In addition there are specific areas such as printing, copying, smoking lounges and the like that should be equipped with dedicated local exhaust ventilation.

D. *Building Bake-out*

Some encouraging research has been completed in California (Department of Health Services, Berkeley) and in Sweden on the use of controlled bake-out procedures. Newly built or renovated buildings have been purged of many volatile organic compounds by using a three to five day bake-out period. During this period, temperatures should be elevated to a range of 80 to 100°F. Ventilation rates also should be kept low. For one or two days after the bake-out period, ventilation rates should be raised to their maximum to flush out the volatiles emitted during the bake-out.

Although this technique has considerable promise, care must be taken to ensure that the heating cycle does not adversely affect construction materials such as wooden frames, doors, metal-wood interfaces, etc. Care also is necessary to ensure that the bake-out procedures utilized do not violate manufacturer warranties on installed equipment or materials.

E. *Material Selection*

Designers and architects are paying increasing attention to the stability of the materials used in buildings such as wood preservatives, sealing compounds, insulation materials, wall coverings, paints, carpets, tiles, particle boards, adhesives and the like. Manufacturers Safety Data Sheets (MSDS) should be obtained for these products from potential vendors, together with such information as chemical formulations, storage, drying times and airing procedures, before installation.

Such requests have caused some suppliers to implement improved product drying and airing out procedures prior to delivery. One commercial carpet manufacturer (Collins and Aikman) recently started marketing carpets with microencapsulated tackifiers. These preclude the use of other adhesives. Early results suggest they avoid much of the odor from new carpets.

F. Foliage Plants

Research by the U.S. National Aeronautics and Space Administration (NASA) has shown that many common foliage plants can remove diverse organic chemicals from indoor air. Using mixtures of activated carbon and potting soil coupled with fan-powered air movement through the soil and across the plant roots appear to be particularly effective in trapping contaminants. Microbial organisms in the soil then digest the contaminants, thereby regenerating the activated carbon.

After considerable success with this technology in the laboratory and in pilot chamber studies, "real world" tests are now underway in a major commercial office building in a joint venture between NASA, the Association of Landscape Contractors of America and HBI. Results of these tests should be available toward the end of 1990.

G. Proactive Monitoring

HBI routinely conducts a detailed investigation of the design and operating practices of building air handling systems. This information is integrated with the data collected from comprehensive air sampling and analysis to establish reference points. Then, at six month intervals, repeat inspections are performed to evaluate changes in air quality over time.

Proactive monitoring permits the effects of remedial actions to be quantified. Conversely, in the event of adverse trends in air quality over time, changes can be implemented to rectify the situation before complaints arise from building occupants.

The benefits of such a preventive approach are substantial:

1. It reduces the chances of a "healthy" building becoming "sick." Problems or potential problems are quickly identified and corrected at minimal expense.
2. It protects against owner liability. In addition to reducing the chances of litigation, proactive monitoring demonstrates that the owner has taken reasonable steps to assure a healthy work environment.
3. It reduces employee absenteeism. Thirty to fifty percent of employee absenteeism in the U.S. is due to upper-respiratory complaints—symptoms that are common in environments characterized by poor indoor air quality.
4. It enhances management's relationship with employees.
5. It improves overall building maintenance and operations. Air quality is improved through regular monitoring of ventilation rates and filtration efficiencies.

6. It is a selling point for private and commercial real estate owners in marketing and advertising their properties.

H. Ventilation Controllers

Some devices already are being marketed as controllers of HVAC equipment based on their sensing capacity for different pollutants. Carbon monoxide monitors linked to exhaust fans have been commonplace for a number of years in many garages. Carbon dioxide sensors controlling fresh air intake rates are technically feasible, though somewhat expensive. More recently, electronic probes have been developed using catalytic sensors that change conductivity based on concentrations of oxidizable volatile gases in the environment. Such probes can be mounted in return air ducts, then linked to the supply fans or louvers, so as to adjust outside air rates as pollutant levels increase.

VI. Conclusion

Over the past few years there has been a dramatic increase in public sensitivity to indoor air quality. We have seen veritable witch-hunts for specific pollutants such as formaldehyde, asbestos, tobacco smoke and radon. HBI's own investigations have identified a multitude of factors that contribute to poor indoor air quality. To concentrate upon any one element of this matrix is inefficient and dangerous. It would be naive to assume that the removal or control of ETS, the most visible indoor air pollutant, would solve the indoor air pollution problems found in "sick buildings." That step ignores the many hidden sources of indoor contamination, and can lead—at least in the short run—to a false sense of security.

HBI's work and experience, and evaluations conducted by NIOSH, indicate that indoor air quality can be improved significantly with proper maintenance of and attention to building air handling systems. Ensuring the introduction of filtered outside air, maintaining effective filtration systems, ongoing monitoring of air quality, cleaning and repairing ductwork and improving the designs of ventilation systems are necessary steps for the achievement of acceptable indoor air quality.

Property owners have feared that the "sick building syndrome" was an intangible condition that defied understanding or cure. In reality, virtually all cases of sick building syndrome can be diagnosed and cured. The two most successful prevention policies to follow are providing basic education to building managers and engineers, and adopting a philosophy based on prevention rather than cure. Integration of a prevention philosophy into a building's initial design is especially important. Other mitigation strategies, such as pollution sensors, foliage plants and building bake-outs should result in incremental improvements. The initial and principal focus, however, should be on a generic engineering approach addressing all pollutants ex ante.

References

American Society of Heating, Refrigeration, & Air Conditioning Engineers, (1989). Standard 62–1989. Ventilation for Acceptable Indoor Air Quality.

Drake, J.W., and D.C. Johnson. Measurement of certain ETS components on long-range 747 flights (*submitted for publication*).

Foliart, D., N.L. Benowitz, and C.E. Becker (1983). Passive absorption of nicotine in airline flight attendants. *N. Eng. J. Med.*, 308 (18): 1105.

Holcomb, L.C. (1988). Impact of environmental tobacco smoke on airline cabin air quality. *Environ. Technol. Letters* 9: 509–514.

Malmfors, T., D. Thorburn and A. Westlin (1989). Air quality in passenger cabins of DC-9 and MD-80 aircraft. *Environ. Technol. Letters* 10: 613–628.

Meluis, J., K. Wallingford, R. Keenlyside, and J. Carpenter (1984). Indoor Air Quality—The NIOSH Experience. *Ann. Am. Conf. Gov. Ind. Hyg.* Vol. 10.

Muramatsu, M., S. Umemura, T. Okada, and H. Tomita (1984). Estimation of personal exposure to tobacco smoke with a newly developed nicotine personal monitor. *Environ. Res.* 35: 218–227.

Muramatsu, M., S. Umemura, J. Fukui, T. Arai, and S. Kira, (1987). Estimation of effect of environmental tobacco smoke on air quality within passenger cabins of commercial aircraft. *Int. Arch. Occup. Environ. Health* 59: 545–550.

National Academy of Sciences (1986a). *The Airliner Cabin Environment: Air Quality and Safety.* National Academy Press, Washington, D.C., p. 303. (Estimation of personal exposure to ambient nicotine in daily environment.)

National Academy of Sciences (1986b). *Environmental Tobacco Smoke: Measuring Exposures and Assessing Health Effects.* National Academy Press, Washington, D.C., p. 337.

Oldaker, G.B. III, and F.W. Conrad, Jr. (1987). Estimation of effect of environmental tobacco smoke on air quality within passenger cabins of commercial aircraft. *Environ. Sci. Technol.* 21: 994–999.

Vieillefond, H., P. Fourn, and R. Auffrer, (1977). Characteristics in atmosphere of long-range transport aircraft cabins. *Aviat. Space Environ. Med.* 48: 503–507.

19
Panel Discussion on Indoor Air Quality

Howard Goodfellow: I would like to expand on the role that ventilation plays in indoor air quality mitigation strategies. The two areas that I will discuss are ventilation regulations and the parameters for the application of mathematical ventilation models.

As discussed by Mr. Robertson, indoor air quality is a function of many different factors. By far the most important is building ventilation and air conditioning systems. Other factors include thermal comfort, airborne contaminants, building materials, quality of outdoor air, building occupancy and use.

There are two types of buildings to consider: conventional and energy efficient. Conventional buildings rely on mechanical and/or natural ventilation through open doors and windows, making the indoor air very near the quality of the outdoor air. Energy efficient buildings reduce the quantity of fresh air, increasing the amount of recirculated air, to reduce energy costs, which results in a build-up of contaminants rather than dilution of contaminants. These "tight" buildings require special filters, air cleaners, humidifiers, etc. to rid the air of the undesirable affects of recycling.

Poor distribution of air will reduce the quality of the air. The position of supply diffusers and return vents can result in short-circuiting air streams. Partitions in occupied areas will inhibit air flow and improper pressure differentials between rooms will create drafts of undesirable directions of air flow.

Inadequate filtration has a direct impact on air quality. Very often filters are underrated or low efficiency, not changed frequently enough, poorly fitted, or ineffectively positioned in the system. Airborne particulate matter is not eliminated and is dispensed throughout the building.

Regular maintenance and proper operation of the HVAC system is essential to maintain air quality. Lack of attention will result in subtle deficiencies precipitating major problems.

Dirty ductwork, untreated stagnant water in condensate trays, closed dampers, thermostats shut off, contaminated intake ducts, and a variety of other situations can easily go unnoticed.

Cost is a consideration which will reduce the effectiveness of a ventilation system. Fresh air is no doubt more expensive to heat or cool than simply recycling the air; however, these costs can be offset by the reduction in indoor air quality problems. Employee absenteeism, complaints and even litigation can be very expensive and quite preventable. In the long run, a properly run ventilation system is cost effective.

The quality of the air is greatly affected by the presence of contaminants, generated by the occupants or by the building itself. Human generated contaminants consist of carbon dioxide, ammonia, organics, odorous gases, dust particles and compounds associated with ETS such as carbon monoxide, nicotine, aldehydes, and a variety of particulate matter. Building generated contaminants consist of organics, odors, outgassing of building materials, formaldehydes, solvents, asbestos and other compounds.

Contaminants can also be introduced through the outdoor air. The location of the intake should be considered to ensure the best quality of outdoor air. Very often intakes are carelessly located above loading docks or adjacent to parking garages. Common outdoor contaminants are SO_2, oxides of nitrogen, ozone, carbon monoxide, and other particulate matter. Many of these are also contained in ETS and it is possible that associated ill-effects could be wrongly attributed to the presence of ETS rather than poor quality outdoor air.

Weather conditions contribute to the quality of the air. Comfort factors such as temperature and relative humidity should be carefully controlled. Humidity levels less than 20% will cause nose and eye irritation, coughing and other respiratory complaints. Very often ETS will be blamed for these symptoms. Pockets of extreme heat and cold are often uncontrollable with commonly used thermostatically controlled systems. It is essential that thermostat locations reflect the temperature of occupied areas. It is not uncommon to find them in elevator shafts, ceiling plenums or open drafty areas. When comfort targets are not achieved it can make the effects of other contaminants that much more pronounced and any visually recognized contaminant will bear responsibility for all ill-effects felt by occupants.

An effective means of addressing contaminant levels is in the ventilation rates specified by the American Society of Heating, Refrigeration and Air-Conditioning Engineers (ASHRAE). It has developed the most widely accepted standard addressing Ventilation for Acceptable Indoor Air Quality. In the late 1960's ASHRAE undertook a program to develop this standard. In 1973, the ASHRAE Standard 62–73 for Natural and Mechanical Ventilation was published which specified "minimum" and "recommended" ventilation rates for occupied areas. Lacking from this standard were air quantities needed for control of temperature and humidity, and exhaust required for source control of pollutants.

The ventilation rates specified were for 100% outdoor air, and the minimum outdoor air quantity was 5 cfm per person.

In 1975 the ASHRAE Standard 90–75 was introduced to encourage design to just meet the minimum ventilation requirement in order to conserve energy. This change actually resulted in a 67% increase in indoor pollution levels and drew attention to ETS particulate concentrations, which also rose dramatically.

In an effort to resolve problems associated with standards 62–73 and 90–75, ASHRAE developed Standard 62–1981, which recommended minimum 5 cfm/person in non-smoking office areas and minimum 20 cfm/person in smoking permitted office areas.

This Standard has recently been revised to 62–1989, and is essentially a guide to preventing indoor air quality problems. The most significant change is the increase to a 15 cfm/person minimum for outside air ventilation rates. This will greatly change the design and operation of buildings in the future.

The other key changes of ASHRAE 62–1989 are:

1. maintainability of HVAC systems is required,
2. outside air used for ventilation must meet federal standards,
3. the required outside air must be delivered to the occupants' breathing zone,
4. control of certain indoor air pollutant sources is mandated, and
5. HVAC design and operation must respond to IAQ loads, not just thermal loads.

The key feature of the revision is that no distinction is made between smoking and non-smoking environments. The minimum ventilation requirement is 15 cfm/person in office areas. ASHRAE's experience is that very few complaints arise at this ventilation rate. Unfortunately many buildings are still operating at 5 cfm/person.

Exhaust ventilation is another means of addressing contaminant control, which involves the designation of smoking areas in buildings and the retrofitting of exhaust systems to those areas. When properly installed, the advantages to this system are no re-entrainment of ETS into the return system of the building, and a minimum of overall air movement is required. From the point of view of basic industrial hygiene principles, this approach is sound. The key is careful design. Poor design can result in more problems than it solves, such as over pressurized ceiling voids, unbalancing of the main air handling system, and short-circulating of the exhaust outlet into fresh air intakes.

In order to determine the exposure of an individual to a contaminant, the airborne concentration must be determined with respect to time. For this to be done, both the contaminant emission rate and the ventilation parameters must be determined.

Emission rates generally vary with time. Smoking is a case where the emission is intermittent with a variable source strength. Both the frequency of emission and the source strength are important in order to predict ambient contaminant concentrations. The ventilation characteristics are also important.

Several of the important parameters which are required for the mathematical ventilation model are:

1. Source air-contaminant emission characteristics and source use (generation rate, etc.),
2. General ventilation rates,
3. Infiltration/exfiltration rates,
4. Air mixing/ventilation efficiency characteristics,
5. Efficiency or air cleaning equipment,
6. Outdoor contaminant levels, and
7. Removal of contaminant by surfaces or chemical transformations.

The application of the mathematical ventilation models permits determination of contaminant concentrations and exposures. This technique will become important as ventilation and contaminant emission databases develop.

Jolanda Janczewski: I'm going to talk about regulation, but a different type, I think. I would like to thank Mr. Robertson for his presentation. He did an excellent job in summarizing the most frequent causes of indoor air pollution problems and, more importantly, he highlighted some of the best solutions we can come up with given our present knowledge. I will note, also, that we have identified trends which are consistent with those that Mr. Robertson discussed during our investigations of indoor air quality problems.

There are just a few points I'd like to make. The first has to do with regulation or the use of effective legislation as a mitigation strategy.

Now, Mr. Robertson did not directly address this in his talk, but effective legislation encompasses all of the points he discussed in his conclusion. We have a good solid body of knowledge and experience that suggests a number of steps that we can take to reduce indoor air pollution. We are in a better position in this field than in risk assessment or a lot of other areas that we've discussed over the last two days. So we can use effective, sound legislation as a good mitigation tool. I therefore would like to make a plea for the incorporation of good science into legislation and policies in order to effectively achieve a healthier indoor environment.

Legislation that points at one pollution source, while often well-intended, is certainly not effective. I think it was Dr. Liao yesterday who stated that ETS does not stand alone. There are many chemicals which exist in the parts per million range in indoor environments. These should certainly be considered when regulating for a cleaner environment. The summary work that Mr. Robertson showed you today makes that perfectly clear. He mentioned in his study that tobacco smoke has been a major contributing factor in air quality problems in only about 3% of the cases he has investigated. NIOSH reports about a 2% contribution. I therefore take strong exception to legislation and policies which address only environmental tobacco smoke. Smoking bans or smoking restrictions ignore the more serious causes of adverse health effects in the indoor environment.

In a study which we conducted consisting of a self-administered survey to U.S. and District of Columbia government workers in the Washington, D.C. metropolitan area, we found that over 80% of the respondents were reporting symptoms consistent with indoor air pollution problems. You should keep in mind that smoking was already eliminated or restricted in all of these government buildings. This study again is consistent with the point that Gray made. It revealed that ETS is not the major problem, and more importantly, that the chosen legislative approach focussing only on ETS mitigation was ineffective in solving the real problem.

Mr. Moschandreas yesterday made an excellent point when he said that many of these types of decisions are being made on less than sufficient scientific information. It's important to provide necessary information to policy developers. The body of knowledge we have now does not become available automatically to a legislative body. We must get it there.

Mr. Robertson has stressed education and I think he's right, but I think he's speaking more to the training of the practitioner involved in the maintaining of indoor air environments. I agree with this, but I also suggest that such education should include a diffusion of knowledge into legislative bodies and the general public. I think that a greater effort in this particular area would help to increase awareness and also regulatory requirements for all of the mitigation strategies which we are going to discuss today.

I have a second and third point, the second being the area of microbial contaminants in indoor environments. Our early investigations showed that biological organism involvement in indoor air pollution was minimal. The rapid increase in sampling technology in recent years gave us an awareness of the importance of microbial contaminants in some indoor environments. I disagree with the statement that Mr. Moschandreas made yesterday, if I understood him correctly, in which he said that ventilation systems are not the source of pollutants. In Mr. Robertson's experience, I think, and certainly in ours, the ventilation system often is a source for substantial microbial growth and distribution. So I think it's vital that we continue to study these particular types of contaminants and that we begin to look more into the possible effects of bioamplification and biomagnification in indoor environments.

The other point I'd like to mention is the "bake-out." Mr. Robertson mentioned this as an area to look into. I don't know whether or not we might be creating a problem which normally would not exist. The use of a bake-out in a new building could possibly release some volatile organic compounds that would not normally be released under ambient conditions. I think that that certainly is an area that we have to look into in the near future. Thank you.

Frank Lunau: There are just one or two points I'd like to make.

First, are we really devoting our efforts to the right end? In a recent Swiss study, as yet unpublished, which involved a random selection of 800 offices from 732,000 offices in 79,000 buildings housing 1.4 million people, about 15% of buildings were mechanically ventilated or air conditioned. That means that what we've been talking about just now only applies to fifteen percent of the total buildings in a reasonably developed country such as Switzerland. Eighty-five percent of the buildings were naturally ventilated. Therefore, we don't want to spend too much effort on the air conditioned large building. I agree entirely with Mr. Robertson that the problems that he has outlined are real ones in those buildings. But there are lots of other buildings, too.

Second, if we're talking about office buildings, the people in them are employed, by and large. Why do we start applying different standards from those which we apply to workers in general? It seems to me to be somewhat illogical to do so if it is health effects we are considering.

Thirdly, dealing now with ETS, we seem to have tacitly admitted, in what we're talking about now, that we're not talking about a health problem, but we're talking about a perception problem. The latest ASHRAE ventilation rates are designed not with control of health effects in mind, but to achieve what people accept as a reasonable quality of air. This is all very well, but it does ignore one point, that cigarette smoking does annoy some people and the extent of their annoyance will be governed, not by the average values in the room, but more by their immediate proximity to a smoker.

I don't think that ventilation can deal with this problem completely. It's more a social and behavioral problem.

Finally, in my view, the perception of air quality by people has probably not been considered enough. Fanger, for example, has produced some extremely interesting results which tend to show that one major factor affecting perception of good indoor air quality is people's sense of smell. This is, I think, something that needs to be considered more.

I've had a note passed to me and I should point out that in the USA 95% of modern offices are air conditioned. I wouldn't dispute that. But we must not forget that this is an international conference, and we are talking about other countries as well and circumstances are not necessarily the same as in the U.S. and Canada.

Milt Meckler: There are some issues I'd like to touch on that hopefully will complement Mr. Robertson's excellent talk.

The term "mitigation," I think, has been primarily used to this point as "what does one do assuming there's a problem or likely to be a problem?" My perspective is as a designer of buildings, principally in the United States, that are air conditioned. A lot of indoor air problems surfaced as we began to design tighter buildings, primarily due to the energy crisis. We are searching now for ways to fix these problems. Personally, I don't think that ASHRAE Standard 62–1989 alone will be the solution. It has to be used in conjunction with another ASHRAE document known as the ASHRAE Commissioning Guideline GPC–1 (public review draft dated June, 1988).

The commissioning process is one that's perhaps better understood in Europe than it is in the United States. Commissioning influences building design and maintenance. It forces you to plan at the early stages of design how you're going to test the system, and how the building manager and operator will be educated concerning the operation of the system.

An issue worth attention from a building designer's perspective is particulates. ASHRAE standards that preceded 62–1989 assumed that outside air became uniformly mixed with the supply air delivered to conditioned spaces. This was not a correct assumption, and particulates clearly stratify in a room. They present a special challenge for ventilation systems. By the way, in our own research focusing on particle size we have found that at least two-thirds of particles could not be attributed to tobacco smoke.

Demetrios Moschandreas: Taking the risk of repeating myself, I will state that poor indoor air quality is not synonymous with low ventilation rates and that good ventilation rates do not ensure good indoor air quality. At a minimum, indoor air quality is driven by both ventilation and source strength.

The objective of this paper is twofold: (1) to provide a qualitative brief outline of mitigation strategies focusing on source control and innovative control systems and (2) to point out that IAQ controls by ventilation is an overrated strategy.

Mitigation strategies are either pro active or post active. Pro active mitigation focuses on *source* control which includes source elimination, modification, redirection, confinement, and substitution. These concepts have been studied extensively and been applied on various sources, such as building materials, combustion sources (including cigarettes), furnishings and natural pollution sources, such as radon. Research on building materials is most fruitful. A few examples are given below: elimination of pollution generating building materials such as granite block (in New Hampshire), or phosphorus-containing bricks (Florida). The resins used for presswood building materials have been modified to reduce their formaldehyde emission rates. Automatic pilots are now used with unvented gas ranges, or in Denmark, the unvented gas ranges were modified to become vented. Several carpet manufacturers have modified the bonding to reduce inhouse emissions. Radon pathways to indoor environments are redirected outdoors, and substitutes for methylene chloride containing paint removers are in the late stages of research. Source control is a successful, long-term mitigation strategy for reducing indoor air pollution. Research on better, less emitting, sources in indoor environments is continuing on its successful path.

Post active mitigation strategies refer to controls after pollutants are found indoors at high levels. Post active controls may be divided into two categories: (1) cleaning systems and (2) ventilation systems. Several innovative cleaning systems are either in the late stages of research or are being used to control the quality of indoor air. In addition to the conventional filters, the IAQ research community is looking forward to learning about several innovative cleaning systems. I will give only a few examples: the pleated dry processed carbon composite (DPCC) based absorbers, the desiccant wheel, and the liquid desiccants. Preliminary results in DPCC absorbers are most promising. Tested with HCHO, they indicate removal efficiencies much greater than conventional absorbing materials. The desiccant wheel, my data indicate, reduces odors, the driving force of ETS analyses. The breakthrough time is a function of regeneration and is being studied. In a recent study, my associates and I have concluded, preliminarily, that liquid desiccants also control pollutants, and they are most effective in controlling biopollutants. These are exciting prospects and are a few of many cleaning systems that are being studied and applied.

In my opinion, the impact of controlling with ventilation, a post active control strategy of indoor air quality, is overestimated for two reasons: (1) buildings with mechanical ventilation systems are not the only indoor environments where individuals are exposed to pollutants, consequently ventilation, when effective, resolves only a portion of the exposure question: and (2) strong sources of indoor pollution can and do cause unacceptably high pollutants concentrations in properly ventilated environments. A most disturbing dichotomy is evident when ETS concerns are studied. The health experts focus on non-smoking housewives, pregnant women and preschool and school age children, yet the exposure and controls reviews in this conference focus on office buildings. Research in residential environments has been performed, major studies have characterized indoor air pollution in the U.S. housing stock. It is my assessment that we know more on exposure to indoor air pollutants in residences than we do in office buildings. But it is not sufficient. I will, therefore, end my brief comment by recommending, for a second time in two days, a statistically designed study to determine population exposure to ETS (the subject of this conference) in both houses and offices.

Frank Powell: I, like Gray Robertson, spend a lot of my time in commercial buildings in the United States. While admittedly anecdotal, my experience confirms the figures that Mr. Robertson cited of his firm and NIOSH's experience that ventilation system design, operation and maintenance is, from our experience, the primary cause of air quality problems in problem buildings that we investigate. And I would submit to you also that in those buildings where the ventilation system is not the cause of the problem it's a part of the cure of the problem.

The second point I'd like to make with respect to ventilation is that mass air flow rates or mass fresh air rates should be at certain levels, but also that air should be distributed properly within the occupied spaces of the buildings and that the level of or concentration of any given pollutant within the space is determined by both those factors in addition to many other factors. I encourage all of you who are working in exposure studies to be very aware of the realities of the distribution of air within spaces and its effect on both mass and local contaminant levels.

Donald Ecobichon: I'll ask if there are any comments or questions from the audience.

John Dilley: A long, long time ago, yesterday afternoon, I stood in front of this microphone and asked the first question of this symposium.

I think I now have an answer, but not to that question. I think I now know what would be a reasonable response to make to an employer's inquiry about the health risk to his nonsmoking employees exposed to the smoke of their smoking colleagues.

I think I can now say that the risk is probably comparable to or less than that due to him allowing his employees with colds to attend work, spreading infection through his workforce, some of whom are at risk to succumb to respiratory or circulatory complications.

What would be his response, I ask myself. If he just brings in a no-smoking policy, then logically he should bring in another policy banning employees with upper respiratory infections from work. However, I think I can predict that his pragmatic response with some degree of accuracy, by referring to a decision made by a UK automotive company that has brought in a no smoking policy for their offices, but not on their production line.

My prediction is that my client will not bring in a policy excluding employees with colds because he will perceive this to cost him too much in lost time. But he could well bow to employee pressure groups and bring in a nonsmoking policy at work, providing that he himself is not a heavy smoker!

To summarize, after this symposium, I doubt I can recommend a nonsmoking policy at work in isolation on the basis of health risks to nonsmokers. What I can do is advise a client to investigate, and where necessary correct, the total environment, physical and psychological, of the work place.

Gray Robertson: I was asked whether I wanted to add anything to wrap up. I wanted to make one point very clear. I totally agree with the observations in, say, Switzerland, where we've done a lot of work ourselves, that most of the buildings are naturally ventilated. Many of us also live in homes that don't have mechanical ventilation with outside air supply. That's fine. The only problem is that most of the focus of legislation against smoking is not suggesting that we stop smoking in our homes. It's smoking in our offices. And as a result of that focus we're being asked to restrict our activities in the office. Yet most of the offices in which we're working are either naturally ventilated or at least capable of being adequately ventilated mechanically. It's the wayward operating nose that's created that problem.

So, while I agree on the naturally ventilated building, you've got a different set of criteria and a different set of things that are important. I think it's very important to recognize that the studies that you've been talking about in the last couple of days on ETS exposure relate to exposure in the home, and yet it's not for the home we're introducing legislation. It's in the office. And the office is fundamentally different from the home. And I think that's a very important factor to leave with, as far as this conference is concerned.

Summary and Concluding Remarks

Joseph M. Wu, Ph.D.
Department of Biochemistry and Molecular Biology
New York Medical College

Introduction

One of the primary objectives of this international symposium has been to provide a forum for a critical review and evaluation of the existing literature on environmental tobacco smoke ("ETS"). A second and at least equally important objective has been to identify new research initiatives and directions that will increase our understanding of the nature and behavior of ETS. Last, but not least, our goal has been to place ETS in the larger indoor air quality context.

ETS Characterization

Delbert Eatough began our program with a presentation on the chemical characteristics of ETS. This is a subject that is all too often glossed over, but it really is one of the keys to understanding the possible health effects of ETS. As Dr. Eatough explained, ETS is a complex mixture of many substances. Its composition differs from that of mainstream tobacco smoke in that it contains fewer combustion products and more distillation products. We often hear references to the gas and particulate phases of ETS, but Dr. Eatough showed us that it often is not easy to tell in which phase a component will be found. Nicotine, for example, is mostly found in the particulate phase of mainstream smoke but in the vapor phase of ETS. There is also good evidence of redistribution and/or transformation of chemicals from one phase to another during the dilution and aging of ETS.

Dr. Eatough noted that there remain many areas of incomplete knowledge so far as the chemistry of ETS is concerned. This is an area that clearly needs more work. A question that arises here is whether we really need to characterize ETS exhaustively in order to understand its possible health effects. Can we, instead, identify a few compounds of primary concern that should be the focus of future research? It is very important for scientists to seek to identify the components of ETS that conceivably could matter in terms of health effects. This was a point that several of the discussants made.

The discussants also noted that the components of indoor air are derived from many different sources. This means that, even if one or more of those components were found to be harmful, one would have to determine whether they were in fact contributed by ETS at significant levels. Those other sources also must be considered in any proper evaluation of possible health risks.

ETS Exposure and Dose

Drs. Goodfellow and Reasor focused on the physical and biological aspects of ETS monitoring.

Dr. Goodfellow's presentation concentrated on components of ETS that have been pursued as possible markers of or surrogates for the entire ETS mixture. He described in that connection some of the inadequacies of individual components in satisfying the ETS marker criteria recommended by the U.S. National Research Council. Several key recommendations for future research were made by Dr. Goodfellow and the panel. Standardized monitoring methods for ETS need to be developed and agreed upon. As Dr. Perry pointed out in an earlier session, many of the instruments traditionally used to gather data are simply incapable of detecting the low levels of ETS components found in indoor environments. Study designs should incorporate information on sampling environments, i.e., the qualitative and quantitative effects of building characteristics, furniture, carpeting and occupant density on ETS concentrations. And researchers should get on with the task of developing multiple markers, both ETS-specific and non-specific, for both the vapor and particulate phases of ETS, to quantify exposure more accurately.

As discussed by Dr. Reasor, current methodologies for biological monitoring of ETS exposure depend primarily on physiochemical and immunological procedures for the detection of nicotine and its metabolite cotinine in biological fluids. Measurements of these compounds are not suitable surrogates for other constituents of ETS. Neither are they good indicators for assessing long-term ETS exposure. Comparisons of urinary cotinine levels between smokers and nonsmokers often have failed to take into consideration the difference in partitioning properties of nicotine in smoking versus exposure to ETS, and they also have neglected to account for the difference in the ability of smokers and nonsmokers to metabolize nicotine.

A second approach to measuring ETS exposure is based upon the ability of concentrated extracts from the urine of nonsmokers to induce mutations in bacteria using the Ames test. Many of these studies have been conducted in artificial settings and have failed to include such confounding factors as dietary habits and occupational specializations of the tested individuals. A third commonly used method involves the detection of covalent adducts in ETS and cellular macromolecules such as protein or DNA.

The discussants emphasized that these measurements invariably represent events in surrogate cells and targets. The actual course of events in tissues alleged to be at risk to ETS is unknown. Furthermore, these assays may or may not reflect multiple and variable exposures and certainly do not include any potential synergistic interactions between ETS-derived compounds and other chemicals known to be present in indoor air.

A number of future research directions were recommended by Dr. Reasor and the panelists. The potential of nicotine-induced cellular adducts should be investigated as a means of providing a basis for assessing long-term exposure to ETS. Additional relevant biological markers that would be as representative of non-nicotine ETS constituents as possible should also be sought. Molecular biological concepts and methods should be incorporated into investigations of health effects claimed to be associated with ETS exposure. Greater use should be made of animal studies to calibrate dose accurately and carefully to dissect out various confounding sources for certain ETS constituents that are alleged to have adverse health effects.

Lung and Other Cancers

We turned then to the highly publicized issue of whether nonsmokers exposed to ETS run an increased risk of developing lung cancer. The latest count shows a total of 23 epidemiologic studies of lung cancer and ETS conducted on three continents. Five of the published studies reported associations between ETS and lung cancer at the 5% level of significance. The other 18 studies reported relative risk increases or decreases that were not statistically significant. After reviewing these studies, Dr. Layard concluded that the results were, at best, weak and inconsistent and did not support an inference of a causal relationship between exposure to ETS and lung cancer.

One of the important areas discussed by Dr. Layard and members of the panel involved the use of a statistical technique known as "meta-analysis." This technique was utilized by the U.S. National Research Council in combining the results of 13 of the published epidemiologic studies in order to arrive at a small but statistically significant increased relative risk of 1.34. The major objection to meta-analysis is that it sometimes has been used, including in connection with ETS, even when the underlying studies are neither reliable nor comparable in design. The 13 studies used in the NRC report displayed a wide variety of exposure indices, study population demographics and methods of disease diagnosis. The studies also suffered from a number of serious individual weaknesses, including lack of questionnaire reliability, absence of histological diagnosis of the primary cancer in all subjects, lack of consistency of results, inadequate statistical evaluation of the data, failure to account for variances in life-style factors such as diet and occupations that might influence the results, and failure to examine or consider such factors as air pollution from heating and cooking sources. Furthermore, in none of these studies were actual measurements of ETS exposure made. In addition, considerations of dosimetry throw the NRC conclusion into considerable doubt. In these circumstances, as Dr. Mantel pointed out, meta-analysis simply reinforces the biases and errors of the underlying studies themselves.

Dr. Layard and several panel members stressed that confounding factors often can lead to misinterpretation and erroneous conclusions. The published work of Koo and coworkers clearly illustrates the importance of such considerations: they found that wives of nonsmoking husbands had "healthier" lifestyles than wives of smoking husbands and concluded that caution is needed when interpreting data on ETS in such circumstances.

Dr. Layard also reviewed the sketchy publications dealing with ETS and cancers other than lung cancer. He concluded that the nine studies that are available provide insufficient data to evaluate the possible effect of ETS. In fact, the data from these studies are even weaker and less consistent than those focusing on lung cancer.

Finally, the discussion of ETS and cancer produced a number of specific recommendations for future research. If questionnaires are to be relied upon to provide data about exposure, investigators must do better in avoiding problems of misclassification—including clarification of the present and past smoking status of declared nonsmokers. More objective measurements of ETS exposure are needed. Further work needs to be done on confounding factors for cancers alleged to be correlated with ETS exposure. And investigators need to develop a more precise determination of the dose-response relationship between ETS exposure and disease pathogenesis. Data of this kind are crucial in confirming or refuting the results of epidemiological studies.

Cardiovascular Disease

Dr. Lawrence Wexler concluded the first day of the conference with a presentation on ETS and cardiovascular disease. Based on a critical evaluation of the seven epidemiologic studies in this area, Dr. Wexler concluded that there is as yet no clear demonstration of any increased risk of cardiovascular disease from exposure to ETS. Perhaps the best evidence to support his conclusion is the work of Schievelbein and Richter. They report that in real-life situations, persons exposed to ETS inhaled approximately 0.01 to 0.02% of the amount of particulate matter taken up by active smokers.

All of the panelists agreed that the existing epidemiologic evidence is inadequate to establish even a statistical association between ETS and cardiovascular disease. Several discussants doubted that an association between ETS exposure and cardiovascular disease could ever be demonstrated, given the extremely low exposure levels and, thus, the biological implausibility of any relationship. Accordingly, there may be little or no reason to pursue further studies in this area. The panelists agreed that attention may be more profitably directed toward factors other than ETS such as diet, weight, cholesterol, stress and blood pressure.

Respiratory Effects in Adults

Dr. Philip Witorsch began the second day of the conference with a paper on ETS and respiratory effects in adults. Dr. Witorsch criticized the studies that have been completed in this area for a variety of design and methodological flaws, including excessive reliance on the use of questionnaires without actual confirmation of ETS exposure and failure to control for confounding variables such as socioeconomic status and occupational hazards.

The discussants agreed that the data are extremely weak in this area and that no relationship has been convincingly demonstrated. At most, ETS exposure may cause transitory irritation or annoyance in adults. This kind of irritation, however, is not specific to tobacco. Several panelists thought that psychological factors play a significant role in determining responses to ETS exposure, especially in sensitive individuals such as asthmatics.

Dr. Witorsch and the panel members concluded that future research should focus on the development of standardized procedures to minimize misclassification and the presence of confounding factors; further investigation of the role of confounding factors in pulmonary function; additional studies of asthmatics claiming to be especially sensitive to ETS; and clarification of the role of psychogenic factors in relation to ETS exposure.

Respiratory Effects in Children

The claim that parents who smoke may harm the health of their children tends to evoke intense emotions. Dr. Raphael Witorsch reviewed 24 epidemiological studies of ETS and respiratory effects in children. The studies generally report a statistical association between exposure to ETS and respiratory effects in children less than two years old but the association tends to diminish and even disappear as the child ages. Factors other than ETS, such as socio-economic status, outdoor air pollution, infections transmitted during day-care attendance, and the use of heating and cooking devices in the home may well account for this association. Other possibilities pointed out by the panelists include inherited susceptibility to childhood respiratory illness as well as in utero effects from active smoking by the mother during pregnancy. The failure of the studies to control adequately for confounding variables, as well as inconsistencies in the design and execution of the studies, make it difficult to reach definitive conclusions.

Dr. Witorsch and the panelists recommended animal toxicological studies to explore the role of maternal smoking during pregnancy and lactation on the respiratory health of offspring; standardization of questionnaire forms and spirometric measurements; and a more detailed analysis of childhood exposure to tobacco smoke coupled with actual measurement of cotinine and other markers for ambient tobacco smoke in body fluids.

Reproductive Effects

Next, Dr. Hood assessed the potential effects of ETS on prenatal development and reproductive capacity. After examining the variety of studies on ETS exposure and (1) the incidence of low birth weight in infants, (2) suboptimal mean birth weight, (3) perinatal mortality, (4) congenital effects and (5) other reproductive parameters, he concluded that the literature is both inconsistent and inconclusive. This conclusion is largely attributable to the fact that most of the studies in this area are epidemiologic in nature, and they exhibit the same types of weaknesses and flaws addressed throughout this symposium. In particular, the epidemiology on reproductive effects fails to consider issues such as the magnitude of dose and duration of exposure, chemical interactions, and variations in individual susceptibility due to differences in genotypes.

Some participants, such as Mr. Leslie, are of the view that epidemiology is simply not helpful in this area, and that meaningful conclusions will result only from experimental work with animals. However, presently existing animal studies lack the quality and comprehensiveness necessary for credible conclusions.

The research needs in this field are many. Dr. Hood reiterated the importance of establishing an objective measure of actual exposure. Work on this problem must include a critical assessment of the time-dependent nature of ETS exposure. In addition, investigators must acquire a better understanding of the contribution of such confounding factors as the infant's sex, racial/ethnic origin, gestational weight gain and caloric intake.

Dr. Hood also urged the increased use of animal studies, although there was some debate among the panelists as to whether it is possible to make meaningful extrapolations from these studies to human populations. Finally, it was suggested that workers need to be more careful in monitoring dose levels in order to minimize toxicity and systemic stress.

Risk Assessment

The next topic presented for discussion was ETS risk assessment. Dr. Gross, our opening presenter, described the steps that must be taken in performing a risk assessment—namely, determining whether a particular agent is causally linked to an adverse health effect; determining the relationship between the level of exposure to the agent and the probability of that exposure's producing an effect; assessment of the extent to which humans actually are exposed to the agent; and describing the nature and the magnitude of the risk to humans, including the degree of uncertainty involved. Dr. Gross emphasized the importance of each of these steps to the validity and reliability of any risk assessment exercise.

Dr. Gross then reviewed the ETS risk assessments that have been published by individuals or groups in the United States. His basic conclusion, which was echoed by many of the subsequent discussants, was that the ETS risk assessments that have been conducted thus far assume incorrectly that ETS has been shown to cause adverse health effects. Dr. Gross pointed out that the unsupportability of that basic assumption, which relates to the hazard identification stage of risk assessment, is a fatal threshold flaw in all of the published ETS risk assessments. He noted further that the available data base on ETS also is deficient for risk assessment purposes in a number of other critical respects, including the absence of reliable dose-response information and the existence of major gaps in the available knowledge base on ETS exposure. In view of these and other considerations, Dr. Gross remarked that the most striking aspect of the ETS risk assessments that have been carried out thus far is that the authors have seen fit to undertake them at all.

The major points made by Dr. Gross in his opening presentation were repeated and elaborated upon by the individual discussants. In addition, several of the discussants, notably Drs. Flamm, Paustenbach and Voytek, emphasized that further work on ETS needs to be conducted with full awareness of the current regulatory environment in the United States and other countries. It is important, but not sufficient, to analyze critically the risk assessments on ETS that have been carried out thus far. Scientists working in this area must proceed to the next stage: we need new, properly conducted studies in order to provide regulators with reliable data on which to base a determination of whether exposure to ETS poses a risk of particular health effects. This challenging task will involve both refinements of epidemiologic methodology and the search for convincing, biologically based dosimetric models.

Indoor Pollution: Sources, Effects and Mitigation Strategies

Gray Robertson wrapped up the symposium by attempting to place ETS in context. He noted that some people seem to think that ETS and indoor air pollution are synonymous. Mr. Robertson demonstrated that this is simply untrue. In fact, only about 2–4% of indoor air quality complaints investigated by Mr. Robertson and the U.S. National Institute for Occupational Safety and Health were traced to ETS. Similarly, the available data indicate that flight attendants on commercial airliners are exposed to only minimal amounts of ETS constituents.

According to Mr. Robertson, poor ventilation is by far the leading cause of indoor air contamination in both buildings and airline passenger cabins. Poor ventilation and inadequate system maintenance allow pollutants such as formaldehyde, carbon monoxide, ozone and other substances to accumulate within buildings and, in the case of fungal and bacterial spores, to multiply.

Adequate ventilation remedies not only the underlying causes of the "sick building syndrome" but also the irritation and annoyance some people experience from high levels of ETS. Contrary to the claims made by the Surgeon General in his 1986 report, Mr. Robertson emphasized that proper ventilation quickly dissipates ETS. High concentrations of ETS are a clue that a serious ventilation problem exists.

The discussants generally agreed with Mr. Robertson's conclusion that ETS is not a significant contributor to indoor air quality problems. Indeed, strategies focusing exclusively on ETS, such as building-wide smoking bans, ignore the more serious causes of adverse health effects in the indoor environment. All applauded the publication of a revised and strengthened ventilation standard for new buildings by the American Society of Heating, Refrigeration and Air Conditioning Engineers (ASHRAE). The participants also emphasized the need for additional strategies based on a philosophy of prevention rather than cure. These strategies include improved design and maintenance of ventilation equipment, building "bake-out," increased attention to the stability and toxicity of building materials, and improved distribution and mixing of air within buildings.

Conclusion

What does all of this mean, and where do we go from here? I would like to leave you with a brief series of observations on those questions.

It is important that we as scientists function as exponents of knowledge rather than as impediments. In the last couple of days, the participants in this conference have been highly critical of much of the research that has been conducted on ETS, particularly the epidemiologic research that has been undertaken. Critical evaluation is, of course, an appropriate scientific activity. It permits us to identify and clear away the scientific underbrush and prepare the way for real progress to be made. Without a critical evaluation of what has gone before, mistakes of the past tend simply to be repeated.

But critical evaluation of already completed research efforts is not sufficient. We must endeavor not simply to be good critics. Our ultimate responsibility is to be advocates of good science. We must be prepared to tackle the difficult tasks of designing and carrying out improved studies capable of resolving the health concerns that have been raised with respect to ETS. It is for that reason that Dr. Ecobichon and I, as co-organizers of this conference, encouraged the presenters and discussants to cast their nets toward the future —to identify important gaps in our knowledge of ETS and to make recommendations concerning the research that needs to be undertaken to eliminate those gaps.

One of the most striking consensus views emanating from this conference is that the published data, when critically examined and evaluated, are inconsistent with the notion that ETS is a health hazard. Accordingly, it appears premature to take any sort of regulatory action with regard to ETS at this point. Clearly, more and better research needs to be done. One of our responsibilities as scientists is, of course, to make sure that regulators have the pertinent facts before them as they consider policy options. Although the science of indoor air pollution is in many respects still in its infancy, the discussions that have occurred here should make clear that ETS is not synonymous with indoor air pollution and that indoor smoking bans will do little, in the vast majority of circumstances, to ensure meaningful and lasting improvements in indoor air quality.

Each of the participants in this conference, and many other scientists throughout the world, have made and can continue to make important contributions to our understanding of ETS and the much larger and more pressing subject of indoor air quality. I am taking away from this conference a renewed enthusiasm for indoor air quality research in my own area, molecular biology. Dr Ecobichon and I certainly hope that the proceedings of this conference will provide to many others fresh views and perspectives that will serve both to stimulate and to guide.

INTERNATIONAL SYMPOSIUM ON ENVIRONMENTAL TOBACCO SMOKE

McGill University
Montreal, Canada
November 3–4, 1989

FRIDAY, NOVEMBER 3, 1989

Introductory Remarks

Donald Ecobichon (Canada)

ETS Characterization

Opening Presentation:
Delbert Eatough (U.S.)

Discussants:
George Feuer (Canada)
John Gorrod (U.K.)
Georg Neurath (W. Germany)
Roger Perry (U.K.)
Mark Reasor (U.S.)

Exposure & Dose

Opening Presentation:
Howard Goodfellow (Canada)
Mark Reasor (U.S.)

Discussants:
Lawrence Holcomb (U.S.)

Roger Jenkins (U.S.)
Yoon Shin Kim (Korea)
Sarah Liao (Hong Kong)
Torbjorn Malmfors (Sweden)
Demetrios Moschandreas (U.S.)
Roger Perry (U.K.)
Joseph Wu (U.S.)

Lung and Other Cancers

Opening Presentation:
Maxwell Layard (U.S.)

Discussants:
G.R. Betton (U.K.)
Edward Field (U.K.)
Austin Gardiner (U.K.)
Irving Kessler (U.S.)
James Kilpatrick (U.S.)
Nathan Mantel (U.S.)
Francis Roe (U.K.)
Alain Viala (France)

Cardiovascular Disease

Opening Presentation:
Lawrence Wexler (U.S.)

Discussants:
Alan Armitage (U.K.)
Joseph Fleiss (U.S.)
Peter Lee (U.K.)
Ross Lorimer (U.K.)
Max Weetman (U.K.)
Philip Witorsch (U.S.)

SATURDAY, NOVEMBER 4, 1989

Respiratory Effects in Adults

Opening Presentation:
Philip Witorsch (U.S.)

Discussants:
Robert Brown (U.K.)
George Feuer (Canada)
Austin Gardiner (U.K.)
Leonard Levy (U.K.)
A. Poole (U.K.)
Benito Reverente (Philippines)

Respiratory Effects in Children

Opening Presentation:
Raphael Witorsch (U.S.)

Discussants:
Robert Brown (U.K.)
Ronald Hood (U.S.)
Jarnail Singh (U.S.)
Frank Sullivan (U.K.)
Lawrence Wexler (U.S.)

Reproductive Effects

Opening Presentation:
Ronald Hood (U.S.)

Discussants:
William Butler (U.S.)
Edward Husting (U.S.)
George Leslie (U.K.)
C.E. Steele (U.K.)
Frank Sullivan (U.K.)
Raphael Witorsch (U.S.)

Risk Assessment

Opening Presentation:
Alan Gross (U.S.)

Discussants:
Peter Atteslander (Switzerland)
Gary Flamm (U.S.)
James Kilpatrick (U.S.)
Maxwell Layard (U.S.)
Peter Lee (U.K.)
Maurice Levois (U.S.)
Torbjorn Malmfors (Sweden)
Dennis Paustenbach (U.S.)
Sorell Schwartz (U.S.)
Tom Starr (U.S.)
Peter Voytek (U.S.)

Indoor Pollution: Sources, Effects and Mitigation Strategies

Opening Presentation:
Gray Robertson (U.S.)

Discussants:
Howard Goodfellow (Canada)
Jolanda Janczewski (U.S.)
Frank Lunau (U.K.)
Milt Meckler (U.S.)
Demetrios Moschandreas (U.S.)
Frank Powell (U.S.)

Summary and Concluding Observations

Joseph Wu (U.S.)

Index